INTEGRATIVE AND COUNSELLING PSYCHOTHERAPY

INTEGRATIVE AND ECLECTIC COUNSELLING AND PSYCHOTHERAPY

Edited by
Stephen Palmer and Ray Woolfe

SAGE Publications
London • Thousand Oaks • New Delhi

Editorial arrangement © Stephen Palmer and Ray Woolfe 2000
Chapter 1 © Henry Hollanders 2000
Chapter 2 © Henry Hollanders 2000
Chapter 3 © Jane Martin and Frank Margison 2000
Chapter 4 © David Bott 2000
Chapter 5 © Katherine Murphy and Maria Gilbert 2000
Chapter 6 © Stephen Paul and Geoff Pelham 2000
Chapter 7 © Clare Austen 2000
Chapter 8 © Stephen Palmer 2000
Chapter 9 © Peter Jenkins 2000
Chapter 10 © Stephen Palmer and Michael Neenan 2000
Chapter 11 © David Crossley and Mark Stowell-Smith 2000
Chapter 12 © William West 2000
Chapter 13 © Colin Lago and Roy Moodley 2000
Chapter 14 © Jenifer Elton Wilson 2000
Chapter 15 © Val Wosket 2000
Chapter 16 © Mary Connor 2000
Chapter 17 © Petruska Clarkson 2000
Chapter 18 © Ian Horton 2000
Chapter 19 © Rhona Fear and Ray Woolfe 2000
Appendix © Ian Horton 2000

First published 2000
Reprinted 2005

All rights reserved. No part of this publication may be reproduced, stored in a retrieval system, transmitted or utilized in any form or by any means, electronic, mechanical, photocopying, recording or otherwise, without permission in writing from the Publishers.

SAGE Publications Ltd
1 Oliver's Yard, 55 City Road
London EC1Y 1SP

SAGE Publications Inc
2455 Teller Road
Thousand Oaks, California 91320

SAGE Publications India Pvt Ltd
B-42 Panchsheel Enclave
Post Box 4109
New Delhi 100 017

British Library Cataloguing in Publication data

A catalogue record for this book is available from the British Library

ISBN 0-7619-5798-7
ISBN 0-7619-5799-5 (pbk)

Library of Congress catalog card number available from the publisher

Typeset by M Rules
Printed and bound in Great Britain by Athenaeum Press Ltd., Gateshead, Tyne & Wear.

To my wife, Sarah (RW)

To those who influenced my childhood, in particular, my parents, grandparents, Sylvie, Frank, Norah, Bob, Fred, Eileen, Sue and Reg (SP)

CONTENTS

The Editors   ix

Notes on Contributors   xi

Preface   xv

PART I   INTRODUCTION   1

1. Eclecticism/Integration: Historical Developments   1
   Henry Hollanders

2. Eclecticism/Integration: Some Key Issues and Research   31
   Henry Hollanders

PART II   THERAPEUTIC APPROACHES   57

3. The Conversational Model   57
   Jane Martin and Frank Margison

4. Integrating Systemic Thinking in Counselling and Psychotherapy   74
   David Bott

5. A Systematic Integrative Relational Model for Counselling and Psychotherapy   93
   Katherine Murphy and Maria Gilbert

6. A Relational Approach to Therapy   110
   Stephen Paul and Geoff Pelham

7. Integrated Eclecticism: A Therapeutic Synthesis   127
   Clare Austen

8. Multimodal Therapy   141
   Stephen Palmer

9. Gerard Egan's Skilled Helper Model   163
   Peter Jenkins

10. Problem-Focused Counselling and Psychotherapy   181
    Stephen Palmer and Michael Neenan

11	Cognitive Analytic Therapy *David Crossley and Mark Stowell-Smith*	202
12	Eclecticism and Integration in Humanistic Therapy *William West*	218

PART III ISSUES 233

13	Multicultural Issues in Eclectic and Integrative Counselling and Psychotherapy *Colin Lago and Roy Moodley*	233
14	Integration and Eclecticism in Brief/Time-Focused Therapy *Jenifer Elton Wilson*	252
15	Integration and Eclecticism in Supervision *Val Wosket*	271
16	Integration and Eclecticism in Counselling Training *Mary Connor*	291
17	Eclectic, Integrative and Integrating Psychotherapy or Beyond Schoolism *Petruska Clarkson*	305
18	Principles and Practice of a Personal Integration *Ian Horton*	315
19	The Personal, The Professional and The Basis of Integrative Practice *Rhona Fear and Ray Woolfe*	329

Appendix. Exercise: Developing a Personal Integration 341
    Ian Horton

Index 345

THE EDITORS

Professor Stephen Palmer PhD is a chartered psychologist (counselling and health), a UKCP registered cognitive-behavioural psychotherapist and a certified REBT supervisor. He is Director of the Centre for Stress Management and the Centre for Multimodal Therapy in London, an Honorary Visiting Professor at the Centre for Health and Counselling Psychology, City University, and Honorary Senior Research Fellow at the University of Manchester. He is a Fellow of the British Association for Counselling and the International Stress Management Association. He is currently President of the Institute of Health Promotion and Education and Honorary Vice-President of the International Stress Management Association (UK). He has written and edited sixteen books including *Integrative Stress Counselling* (with Milner, Cassell) and the *Handbook of Counselling* (with McMahon, Routledge) and edits three book series including *Brief Therapies* (Sage).

Ray Woolfe took early retirement in 1997 from his post as Senior Lecturer in Counselling Studies at Keele University and now works in private practice as a chartered counselling psychologist offering therapy, supervision and training. He is currently in advanced training as a psychodynamic psychotherapist. He has contributed widely to the literature on counselling and his publications include the *Handbook of Counselling Psychology*, the major textbook on counselling psychology in the UK. He is actively involved within the British Psychological Society with the accreditation both of individuals and of courses and is a Fellow of the British Association for Counselling. He is a Strategic Director for the Professional Development Foundation, London.

NOTES ON CONTRIBUTORS

Clare Austen is a Chartered Counselling Psychologist. A former lecturer in counselling with a background in adult mental health and child and family psychiatry, she now divides her time between working in primary care and private practice.

David Bott is a Senior Lecturer in Counselling and Therapy at the University of Brighton. He is a UKCP registered systemic psychotherapist and a BAC accredited counsellor, practising independently and working with individuals, couples and families. His publications include a number of papers which address the relationship between theories and models of counselling and psychotherapy.

Professor Dr Petruska Clarkson, PHYSIS and Surrey University, FBAC, FBPS, CPsychol, UKCP registered Psychotherapist and accredited Supervisor with almost 30 years' international experience, over 150 publications, the original designer of the first UK MSc level Integrative Psychotherapy course, first Chair of the British Institute for Integrative Psychotherapy. Author of *The Therapeutic Relationship* and *Ethics: Working with Ethical and Moral Dilemmas in Psychotherapy*.

Dr Mary Connor is Head of Individual and Organisation Development Studies at the University College of Ripon and York St John and she is also an Honorary Fellow of the University of York. She has developed an integrative model (*Training the Counsellor*, Routledge, 1994) which encapsulates her experience of 20 years as a counsellor trainer.

David Crossley's first degree is in theology and religious studies before qualifying in medicine. He trained first as a GP and subsequently in psychiatry and psychotherapy and has several publications in the field of psychiatry. He also has worked as a teacher and medical officer in Africa. Currently he is Senior Registrar in Psychotherapy in Liverpool.

Jenifer Elton Wilson is a Chartered Counselling Psychologist and UKCP Registered Psychotherapist. In 1996, Jenifer published a book on the subject of *Time-Conscious Psychological Therapy: A Life Stage to go Through*. She has, for several years, taught Masters Courses in Integrative

Psychotherapy and Counselling. Previously, she was the first Chair of the BPS Division of Counselling Psychology and is at present Chair of the Training Committee of that division. She established an expanded counselling and psychological service at the University of the West of England, Bristol. She retired from UWE in September 1997 and immediately took up the post of Head of the Doctoral Department at Metanoia. She is in private practice as a therapist, a clinical supervisor, a consultant and a freelance trainer.

Rhona Fear MA is a counsellor in private practice in Worcestershire. Her interest in the relationship between counsellors' choice of theoretical orientation and their underlying personal philosophy developed as a consequence of an interest in the integration debate and her search for a personal integrative approach. She is the author of a number of papers on these subjects.

Maria C. Gilbert MA, CPsychol, UKCP registered integrative psychotherapist is currently the Head of the Integrative Psychotherapy Training and Supervision Training at the Metanoia Institute in West London. She has a private practice as a clinician, consultant and supervisor and has recently co-authored *Brief Therapy with Couples: An Integrative Approach*.

Dr Henry E. Hollanders has had many years experience in the field of counselling, having worked in pastoral, community, medical and educational settings. He is currently a lecturer at the University of Manchester, where he directs the Masters in Counselling programme (MA in Counselling Studies). His counselling practice is based at Pendle in Lancashire and the city of Manchester.

Ian Horton is a Principal Lecturer and Course Director of the Integrative Diploma/MA in Therapeutic Counselling/Psychotherapy at the University of East London (Psychology Department). He is a BAC accredited practitioner, Chair of UK Register of Counsellors and a Fellow of BAC.

Peter Jenkins is Senior Lecturer in Counselling Studies at the University of Central Lancashire. He is the author of *Counselling, Psychotherapy and the Law* (Sage, 1997) and co-author, with Debbie Daniels, of *Therapy with Children* (Sage, in press).

Colin Lago is the Director of Counselling Service at Sheffield University. He has long been interested in and concerned about enhancing the effectiveness and provision of transcultural counselling and has authored several books including *Race, Culture and Counselling* (O.U. Press, 1996). He is a Fellow and Accredited Member of BAC.

Dr Frank Margison MB ChB, MD, FRCPsych has been a Consultant Psychiatrist in Psychotherapy at Gaskell House Psychotherapy Service in Manchester since 1983. He has been involved in training and research in the Conversational Model for 20 years and before that worked on the mother–baby relationship during psychiatric illness.

Dr Jane Martin BA, Cert. Ed, MB ChB, MRCPsych is a Specialist Registrar in Psychotherapy at Gaskell House Psychotherapy Service in Manchester. After gaining a degree in modern languages she worked as a teacher, lecturer and college counsellor, before deciding to study medicine in her thirties. She plans to become a Consultant Psychiatrist in Psychotherapy in the NHS.

Roy Moodley is currently a freelance trainer in multicultural psychotherapy and counselling. He was Assistant Director for Research and Development at Thomas Danby College, Leeds and is now completing a PhD in psychotherapy at the University of Sheffield. He has published papers on race, counselling and psychotherapy; masculinity and management; access to HE.

Katherine Murphy MSc (psychotherapy) is a UKCP registered integrative psychotherapist. She is involved both in clinical practice and the education of psychotherapists and workbased counsellors, and has a passionate interest in what constitutes appropriate preparation for the practice of the art and craft of therapeutic endeavours.

Michael Neenan is Associate Director of the Centre for Stress Management in Hayes, Kent. He is an accredited therapist in cognitive-behaviour therapy (CBT) and rational emotive behaviour therapy (REBT) and is co-chair of the Association of REB therapists. He is on the editorial boards of *Counselling*, the journal of the British Association of Counselling and *Stress News*, the journal of the International Stress Management Association (UK). He has co-authored six books on REBT.

Stephen Paul is trained in counselling and psychotherapy. He is Principal Lecturer in Psychology and Programme Leader for Counselling and Psychotherapy courses at Leeds Metropolitan University. His therapeutic work includes seven years in Child and Adolescent Psychiatry, a Headship of a Special School for children and young people with emotional and behavioural problems and almost 20 years of therapy with adults in a variety of settings.

Geoff Pelham PhD is Course Leader of the Therapeutic Counselling Programme based at Leeds Metropolitan University and Park Lane College. The Relational Approach is the core model on the Diploma which is BAC accredited. He is a BAC accredited counsellor and trainer. He also works as a therapist and supervisor in private practice.

Mark Stowell-Smith works as a Psychotherapist in the St Helens and Knowsley Hospital Trust. His first degree is in history and philosophy and he has completed subsequent degrees in psychology. He originally trained as a Psychiatric Social Worker and worked in the forensic field. He has published work in this area and retains an interest in the application of psychotherapeutic approaches to forensic issues.

William West is a full-time lecturer in Counselling Studies at Manchester University where he teaches on the Advanced Diploma, MA and PhD programmes. He has an MA and PhD in Counselling Studies from Keele University and maintains a small private practice. His current research and writing interests include therapy and spirituality, integrative medicine and supervision. He is a member of the BAC research and evaluation subcommittee.

Val Wosket is Head of Scheme for Counselling Studies at the University College of Ripon and York St John, where she is Course Director for the Graduate Diploma in Counselling and the Certificate/Diploma in Counsellor Supervision. She is an accredited counsellor (BAC), author of *The Therapeutic Use of Self: Counselling Practice, Research and Supervision* (Routledge, 1999) and co-author of *Supervising the Counsellor: A Cyclical Model* (with Steve Page, Routledge, 1994).

PREFACE

A term now in regular use to describe the zeitgest or spirit of our age is 'post-modernist'. The essence of post-modernism is a decline in the belief of purist approaches to understanding physical, biological and social phenomena. This has permeated the whole field of human endeavour in disciplines as wide ranging as medicine, chemistry, architecture, art and politics. In the latter field, for example, the traditional boundaries between left and right have been largely obscured. Where once there was a belief in purist solutions, now there is only doubt and a resort to a more flexible and pragmatic approach to understanding the world in which we live.

Counselling and psychotherapy are not immune from this tendency. A domain which has always been prone to doctrinal differences and separatist tendencies is now increasingly coming to accept that there is little evidence that any one therapeutic method is superior to all others for all types of problems and all types of clients or patients. This has led to a growing interest in flexibility of response and bringing together ideas from disparate schools. The terms integrative and eclectic have come to be used increasingly to describe this process.

This development has been reflected in the appearance of a number of major American texts and accompanied by a growing British literature on the subject, in addition to the establishment first of an International Society for the Exploration of Psychotherapy Integration and its British branch, the British Institute of Integrative Psychotherapy.

Inherent within these developments is the idea that change is a constantly occurring process. Thus the accounts in this book are to be understood as a statement of the field at the present time. Some of the approaches discussed are now well established and likely to be around for the forseeable future, while others are still in an active phase of development. This diversity reflects the nature of the field.

The chapters are divided into three parts. Part I, Introduction, offers a detailed account of the history and origins of the growth of integration and eclecticism. This incorporates an extensive review of both the British and American literature and traces the development of a variety of the key models. The key issues in the eclectic/integrative approach are introduced and discussed.

Part II, Therapeutic Approaches, offers detailed discussion of some of the key therapies encompassed within the subject of integration/

eclecticism. Inevitably, the choice is selective. It is not possible to include every approach. Nevertheless we think that the section incorporates a range of approaches from those which are well established to others which are still struggling towards greater institutional support. We leave it to the reader to decide which approach falls into which category.

In Part II the authors were asked to do the following:

- Discuss the origins of the approach, who developed the theory, when and where.
- Describe the major central concepts and if these derived from more than one tradition, how these are reconciled.
- Explain the basic assumptions about human nature and individual development.
- Explain how psychological disturbance is acquired and perpetuated and how the individual may move from psychological disturbance to psychological health.
- Identify the goal of the therapeutic method.
- Describe how the theory is related to the practice, including a discussion of the change process and the therapeutic relationship.
- Describe the format of a typical session.
- Give some account of indications and contraindications of who would find the approach helpful or unhelpful and the type of problems which are most amenable to being treated by the approach.
- Offer a case study describing the application of the approach in practice.
- Look at wider implications in relation to the range of settings and modalities in which the approach can be used.
- Speculate on future developments.

In Part III, Issues, there are chapters focusing on training, supervision and multicultural issues, in addition to discussions on what integration might mean at a more individual level.

Our hope is that the book will offer a comprehensive account of what is meant by integration/eclecticism, explain the key issues and ideas and demonstrate how they are represented in practice in the UK.

PART I

INTRODUCTION

1
ECLECTICISM/INTEGRATION
Historical developments

Henry Hollanders

In this chapter the historical developments of the movement towards eclecticism and integration in the field of counselling/psychotherapy will be traced from 1930 through to the first half of the 1990s. Publications relating to eclecticism/integration will be referred to and those that seem to have had some significant effect on the movement will be briefly reviewed. The main events in the development of the movement, and the work of some of the influential figures, will all be highlighted. Some more specific issues related to eclecticism and integration, together with an overview of research, will be dealt with in the next chapter.

Setting the scene

While psychotherapy as a discrete discipline has a relatively short history of little more than one hundred years (Freedheim, 1992), the role of the psychotherapist reaches back across the ages to the earliest days of human existence (Ehrenwald, 1976). In this more general, non-specific sense the history of counselling and psychotherapy is interwoven with the history of the way in which human beings have managed, and have been managed by, the psyche. Its central concern can be considered to be the making whole of the inner being or soul (Bettelheim, 1983), and as such the history of psychotherapy is the history of that age-old endeavour.

In the much narrower sense of a movement or discipline, psychotherapy has a short history. In a preface to the most comprehensive recent history of psychotherapy (from a mainly American perspective), Freedheim (1992) refers to the facts that many of the chapters making up the book cover aspects of psychotherapy that are less than fifty years old and that they are written by living authors who are themselves among the originators of the systems about which they are writing. Thus 'the perspective of time, which can be helpful in assessing historical influences, is non-existent for many of the topics covered' (Freedheim, 1992: xxviii). Nevertheless, in spite of psychotherapy's comparatively short life, a great complexity of ideas, approaches and movements has developed, which has inevitably been influenced and shaped by the social, economic, political and cultural climates in which it has been formed (Buss, 1975; Cushman, 1990; VandenBos et al., 1992; Pilgrim, 1997). It is only in the context of these other 'histories' that the history of psychotherapy can be properly presented. Such a task, however, is way beyond the scope of this review, which has as its more modest aim the provision of an outline of the developments of just one strand in this complex tapestry – the even more recent movement towards integration in psychotherapy and counselling.

Early history: schools and segregation

The early history of psychotherapy and counselling is dominated by the development of different schools, each one eager to present its case against the others and each with its own language, which only those committed to its ideas would be likely to understand. The resulting cacophony has been likened by Messer (1987) to the Tower of Babel. A separatist, denominational spirit prevailed in which theory, mainly in the form of dogmatics and lacking any substantial research base, was propounded within an adversarial culture, characterized by Larson (1980) as 'dogma eat dogma'. Perls's (1969) unedifying description of psychoanalysis as 'crap' and the more sophisticated but no less vitriolic attacks on psychoanalysis by prominent behaviourists (e.g. Eysenck, 1960; Wolpe and Rachman, 1960) serve as examples of the ethos of this period. In assigning such attitudes to an earlier period, however, it is not intended to imply that the field is currently beyond them. Disputes between orientations remain, which even now may take the form of ridicule rather than reasoned debate, as evidenced by Clarke's caricature of the work of Ellis (Clarke, 1990).

Kuhn's (1970) description of a discipline prior to the development of a shared paradigm, which gives definition to the field and around which an identifiable community is built, offers a remarkably accurate picture of this period.

The early development of eclectic attitudes: the movement towards desegregation 1930–1960

Even within the adversarial climate described above, another attitudinal strand can be traced. A body of therapists working at grass-roots level was beginning to recognize elements in approaches other than their own that needed to be heard. This diverse and ill-defined group has been termed a 'therapeutic underground' (Goldfried and Davison, 1976; Wachtel, 1977) to which belonged all who, while outwardly and publicly espousing a single orientation, were prepared, in the privacy of their own study and practice, to open themselves to influences from other approaches.

There is no way of knowing the numbers involved but evidence for the existence of such a group is drawn from the way in which, every now and then, a plea to colleagues to consider the possibilities of rapprochement and even integration would be made first by one and then another. Voices were raised intermittently, and at first were generally unheeded, but they were there. As early as 1932 a voice sounding an eclectic/integrative note was raised by French (1933) in an address delivered to a meeting of the American Psychiatric Association. It was an attempt to persuade colleagues of the similarities he considered to exist between two seemingly incompatible sets of concepts, namely Freudian psychoanalysis and Pavlovian conditioning. The address was published in the following year together with some of the reactions, some sympathetic but mostly hostile, to this attempt at rapprochement. Essentially French was seeking to translate the concepts of one orientation into the language of the other. Given that Pavlov acknowledged the possibility of associations existing outside of awareness (Pavlov, 1927), it seemed not an unreasonable task to attempt by someone with goodwill towards another way of 'seeing'. Few had the same goodwill, however, and though Kubie (1934) continued the task in the following year, and Shoben (1949) took it up again some time later, by far the greatest efforts of the theorists of this time were devoted to establishing and developing their own orientations as 'superior' systems. Nevertheless, French had begun what was later to become a major focus for those concerned to bring the orientations closer together, namely the integration of psychoanalysis with behaviourism.

Another attempt at rapprochement, and from a different perspective to that of French, was made by Rosenzweig in 1936. This could be described as a basic common factors approach, with Rosenzweig pointing to some commonalities across orientations. He focused on the importance of the personality of the therapist, whatever his theoretical orientation, and on the usefulness of any kind of intervention, behavioural or dynamic, that contributed to a new perspective on the problem. The point of entry into the dysfunctional system, whether it be at the point of problematic behaviour or of emotional distress arising out of internal conflict, is not of primary importance since change in any one aspect of human functioning is bound to exert a synergistic influence on all other aspects.

The 'common factors' theme emerged again four years later at a meeting of a group of psychotherapists held informally during a conference of the American Orthopsychiatric Association. As described by Watson (1940) this meeting was for the purpose of exploring the therapeutic factors that the members held in common with each other. Following the discussion Watson drew the conclusion that agreement between them was 'greater in practice than in theory' (p. 708). This seems to imply that what was later to be described as 'technical eclecticism' was already in operation at some level by this time.

In 1950 Fiedler (1950a, 1950b) published his findings from a study showing that less experienced therapists tended to hold much more tenaciously to theoretical allegiances than did their more experienced counterparts, and that experienced therapists from different orientations were closer to each other than they were to inexperienced colleagues within their own orientation.

In the same year Dollard and Miller (1950) published their widely acclaimed *Personality and Psychotherapy*. This work has an enduring quality and is still in print. To some extent it informed the latter work of Wachtel in this area and deserves some more detailed attention here.

J. Dollard and N.E. Miller Personality and Psychotherapy, An Analysis in Terms of Learning, Thinking and Culture *(1950)*

This work represents a major attempt at bringing together concepts from psychoanalysis and behavioural theory, and thus continues the task begun 17 years earlier by French. It goes beyond French, however, in that it is more than an attempt at translation; rather it seeks to demonstrate the possibility of an integration of a number of concepts from these two diverse orientations. In particular it focuses on the *learned* nature of the neuroses, involving the *learning* of repression, unconscious conflicts and symptoms. Therapy involves *new learning* which can take place under certain conditions and includes a proper selection of patients who are able to learn, the use of free association, transference, labelling (in the sense of teaching patients to think about new topics), teaching discrimination between the roles of the past and of the present, and a concentration on the gains that can be obtained from the restoration of the 'higher mental processes'. Though the therapeutic process, as Dollard and Miller describe it, remains largely psychoanalytic, the therapist is seen as 'a special kind of teacher' and some behavioural procedures are introduced, particularly the use of homework assignments and techniques for the reinforcement of desired behaviours.

Dollard and Miller's project was funded by the Institute of Human Relations at the University of Yale and, although the book was published in 1950, work on it had begun before the involvement of the USA in World

War II. Originally it took the form of lectures to classes and discussions with colleagues. Since this implies an early interest among a wider group of people than just the two authors heading the project, it supplies further support for the existence of an 'underground' group of therapists prepared to reach across orientational boundaries at a time when conflict between the orientations was rife.

Gathering momentum: the eclectic movement in the 1960s and 1970s

The 1960s: the 'underground' begins to emerge

Momentum in the movement towards the desegregation of the orientations, began to grow in the 1960s. 'Schoolism' was still rife, but even so a surprising number of practitioners were prepared to identify themselves as eclectic when surveyed (see Chapter 2). Clearly, there was a realization among many that the segregation of the therapies was both unhelpful and unrealistic. The increasing volume of psychotherapeutic literature meant that a reservoir of therapeutic interests and ideas was being created, into which flowed contributions from all the major approaches. A 'back-flow' from the reservoir into the various contributing streams was beginning to occur. While those theoreticians bathing in the purist waters some way upstream remained unaffected, it was becoming more evident that considerable numbers in each 'orietational tributary' were beginning to be influenced by the back-flow. If the theorists were unable, or unwilling, to seek integration at their level, a growing number of 'artful' therapists from both the psychodynamic and behavioural orientations were blending together techniques at the level of practice (London, 1964).

Psychodynamicists and behaviourists

For those concerned with the integration of the therapies the main efforts continued to be directed towards effecting some kind of marriage between psychoanalysis and behaviour therapy. If a 'marriage' was a rather optimistic metaphor at this stage of development, then, perhaps, at least a genial and mutually beneficial co-habitation could be hoped for.

Throughout the 1960s a steady growth of interest in taking up the challenge of bringing about some kind of integration between these two still disparate orientations can be detected in the literature (e.g. Alexander, 1963; Marmor, 1964; Marks and Gelder, 1966; Wolf, 1966; Weitzman, 1967; Bergin, 1968; Brady, 1968; Kraft, 1969).

In 1966, in a study of the respective merits of insight therapy and the use of desensitization, Paul (1966) argued that the central concern in any approach to therapy should be: 'What treatment, by whom, is most effective for this individual, with that specific problem, under which set of circumstances?' This compound question has been repeatedly asked in the counselling and psychotherapy literature and is an important focus of the integrative project today.

The humanists

The 1960s saw the entry of the humanists into the eclectic/integrative debate. In 1951 Carl Rogers had written somewhat dismissively of eclecticism and in favour of adherence to a single school of thought. At that time he considered the insufficient objective evidence available to theorists made the development of markedly different hypotheses inevitable. Any attempt at reconciling them through compromise would result in 'a superficial eclecticism which does not increase objectivity and which leads nowhere' (Rogers, 1951: 8).

By the early 1960s, however, Rogers (1963) recognized that the psychotherapeutic domain was in chaos because of the growing number of conflicting approaches entering the fray, some of which did not fit into any recognizable mainstream orientation. Acknowledging that the hitherto self-contained orientations in which therapists had conducted their endeavours were breaking down in the realm of practice, he considered that the time was now right for the inevitable limitations of single orientations to yield to a more rigorous and direct process of observation of what actually transpires in the course of therapy. In many respects Rogers was ahead of the field in this direction, in that he was not advocating simply melding existing theoretical approaches, but rather that closer attention should be given to research allowing new insights into the process of therapy to emerge.

In 1965 Rogers made the now famous teaching film with Shostrom, Perls and Ellis (Shostrom, 1965) in which the three psychotherapies (Client-Centred, Gestalt and Rational Emotive Therapy) were demonstrated with a single client (Gloria). This was not in any way an attempt at integrating the therapies. Rather it sought to demonstrate the differences in the approaches taken by each therapist. However, it does represent, in pluralistic fashion, a readiness on behalf of each therapist to see the others' approaches as valid in their own right simply by virtue of appearing together in the same film under the same general title. It is perhaps a little ironic that the client herself engaged in some therapeutic integrating in her final summary of her experience by pointing out that the overall process had been beneficial to her, having begun with the empathic warmth of Rogers, continued with the challenging techniques of Perls and finished with the more action-oriented approach of Ellis – a process later to be built into an influential eclectic framework by Egan (1975).

In the second half of the decade another humanist, C.H. Patterson (1967), focused on the points of convergence and divergence between the different therapeutic approaches. Sloane (1969) added client-centred therapy to a review of the convergent paths of behaviour therapy and psychotherapy, arguing that a major factor common to all three therapeutic approaches was the principles of learning.

Two influential figures in the eclectic movement in the 1960s: J. Frank and A.A. Lazarus

J. FRANK AND A COMMON FACTORS APPROACH   Jerome Frank published *Persuasion and Healing* in 1961, a work described by Arkowitz (1992: 277) as 'one of the most influential early writings on common factors'. Exploring much more widely than the realm of psychotherapy, Frank looked at the process of change as it can be observed in forms of primitive healing, placebo effects in medicine, brainwashing, religious conversion and faith healing in a number of different cultures. He considered that the prime influences in effecting change in individuals are emotional arousal, an increase in self-esteem, the raising of hope and an expectation of change, the facilitation of some new ways of seeing the problem, and some focused activity in which to engage. These, he suggests, are factors common in some form, either explicitly or implicitly, to all approaches to psychotherapy.

A.A. LAZARUS AND TECHNICAL ECLECTICISM   The term 'technical eclecticism' was introduced by Lazarus in 1967. Though still working within the behavioural orientation at this time, Lazarus became dissatisfied with what he called 'narrow-band behaviour therapy' and sought to incorporate into his repertoire of techniques some procedures that were considered to be outside the boundaries of traditional behaviour therapy (Lazarus, 1981). This expanded version of behaviour therapy he later referred to as 'broad-spectrum behaviour therapy' (Lazarus, 1971). Clearly these were steps on the way to an even more broadly eclectic position. But it was not until the mid-1970s that the technically eclectic approach of Multimodal Behaviour Therapy was presented in published form to the therapeutic community (Lazarus, 1976), and later still that the even more fully technically eclectic Multimodal Therapy (1981) was introduced.

The 1970s: eclectics/integrationists 'coming out'

Surveys in the 1970s

A number of surveys of therapists were conducted in the 1970s, which for the most part showed a growing trend among therapists to describe their theoretical orientation as eclectic/integrative. These surveys will be reviewed in the following chapter.

Psychodynamic and behavioural integration in the 1970s: a continuing theme

The momentum towards the search for integration continued to increase throughout the 1970s. The number of publications with an eclectic/integrative concern grew steadily, with the main focus of interest remaining on the psychoanalytic/psychodynamic and behavioural orientations. Moreover, other factors were coming into play as socio-economic influences were being brought to bear on psychotherapists. In particular, third-party funding was throwing greater emphasis on accountability and effectiveness, and therapists were having to consider the use of briefer forms of therapy (London, 1983; Garfield and Bergin, 1986; VandenBos et al., 1992).

In some respects these issues were more pertinent to the psychodynamic therapists whose work with clients/patients was usually spread over many sessions and often over many years. Messer (1986) and Arkowitz (1992) suggest that the response to this pressure had the side effect of moving some psychodynamic approaches more in the behavioural direction. Malan (1976) introduced the concept of focused treatment and goal setting in a brief psychodynamic approach; Blanck and Blanck (1976) argued that there should be a place in the psychodynamic approach for a greater appreciation by therapists of the adaptive efforts made by clients/patients in coping with their problems. Shengold (1979), in working with the victims of child abuse, sought to pay more attention than was usual in the psychodynamic tradition to the effects of actual events on people's lives.

On the behavioural side, behaviour therapists like Lazarus were beginning to feel the impact of cognitive therapy as developed by Ellis, in the form of rational-emotive therapy, and by Beck, whose work on depression was by now attracting considerable interest (Beck, 1967). Arnkoff and Glass (1992) note the rapid growth in the 1970s of the number of therapists of all orientations interested in cognitive interventions. They suggest that one reason for this interest was a growing dissatisfaction among behaviour therapists 'with techniques that did not target the internal dialogue that they saw their clients engaging in and that seemed to maintain maladaptive behaviour' (p. 659). This interest shown by behaviour therapists in cognitive interventions moved them a little closer to the more recent developments in the psychodynamic therapies and thus increased the potential for integration. Interestingly, Arnkoff and Glass (1992), following Dobson and Block (1988), suggest that cognitive techniques were also drawing attention from many psychoanalytically trained therapists who were dissatisfied with the primacy awarded to the unconscious, with the emphasis on history rather than on current behaviour, and with the long-term nature of psychoanalytic therapy. This growing interest on both sides of the psychoanalytic behavioural divide provided cognitive therapy with a potentially pivotal role in the process of integration. This integrative potential of cognitive learning methods for bringing together 'internalism' (Freudian and neo-Freudian; humanistic and existential approaches) and 'behaviourism' (from Watson to Skinner), was noted by Rimm and Masters (1979).

Some contributions to the psychodynamic behavioural integration debate in the 1970s

Marmor (1971) argued that all psychotherapy is basically a learning process and that the psychodynamically oriented approaches and the behavioural approaches 'simply represent different teaching techniques' (p. 26). While he acknowledges that the different techniques are based on differences in goals and differences of assumptions about the nature of psychotherapy, he considers that the common factor between the two orientations is to be found in the basic processes involved in learning.

Birk and Brinkley-Birk (1974) presented a case for complementarity between the two orientations, with psychodynamic therapy providing insight and behaviour therapy contributing the actual procedures for effecting change.

Sloane et al. (1975), in a study on the activities of psychodynamic and behavioural therapists, found some remarkable similarities between the two groups. Both groups demonstrated comparable degrees of warmth and acceptance towards their clients, both facilitated comparable degrees of depth of self-exploration in their clients and both used interpretative and clarifying statements to the same extent.

Feldman (1979) presented a conceptual model of some of the intrapsychic and interpersonal forces that stimulate and maintain repetitive, non-productive marital conflict behaviour, in which he sought to integrate concepts derived from psychoanalytic and social learning theory within a family systems framework.

An integrative landmark in the 1970s: Paul Wachtel and cyclical dynamics

Psychoanalysis and Behaviour Therapy: Toward an Integration was published by Wachtel in 1977. It is described by Arkowitz (1992: 267) as 'the most comprehensive and successful attempt to integrate behavioural and psychodynamic approaches and one of the most influential books in the entire field of psychotherapy integration'. Wachtel (1977) confessed that, ironically, the book had its origins in his desire as a psychoanalytical therapist to put behaviour therapists 'in their place'. Being convinced that 'behaviour therapy was foolish, superficial, and possibly even immoral' (p. xvii), he decided to take the opportunity offered him to write a paper for a symposium (that, in the end, was never held) attacking the dangers of behaviour therapy. This led him to consider in depth for the first time what behaviour therapy really involved. The result was a very serious contribution on the integration of the two approaches.

The two main themes underlying the arguments in the book are described by Wachtel as, first, 'in order to help, we must *help*' (p. xviif., original emphasis). He is critical of the stance of minimal intervention which characterizes much of the clinical practice in the psychoanalytic tradition, and probably in the humanist and existential traditions as well. The second underlying theme is the need to develop a theory of personality that 'substitutes for the traditional psychoanalytic imagery (e.g. "archaeological" layering, superficial surfaces that mask deep and genuine inner cores) a conception of cyclical events that confirm themselves by a complex set of feedback processes in which the co-operation of other people is essential' (p. xviii).

The psychoanalytic approaches that Wachtel considered to be most favourable to his purpose of integrating the two orientations were the interpersonal approaches of Sullivan, Horney and Erikson. These, he believes, allow room for the current interpersonal context of the individual to be worked with in therapy and provide better opportunities for more therapist activity. He continues to emphasize the psychoanalytical concepts of the unconscious, dynamic conflict and the importance of meanings and fantasies in the inner world in influencing interactions with the outer world. To these, however, he adds a concern with the present environmental context in which problematical behaviour takes place, the importance of present as well as past interpersonal influences, and an emphasis on the use of active interventions by the therapist in working together with the patient/client towards identified goals.

Although it is in a later work that Wachtel uses the term 'cyclical dynamics' (1987), the concept is a central feature here. Early patterns are reproduced in present interpersonal contexts with the effect of pulling in 'accomplices' who are 'prompted' to respond in a way that confirms the pattern and ensures that a further cycle follows. Thus 'rather than having been locked in, in the past, by intrapsychic structuring, the pattern seems from this perspective to be continually being formed, but generally in a way that keeps it quite consistent through the years' (p. 53). It follows that if the pattern is being continually re-formed, it can be interupted with appropriate interventions. Interpretations aimed at facilitating insight into origins and current motivations are one form of intervention with which Wachtel is in full agreement, but he considers it to be essential to be more active since 'such interpretative efforts may be undermined if they are not combined with efforts aimed more directly at bringing about new behaviour in day-to-day situations' (p. 71).

Widening the eclectic/integrative scene in the 1970s: the humanistic and cognitive therapies

HUMANISTIC CONTRIBUTIONS A humanistic perspective on integration was offered by a number of writers during the 1970s. Truax and Mitchell (1971) focused on the fact that whatever the theoretical orientation of the therapist every process of therapy has an interpersonal dimension. They stress the importance of the part played by the personal characteristics of the therapist in the process of change and suggest that this is a factor needing research across the orientations.

Martin (1972) sought to bring together a view of learning theory with a client-centred approach. Thoresen (1973) suggested that behavioural techniques could serve humanistic ends, since the philosophy underpinning the behavioural approach was not essentially different from that underpinning the humanistic therapies. It is worth noting that this is a clear departure from the position taken up by Rogers who considered that it was precisely at the level of philosophy that the two approaches were mutually exclusive (Rogers, 1980).

Appelbaum (1976), writing from a psychoanalytic perspective, expressed the view that Gestalt therapy could be usefully added to a psychoanalytic approach and later widened his interest to other aspects of the humanistic therapies (1979).

Areas of potential integration between behaviourism and humanism were explored by contributors from each orientation in a volume edited by Wandersman et al. in 1976. In the same year Lazarus published *Multimodal Behavior Therapy* (1976) which not only provided a framework for behavioural and cognitive elements, but also included some elements from the more humanistic approaches (e.g. Gestalt). This was also a theme taken up by Davison (1978) when, addressing members of the Association for the Advancement of Behaviour Therapy, he advocated that behaviour therapists should consider the possibility of using some humanistic procedures to enhance their clinical work.

COGNITIVE THERAPY AND INTEGRATION   Though, in a formal sense, the cognitive approaches were the most recent of therapies, by the mid-1970s they were already finding their way into the integration debate, as noted above. The juxtaposition of three orientations in a question posed by Arkowitz, which serves as the title of a paper (1978): 'Are Psychoanalytic Therapists Beginning to Practice Cognitive Behavior Therapy or is Behavior Therapy Turning Analytic?' shows that by the end of the 1970s the issues of integration could not be discussed without some recognition of the part to be played by cognitive therapy.

Gerard Egan and The Skilled Helper: *an eclectic framework*

The first edition of *The Skilled Helper* was published in 1975. Egan began from an essentially humanistic position and then moved progressively towards a more action-oriented form of helping. His work, described as a problem management approach, is basically an eclectic framework into which is built concepts from psychology and sociology as well as from the major therapies. The counselling process is presented as having three main stages: Exploration, Understanding and Action (later to be retitled: Present Scenario, Preferred Scenario, and Getting There), with each stage having a set of skills appropriate to the process. The elements of insight and action can be readily identified in the approach, especially in its early form. The book, however, has gone through five editions and the approach has become more refined and more action oriented with each edition. Egan's approach has been a major influence on training programmes for counsellors, particularly in the UK.

Other contributions to the integration debate in the 1970s

Some contributors to the debate called not so much for an integration of existing orientations as for a new orientation altogether. For example, Feather and Rhoads (1972a, 1972b), though beginning with a view to exploring the integration of behaviour and psychoanalytic therapy, argue that in the end these diverse ways of understanding psychological and emotional disorder probably serve only to indicate a lack of very much real understanding at all. They emphasize the importance of continuing to search for a more all-embracing theory of psychotherapy which will go beyond a mere merging of what already exists.

Others had a more pluralistic perspective, acknowledging the usefulness of all the therapies. Hunt (1976) serves as an example of this, arguing that rather than merging therapies in order to reduce their number, they should each be seen as contributing to a fuller understanding of human beings, rather like laser beams operating together to produce a hologram.

Developing an identity: the 1980s and 1990s

Rapprochement, eclecticism and integration in counselling and psychotherapy became central themes in the 1980s and early 1990s, and it was during this period that the eclectic and integration movement emerged with an identity in its own right.

Surveys of therapists in the 1980s and 1990s

The number of surveys of therapists which included a section on theoretical orientation increased from four in the 1970s to 14 in the 1980s. Interest was still largely focused on clinical psychologists, but a number of surveys drew samples from other bodies of practitioners. These will be reviewed more fully in the following chapter, but it should be noted here that overall the surveys show the number of therapists reporting themselves to be eclectic/integrative continuing to rise during this period.

Increasing numbers of publications

In addition to the surveys carried out, the number of publications with an eclectic/integrative interest multiplied. There were over 200 publications related to the integration of counselling and psychotherapy between 1980 and 1992, and many more if extended references and parts of publications are included (Hollanders, 1996). Only a few of what may be considered to be the main contributions will be mentioned here.

Integration of psychoanalytic and behaviour therapy: an incomplete project

Interest in the integration of these two orientations continued throughout the 1980s and 1990s. Marmor and Woods (1980) edited a volume on *The Interface between the Psychodynamic and Behavioural Therapies* in which it was argued that neither approach can encompass all that is needed in addressing the human condition. In many respects this sets out the case for a more pluralistic approach rather than for an integration of the orientations into one superordinate theory of therapy. This theme was subsequently illustrated by Cohen and Pope (1980) who presented a case study in which a client/patient underwent therapy with a psychoanalytic therapist and a behavioural therapist concurrently. Each therapist co-operated fully with the other and significant progress was considered to have been made.

The subject of resistance in the therapeutic process was explored by Wachtel (1982) from an integrative perspective by seeking to elicit the experience of established therapists from different orientations in the hope that a common understanding of the problem may emerge. Other contributions concerned with the psychoanalytic/behavioural dimensions of integration included Rhoads (1981), Arkowitz and Messer (1984) and Messer (1986).

Clearly, the task of integrating the concepts of psychoanalysis and behaviour therapy has not yet been achieved to any extent that convinces all within these two diverse orientations of the validity of the project. Moreover, there are indications that many of those committed to integration in psychotherapy and counselling are now looking in directions which take them beyond the bounds of an integration of existing 'pure form' approaches (see Chapter 2).

The humanistic and cognitive therapies

The humanistic and cognitive therapies continued to make their respective voices heard in the debate in the 1980s and 1990s. The relationship between psychoanalytic *concepts* and Gestalt *practice* as a basis for rapprochement between the two approaches was the subject of a paper by Nielsen (1980). One year later Arnkoff (1981) explored the possibility of using the Gestalt technique of the empty chair within a cognitive therapy framework. He considered that the resulting progress made by clients was greater than would have been expected using cognitive techniques alone. In the following year a fuller discussion of the overlaps between cognitive therapy and humanistic therapy was presented by Bohart (1982).

An attempt at the integration of cognitive-behavioural therapy with the interpersonal psychoanalytic approaches was illustrated by Anchin (1982), and Horowitz (1988) produced what he described as 'a new synthesis' of the more recent forms of psychoanalysis, including ego psychology (e.g. Hartman, 1964), self-psychology (e.g. Kohut, 1984) and object relations theory (e.g. Winnicott, 1965), with new developments in cognitive psychology (e.g. Baars, 1986).

In 1991 Kahn focused on the relationship between client and therapist within the humanistic and psychoanalytic traditions. He presented the work of Kohut as a point at which the psychoanalytic concepts developed by Freud and later by Gill could meet the humanistic approach developed by Rogers. He described what he considered an integration of the work of Freud, Gill, Kohut and Rogers would mean in terms of the therapeutic relationship. He concluded in a truly integrative fashion:

> At the moment of the existential encounter between therapist and client, the client's whole world is present. All of the client's significant past relationships, all their most basic hopes and fears, are there and are focused upon the therapist. If we can make it possible for them to become aware of their world coming to rest in us, and if we can be there, fully there, to receive their awareness and respond to it, the relationship cannot help but become therapeutic. (Kahn, 1991: 160)

An attempt to bring together object relations theory with Gestalt techniques was made in 1996 by Glickauf-Hughes et al., coming to the conclusion that 'therapeutic gains are most likely to be noted where gestalt techniques are used in tandem with techniques recommended by Object relations theorists (Kohut, 1977; Winnicott, 1965) such as empathy with the client's feelings and attunement to their needs' (p. 67).

Common factors

What has become known as the common factors approach to integration emerged as a major focus during the 1980s. This was spurred on by research that seemed to show the equivalence of outcomes among the mainstream approaches (Luborsky et al., 1975; Smith et al., 1980; Landsman and Dawes, 1982; Stiles et al., 1986). If no therapy is superior to any other in terms of the overall outcomes achieved, then whatever is effective can be found in all. Karasu (1986), who identified more than 400 different approaches to psychotherapy, also identified three common factors shared by all approaches: affective experiencing, cognitive mastery and behavioural reformulation.

Goldfried (1982) sought to identify 'converging themes' from the psychoanalytic, behavioural and humanistic orientations, focusing particularly on trends in practice as described by therapists from the different approaches. This work has an historical perspective, being largely reprinted articles grouped in a sequence that is intended to show the development of interest in rapprochement and integration since the 1930s, with an overview of the period provided by Goldfried and Padawar (1982).

Others have looked for the agents of effective change in the therapeutic relationship formed between the client and the counsellor/therapist (e.g. Bordin, 1979; Clarkson, 1990). Among these lines Friedman (1985), greatly influenced by the work of Buber (1937), focused on the nature of the dialogue in the different orientations as the healing agent. Called by Friedman the 'dialogue of touchstones', it is possible that the 'I – Thou' moments in therapy which produce deep personal insight can take place in any therapeutic process regardless of the theoretical orientation of the therapist, though the theoretical framework in which therapy takes place may influence the way in which such moments are used.

Developing eclectic/integrative approaches

An area of interest that grew rapidly during this period was the development of eclectic/integrative therapies that drew from the major orientations but were approaches in their own right. Lazarus's Multimodal Therapy (Lazarus, 1981, 1986), Garfield's Eclectic Therapy (Garfield, 1980), and later his brief therapy (Garfield, 1989), Beutler's systemic approach to eclectic therapy (Beutler, 1983) and Andrews (1988, 1989, 1991) 'self-confirmation model' are all examples of the eclectic approaches being developed at this time. These tended to be much more empirical in nature than the mainstream theoretical orientations.

In 1989 Mahrer published what Norcross, who had been invited to write the Foreword, described as 'a new and incisive book' (p. 11). Six strategies for integrating the psychotherapies were considered in some depth:

- the integrative development of substantive new theories of psychotherapy;
- the integration of concretely specific operating procedures;
- the integration of therapeutic vocabularies;
- the integrative super-framework;
- the integration of commonalities across approaches;
- diagnose-the-problem and prescribe-the-treatment.

Mahrer recommended that the first two strategies, together with a limited version of the third, should be pursued and that the rest should be abandoned. Norcross, however, takes issue with the way in which Mahrer describes his last strategy, commenting:

> His conceptualisation of the sixth strategy – Diagnose-the-Problem and Prescribe-the-Treatment – is off the mark. This meaning of integration, for me, is Understand-the-Person and Orient-Therapy-to-the-Person. We obviously cannot fully appreciate a person solely through DSM-III (DSM-IIIR), but need to understand a client's phenomenal world and interpersonal drama. This clinical understanding, not discrete diagnoses, can be translated into more prescriptive therapeutic stances and interventions. (Norcross in Mahrer, 1989: 14)

An approach to integration based on the assimilation model began to be developed by Stiles and his colleagues (Stiles et al., 1992) at Miami University in the late 1980s and early 1990s. Since this arose directly out of the British Sheffield Psychotherapy Project (Shapiro and Firth, 1987; Stiles et al., 1990), more detailed reference will be made to it later in this chapter when specifically British contributions will be considered.

Eclectic and integrative handbooks

A major publication was Norcross's *Handbook of Eclectic Psychotherapy* in 1986, and the subsequent companion volume *A Case Book of Eclectic Psychotherapy* in 1987. By collecting together contributions relating to history, philosophy, current trends and developing approaches, Norcross gave eclecticism the shape and standing as an multi-faceted orientation that it had been striving for but had hitherto lacked. Though optimistic in tone the Handbook is nevertheless realistic, providing a critique of the leading approaches (Dryden, 1986) and a careful examination of the complexities of seeking to integrate orientations which have different 'visions of reality' (Messer, 1986).

It is indicative of the developments continuing to take place in this field that a new version of the Handbook was produced in 1992 (Norcross and Goldfried, 1992). This is essentially an update, but its title has now become the *Handbook of Psychotherapy Integration* and of the eight eclectic approaches featured in the 1986 version, only four remain. Lazarus's 'Multimodal Therapy', Beulter's 'Systematic Eclectic Psychotherapy', Garfield's 'Eclectic Psychotherapy' and Prochaska and DiClemente's 'Transtheoretical Approach' are all retained.

Two new approaches in the 1992 Handbook are those developed by Beitman (1992) and Wachtel and McKinney (1992). There are also two new sections in the 1992 version of the Handbook: 'Integrative Psychotherapies for Specific Disorders' and 'Integrative Treatment Modalities'. Both represent some significantly new directions being taken by the eclectic/integration movement in recent times. The former is indicative of the trend away from theoretical orientations and towards effective 'treatments' for particular problems. This may involve the production of 'treatment manuals' that do not regard the dogmatic boundaries of the individual approaches. The latter is indicative of the movement towards the integration of psychotherapy and counselling with other disciplines in 'treatment planning', most notably pharmacotherapy and applied psychology research.

A second major Handbook was that of Stricker and Gold (1993): *Comprehensive Handbook of Psychotherapy Integration* which includes sections on 'the integration of traditional and nontraditional approaches', and 'psychotherapy integration with specific populations'.

Integration reflected in the journals

Psychotherapy and counselling related journals grew rapidly in number in the 1980s and early 1990s. Not only were many of them making space for papers on topics related to rapprochement, eclecticism and integration (e.g. *Psychotherapy*, 29, 1, an issue devoted to the future of psychotherapy included papers on psychotherapy integration (Goldfried and Castonguay, 1992) and technical eclecticism (Lazarus, 1992)), but some were also devoting special issues to exploring the theme in depth (e.g. *Cognitive Therapy and Research*, special issue, 1980; *Behavior Therapy*, special issue, 1982; *British*

Journal of Clinical Psychology, special issue, 1983). *The British Journal of Guidance and Counselling* devoted most of a 1989 issue (17, 3) to eclecticism and integration, but it may be indicative of the lack of development in this direction among British counsellors/therapists that all but one of the main contributors came from the USA. The developments in the UK will be returned to later. Although the *Journal of Cognitive Psychotherapy: An International Quarterly*, first published in 1987, was concerned with a particular approach, one of its declared intentions was to explore the possibility of the integration of cognitive therapy with other therapeutic approaches. The first journal to be specifically devoted to the exploration and study of eclecticism in psychotherapy was the *International Journal of Eclectic Psychotherapy*, published in 1985. Significantly, it was renamed in 1987 to become the *Journal of Integrative and Eclectic Psychotherapy*. An important new journal, the *Journal of Psychotherapy Integration*, is referred to below in connection with the formation of the Society For The Exploration of Psychotherapy Integration (SEPI).

Networks and associations

The growth of interest in eclecticism and integration, together with the recognition that such interest is respectable, at least among a good proportion of the psychotherapeutic population, led to more open discussion between practitioners with a desire to foster a network of interested parties. Goldfried and Newman (1992) refer to a two-day conference that took place in 1981, attended by Garfield, Goldfried, Horowitz, Imber, Kendall, Strupp, Wachtel and Wolfe. The conference had as its agreed primary objective the initiation of a dialogue between these therapists of different orientations who, nevertheless, had an interest in rapprochement and possible integration. Working at the level of practice as well as theory, they agreed that if it was possible actual clinical material would be discussed from different perspectives.

About the same time, the International Academy of Eclectic Psychotherapists was formed 'to bring psychotherapy into a new era, through closer collaboration of eminent professionals of diverse expertise' (Dryden, 1984: 362).

International conferences sponsored by well-established professional associations also began to focus on the theme of rapprochement (e.g. the World Congress of the Adler Society held in Vienna in 1982 was given over to the consideration of contributions from representatives of different orientations).

In 1986, recognizing the need for urgent research to be carried out into the development of integration in psychotherapy, the Affective and Anxiety Disorders Branch of the Division of Clinical Research at the American National Institute of Mental Health (NIMH) invited 14 eminent integrationist therapists to a two-day workshop. Their task was 'to consider the key issues associated with psychotherapy integration in order to advise the NIMH on guidelines for launching a program to stimulate relevant empirical research' (Wolfe and Goldfried, 1988: 448). A report on the recommendations and conclusions from the workshop stated:

> Some sort of desegregation is needed to break down the barriers between schools of therapy and to identify both the robust principles of change that cut across orientations as well as the unique contributions that each particular approach may offer. Only then will it be possible to compile research findings that, although they may originate from a given orientation, are not irrevocably embedded in that particular school of thought. These findings, in turn, may ultimately be used to construct a new conceptual system close enough to the research data and clinical observations to be used for selecting the interventions that are most likely to be effective with various clinical problems. (Wolfe and Goldfried, 1988: 451)

Here common factors, elements unique to each orientation and research data are all envisaged as coming together in the creation of a new, more comprehensive form of therapy. There is an acknowledgement in the report, however, that this is still only a very distant prospect.

The most significant event in the development of a professional identity for those who were concerned to pursue integration through exploration of the issues with other therapists was the formation of the Society for the Exploration of Psychotherapy Integration (SEPI). The first newsletter of the society was produced in 1983 and in 1991 it published the first issue of its official journal, the *Journal of Psychotherapy Integration*. The journal continues to contain the newsletter which serves to pass information between groups of therapists. The directory of the society's membership for 1990–91 contained 537 names, and although 465 of them were from the USA there was an international membership of 72 from 14 countries outside the USA, including 10 from the UK. In 1991 the first international conference of SEPI to be convened outside the USA was held in London.

Much of the preceding outline of historical developments has focused on the American scene. That is where the modern integrative movement had its origins, and where the main developments have taken place. Nevertheless, there has been a steady growth of interest in eclecticism and integration in the UK, and some significant contributions have come from British practitioners. We now turn our attention to reviewing briefly a number of British contributions to the debate (some of these will be covered in more detail later in this book).

Eclecticism and integration: British contributions

Pilgrim (1990) tentatively suggests that one of the reasons for the development of eclecticism in Britain was that British psychologists/therapists were acculturated generally not to theorize too much: 'At the risk of overgeneralizing about my own culture, the British tend to treat emotionality *and* elaborate intellectual theorising with equal suspicion' (p. 7).

Clearly this is an over-generalization and falls into the trap of thinking of eclecticism as a refuge for the theoretically 'woolly' practitioner. While it has to be acknowledged that this may be so in some (perhaps many) instances, it does not take sufficiently into account those therapists who allowed their theory to be guided by practice, and who thus found that not every client in every situation fitted well into a single theoretical position. This is a long way from a lack of concern for theory. Rather, it implies a theoretical integrity which is flexible instead of dogmatic, and which places greater value on open-ended exploration of the integration of theory and practice, than on defending some cherished but closed theoretical position. It is the concern for theory that is grounded in, arises out of, and feeds back into practice, that has been the motivation behind many of the British contributions to integration.

Heron's six-category intervention

Although Heron's (1982) six-category intervention analysis has not been formulated into a specific approach, it does provide an eclectic framework. Based on the work of Blake and Moulton (1972), Heron suggests there are six basic intervention categories: prescriptive, informative, confronting, cathartic, catalytic and supportive. The first three are grouped under the heading of 'authoritative' and the last three are termed 'facilitative'. These categories are not the property of any one approach, but rather are likely to be found in most approaches in some form. The truly skilful practitioner (whatever her theoretical orientation), will be proficient at working within each of these categories, and will be able to move 'elegantly and cleanly' from one to another as the situation requires. Moreover, she will know which category she is working in at any point in the process, and be able to give an explanation of the rationale behind the practice.

Hobson's conversation therapy

Although the Conversational Model, developed by Hobson (1985), is not usually included in the integrative literature, it does, nevertheless, have a strong eclectic ethos.

Hobson himself had a Jungian training, and this is evident in his approach, but he also draws on object-relations theory, the existential philosophy of Buber (1937), cognitive psychology, systems theory, and the work of Rogers (1951). In addition to this, his use of philosophy, literature and poetry (another form of integration) is a prominent feature of his presentation of his work. Moreover, Hobson expressly endorses eclecticism:

> In the present state of knowledge no one of very many theories can be sufficient. In doing his best to assess what methods are appropriate for what patients, with what therapists, in what situations, a psychotherapist needs to use different frameworks. This eclectic approach calls for a paragon with wide theoretical

knowledge, long experience, and a clarity and flexibility of intellect as well as sensitive feeling.... The Conversational Model can be elaborated in many ways using different theoretical principles incarnated in varied personal styles. (Hobson, 1985: 209)

Hobson's model has been used in a number of research projects. Most notably it was the relationship-oriented approach used in the influential Sheffield Psychotherapy Project (see below).

Arising out of the Sheffield project, an attempt was made to adapt Hobson's approach to a brief therapy format involving just two sessions, plus one follow-up session (Barkham, 1989; Barkham and Hobson, 1989).

Some research currently being carried out in the School of Psychiatry and Behavioural Sciences at the University of Manchester is also making use of Hobson's approach, with some adaptations from Ryle's Cognitive Analytic Therapy. This is basically an outcome study using randomized control trials seeking to assess the effectiveness of this form of therapy with patients who have previously been considered unsuitable for psychotherapeutic treatment (e.g. treatment resistant outpatients).

In the light of its use in such projects it is surprising that the approach does not receive more attention in the eclectic/integrative literature.

Dyne and eclectic endeavours

Dyne (1985), another British contributor to the debate, sees eclecticism as *an attitude leading to engagement in a process* rather than as a *position*. According to Dyne, the eclectic attitude will manifest its 'life and value' through an active involvement in a number of 'easily identifiable and related endeavours' (p. 121). Each endeavour has the quality of a search, a seeking out of that which deepens and broadens vision and enables the seeker to move closer to a more integrated and unified field of knowledge and practice. The search, however, will not result in finding a position in which the seeker may rest, relieved of any necessity for further endeavour. Rather, the one who possesses a truly eclectic attitude will be engaged in an unending process of experimentation with 'ideas and techniques in order to understand, investigate, question, support, extend and develop the state of knowledge in the field' (p. 122).

Dyne (1985) identifies three related endeavours in which the eclectic will be engaged.

First is the search in any direction that 'seems likely to yield information, concepts, suggestions and paradigms that may cast useful light on the nature of human beings' (p. 121). He cites Freud, Rank, Adler, Jung and Fromm as examples of those who have been truly eclectic in this multi-disciplinary sense.

The second endeavour of eclecticism is to seek to establish inner coherence in related areas of concern, and to 'uncover fundamental structures and lines of inter-connectedness that underpin the whole field' (p. 121). In this endeavour eclecticism is moving closer to what is now considered by some to be integration.

The third endeavour is described as 'the integration of theory and practice' (p. 122). Dyne expresses the conviction that as there is a free-flowing, two-way interaction between theory and practice, with each continually informing the other, there will be a growing recognition of the impossibility of an emergence of a single, universally applicable theory or way of practice. He contends that each individual practitioner must be free 'to be self-responsible for the selection and synthesising of materials according to his or her own sense of truth' (p. 122).

Ryle and Cognitive Analytic Therapy (CAT)

A thoroughly British integrative approach is Ryle's Cognitive Analytic Therapy (Ryle, 1990). Ryle's early work as a GP and then as a medic in a university health service confirmed to him the high level of emotional and psychological disturbance in the population. In the context of this experience, he developed a research interest in the neuroses and in psychotherapy as a form of treatment and subsequently undertook a training in psychoanalytic (object relations) therapy. He confessed, however, to being unhappy with some aspects of the theoretical structure of psychoanalysis and began in his research work to make increasing use of Kelly's repertory grid technique, which he considered to be essentially cognitive. Thus, although the basis of his therapeutic approach continued to be psychoanalytic, his exposure to personal construct therapy and, at the same time, to the developments in cognitive and behavioural therapy, 'generated an increasing interest in integrating the diverse theoretical and practical approaches competing for the psychotherapeutic field' (p. 1).

One of Ryle's concerns was that the language of psychotherapy should be comprehensible to therapists and clients alike, and in this respect he considered cognitive therapy to have a great advantage over psychoanalytic formulations (Ryle, 1987). Arising out of his clinical work Ryle (1979) believed he could identify three main patterns of neurotic repetition which satisfactorily account for a wide range of neurotic phenomena. He labelled these three patterns as 'traps', 'dilemmas' and 'snags'. The origins of these patterns are to be found in 'reciprocal role procedures' developed in relation to significant others in early life. The aim of psychotherapy, then, is the empathic uncovering of these patterns so that they can be recognized not only in the therapy session but in the client's daily life. To facilitate this a psychotherapy file, together with a diary of moods and behaviour, is kept by the client. As the approach developed, a method of using diagrams as a visual presentation of the neurotic patterns, their origins and the way out (sequential diagrammatic reformulation, SDR) was incorporated into its repertoire of techniques. Since the sessions span a period of about sixteen weeks, the approach may be considered to be a form of brief therapy and as such it is focused on agreed 'target problems' (TPs).

From this it can be seen that CAT is a creative integration of cognitive and psychoanalytic therapies. The theory is essentially psychodynamic and the method is, to a large extent, cognitive but with some very distinctive and unique elements.

The main centre for the training of CAT therapists is in London at the United Medical and Dental Schools of Guy's and St Thomas Hospitals (UMDS) but more recently training has also become available in Liverpool and Manchester (Fisher, 1993). There is evidence, however, that interest in it is growing not only in this country but also overseas (e.g. Finland and Greece – Ryle, 1990). By 1991 the Association of Cognitive Analytic Therapists (ACAT) had been formed in conjunction with the Department of Psychiatry UMDS (Ryle, 1991).

The Assimilation Model

The Assimilation Model was developed by Stiles et al. (1992) and arose out of the work done in the Sheffield Psychotherapy Project. This model views disturbance as an inability to assimilate problematic experiences. The purpose of psychotherapy is to facilitate assimilation. The process of assimilation can be traced through a number of stages from 0 to 7:

0   In the disturbed state the problematic experience is *warded off*;
1   *Unwanted thoughts* and strong negative feelings emerge in the second stage of assimilation;
2   *Vague awareness* grows and the client acknowledges the existence of a problematic experience, accompanied by acute emotional pain;
3   A clear *problem statement* is achieved giving something that can be worked, but affect remains negative;
4   *Understanding/insight* is gained and the problematic experience is placed into a schema, formulated, understood, with clear connective links which are likely to produce some painful affect but also some relief;
5   *Application/working through* follows as insight is used to work on aspects of the problem, utilizing a number of problem-solving processes, often without complete success but with positive affect;
6   This leads to *problem solution* in which the client achieves a successful solution for a specific problem and experiences very positive affect;
7   *Mastery* is the final stage in which the client is able successfully to use solutions in new situations with an eventual 'it's nothing to get excited about' attitude.

It is believed that in any form of therapy these stages of assimilation can be traced across sessions. Research into the model has been carried out by the largely British Sheffield Psychotherapy Project research team using the 'cross-over' design described in the next chapter. It was found that progress on a particular problem is more likely to be steady if exploratory techniques are used first, followed by prescriptive techniques. However, the attempt to measure each problem's level of assimilation failed. The researchers (Stiles et al., 1992) suggest that the failure reflects the raters' difficulty in understanding the client's experience of the problem and that any future attempt would require raters who have an intimate familiarity with the case being studied.

Clarkson and the multiplicity of therapeutic relationships

The therapeutic relationship is a central feature common to all forms of therapy and developing an understanding of its nature and usefulness is being seen increasingly as the single most likely focus for the future process of integration (Hynan, 1981; Friedman, 1985; Hinshelwood, 1990; Clarkson, 1990, 1995; Gergen, 1995, 1996). One integrative approach based essentially on the nature of the therapeutic relationship is that described by Clarkson and Lapworth in 1992 and more fully by Clarkson in 1995. Systemic integrative psychotherapy presents a complex pattern of inter-relationships between four dominant variables (client, therapist, environment and time), five modes of therapeutic relationships (the working alliance; the transferential-countertransferential relationship; the developmentally needed/reparative relationship; the person-to-person or real relationship; and the transpersonal relationship), and seven conceptualized levels of human experience and behaviour. In practice there will be variations in the relationship over time, with different aspects of the relationship needed at different levels of therapy.

Fear and Woolfe: the vicious circle

The importance of the discovery and development of an 'owned' personal perspective as the foundation for integration is emphasized by Fear and Woolfe (1996). Using the mythopoetic concept of 'visions of reality' (i.e. romantic, tragic, ironic and comic), as developed by the literary critic Northrop Frye (1957) and adapted to the counselling/psychotherapeutic world first by Shafer (1976), and then by Messer (1986, 1989, 1992), Fear and Woolfe (1996: 403) suggest that the individual counsellor must struggle 'to find a theory or mix of theories that best aligns to his or her vision of reality'. While acknowledging that those most likely to respond positively to the challenge of integration are those 'whose vision of reality is more flexible, who take some part of each' (p. 403), they insist that the task of the individual therapist in developing 'personal theoretical integration' is 'to search for a concept [of integration] that fits their particular vision of reality' (p. 404). Clearly such a task involves not only the adoption of a personally appropriate and coherently open theoretical system, but also the discovery and personal ownership of the philosophy on which it is built. The approach presented by Fear and Woolfe is one based on Wachtel's cyclical psychodynamics (Wachtel, 1991; Gold and Wachtel, 1993) and brings together psychodynamic attachment theory (Holmes, 1993) with cognitive behavioural techniques.

Conclusion

Clearly, interest in integration is growing in Britain. The above contributions are only part of the picture. Even among those who retain a firm stand within one or other of the single 'pure form' approaches there is a discernible shift away from a dogmatic attitude towards a greater readiness to listen to what others have to say.

The substantial growth of the eclectic/integrative movement, however, should not blind us to the difficulties involved in such a project. Growing popularity does not mean anything in itself. There are many issues that cannot simply be fudged in order to gain some kind of superficial syncretism. Some of these key issues in the debate will be explored in the following chapter.

References

Alexander, F. (1963): 'The dynamics of psychotherapy in light of learning theory', *American Journal of Psychiatry*, 120: 440–8.

Anchin, J.C. (1982) 'Sequence, pattern and style: integration and treatment implications of some interpersonal concepts', in J.C. Anchin and D.J. Kiesler (eds), *Handbook of Interpersonal Psychotherapy*. Elmsford, NY: Pergamon.

Andrews, J.D.W. (1988) 'Self-confirmation theory: a paradigm for psychotherapy integration: 1. Content analysis of therapeutic styles', *Journal of Integrative and Eclectic Psychotherapy*, 7: 359–84.

Andrews, J.D.W. (1989) 'Psychotherapy of depression: a self-confirmation model', *Psychological Review*, 96: 576–607.

Andrews, J.D.W. (1991) *The Active Self in Psychotherapy: An Integration of Therapeutic Styles*. Boston: Allyn & Bacon.

Appelbaum, S.A. (1976) 'A psychoanalyst looks at gestalt therapy', in C. Hatcher and P. Himmelstein (eds), *The Handbook of Gestalt Therapy*. New York: Jason Aronson.

Appelbaum, S.A. (1979) *Out in Inner Space: A Psychoanalyst Explores the Therapies*. Garden City, NY: Anchor.

Arkowitz, H. (1978) 'Behavior therapy and psychoanalysis: compatible or incompatible?', symposium, the Convention of the Association for Advancement of Behavior Therapy, Chicago.

Arkowitz, H. (1992) 'Integrative theories of therapy', in D.K. Freedheim (ed.), *History of Psychotherapy: A Century of Change*. Washington, DC: American Psychological Association.

Arkowitz, H. and Messer, S.B. (eds) (1984) *Psychoanalytic and Behavior Therapy: Is Integration Possible?* New York: Plenum.

Arnkoff, D.B. (1981) 'Flexibility in practicing cognitive therapy', in G. Emery, S.D. Hollon and R.C. Bedrosian (eds), *New Directions in Cognitive Therapy*. New York: Guilford Press. pp. 203–23.

Arnkoff, D.B. and Glass, C.R. (1992) 'Cognitive and integrative therapies', in D.K. Freedheim (ed.), *History of Psychotherapy: A Century of Change*. Washington, DC: American Psychological Association.

Baars, B.J. (1986) *The Cognitive Revolution in Psychotherapy*. New York: Guilford Press.
Barkham, M. (1989) 'Exploratory therapy in two-plus-one sessions. I—Rationale for a brief psychotherapy model', *British Journal of Psychotherapy*, 6 (1): 81–8.
Barkham, M. and Hobson, R.F. (1989) 'Exploratory therapy in two-plus-one sessions. II—Single case study', *British Journal of Psychotherapy*, 6 (1): 89–100.
Beck, A.T. (1967) *Depression: Clinical, Experimental, and Theoretical Aspects*. New York: Hoeber.
Beitman, B.D. (1992) 'Integration through fundamental similarities and useful differences among the schools', in J.C. Norcross and M.R. Goldfried (eds), *Handbook of Psychotherapy Integration*. New York: Basic Books.
Bergin, A.E. (1968) 'Technique for improving desensitization via warmth, empathy and emotional re-experiencing of hierarchy events', in R. Rubin and C.M. Franks (eds), *Advances in Behavior Therapy*. New York: Academic Press.
Bettelheim, B. (1983) *Freud and Man's Soul*. New York: Alfred A. Knopf.
Beutler, L.E. (1983) *Eclectic Psychotherapy: A Systematic Approach*. New York: Pergamon.
Birk, L. and Brinkley-Birk, A. (1974) 'Psychoanalysis and behavior therapy', *American Journal of Psychiatry*, 131: 499–510.
Blake, R. and Moulton, J. (1972) *The D/D Matrix*. Austin, Texas: Scientific Methods.
Blanck, G. and Blanck, R. (1976) *Ego Psychology*, vol. 1. New York: Columbia University Press.
Bohart, A. (1982) 'Similarities between cognitive and humanistic approaches to psychotherapy', *Cognitive Therapy and Research*, 6: 240–9.
Bordin, E.S. (1979) 'The generalizability of the psychoanalytic concept of the working alliance', *Psychotherapy: Theory, Research, and Practice*, 16: 252–60.
Brady, J.P. (1968) Psychotherapy by combined behavioral and dynamic approaches', *Comprehensive Psychiatry*, 9: 536–43.
Buber, M. (1937) *I and Thou*. Edinburgh: T. & T. Clark.
Buss, A. (1975) 'The emerging field of the sociology of psychological knowledge', *The American Psychologist*, 19: 43–55.
Clarke, L. (1990) 'Rational emotive therapy', *British Journal of Psychotherapy*, 7 (1): 86–93.
Clarkson, P. (1990) 'A multiplicity of psychotherapeutic relationships', *British Journal of Psychotherapy*, 7 (2): 148–63.
Clarkson, P. (1995) *The Therapeutic Relationship*. London: Whurr Publishers.
Cohen, L.H. and Pope, B. (1980) 'Concurrent use of insight and desensitisation therapy', *Psychiatry*, 43: 146–54.
Cushman, P. (1990) 'Why the self is empty: toward a historically situated psychology', *American Psychologist*, 45: 599–611.
Davison, G.C. (1978) *Theory and Practice in Behavior Therapy: An Unconsumated Marriage*. New York: BMA Audio Cassettes.
Dobson, K.S. and Block, L. (1988) 'Historical and philosophical bases of the cognitive-behavioral therapies', in K.S. Dobson (ed.), *Handbook of Cognitive-Behavioral Therapies*. New York: Guilford Press.
Dollard, J. & Miller, N.E. (1950) *Personality and Psychotherapy: An Analysis in Terms of Learning, Thinking and Culture*. New York: McGraw-Hill.
Dryden, W. (1984) 'Issues in the eclectic practice of individual therapy', in W. Dryden, (ed.), *Individual Therapy in Britain*. London: Harper and Row.
Dryden, W. (1986) 'Eclectic psychotherapies: a critique of leading approaches', in J.C. Norcross (ed.), *A Handbook of Eclectic Psychotherapy*. New York: Brunner/Mazel.

Dyne, D. (1985) 'Questions of "training" – a contribution from a peripatetic cousin', *Free Associations*, 3.
Egan, G. (1975, 1982, 1986, 1990, 1993): *The Skilled Helper*. Pacific Grove: Brooks/Cole.
Ehrenwald, J. (1976) *The History of Psychotherapy: From Healing Magic to Encounter*. New York: J. Aronson.
Eysenck, H.J. (1960) *Behaviour Therapy and the Neuroses*. London: Pergamon.
Fear, R. and Woolfe, R. (1996) 'Searching for integration in counselling practice', *British Journal of Guidance and Counselling*, 24: 399–411.
Feather, B.W. and Rhoads, J.M. (1972a) 'Psychodynamic behavior therapy: 1. Theory and rationale', *Archives of General Psychiatry*, 26: 496–502.
Feather, B.W. and Rhoads, J.M. (1972b) 'Psychodynamic behavior therapy: 2. Clinical aspects', *Archives of General Psychiatry*, 26: 503–11.
Feldman, L. (1979) 'Marital conflict and marital intimacy: an integrative psychodynamic-behavioral-systemic model', *Family Process*, 18: 69–78.
Fiedler, F.E. (1950a) 'The concept of the ideal therapeutic relationship', *Journal of Consulting Psychology*, 14: 239–45.
Fiedler, F.E. (1950b) 'Comparison of therapeutic relationships in psychoanalytic, nondirective, and Adlerian therapy', *Journal of Consulting Psychology*, 14: 436–45.
Fisher, M. (1993) 'Cognitive-analytic therapy: a personal view', *Counselling: Journal of the British Association for Counselling*, 4 (4): 281–3.
Frank, J.D. (1961) *Persuasion and Healing*. Baltimore: Johns Hopkins University Press.
Freedheim, D.K. (ed.) (1992) *History of Psychotherapy: A Century of Change*. Washington, DC: American Psychological Association.
French, T.M. (1933) 'Interrelations between psychoanalysis and the experimental work of Pavlov', *American Journal of Psychiatry*, 89: 1165–1203.
Friedman, M. (1985) *The Healing Dialogue in Psychotherapy*. New Jersey: Jason Aronson.
Frye, N. (1957) *Anatomy of Criticism*. Princeton, NJ: Princeton University Press.
Garfield, S.L. (1980) *Psychotherapy: An Eclectic Approach*. New York, Wiley.
Garfield, S.L. (1989) *The Practice of Brief Psychotherapy*. New York: Pergamon.
Garfield, S.L. and Bergin, A.E. (1986) 'Introduction and historical overview', in S.L. Garfield and A.E. Bergin (eds), *Handbook of Psychotherapy and Behaviour Change*, 3rd edn. New York: Wiley.
Gergen, K.L. (1995) *Realities and Relationships*. Cambridge, MA: Harvard University Press.
Gergen, K.J. (1996) Unpublished transcript of a tape recording of a keynote address delivered at the World Congress on Psychotherapy, Vienna, July.
Glickauf-Hughes, C., Riviere, S.L., Clance, P.R. and Jones, R.A. (1996) 'An integration of object relations theory with gestalt techniques to promote structuralisation of the self', *Journal of Integrative Psychotherapy*, 6, (1): 39–69.
Gold, J.R. and Wachtel, P.L. (1993) 'Cyclical psychodynamics', in G. Stricker and J.R. Gold (eds), *Comprehensive Handbook of Psychotherapy Integration*. New York: Plenum Press.
Goldfried, M.R. (1982) *Converging Themes in Psychotherapy: Trends in Psychodynamic, Humanistic and Behavioral Practice*. New York: Springer.
Goldfried, M.R. and Castonguay, L.G. (1992) 'The future of psychotherapy integration', *Psychotherapy*, 29 (1): 4–10.

Goldfried, M.R. and Davison, G.C. (1976) *Clinical Behavior Therapy*. New York: Holt, Rinehart and Winston.

Goldfried, M.R. and Newman, C.F. (1992) 'A history of psychotherapy integration', in J.C. Norcross and M.R. Goldfried (eds), *Handbook of Psychotherapy Integration*. New York: Basic Books.

Goldfried, M.R. and Padawer, W. (1982) 'Current status and future directions in psychotherapy', in M.R. Goldfried (ed.), *Converging Themes in Psychotherapy: Trends in Psychodynamic, Humanistic, and Behavioral Practice*. New York: Springer.

Hartman, H. (1964) *Essays on Ego Psychology: Selected Problems in Psychoanalytic Theory*. New York: International Universities Press.

Heron, J. (1982) 'A six-category intervention analysis', in A.W. Bolger (ed.), *Counselling in Britain*. London: Batsford Academic and Educational Ltd.

Hinshelwood, R.D. (1990) Editorial, *British Journal of Psychotherapy*, 7 (2): 119–20.

Hobson, R.F. (1985) *Forms of Feeling*. London: Routledge.

Hollanders, H.E. (1996) 'Eclecticism integration among counsellors in Britain in relation to Kuhn's concept of paradigm formation'. PhD Thesis, University Library, University of Keele.

Holmes, J. (1993) *John Bowlby and Attachment Theory*. London: Routledge.

Horowitz, M.J. (1988) *Introduction to Psychodynamics: A New Synthesis*. London: Routledge.

Hunt, H.F. (1976) 'Recurrent dilemmas in behaviour therapy', in G. Serban (ed.), *Psychopathology of Human Adaptation*. New York: Plenum.

Hynan, M.T. (1981) 'On the advantage of assuming that the techniques of psychotherapy are ineffective', *Psychotherapy: Theory, Research & Practice*, 18: 11–13.

Kahn, M. (1991) *Between Therapist and Client: The New Relationship*. New York: W.H. Freeman.

Karasu, T.B. (1986) 'The specificity versus nonspecificity dilemma: toward identifying therapeutic change agents', *American Journal of Psychiatry*, 143: 687–95.

Kohut, H. (1977) *Restoration of the Self*. New York: International Universities Press.

Kohut, H. (1984) *How Does Analysis Cure?*, A. Goldberg (ed.) with the collaboration of S. Stepansky. Chicago and London: University of Chicago Press.

Kraft, T. (1969) 'Psychoanalysis and behaviorism: a false antithesis', *American Journal of Psychotherapy*, 23: 482–7.

Kubie, L.S. (1934) 'Relation of the conditioned reflex to psychoanalytic technique', *Archives of Neurology and Psychiatry*, 32: 1137–42.

Kuhn, T.S. (1970) *The Structure of Scientific Revolutions*, 2nd edn. Chicago: University of Chicago Press.

Landsman, J.T. and Dawes, R.M. (1982) 'Smith and Glass' conclusions stand up under scrutiny', *American Psychologist*, 37: 504–16.

Larson, D. (1980) 'Therapeutic schools, styles and schoolism: a national survey', *Journal of Humanistic Psychology*, 20: 3–20.

Lazarus, A.A. (1967) 'In support of technical eclecticism', *Psychological Reports*, 21: 415–16.

Lazarus, A.A. (1971) *Behavior Therapy and Beyond*. New York: McGraw-Hill.

Lazarus, A.A. (1976) *Multimodal Behavior Therapy*. New York: Springer.

Lazarus, A.A. (1981) *The Practice of Multi-Modal Therapy*. New York: McGraw-Hill.

Lazarus, A.A. (1986) 'From the ashes', *International Journal of Eclectic Psychotherapy*, 5: 241–2.

Lazarus, A.A. (1992) 'Multimodal therapy: technical eclecticism with minimal integration', in J.C. Norcross and M.R. Goldfried (eds), *Handbook of Psychotherapy Integration*. New York: Basic Books.
London, P. (1964) *The Modes and Morals of Psychotherapy*. New York: Holt, Rinehart and Winston.
London, P. (1983) 'Ecumenism in psychotherapy', *Contemporary Psychology*, 28 (7): 507–8.
Luborsky, L., Singer, B. and Luborsky, L. (1975) 'Comparative studies of psychotherapies: is it true that "Everybody has won and all must have prizes?"', *Archives of General Psychiatry*, 32: 995–1008.
Mahrer, A. (1989) *The Integration of Psychotherapies: A Guide for Practicing Therapists*. Human Sciences Press.
Malan, D.H. (1976) *The Frontier of Brief Psychotherapy*. New York: Plenum.
Marks, I.M. and Gelder, M.G. (1966) 'Common ground between behaviour therapy and psychodynamic methods', *British Journal of Medical Psychology*, 39: 11–23.
Marmor, J. (1964) 'Psychoanalytic therapy and theories of learning', in J. Masserman (ed.), *Science and Psychoanalysis*, vol. 7. New York: Grune and Stratton.
Marmor, J. (1971) 'Dynamic psychotherapy and behavior therapy: are they irreconcilable?', *Archives of General Psychiatry*, 24: 22–8.
Marmor, J. and Woods, S.M. (eds) (1980) *The Interface between the Psychodynamic and Behavioral Therapies*. New York: Plenum.
Martin, C.G. (1972) *Learning-based Client-centred Therapy*. Monterey, CA: Brooks/Cole.
Messer, S.B. (1986) 'Behavioral and psychoanalytic perspectives at therapeutic choice points', *American Psychologist*, 41: 1261–72.
Messer, S.B. (1987) 'Can the Tower of Babel be completed? A critique of the common language proposal', *Journal of Integrative and Eclectic Psychotherapy*, 6 (2): 195–9.
Messer, S.B. (1989) 'Integration and electicism in counselling and psychotherapy: cautionary notes', *British Journal of Guidance and Counselling*, 17: 275–85.
Messer, S.B. (1992) 'A critical examination of belief structures in integrative and eclectic psychotherapy', in J.C. Norcross and M.R. Goldfried (eds), *Handbook of Psychotherapy Integration*. New York: Basic Books.
Nielsen, A.C. (1980) 'Gestalt and psychoanalytic therapies: structural analysis and rapproachment', *American Journal of Psychotherapy*, 34: 534–44.
Norcross, J.C. (1986) 'Eclectic psychotherapy: an introduction and overview', in J.C. Norcross, *Handbook of Eclectic Psychotherapy*. New York: Brunner/Mazel.
Norcross, J.C. (ed.) (1987) *A Case Book of Eclectic Psychotherapy*. New York: Brunner/Mazel.
Norcross, J.C. and Goldfried, M.R. (eds) (1992) *Handbook of Psychotherapy Integration*. New York: Basic Books.
Patterson, C.H. (1967) 'Divergence and convergence in psychotherapy', *American Journal of Psychotherapy*, 21: 4–17.
Paul, G.L. (1966) *Insight versus Desensitization in Psychotherapy*. California: Stanford University Press.
Pavlov, I.P. (1927) *Conditioned Reflexes*. Oxford: Oxford University Press.
Perls, F.S. (1969) *Gestalt Therapy Verbatim*. Moab, UT: Real People Press.
Pilgrim, D. (1990) 'British psychotherapy in context', in W. Dryden (ed.), *Individual Therapy: A Handbook*. Milton Keynes: Open University Press.
Pilgrim, D. (1997) *Psychotherapy and Society*. London: Sage.

Rhoads, J.M. (1981) 'The integration of behavior therapy and psychoanalytic theory', *Journal of Psychiatric Treatment and Evaluation*, 3: 1–6.

Rimm, D.C. and Masters, J.C. (1979) *Behavior Therapy: Techniques and Empirical Findings*, 2nd edn. San Diego, CA: Academic Press.

Rogers, C.R. (1951) *Client-centred Therapy*. Boston: Houghton Mifflin.

Rogers, C.R. (1963) 'Psychotherapy today, or where do we go from here?', *American Journal of Psychotherapy*, 17: 5–15.

Rogers, C.R. (1980) *A Way of Being*. Boston: Houghton Mifflin.

Rosenzweig, S. (1936) 'Some implicit common factors in diverse methods in psychotherapy', *American Journal of Orthopsychiatry*, 6: 412–15.

Ryle, A. (1979) 'The focus in brief interpretive psychotherapy: dilemmas, traps and snags as target problems', *British Journal of Psychiatry*, 13: 46–64.

Ryle, A. (1987) 'Cognitive psychology as a common language for psychotherapy', *Journal of Integrative and Eclectic Psychotherapy*, 6 (2): 168–72.

Ryle, A. (1990) *Cognitive-Analytic Therapy: Active Participation in Change – A New Integration in Brief Psychotherapy*. Chichester: Wiley.

Ryle, A. (1991) Reformulation (revised 1991), CAT Course Notes.

Shafer, R. (1976) *A New Language for Psychoanalysis*. New Haven: Yale University Press.

Shapiro, D.A. and Firth, J. (1987) 'Prescriptive vs. exploratory psychotherapy: outcomes of the Sheffield Psychotherapy Project', *British Journal of Psychiatry*, 151: 790–9.

Shengold, L.L. (1979) 'Child abuse and deprivation: soul murder', *Journal of the American Psychoanalytic Association*, 27: 533–9.

Shoben, E.J. (1949) 'Psychotherapy as a problem in learning theory', *Psychological Bulletin*, 46: 366–92.

Shostrom, E. (ed.) (1965) *Three Approaches to Psychotherapy*. Orange, CA: Psychological Films. Film no. 1.

Sloane, R.B. (1969) 'The converging paths of behavior therapy and psychotherapy', *American Journal of Psychiatry*, 125: 877–85.

Sloane, R.B., Staples, F.R., Cristol, A.H., Yorkston, N.J. and Whipple, K. (1975) *Psychotherapy versus Behavior Therapy*. Cambridge, MA: Harvard University Press.

Smith, M.L., Glass, G.V. and Miller, T.J. (1980) *The Benefits of Psychotherapy*. Baltimore: Johns Hopkins University Press.

Stiles, W.B., Elliot, R., Llewelyn, S.P., Firth-Cozens, J., Margison, F., Shapiro, D.A. and Hardy, G. (1990) 'Assimilation of problematic experiences by clients in psychotherapy', *Psychotherapy*, 27: 411–20.

Stiles, W.B., Meshot, C.M., Anderson, T.M. and Sloan, W.W. (1992) 'Assimilation of problematic experiences: the case of John Jones;, *Psychotherapy Research*, 2 (2): 81–101.

Stiles, W.B., Sharpiro, D.A. and Elliot, R. (1986) 'Are all psychotherapies equal?', *American Psychologist*, 41: 165–80.

Stricker, G. and Gold, J.R. (eds) (1993) *Comprehensive Handbook of Psychotherapy Integration*. New York: Plenum.

Thoresen, C.E. (1973) 'Behavioral humanism', in C.E. Thorensen (ed.), *Behavior modification in Education*. Chicago: University of Chicago Press.

Truax, C.B. and Mitchell, K.M. (1971) 'Research on certain therapist intervention skills in relation to process and outcome', in A.E. Bergin and S.L. Garfield (eds), *Handbook of Psychotherapy and Behavior Change: An Empirical Analysis*. New York: Wiley.

VandenBos, G.R. Cummings, N.A. and DeLeon, P.H. (1992) 'A century of psychotherapy: economic and environmental influences', in D.K. Freedheim (ed.), *History of Psychotherapy: A Century of Change*. Washington, DC: American Psychological Association.

Wachtel, P.L. (1977) *Psychoanalysis and Behavior Therapy: Toward an Integration*. New York: Basic Books.

Wachtel, P. (1982) *Resistance: Psychodynamic and Behavioral Approaches*. New York: Plenum.

Wachtel, P. (1987) *Action and Insight*. New York: Guilford Press.

Wachtel, P.L. (1991) 'From eclecticism to synthesis: Towards a more seamless psychotherapeutic integration', *Journal of Psychotherapy Integration*, 1: 43–54.

Wachtel, P.L. and McKinney, M.K. (1992) 'Cyclical psychodynamics and integrative psychodynamic therapy', in J.C. Norcross and M.R. Goldfried (eds), *Handbook of Psychotherapy Integration*. New York: Basic Books.

Wandersman, A., Poppen, P.J. and Ricks, D.F. (eds) (1976) *Humanism and Behaviorism: Dialogue and Growth*. Elmsford, NY: Pergamon.

Watson, G. (1940) 'Areas of agreement in psychotherapy', *American Journal of Orthopsychiatry*, 10: 698–709.

Weitzman, B. (1967) 'Behavior therapy and psychotherapy', *Psychological Review*, 74: 300–17.

Winnicott, D.W. (1965) *Maturational Processes in the Facilitating Environment*. London: Karnac Books and the Institute of Psychoanalysis.

Wolf, E. (1996) 'Learning theory and psychoanalysis', *British Journal of Medical Psychology*, 39: 1–10.

Wolfe, B.E. and Goldfried, M.R. (1988) 'Research on psychotherapy integration: recommendations and conclusions from an NIMH workshop', *Journal of Consulting and Clinical Psychology*, 22: 448–51.

Wolpe, J. and Rachman, S. (1960) 'Psychoanalytic "evidence": a critique based on Freud's case of Little Hans', *Journal of Nervous and Mental Disease*, 131: 135–48.

2
ECLECTICISM/INTEGRATION
Some key issues and research

Henry Hollanders

Those who go beyond a merely cursory glance at the developments outlined in the previous chapter will very quickly recognize that to grapple seriously with the eclectic/integrative issues requires both intellectual rigour and a commitment to competent creative practice. In the first part of this chapter, nine issues that have been central to the debate will be discussed. Following this, in the second part of the chapter, some research relevant to eclecticism/integration will be briefly reviewed.

Nine key issues

Issue 1 Definitions: eclecticism and integration

The terms 'eclecticism' and 'integration' have often been used interchangeably. Although the earlier literature did encompass both without making a sharp distinction between them, as the debate has progressed it has become necessary to provide clearer definitions.

ECLECTIC AND ECLECTICISM The 1920 edition of *Webster's New International Dictionary* gives a definition and explanation of eclecticism which, because of its historical interest, is worth quoting at length:

> Eclecticism: . . . the practice of choosing doctrines from various or diverse systems of thought in the formation of a body of acceptable doctrine. . . . Eclecticism, like syncretism and skepticism, appears only where several powerful, antagonistic systems are in the field, hence in an era of developed historical consciousness. Unlike skepticism, it does not doubt all systems because of the antagonistic reasonableness of each; unlike syncretism, it does not modify all for the sake of mutual consistency; rather it selects from each its psychologically satisfying doctrines and thus gains whatever consistency the eclectic system may have from the inner conformity of the eclectic's own temperament. (Webster's, 1920)

It is interesting to note that this definition, published before the flowering of the debate in the field of counselling, places the locus of eclecticism within the individual, giving the main criterion for the selection of diverse elements as an *'inner conformity'* with *'the eclectic's own temperament'*.

Briefer and more recent definitions, with particular reference to counselling and psychotherapy, have had a more functional emphasis. According to these eclecticism is selecting:

> Whatever is considered best in all systems. (Reber, 1985: 224)
>
> Whatever therapeutic procedures seem most applicable to the case. (Reber, 1985: 224)
>
> That which works. (Brammer and Shostrom, 1982: 35)
>
> Concepts drawn from two or more systems of thought, or schools of psychology. (Bruno, 1986: 69)

INTEGRATION   The English verb 'to integrate' derives from the Latin *'integrare'* meaning 'to make whole, to renew'. Integration, therefore, is the act or process of combining 'parts into a whole' and/or completing something that is not yet complete 'by the addition of parts' (*Oxford English Dictionary*, 1991).

Reber (1985) identifies a number of uses to which the term is put, usually with qualifiers (e.g. 'cultural' integration), but the factor common to them all is the concept of 'blending' different parts into a whole.

ECLECTICISM *VERSUS* INTEGRATION?   The above definitions make it clear that while the two terms have a considerable area of overlap, there is a fundamental difference between them. *'Eclecticism'* is a process of *selecting out*, with the implication of taking something apart, whereas *'integration'* is the process of *bringing together*, with the implication of making something whole and new.

Drawing on a number of studies (Norcross and Napolitano, 1986; Norcross and Prochaska, 1988; Wolfe and Goldfried, 1988) Norcross and Grencavage (1989) provide a summary of the differences between eclecticism and integrationism in counselling and psychotherapy.

Eclecticism is seen as:

- primarily technical;
- using and applying the parts that already exist, basically in the same form;
- atheoretical but empirical;
- realistic.

Integrationism, on the other hand, is considered to be:

- primarily theoretical in its development;
- the creation of something new by blending elements together into a unified whole;
- more theoretical than empirical;
- idealistic.

Watchel (1991) describes the difference between the two in terms of 'pieces' and 'synthesis'. Eclectics use pieces from different approaches, but they remain recognizable and separate as pieces. Integrationists seek a synthesis – a more 'seamless' approach.

ECLECTICISM *AND* INTEGRATION?   In spite of the growing emphasis on difference, there is a tendency in some of the literature to merge the two concepts. Thus Patterson (1980: 571) considers that: 'Eclecticism is . . . or should be, a systematic, integrative, theoretical position . . . attempting to integrate or synthesise the valid or demonstrated elements of . . . narrower or more restricted theories.'

Norcross (Dryden, 1991) rather loosely joins eclectic and integrative therapy together in an interview with Windy Dryden, stating that: 'When I speak about integrative therapy in this context I am referring to technically eclectic therapies' (p. 16).

Beitman (1990) considers technical eclecticism to be *'a form of Integration'* (p. 52); Norcross and Newman (1992) describe *'three routes to Integration'* (p. 10), one of which is *'Technical Eclecticism'*.

There appears, then, to be some confusion over the uses of the terms. Sometimes they are used as though synonymous (e.g. Dyne, 1985) and sometimes as though they denote two distinct, almost opposite, attitudes (e.g. Wolfe and Goldfried, 1988). Some see a form of eclecticism as a route to integration (e.g. Norcross in Dryden 1991) and some see it as quite distinct and different in its direction (e.g. Lazarus, 1990).

To some degree a blurring of the boundary between eclecticism and integrationism is almost inevitable since the two concepts are bound to merge at some point. In practice, the eclectic has to find some way of *putting together* the parts that have been selected out and, similarly, the integrationist must first *select out* the elements to be blended together into a new whole.

Figure 2.1 illustrates the different uses of the terms and the overlap between them.

A and C can be described as the 'eclectic wing' and the 'integrative wing', respectively (Watchtel, 1991). Those who place themselves in either A (e.g. Lazarus, 1990) or C (e.g. Beitman, 1990; Wachtel, 1991) are likely to reject the opposite term as a description of their position. Those who place themselves in B (e.g. Norcross in Dryden 1991) may use either term to describe their position. 'The Integration Movement' (formerly the 'Eclectic Movement') is a term used to encompass the whole.

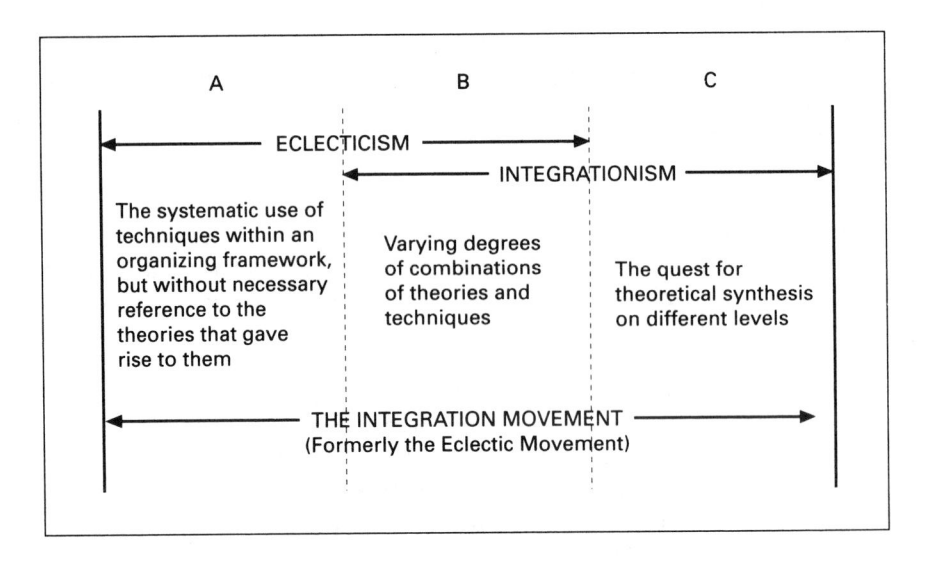

```
         A              B              C
    ←──── ECLECTICISM ────→
              ←──── INTEGRATIONISM ────→
    
    The systematic use of
    techniques within an    Varying degrees
    organizing framework,   of combinations   The quest for
    but without necessary   of theories and   theoretical synthesis
    reference to the        techniques        on different levels
    theories that gave
    rise to them
    
    ←────────── THE INTEGRATION MOVEMENT ──────────→
              (Formerly the Eclectic Movement)
```

Figure 2.1 *Eclecticism, integrationism and the integration movement*

Issue 2 The incommensurability of paradigms

Kuhn (1970) used the term 'the incommensurability of paradigms' to express the idea that an individual cannot view the world in two fundamentally different ways at the same time. The notion of the incommensurability of paradigms strikes at the heart of the integration movement, raising the issue of whether integration is a viable project at all.

The underpinning theories of each of the mainstream 'purist' approaches are internally consistent (i.e. consistent within themselves and consistent with the philosophical presuppositions on which they are built). They may also be consistent externally with each other at some points, but overall they are not commensurable. For example, each approach has its own way of understanding how people are constituted. Its theory and practice proceeds on the basis that people are constituted in this particular way rather than in that particular way. They cannot be considered to be constituted in two different ways at the same time.

Somewhat like a gestalt, a paradigm provides us with a coherent way of construing and understanding data. Just as it is impossible to 'see' two gestalts at the same time, so you cannot be within two paradigms at once. You can experience a gestalt *shift* but not a gestalt *integration*. This was the main thrust of Hinshelwood's (1986) objection to Dyne's (1985) call for an eclectic/integrative approach to the training of therapists. Some theories just cannot be reconciled – you cannot integrate, you can only make a choice between them. Thus, integration with intellectual integrity becomes impossible.

This objection, however, only carries weight when levelled against theoretical integration. It has little relevance when directed against other forms of integration, such as the integration of techniques. A whole range of techniques may be compatible with a number of very different theoretical positions, and these can be employed within a framework for practice without necessarily compromising theoretical integrity.

Issue 3   Integration or pluralism?

An issue that takes us in a different direction from that discussed above (the incommensurability of paradigms), is the relationship between integration and pluralism.

This raises a question that needs urgent and serious attention from integrationists. Can integration be in step with a post-modern society in which the search for absolutes has been abandoned in favour of constructionism?

In such a society there is no 'truth' in itself, only a multitude of different constructions of 'what is' (Gergen, 1992, 1995, 1996). If this is so, to search for some superordinate theory of psychotherapy, some integrated 'whole' which will encompass everything and provide a final definition of the field, would be swimming against the prevailing philosophical tide.

Pluralism, however, does not present us with the same difficulties. The *Oxford English Dictionary* (1991) defines pluralism as: 'Philos: a system that recognises more than one ultimate principle or kind of being; (in moral philosophy) the theory that there is more than one value and that they cannot be reduced to one another.'

According to Ayer (1982: 13) pluralism is built on the denial: 'that there is a single world, which is waiting there to be captured, with a greater or lesser degree of truth, by our narratives, our scientific theories or even our artistic representations'. A consequence of this denial is that:

> There are as many worlds as we are able to construct by the use of different systems of concepts, different standards of measurement, different forms of expression and exemplification. Our account of any one such world may be more or less accurate, our representations more or less acceptable, but when two rival systems come into conflict there may be no way of adjudication between them. In that case there is no sense in asking which is right. (Ayer, 1982: 13)

Samuels (1989) adopts a pluralistic approach to the psychotherapeutic field arguing that:

> Each school may be seen as relatively autonomous from the other schools, and its theory as having its own strengths and weaknesses. It is a case of taking it in turns to be the dominant theorist, and of accepting that, in some ways and in some situations, the other guy has a more utilizable (more true?) theory. (Samuels, 1989: 12)

On this basis pluralists may well enter into each other's theories in order to make use of them, but this is different from pulling out bits and pieces from them.

Paradoxically, Samuels (1993) insists that pluralism is also concerned with oneness, with 'a unified version of the field, a cohesive vision of psychotherapy'. Alongside religion, philosophy and politics, psychotherapy must take part in 'humanity's age-old struggle . . . to hold the tension between the One and the Many' (p. 320).

In keeping with this view, Samuels (1991: 320) argues that it is only by setting out the debates and disputes between the schools that the field becomes defined. A dispute can only arise between parties that have commonalties as well as differences: 'If behaviourists and analysts have an argument then, provided there is enough in common for them to have an argument, they are also part of the same field'.

It is, then, 'competition' and 'bargaining' between schools in a spirit of 'passion' and 'tolerance' that characterizes the pluralist approach, and it is precisely this that gives a sense of all being part of the one field (Samuels, 1991).

Schacht (1984) had earlier made the same point from a slightly different perspective by presenting the pluralistic position as one which 'cherishes contradictions as spurs to the creation of knowledge and as antidotes to the suffocating intellectual effects of an a priori assumption of unity' (p. 125).

Walsh and Peterson (1985) took up a similar position. After considering, and rejecting, the possibility of a synthesis of the major theoretical viewpoints in psychotherapy, they concluded that pluralism, with its emphasis on cross-fertilization and cross-school competition is 'the most cognitively responsible yet comprehensive view available at this time' (p. 151).

While Samuels sets pluralism over against eclecticism and integration, others see them as compatible positions.

Schacht (1984) points out that eclecticism may well lead to a new and creative theory of therapy that will then take its place within the pluralistic community of therapeutic theories.

Norcross (Dryden, 1991) anticipates pluralism becoming a 'megatrend' in psychotherapy and considers it to be an antecedent of integration. Norcross and Newman (1992), aware of the danger warned against by a number of observers that the integrative approaches could become just another group of therapies competing with the rest in the same spirit of partisanship (Arkowitz, 1991, 1992; Arnkoff and Glass, 1992; Lazarus et al., 1992; Wachtel and McKinney, 1992), express the hope that the integration movement will 'engender an open system of informed pluralism, deepening rapprochement, and empirically grounded practice' (Norcross and Newman, 1992: 32).

Such a hope only has meaning inasmuch as it has reference to integration in its broadest sense. It would clearly be self-contradictory if applied to integrationism as the search for a superordinate theory.

Issue 4 The locus of integration

On the assumption that some form of integration is viable, another issue in the debate has been around the question: 'Where does integration take place?' Broadly, there are three possibilities:

1. *Externally* (i.e. primarily outside the practitioner).
2. *Internally* (i.e. primarily within the individual practitioner).
3. *Within the relationship* (i.e. primarily in 'the Between' person and person).

EXTERNALLY (I.E. PRIMARILY OUTSIDE THE PRACTITIONER) There are at least three versions of this possibility. One version points to the need for the development of a meta-theory which will bring together elements from many different theories into a coherent whole which can be presented as a (perhaps 'the') comprehensive approach to psychotherapy. This is usually referred to as 'theoretical integration'. One example of an approach in which theoretical integration has been attempted is Cognitive Analytic Therapy (Ryle, 1990).

A second version of this 'external' perspective is to focus not so much on the development of an *integrative theory* as on the production of a recognizable *eclectic/integrative framework* within which proven effective techniques can be brought together in a systematic way. The framework gives a sense of ordered progression through the process of therapy and guides the therapist in the use and timing of techniques. Such frameworks do not usually make many theoretical demands and each practitioner will bring her own theoretical preferences to it. This has been variously called technical eclecticism, systematic eclecticism or technically prescriptive eclecticism, and is usually set over against 'haphazard eclecticism' or 'syncretism'. An example of technical eclecticism is Lazarus's Multimodal Therapy (Lazarus, 1981).

A third version of the 'external' perspective is to seek first to isolate the factors in each single approach which can be shown to be effective, and then to build them into a new integrative approach which presumably will be even more effective. Based on the available evidence that there seems to be an equivalence of outcomes across approaches (i.e. no single approach can be shown to be substantially more effective than the others (Luborsky et al., 1975; Smith et al., 1980; Lambert et al., 1986)), the quest for the effective elements has focused on the commonalities across the therapies. The approaches developed by Garfield (1992) and Beitman (1992) have both sought to make use of the supposed 'common factors' concept, but neither can claim any substantial research evidence to show that their approach is more effective than any of the other therapies.

Whether primarily concerned with theories, techniques or common factors, the emphasis here is on the production of an external system which may be recognized as an approach in itself (e.g. Cognitive Analytic

Therapy or Multimodal Therapy). As such it can be readily explained to clients and taught to trainees.

An important element in each of the above perspectives is the need to develop a strong research base. How can we know which theories to integrate in order to produce an effective form of therapy? Or how can we know which techniques work best, with which people, with which particular problems? Or how can we determine the effective common factors?

Ideally, research provides us with the answer. I say ideally because it is evident that at present we do not have a sufficiently comprehensive research base to enable us confidently to predict individual outcomes. Some would seriously doubt that we could ever arrive at such a position. To predict the effect of a drug on a particular person is a difficult enough task, but to predict the outcome of interpersonal processes in which two unique individuals are engaged is infinitely more difficult, with the possibility of multitudinous confounding variables. Lambert (1992), in his contribution to a recent *Handbook of Psychotherapy Integration* (Norcross and Goldfried, 1992), notes that 'despite the fact that the plurality of therapists subscribe to an eclectic approach . . . there is not sufficient outcome research on eclectic psychotherapies to base a chapter on these data' (p. 94).

In our present situation the view of Beitman (1990), who remains unconvinced that the current body of research is extensive enough and sufficiently unambiguous to be a clear guide to practice, is probably most realistic. He continues to maintain that although research may be making some progress, 'individual personality plays a great part in therapeutic choice' (p. 68).

This leads us to the second possible answer to the question 'Where does integration take place?'.

INTERNALLY (I.E. PRIMARILY IN THE INDIVIDUAL PRACTITIONER) The emphasis here is on the individual practitioner developing her own form of integration, and probably doing so over and over again with each new client. Of course, in one sense, this may be little more than flying by the seat of your pants, grabbing wildly at whatever comes to hand to do and then rationalizing it as being the product of a personal integrative process. No one would openly espouse this as a valid approach to integration.

However, another more respectable version of internal integration refers us to the whole process involved in being a reflective practitioner. Initially, choices of intervention are likely to be made on the basis of personal preference, training, experience and any assessment procedures that have been previously undertaken (Steiner, 1978; Norcross and Prochaska, 1982; Dryden, 1984). The way in which these choices are worked out in practice in any one session will depend on a wide range of variables (including the current life experience of both the therapist and the client). Following the session, the whole process of choice of intervention, application and the resultant outcome will become the object of reflection by the practitioner both individually and in conjunction with others in supervision.

It is important that this reflection should be as widely informed as possible, by the experience of others, the literature, varied ongoing training, etc. Through this reflective process, over and over again, the experience of the therapist will be integrated into her whole approach to therapy, deepening the 'internal reservoir' that is there to be drawn from in each new situation.

In practice therapy may go in quite different directions with different clients, but the reflective process will remain the same.

In some respects, this may seem to resemble a kind of 'intuitive' approach. It is important to recognize, however, that it does not absolve the therapist from the responsibility of being able, at any point in the process of therapy, to give a coherent rationale for what is being done which is consistent over time.

Now, of course, this description of the reflective process involved in internal integration could be applied to any responsible therapist working within any approach. However, it is a more pertinent, more urgently demanding and, perhaps, a more risky process when the therapist is an integrationist whose practice is not 'held' within a particular approach. On the other hand, it is also likely to be a more freely creative process opening up possibilities that could not be seen from the more restricted confines of a single 'purist' approach.

WITHIN THE RELATIONSHIP (I.E. PRIMARILY IN 'THE BETWEEN' PERSON AND PERSON) A third answer to our question 'Where does integration take place?' points us to the relationship as it develops between therapist and client. The idea here is that it is the client who indicates what is needed, and that she does so by the way in which she relates to the therapist. The therapist, sensitive to the relationship needs of the client, will respond, hopefully, in a way which is appropriate to that particular client. Such needs may change as the therapy progresses and a proper understanding of the unfolding relationship and the appropriate responses to it may well take the therapist beyond the bounds of a single therapeutic approach. Clarkson (1990) held out the relationship as the main area of integration in a paper published in the strongly psychodynamic *British Journal of Psychotherapy*. This received enthusiastic editorial support from the Kleinian analyst Hinshelwood (1990), who had hitherto considered the search for a valid eclecticism to be an 'impossible project' (Hinshelwood, 1986):

> Clarkson's careful analysis of the various levels of the psychotherapeutic relationship is an attempt to find a perspective from which an overview might become possible. She contends that all therapeutic relationships have five levels even though the different psychotherapies prioritise different levels. This offers a way of circumventing the inherent contradictions and incompatibilities that exist between different psychotherapies; instead of incompatibilities we have different priorities and emphasis. And this leaves a way open for the beginnings of a possible integration of psychotherapies. (Hinshelwood, 1990: 129)

It will be recognized that none of the answers given so far to the question 'Where does integration take place?' totally exclude the others. Thus, a fourth response is needed which can combine aspects of all three of the previous answers, in true integrative fashion.

A COMBINATION OF ALL THREE   A metaphoric formulation of an integrated response could go something like this: As a therapist you will have your own position which will function as a secure 'home' base (a preferred 'external' approach). You should not be neurotic about this, however, by staying agoraphobically bound to the house. Never making excursions into the rich 'bustle' of therapeutic activity in the street outside (and even in the supermarket!) is likely to restrict usefulness in practice as much as its disordered counterpart restricts enjoyment in life. Healthy functioning as a therapist means having an enthusiastic curiosity about other people's houses and neighbourhoods as well as your own, so that visits are frequently made to collect interesting and useful items that can be brought back to furnish your own house more richly. In the process you may discover that what you thought would go nicely with existing items doesn't fit very well at all when you try to find a place for it back home – so you may have to jettison it. On the other hand it may fit very well indeed, even better than an old existing item which you may, then, decide has had its day. How you set out, arrange and rearrange all these collected items will depend to some degree on your personal preference ('internal' integration), but if you are sensitive, it will also depend to a considerable extent on who is visiting you that day – their personality, their difficulties and the relationship that has developed between the two of you (the relationship as the locus of integration).

Of course, there are some things that are so much a part of the structure of the house that they cannot be rearranged. So if you are considering removing a retaining wall it would be as well to have a good strong supporting beam to hand lest the whole building collapses and you find yourself bewilderingly homeless – a kind of wandering therapeutic refugee.

I hope the metaphor hasn't been overdone, and that the point has been well made!

Issue 5 *Integration – a position or a process?*

Linked with the above discussion is a question related to *the aim* of the integration movement. Is it to produce integrative *positions* in the form of integrative approaches, perhaps with the eventual aim of producing one single integrative approach which will give definition to the whole field? Or is it to engage in an integrative *process* which is an unending project, and is not intended to have a point of termination in a final definitive approach?

INTEGRATION AS A POSITION   Integration may be seen by some as a position to be arrived at. As such the integrative task is likely to take the form of bringing together two or more 'purist' approaches to produce a new integrative approach in its own right. Or, much more ambitiously, it may take the form of a search for a superordinate theory which will replace all other theories, and provide the whole field with a paradigm which will define the 'profession' of psychotherapy.

It is generally agreed that a single paradigm for the whole field is not going to be brought about in the foreseeable future (and perhaps never!). If this is the case, then, according to this view, the integrationist is left with the less ambitious but more immediate task of bringing together two or more existing approaches to create new integrative models.

This whole 'positions' approach to integration, however, is open to the criticism that it is simply continuing to proliferate approaches, thus compounding the chaos it was seeking originally to reduce. To date it has succeeded only in managing to introduce some new integrative models into the field without replacing any of those that already existed.

INTEGRATION AS A PROCESS   For others, however, integration may take on the aspect of a *process* which is not intended to terminate in the creation of new integrative approaches. Rather, it is to be pursued as a quest that has no end. In this sense it is comparable with Dyne's (1985) first endeavour of eclecticism, which is: 'to go on searching in any direction that seems likely to yield information, concepts, suggestions and paradigms that may cast useful light on the nature of human beings' (p. 121).

Clarkson (1992) eloquently picks up the same theme:

> One of the most underlying values is that integration is an ongoing process in a continual state of development and evolution. Fixed syllabuses or fixed 'goalposts' are intrinsically antithetical to an orientation which is by its very nature perpetually questioning its own assumptions, developing its own ideas and responding to developments in the wider field.... Sometimes one must stop in order to catch one's breath and commit some fraction of an ongoing dynamic process to the constraints of words on paper.... But integration never stops for long. (Clarkson, 1992: 290)

And it is in this spirit that McLeod and Wheeler (1995: 287) encourage a continuing dialogue between different approaches: 'It may never be possible to achieve coherent integration, to create the "grand theory", but let the dialogue continue'.

When integration is seen as a process in this sense the danger highlighted by Arkowitz (1992) of the introduction of a new range of integrative approaches onto the scene, thus creating further confusion in the marketplace, is likely to be avoided.

Issue 6   A question of commitment

The question here is 'How can an eclectic or integrationist gain a sense of identity and commitment?' It is a question that was addressed challengingly by Szasz (1974):

The eclectic psychotherapist is, more often than not, a role player; he wears a variety of psychotherapeutic mantles, but owns none and is usually comfortable in none. Instead of being skilled in a multiplicity of therapeutic techniques, he suffers from what we may consider, after Erikson, 'a diffusion of professional identity'. In sum, the therapist who tries to be all things to all people may be nothing to himself; he is not 'at one' with any particular method of psychotherapy. If he engages in intensive psychotherapy, his patient is likely to discover this. (Szasz, 1974: 41)

Practitioners who adhere to a single school have a kind of ready-made identity which indicates where their allegiance lies. To speak of oneself as humanistic or psychodynamic is immediately to take on a certain broad identity and to give some indication of the philosophy held and the mode of practice likely to be engaged in. To speak of oneself as eclectic or integrative, however, does not carry the same potential for identification. Indeed, for Szasz (above) these terms only indicate an absence of identity and a lack of commitment.

Identity and commitment, however, need not be seen as the province of single schools alone. Interestingly, Prochaska (1984) has applied Perry's (1970) model of intellectual and ethical development to the development of psychotherapists. Following this scheme the process of development runs through four primary stages: 'dualistic', 'multiplistic', 'relativistic' and finally 'committed'. In this view the committed practitioner is one who is not holding tenaciously to a single approach (a dualistic 'I'm right and you're wrong' attitude), but rather one who accepts with a certain humility the validity of different systems. The commitment is not to a narrow school but to the whole project of therapy. Thus, according to Prochaska, the questions with which the committed practitioner is centrally concerned are: 'what is the best way to be in therapy; what is the most valuable model we can provide for our clients, our colleagues, and our students, and how we can help our clients attain a better life' (Prochaska, 1984: 367).

Issue 7 The sociology of integration

Each of the mainstream schools of counselling/psychotherapy (psychodynamic, humanistic, etc.) has developed, albeit for the most part in a limited way, its own community of practitioners, its specialist journals and its own training programmes. To some extent at least, a professional collegiate life has developed within each school 'community'. One consequence of this development is that the practitioner who has committed both time and money in pursuit of becoming a member of such a community is likely to have a strong personal interest in its continued well-being. Those who draw their identity from belonging to one or other of these mainstream 'communities' are unlikely to give up such an investment easily. This is especially so if very little is offered in its place, and until recently the integration movement had little to offer by way of a community. No professional network has been available for integrative practitioners to identify with. However, the emergence of the Society for Psychotherapy

Integration (SEPI), with its provision of a journal, national and international networks and conferences, may be considered to be a very significant step towards the creation of an alternative 'community' of practitioners.

The way in which a professional community functions is an area of study that has been almost entirely neglected in the integration debate (Goldfried et al., 1992). I would like to suggest that it is an area which requires considerable attention if we are to understand the sociology of the psychotherapeutic field and its influences on the process of integration.

Issue 8   The language of integration

The social and professional communities referred to above are also language communities. Each community has developed its own specialized language which hinders understanding between practitioners from different schools and prevents progress in the possible integration of concepts.

The problems involved in developing a common language for psychotherapy were the subject of a special edition of the *Journal of Integrative and Eclectic Psychotherapy* (1987, 6). Driscoll (1987) called for the adoption of ordinary language as the language of psychotherapy, with the elimination as far as possible of terminology that had meaning only for a particular group of practitioners. Ryle (1987) argued for the widespread adoption of a cognitive-experimental language, and Strong (1987) for the language of social influence.

Messer (1987), on the other hand, was neither optimistic nor enthusiastic about the achievement of such a common language since he considered that though there would be some advantages, the replacement of the various theory-based languages would mean the loss of 'the associative richness and creative diversity they encompass' (p. 198). Nevertheless, he concluded his contribution by 'offering some very modest suggestions in the service of breaching the barriers among the different language communities' (p. 198). These 'offerings' included a recommendation to develop multilingualism in which practitioners learn more than one psychotherapeutic language to aid the permeation of ideas from one theory to another; a call for clarity in language and thought, with the implication that all unnecessarily obscure and jargonistic terminology, so characteristic of most psychotherapy schools, be abandoned; and the straightforward use of the vernacular when communicating with those from other psychotherapy camps.

Issue 9   The integrationist – charlatan or statesperson?

Does the integrationist have a role to play within the whole field of counselling and psychotherapy? Clearly, this question has been answered in the negative by Szasz (1974) and others (e.g. Rogers, 1951; Kennedy, 1977) who treated the integrationist with great suspicion, considering her to be more of a charlatan than a bona-fide therapist. There is no doubt, however, that as we approach the end of the millennium integration is commanding more attention and respect than at any other time. Nevertheless, there remains an impression in the hearts and minds of many that the movement has not yet quite found its way. It has still to establish a direction and role within the field as a whole. Currently, some see that role simply as continuing to foster the development of new integrative approaches. Others may have the grander vision of creating an all-embracing theory as a way of finally defining what it is all about.

I suggest, however, that the role of the integrationist is to be sought in quite a different direction. Her task is to develop connectedness with the different parts of the field, to stand between the various schools, to encourage dialogue and debate, and to find ways of helping each to discover and respect the contributions of the other. In short, her role is to serve as a kind of 'statesperson' within the field.

Understood thus, the integrationist will support what already exists and will recognize the importance of each distinctive school pushing its own frontiers further. There are therapeutic pathways that only the psychodynamicist can explore and others that only the cognitivist or behaviourist, with their specialist perspectives, can uncover. If this is so, the integrationist's role will be along the lines of a kind of translator and interpreter of the ensuing developments to the field as a whole so that their implications can be fully explored.

Seen in this way the integrationist has the high task not of creating integrated approaches, but of undertaking a 'cohesive' role which will aim at facilitating a growing sense of unity *within continuing diversity*, to enable the 'many' to have a sense of relatedness to the 'one'.

This may not only be a high task, it may, in the end, prove to be an impossible one if the spirit of 'schoolism' prevails. It is, however, an increasingly urgent task as we attempt to form ourselves into a 'unified' profession alongside other more established professions.

Alongside the above issues are those related to the nature of integrative training and supervision. These centrally important areas will be dealt with in later chapters of this book.

Eclectic/integrative research

While the importance of research is acknowledged in most of the eclectic/integrative literature, it is generally agreed that insufficient substantial outcome research into eclectic/integrative approaches has been undertaken (Barkham, 1992; Lambert, 1992; Glass et al., 1993).

Research into eclecticism/integration can be broadly divided into three areas;

- therapist attitudes and orientations;
- integrative approaches;
- the comparative effectiveness of single approaches and techniques.

Each of these areas can only be briefly reviewed here.

Research concerned with therapist attitudes and orientations

THE THEORETICAL ORIENTATION OF THERAPISTS   A number of studies have focused on the reported theoretical orientation of therapists. Most of these have been carried out in the USA and have tended to concentrate on discrete therapeutic groups (mostly clinical psychologists). A few studies, however, have been undertaken in the UK, including a comprehensive survey of the membership of the British Association For Counselling. Table 2.1 summarizes the results of a number of surveys carried out both in the USA and the UK. It should be noted that the percentage figure in the final column refers only to those therapists who explicitly adopted the label 'eclectic' or 'integrative' as a description of their theoretical orientation. When those who reported multiple approaches without adopting the eclectic label are taken into account the percentage of eclectics (by implication) rises (Jensen et al., 1990; O'Sullivan and Dryden, 1990; Vasco et al., 1992; Hollanders, 1996). When the reported use of techniques from a whole range of approaches is included the number of eclectics (again, by implication) increases very considerably (Vasco et al., 1992; Hollanders, 1996).

Table 2.1   *Studies showing percentage of eclectic therapists*

Study	Population	n	% eclectic
Garfield and Kurtz (1975)	Division 12 APA	855	55
Jayaratne (1978)	Clinical social workers	489	55
Norcross and Prochaska (1982)	Division 12 APA	479	31
Prochaska and Norcross (1983)	Division 29 APA	410	30
Norcross, Prochaska and Gallagher (1989)	Division 12 APA	579	29
Jensen, Bergin and Greaves (1990)	Clinical psychologists; family therapists; psychiatrists; social workers	423	56
O'Sullivan and Dryden (1990)	S.E. Thames Health Region, clinical psychologists	81	31.6
Norcross, Dryden and Brust (1992)	BPS, Clinical Psychology Division	993	27
BAC Membership Survey (1993)	BAC members	2,500	32
Hollanders (1996)	Multiple groups of British practitioners	309	46.9

ECLECTICISM OR INTEGRATION: THERAPISTS' PREFERENCE   In a study of 113 eclectic therapists, Norcross and Prochaska (1988) found that though respondents had earlier identified themselves as 'eclectic', 40 per cent of the sample favoured the term 'integrative'. Of the remaining 60 per cent, the term 'eclectic' was preferred by 25 per cent and 35 per cent indicated no preference at all. Among the reasons given for the 'integration' option were:

'Eclecticism has a more pejorative flavor'; 'Integrative implies a more active intellectual stance'; 'Integrationism has a positive emotional loading'. On the other hand, those who preferred the 'eclectic' label did so because: 'Eclectic permits greater freedom of choice and reorganization; integration implies less flexibility once an integration has been achieved'; 'Integration implies at the outset that one has a comprehensive plan and can predict an entire course of therapy. This promises too much'; 'Integration suggests that even incompatible approaches can be combined, which I find misleading'.

INFLUENCES ON THERAPISTS IN CHOOSING AN APPROACH   In a survey of 479 American clinical psychologists, Norcross and Prochaska (1983) asked respondents to identify the influences on them in choosing their theoretical orientation. Table 2.2. shows some of the results.

Table 2.2 *Influences on selection of theoretical orientation*

Influence	M	SD
Clinical experience	4.2	0.7
Values and personal philosophy	3.8	0.9
Graduate training	3.6	1
Postgraduate training	3.4	1.2
Life experiences	3.3	1.1
Internship	3.3	1.1
Its ability to help me understand myself	3	1.3
Type of clients I work with	2.8	1.2
Orientation of friends/colleagues	2.8	1.1
Outcome research	2.7	1.2
Family experiences	2.5	1.2
Own therapist's orientation	2.4	1.4
Undergraduate training	2.2	1.1
Accidental circumstances	1.7	0.9

1 = no influence. 2 = weak influence. 3 = some influence. 4 = strong influence. 5 = primary influence.
Source: Norcross and Prochaska, 1983

Norcross and Grencavage (1989) later expressed disappointment that 'outcome research' came only tenth on the list, showing between 'weak' and 'some influence'. It can be argued, however, that 'clinical experience', the strongest influence reported, is in itself a form of research which is bound to include reflection on outcome.

OBSTACLES TO INTEGRATION   In 1988 Norcross and Thomas surveyed the membership of the Society for the Exploration of Psychotherapy Integration (SEPI), seeking to solicit an answer to the question: 'What's stopping psychotherapy integration now?' Fifty-eight prominent integrationists responded, ranking 'intrinsic investment of individuals in their private perceptions and theories' as first on the list of obstacles. Next came 'inadequate commitment to training in more than one psychotherapy'. 'Approaches have divergent assumptions about psychopathology and health' came third. Inadequate research and the absence of a common language came third and fourth, respectively.

Research concerned with integrative/eclectic approaches

THE SHEFFIELD PSYCHOTHERAPY PROJECT   The relationship between the psychodynamic and the cognitive-behavioural therapies became a focus of the widely acclaimed Sheffield Psychotherapy Project (Firth et al., 1986; Shapiro and Firth, 1987). This is of interest to the integrationist for two reasons: first, because the 'psychodynamic' approach was based on Hobson's Conversational Model, which has a strongly integrative perspective; second, because one conclusion drawn from the study has clear implications for integration.

The project used a 'cross-over' procedure in which the participating clients were given two types of individual therapy, described as:

> (i) 'Exploratory'/relationship oriented, based upon Hobson's conversational model, with a psychodynamic basis
> (ii) 'Prescriptive', cognitive-behavioural therapy including anxiety control training, self-management procedures, a job-strain package, and cognitive restructuring. (Firth et al., 1986: 170)

The clients were assigned randomly to one of two treatment sequences, either Exploratory-Prescriptive or Prescriptive-Exploratory. The therapy was confined to eight weekly sessions of one method followed by eight weekly sessions of the other method, with the two phases being separated by a 'cross-over' time of three to six weeks. Assessment of effectiveness of the differently ordered therapies was made by non-clinician researchers using both structured interviews and self-assessments, prior to therapy, between phases, at the end of both phases, and at a three month follow-up. Both forms of therapy were reported as being therapeutically beneficial but there seemed to be some advantages to the Exploratory-Prescriptive sequence. One conclusion reached by the research team has some practical implications for psychodynamic, cognitive-behavioural and integrative (pluralistic?) practitioners:

> In centres where both prescriptive and exploratory therapies are recognised as useful, it is unusual for the same therapist to practice both. However, if one implication of the outcome literature's failure to establish one approach's superiority over another (Smith et al., 1980; Lambert et al., 1986) is that therapists need a range of skills, then the challenge of working in two distinct modes can only be beneficial. (Firth et al., 1986: 176)

MULTIMODAL THERAPY   A number of research projects have focused on multimodal therapy (MMT), with varying degrees of rigour. These include a study involving 84 adult 'neurotic patients' suffering variously from obsessive-compulsive disorders and phobias (Kwee et al., 1986). A nine-month follow-up showed improvement in 64 per cent of obsessive-compulsive sufferers and 55 per cent of phobics.

Lazarus (1992) reports conducting a number of outcome and follow-up studies, including a three-year follow-up of 20 'complex cases' who had made considerable progress in MMT. The cases included 'extreme' agoraphobia, pervasive anxiety, panic disorder, obsessive-compulsive disorder, and marital and family problems. The follow-up indicated that 14 out of the 20 had either maintained the gains or had made further gains without recourse to additional therapy.

Another follow-up study involved 100 clients who had previously failed to respond to a minimum of three different therapeutic approaches and who were considered 'intractable' by their former therapists. The follow-up showed the 61 per cent achieved 'objective and unequivocal benefits' from MMT conducted by Lazarus (Lazarus, 1992).

COGNITIVE ANALYTIC THERAPY   An example of a major British integrative approach is Cognitive Analytic Therapy (CAT). Research into the effectiveness of this approach is increasing, though it is still very limited in its scope.

Brockman et al. (1987) compared treatment outcomes between 18 clients receiving psychoanalytical therapy with 30 clients who received CAT. The Beck Depression Inventory was one of the major measures used in this study and on that basis the two approaches were found to be equally effective. CAT was found to have a slight advantage on a measure of cognitive change in relation to self-attitude, using a repertory grid technique. Since this clearly favours the specific cognitive emphasis in CAT it cannot be considered a true comparison.

An outcome study (Treasure et al., 1995) compared CAT with an 'educational-behavioural' approach in the treatment of 30 anorexic outpatients. Patients were randomly allocated to either of the approaches and treatment was conducted over a period of 20 weeks. Although the therapists who administered the treatment were described as 'inexperienced', supervision by experienced therapists was provided on a weekly basis. Weight gains were achieved by patients in each treatment group, and a one-year follow-up showed that these had been maintained. On the basis of weight gain, no significant difference was found between the therapies, but CAT patients reported greater subjective, intrapersonal (e.g. self-image) improvement than those in the educational-behavioural treatment group. Since the intrapersonal dimension was not a major focus of the educational-behavioural approach this result should not surprise us.

Overall, research into the eclectic/integrative approaches has not been strong and the caution expressed by Lambert in 1992 is still pertinent today:

Despite the seeming compatibility of psychotherapy research and eclectic psychotherapy, there is little evidence that eclectic therapies are being carefully researched. Before claims of superiority based on integration of the best from single-school approaches can be supported, empirical investigations will need to be conducted. Until such investigations have been conducted, eclectic practitioners would do well to be more modest in their claims for superiority. (Lambert, 1992: 121–2)

The comparative effectiveness of single approaches and techniques

Roth and Fonagy (1996) have produced an excellent overview of psychotherapy research to which readers with an interest in this area are referred. Here we can only draw attention to a few of their findings that may concern integrationists, focusing on the two broad areas of depression and anxiety.

DEPRESSION   While the research evidence would seem to suggest that cognitive-behavioural therapy (CBT) is likely to be more effective than less structured psychotherapy treatments, direct comparisons show only small differences among the different forms of therapy.

Evidence from the 'best-designed' studies suggests that CBT, interpersonal therapy and dynamic exploratory therapy (as used in the Sheffield Project, i.e. based on Hobson's Conversational Model) have some efficacy in treating depressed patients.

Brief dynamic therapy does not fare very well in the research studies conducted so far and seems to be less effective than cognitive therapy (Steuer et al., 1984; Covi and Lipman, 1987), cognitive therapy and medication combined (Covi and Lipman, 1987) and behaviour therapy (McLean and Hakstian, 1979). Indeed, no study shows a greater effectiveness of brief dynamic therapy over other therapies, and a number of studies show it to be less effective. However, Roth and Fonagy (1996) counsel caution in interpreting the data: 'Firm conclusions regarding the efficacy of brief dynamic techniques are not possible without further and better-designed research' (p. 90).

There are some indications of the effectiveness of supportive counselling, compared to psychiatric intervention and CBT treatment from a clinical psychologist, in treating depressed patients in a primary care context (Scott and Freeman, 1992).

ANXIETY   Behavioural treatments (e.g. systematic desensitization, exposure procedures and especially in vivo techniques) seem to be particularly effective when dealing with specific phobic reactions (Emmelkamp, 1994). Using such techniques some significant improvement can be gained in two to four sessions (e.g. with dental phobics, Liddell et al., 1994; with animal phobics, Ost et al., 1991). The evidence would seem to suggest that with this group of clients the added use of cognitive techniques does not increase the effectiveness of the interventions.

A slightly different picture emerges, however, when dealing with generalized anxiety disorder (GAD). Here, CBT would seem to be more effective than behaviour therapy alone (Butler et al., 1991). In an interesting study comparing CBT with analytical psychotherapy and anxiety management training administered over a six-month period, Durham et al. (1994) found that 81 per cent of those who received CBT were at least moderately improved, compared to 80 per cent of those who received anxiety management and 74 per cent who received analytical psychotherapy. At a six-month follow-up, 76 per cent of those who received CBT had maintained at least moderate gains. This contrasts with only 49 per cent of those who received anxiety management and 42 per cent of those who received analytical psychotherapy.

Another form of anxiety with which CBT seems to have some success is panic disorder. Beck et al. (1994) contrasted CBT with person-centred supportive therapy in treating 33 patients. CBT was administered over a period of 12 weeks but was assessed at eight weeks, and the person-centred therapy was offered over eight weeks and then assessed. Those receiving person-centred therapy had the opportunity to cross over to CBT after eight weeks for a further 12 weeks of treatment. At the eight-week assessment 71 per cent of the CBT patients were panic-free compared to only 25 per cent of the person-centred treated patients. Almost all the person-centred group crossed over to CBT after eight weeks. At a one-year follow-up, 87 per cent of those who received CBT and 79 per cent of those who had crossed over had maintained their gains.

A study of Shear et al. (1994), however, indicates the need for caution before drawing firm conclusions. Here, 15 sessions of CBT conducted according to a manual were contrasted with 15 sessions of what is described as 'non-prescriptive' therapy. This consisted entirely of reflective listening. All those taking part, however, received three initial sessions devoted to education about anxiety and the identification of triggers of panic reactions. At the end of the treatment and at a six-month follow-up no significant differences were found between those receiving the different therapies. The effect of the first three sessions, however, is unclear and it is possible that they provided a directed focus for the non-prescriptive group.

Conclusion

This brief review is intended only to point to the need for an interest in what is going on in the realm of research. In spite of the non-rigorous and non-conclusive nature of so many of the studies, they are beginning to provide some insight into what may be effective in dealing with some problems.

The relevance of this to the whole movement towards integration is obvious enough to require little further comment.

The need to do whatever we can to understand and to be open to what works best for clients with particular problems is clearly already an ethical requirement. It may soon become a legal requirement if, following a case in the USA, therapists are to be sued for not offering the most effective treatment to those seeking their help.

References

Arkowitz, H. (1991) 'Introductory statement: psychotherapy integration comes of age', *Journal of Psychotherapy Integration*, 1 (1): 1–3.
Arkowitz, H. (1992) 'Integrative theories of therapy', in D.K. Freedheim (ed.), *History of Psychotherapy: A Century of Change*. Washington, DC: American Psychological Association.
Arnkoff, D.B. and Glass, C.R. (1992) 'Cognitive and integrative therapies', in D.K. Freedheim (ed.), *History of Psychotherapy: A Century of Change*. Washington, DC: American Psychological Association.
Ayer, A.J. (1982) *Philosophy in the Twentieth Century*. London: Unwin.
BAC (1993) 'BAC membership survey', *Counselling: Journal of the British Association for Counselling*, 4 (4).
Barkham, M. (1992) 'Research on integrative and eclectic therapy', in W. Dryden (ed.), *Integrative and Eclectic Therapy: A Handbook*. Buckingham: Open University Press.
Beck, J.G., Stanley, M.A., Baldwin, L.E., Deagle, E.A. and Averill, P.M. (1994) 'Comparison of cognitive therapy and relaxation training for panic disorder', *Journal of Consulting and Clinical Psychology*, 62: 818–26.
Beitman, B.D. (1990) 'Why I am an integrationist (not an eclectic)', in W. Dryden and J.C. Norcross (eds), *Eclecticism and Integration in Counselling and Psychotherapy*. Loughton: Gale Centre Publications.
Beitman, B.D. (1992) 'Integration through fundamental similarities and useful differences among the schools', in J.C. Norcross and M.R. Goldfried (eds), *Handbook of Psychotherapy Integration*. New York: Basic Books.
Brammer, L.M. and Shostrom, E.L. (1982) *Therapeutic Psychology: Fundamentals of Counselling and Psychotherapy*, 4th edn. Englewood Cliffs, NJ: Prentice-Hall.
Brockman, B., Poynton, A., Ryle, A. and Watson, J.P. (1987) 'Effectiveness of time-limited therapy carried out by trainees: comparison of two methods', *British Journal of Psychiatry*, 151: 602–10.
Bruno, F.J. (1986) *Dictionary of Key Words in Psychology*. London and New York: Routledge & Kegan Paul.
Butler, G., Fennell, M., Robson, P. and Gelder, M. (1991) 'Comparison of behavior therapy and cognitive behavior therapy in the treatment of generalized anxiety disorder', *Journal of Consulting and Clinical Psychology*, 99: 167–75.
Clarkson, P. (1990) 'A multiplicity of psychotherapeutic relationships', *British Journal of Psychotherapy*, 7 (2): 148–63.
Clarkson, P. (1992) 'Systematic integrative psychotherapy training', in W. Dryden (ed.), *Integrative and Eclectic Psychotherapy: A Handbook*. Buckingham: Open University Press.
Covi, L. and Lipman, R.S. (1987) 'Cognitive-behavioral group psychotherapy combined with imipramine in major depression', *Psychopharmacology Bulletin*, 23: 173–6.

Driscoll, R. (1987) 'Ordinary language as a common language for psychotherapy', *Journal of Integrative and Eclectic Psychotherapy*, 6: 184–94.

Dryden, W. (1984) 'Issues in the eclectic practice of individual therapy', in W. Dryden (ed.), *Individual Therapy in Britain*. London: Harper and Row.

Dryden, W. (1991) *A Dialogue with John Norcross: Towards Integration*. Milton Keynes: Open University Press.

Durham, R.C., Murphy, T., Allan, T., Richard, K., (1994) 'Cognitive therapy, analytic psychotherapy and anxiety management training for generalised anxiety disorder', *British Journal of Psychiatry*, 165: 315–23.

Dyne, D. (1985) 'Questions of "training" – a contribution from a peripatetic cousin', *Free Associations*, no. 3.

Emmelkamp, P.M.G. (1994) 'Behavior therapy with adults', in A.E. Bergin and S.L. Garfield (eds), *Handbook of Psychotherapy and Behaviour Change*, 4th edn. New York: Wiley.

Firth, J.A., Shapiro, D.A. and Parry, G. (1986) 'The impact of research on practice of psychotherapy', *British Journal of Psychotherapy*, 2: 169–79.

Garfield, S.L. (1992) 'Eclectic psychotherapy: a common factors approach', in J.C. Norcross and M.R. Goldfried, *Handbook of Psychotherapy Integration*. New York: Basic Books.

Garfield, S.L. and Kurtz, R. (1975) 'Clinical psychologists: A survey of selected attitudes and views', *The Clinical Psychologist*, 28 (2): 6–9.

Gergen, K.J. (1992) 'Towards a postmodern psychology', in S. Kvale (ed.), *Psychology and Postmodernism*. London: Sage.

Gergen, K.J. (1995) *Realities and Relationships*. Cambridge, MA: Harvard University Press.

Gergen, K.J. (1996) Unpublished transcript of a tape of a keynote address delivered at the World Congress on Psychotherapy, Vienna, July.

Glass, C.R., Victor, B.J. and Arnkoff, D.B. (1993) 'Empirical research on integrative and eclectic psychotherapies', in G. Striker and J.R. Gold (eds), *Comprehensive Handbook of Psychotherapy Integration*. New York: Plenum.

Goldfried, M.R. Castonguay, L.G. and Safran, J.D. (1992) 'Core issues and future directions in psychotherapy integration', in J.C. Norcross and M.R. Goldfried (eds), *Handbook of Psychotherapy Integration*. New York: Basic Books.

Hinshelwood, R.D. (1986) 'Eclecticism: the impossible project – a response to Deryck Dyne', *Free Associations*, 5: 23–7.

Hinshelwood, R.D. (1990) 'Editorial', *British Journal of Psychotherapy*, 7 (2): 119–20.

Hollanders, H.E. (1996) 'Eclecticism/integration among counsellors in Britain in relation to Kuhn's concept of paradigm formation'. PhD Thesis, University Library, University of Keele.

Jayaratne, S. (1978) 'Characteristics and theoretical orientations of clinical social workers: a national survey', *Journal of Social Service Research*, 4 (2): 17–30.

Jensen, J.P., Bergin, A.E. and Greaves, D.W. (1990) 'The meaning of eclecticism: new survey and analysis of components', *Professional Psychology Research and Practice*, 21: 124–30.

Kennedy, E. (1977) *On Becoming a Counsellor*. Dublin: Gill and Macmillan.

Kuhn, T.S. (1970) *The Structure of Scientific Revolutions*, 2nd edn. Chicago: University of Chicago Press.

Kwee, M.G.T., Duivenvoorden, H.J., Trijsburg, R.W. and Thiel, J.H. (1986) 'Multimodal therapy in an inpatient setting', *Current Psychological Research and Reviews*, 5: 344–57.

Lambert, M.J. (1992) 'Psychotherapy outcome research: implications for integrative and eclectic therapies', in J. C. Norcross and M.R. Goldfried (eds), *Handbook of Psychotherapy Integration*. New York: Basic Books.

Lambert, M.J., Shapiro, D.A. and Bergin, A.E. (1986) 'Evaluation of therapeutic outcomes', in S.L. Garfield and A.E. Bergin (eds), *Handbook of Psychotherapy and Behaviour Change*, 3rd edn. New York: Wiley.

Lazarus, A.A. (1981) *The Practice of Multi-Modal Therapy*. New York: McGraw-Hill.

Lazarus, A.A. (1990) 'Why I am an eclectic (not an integrationist)', in W. Dryden and J.C. Norcross (eds), *Eclecticism and Integration in Counselling and Psychotherapy*. Loughton: Gale Centre Publications.

Lazarus, A.A. (1992) 'Multimodal therapy: technical eclecticism with minimal integration', in J.C. Norcross and M.R. Goldfried (eds), *Handbook of Psychotherapy Integration*. New York: Basic Books.

Lazarus, A.A., Beutler, L.E. and Norcross, J.C. (1992) 'The future of technical eclecticism', *Psychotherapy*, 29 (1): 11–20.

Liddell, A., di Fazio, L., Blackwood, J. and Ackerman, C. (1994) 'Long-term follow-up of treated dental phobics', *Behavior Research and Therapy*, 32: 605–10.

Luborsky, L., Singer, B. and Luborsky, L. (1975) 'Comparative studies of psychotherapies: is it true that "Everybody has won and all must have prizes?"', *Archives of General Psychiatry*, 32: 995–1008.

McLean, P.D. and Hakstian, A.R. (1979) 'Clinical depression: comparative efficacy of outpatient treatments', *Journal of Consulting and Clinical Psychology*, 47: 818–36.

McLeod, J. and Wheeler, S. (1995) 'Person-centred and psychodynamic counselling: a dialogue', *Counselling, The Journal of BAC*, 6: 283–7.

Messer, S.B. (1987) 'Can the Tower of Babel be completed? A critique of the common language proposal', *Journal of Integrative and Eclectic Psychotherapy*, 6 (2): 195–9.

Norcross, J.C. and Goldfried, M.R. (eds) (1992) *Handbook of Psychotherapy Integration*. New York: Basic Books.

Norcross, J.C. and Grencavage, L.M. (1989) 'Eclecticism and integration in counselling and psychotherapy: major themes and obstacles', *British Journal of Guidance and Counselling*, 17 (3): 227–47.

Norcross, J.C. and Napolitano, G. (1986) 'Defining our journal and ourselves', *International Journal of Eclectic Psychotherapy*, 5: 249–55.

Norcross, J.C. and Newman, C.F. (1992) 'Psychotherapy integration: setting the context', in J.C. Norcross and M.R. Goldfried (eds), *Handbook of Psychotherapy Integration*. New York: Basic Books.

Norcross, J.C. and Prochaska, J.O. (1982) 'A national survey of clinical psychologists: affiliations and orientations', *The Clinical Psychologist*, 35 (3): 1–6.

Norcross, J.C. and Prochaska, J.O. (1983) 'Clinicians' theoretical orientations: Selection, utilization and efficacy', *Professional Psychology: Research and Practice*, 14(2): 197–208.

Norcross, J.C. and Prochaska, J.O. (1988) 'A study of eclectic (and integrative) views revisited', *Professional Psychology: Research and Practice*, 19 (2): 170–4.

Norcross, J.C. and Thomas, B.L. (1988) 'What's stopping us now? Obstacles to psychotherapy integration', *Journal of Integrative and Eclectic Psychotherapy*, 7: 74–80.

Norcross, J.C., Prochaska, J.O. and Gallagher, K.M. (1989) 'Clinical psychologists in the 1980s: I. Demographics, affiliations, and satisfactions', *The Clinical Psychologist*, 42 (2): 29–39.

Norcross, J.C., Dryden, W. and Brust, A.M. (1992) 'British clinical psychologists: I. A national survey of the BPS clinical division', *Clinical Psychology Forum*, 40: 19–24.

Ost, L.G., Salkovskis, P. and Hellstrom, K. (1991) 'One session therapist directed exposure vs self-exposure in the treatment of spider phobia', *Behavior Therapy*, 22: 407–22.

O'Sullivan, K.R. and Dryden, W. (1990) 'A survey of clinical psychologists in the South East Thames Health Region: activities, role and theoretical orientation', *Clinical Psychology Forum*, October.

Patterson, C.H. (1980) *Theories of Counselling and Psychotherapy*, 3rd edn. New York: Harper and Row.

Perry, W. (1970) *Forms of Intellectual and Ethical Development in the College Years: A Scheme*. New York: Holt, Rinehart and Winston.

Prochaska, J.O. (1984) *Systems of Psychotherapy: A Transtheoretical Analysis*, 2nd edn. Homewood, IL: Dorsey Press.

Prochaska, J.O. and Norcross, J.C. (1983) 'Clinicians' theoretical orientations: selection, utilization, and efficacy', *Professional Psychology: Research and Practice*, 14 (2): 197–208.

Reber, A.S. (1985) *Dictionary of Psychology*. Harmondsworth: Penguin.

Rogers, C.R. (1951) *Client-centred therapy*. Boston: Houghton Mifflin.

Roth, A. and Fonagy, P. (1996) *What Works for Whom? A Critical Review Of Psychotherapy Research*. New York & London: Guilford Press.

Ryle, A. (1987) 'Cognitive psychology as a common language for psychotherapy', *Journal of Integrative and Eclectic Psychotherapy*, 6 (2): 168–72.

Ryle, A. (1990) *Cognitive-Analytic Therapy: Active Participation in Change – A New Integration in Brief Psychotherapy*. Chichester: Wiley.

Samuels, A. (1989) *The Plural Psyche: Personality, Morality and the Father*. London & New York: Routledge.

Samuels, A. (1991) 'Pluralism and training', *Journal of the British Association of Psychotherapists*, 22: 3–17.

Samuels, A. (1993) 'What is a good training?', *British Journal of Psychotherapy*, 9 (3): 317–23.

Schacht, T.E. (1984) 'The varieties of integrative experience', in H. Arkowitz and S.B. Messer (eds), *Psychoanalytic Therapy and Behaviour Therapy: Is Integration Possible?* New York: Plenum.

Scott, A.I.F. and Freeman, C.P.L. (1992) 'Edinburgh primary care depression study: treatment outcome, patient satisfaction and cost after 16 weeks', *British Medical Journal*, 304: 883–7.

Shapiro, D.A. and Firth, J. (1987) 'Prescriptive vs. exploratory psychotherapy: outcomes of the Sheffield Psychotherapy Project', *British Journal of Psychiatry*, 151: 790–9.

Shear, M.K., Pilkonis, P.A., Cloitre, M. and Leon, A.C. (1994) 'Cognitive behavioral treatment compared with non-prescriptive treatment of panic disorder', *Archives of General Psychiatry*, 51: 395–401.

Smith, M.L., Glass, G.V. and Miller, T.J. (1980) *The Benefits of Psychotherapy*. Baltimore: Johns Hopkins University Press.

Steiner, G.L. (1978) 'A survey to identify factors in therapists' selection of a theoretical orientation', *Psychotherapy: Theory, Research and Practice*, 15: 371–4.

Steuer, J., Mintz, J., Hammen, C., Hill, M.A., Jarvick, L.F., McCarley, T., Motoike, P. and Rosen, R. (1984) 'Cognitive-behavioral and psychodynamic group psychotherapy in treatment of geriatric depression', *Journal of Consulting and Clinical Psychology*, 52: 180–92.

Strong, R.S. (1987) 'Interpersonal theory as a common language for psychotherapy', *Journal of Integrative and Eclectic Psychotherapy*, 6 (2): 173–84.

Szasz, T.S. (1974) *The Ethics of Psycho-Analysis: The Theory and Method of Autonomous Psychotherapy*. London: Routledge and Kegan Paul.

Treasure, J., Todd, G., Brolly, M., Tiller, J., Nehmed, A. and Denman, F. (1995) 'A pilot study of a randomised trial of cognitive analytical therapy versus behavioral therapy for adult anorexia nervosa', *Behaviour Research and Therapy*, 33: 363–7.

Vasco, A.B., Garcia-Marques, L. and Dryden, W. (1992) 'Eclectic trends among Portuguese psychotherapists', *Journal of Psychotherapy Integration*, 2 (4): 321–31.

Wachtel, P.L. (1991) 'From eclecticism to synthesis: towards a more seamless psychotherapeutic integration', *Journal of Psychotherapy Integration*, 1 (1): 45–54.

Wachtel, P.L. and McKinney, M.K. (1992) 'Cyclical psychodynamics and integrative psychodynamic therapy', in J.C. Norcross and M.R. Goldfried (eds), *Handbook of Psychotherapy Integration*. New York: Basic Books.

Walsh, B.W. and Peterson, L.E. (1985) 'Philosophical foundations of psychological theories: the issue of synthesis', *Psychotherapy*, 22: 145–53.

Webster's New International Dictionary (1920).

Wolfe, B.E. and Goldfried, M.R. (1988) 'Research on psychotherapy integration: recommendations and conclusions from an NIMH workshop', *Journal of Consulting ad Clinical Psychology*, 22: 448–51.

PART II

THERAPEUTIC APPROACHES

3
THE CONVERSATIONAL MODEL

Jane Martin and Frank Margison

The Conversational Model integrates psychodynamic, interpersonal and humanistic approaches to therapy. Integration suggests that the elements are part of one combined approach to theory and practice, as opposed to eclecticism which draws ad hoc from several approaches in the approach to a particular case.

This model of therapy was developed by Dr Robert Hobson, Reader in Psychotherapy at the University of Manchester and a former Training Analyst of the Society of Analytical Psychology in London. Drawing on several traditions, it now represents a tradition, which may be termed psychodynamic interpersonal (PI). It is rooted in the psychodynamic concepts of the unconscious or barely conscious underpinnings of relationships, with particular links to Jung. It has been influenced by interpersonal models of ego psychology, in particular the work of Harry Stack Sullivan. The model also overlaps with the Rogerian approach, in terms of respect for the person, but this approach emphasizes active exploration within a conversation.

Dr Hobson describes the 30 year evolution of his model of therapy in *Forms of Feeling* (1985). In vivid language, rich with imagery and quotations from literature, philosophy, psychology and religion, he eloquently reveals 'the heart of psychotherapy'. Central to the model is the notion of the therapist's task of assisting the patient or client toward developing a deep and whole sense of self by means of a personal conversation. The word is used with the wide meaning of 'the action of living or having one's being in a place or among persons' (OED). In a therapeutic conversation, two persons come together and create a relationship. Within this relationship, the patient may begin the process of personal problem solving.

Development of the therapy

Robert Hobson was born and brought up in the Rossendale Valley in North-East Lancashire, attended medical schools in Cambridge and Manchester, and trained in psychiatry at the Bethlem Royal and Maudsley Hospitals in London. In developing the Conversational Model he has drawn upon many and diverse influences upon his life and career, not least his actual personal conversations with teachers, colleagues and friends.

Though he trained as a Jungian analyst, Hobson has always had his feet firmly planted in the real world of the National Health Service, where he was responsible for psychiatric in-patients throughout his career. If done well, he believed the Conversational Model should form the basis of any psychiatric interview. He regarded psychotherapy as an important component of the treatment of serious mental illnesses such as schizophrenia and bipolar affective disorder. In his paper 'The Messianic Community' (1979) he describes his experience of setting up a therapeutic community for profoundly disturbed patients, an enterprise in which he was strongly influenced by the 'living-learning' concept described by Maxwell Jones.

In Hobson's view, psychotherapy is seen both as an art and a science. Throughout, he has invited scientific appraisal and scrutiny of his poetic vision. In 1974 he returned to Manchester, where he continued his pioneering approach to the use of audio and video taping of therapeutic sessions for research and teaching purposes. Since then, training packages making use of videotape have been produced (Margison, 1984) and the model has been researched extensively (Barkham et al., in press).

Theory and basic concepts

During the 1950s Dr Hobson visited Carl Jung in Switzerland. Though he moved away from a strictly Jungian perspective, Hobson distilled some core elements of Jung's actual clinical work to incorporate into his own model. Central among these are the importance of a 'symbolical attitude', the Jungian focus on the immediate present, or 'here and now', and the concept of the 'dialectical meeting' (or conversation).

Literary influences, in particular Wordsworth and the Romantic poets, have been important; central to the model is a particular kind of feeling-based, associative language. The linguistic emphasis also reflects the influence of Wittgenstein. Further input from the realm of philosophy comes from Martin Buber, whose notion of 'I–Thou' meeting was inspirational for Hobson.

Drawing on great religious writers such as St John of the Cross, Hobson has also extended the reach of psychotherapy into the spiritual domain. The Christian influence is seen in the idea of 'aloneness togetherness' as opposed to 'loneliness', where the image of being forsaken has deep resonance in Christian culture.

Designed for those people whose problems or symptoms arise from disturbances in interpersonal relationships, the Conversational Model assumes that such disturbances can only be explored and modified effectively within another relationship: the therapeutic one. This relationship is fluid and dynamic; it grows and deepens via the gradual development of a mutual language of understanding which Dr Hobson calls a 'feeling language', within which the 'moving metaphor' assumes fundamental importance. Patient and therapist strive to meet in a relationship of 'aloneness togetherness' and therapeutic growth takes place in the space between them.

The aim is to promote a sense of being connected, but not of fusion. There is mutuality in the relationship, but it is nevertheless an 'asymmetrical mutuality', wherein the therapist must not lose sight of the patient's vulnerability.

Forms of Feeling is a remarkable and unique work. Quoting Wordsworth, Hobson sets out to 'choose incidents and situations from common life, and to relate or describe them throughout, in a selection of language really used by men; and at the same time to throw over them a certain colouring of imagination whereby ordinary things should be presented to the mind in an unusual way' (Hobson, 1985: xi). He takes familiar words such as 'experience', 'feeling', 'actions' and 'acts', 'signs and symbols', presenting them to us, his readers, to explore and wonder at their meanings. The best of poets will choose their terms with the same exact precision as the scientist who seeks to find truth. Every word Robert Hobson writes is packed with significance: 'I can only find myself in and between me and my fellows in a human conversation' (Hobson, 1985: 135)

A crucial aim in psychotherapy is to recreate self-esteem, so as to feel at ease with 'myself'. Hobson's model assumes that persons who seek psychotherapy have had to endure a disruption to their sense of personal existence. In developing his ideas on how we form a sense of self, he was interested in Piaget's observations of infant play. There are parallels with Winnicot's Attachment Theory in Hobson's notion of the importance of the mother's attunement to the baby's early attempts to engage her in a rudimentary kind of conversation, characterized by facial expression and body movement. This aspect of the theory underpinning the Conversational Model has been particularly developed and described by a long-time friend and colleague of Hobson, Professor Russell Meares of the University of Sydney (Meares, 1993). In the early weeks of life, the baby's concept of self is seen as consisting solely of a subjective, existential 'I'. By the age of about 15 to 18 months, the infant is able to point to his own image in the mirror and seems to recognize it as an objective self – a 'me'. The crucial point about this process of development of a sense of self is that it occurs interpersonally. If all goes well, it is the mother (or caregiver) who, in her responses to the baby's 'proto-conversation', has played out the role of the 'me' during those early months. She has been the baby's 'fellow'. This idea of a duplex self (I/me) has much in common with the writings of William James (1962), but Hobson has extended it, with the emergence of a sense of 'myself'.

'Myself' grows in the context of a continuing sense of the presence of the other, as the child becomes interested in physical objects in the outside world, and begins to play with them in a symbolical way. This symbolic play develops optimally if the mother is sufficiently attuned to her child to allow a space between them to grow. The space must be sufficiently wide for the child to gain a sense of his own boundaries, yet mother and child must remain close enough to preserve a sense of relatedness. In Hobson's terms, they are alone together. As the young child plays, he talks to himself in a curious kind of play language, which is wandering, non-grammatical and rich with symbols – quite different from the 'linear' language of everyday speech, which uses signs more than symbols. Some time between the ages of 5 and 7 years, we no longer hear this language spoken aloud when the child is playing. It has been internalized, along with a sense of a more complex feeling 'self'. Pure examples of these two forms of language may be observed in legal documents, representing the linear language of the external world, and poetry, the essence of a feeling language. But for the most part we use a mixture of the two, with the language of that inner world embedded in everyday language in the form of metaphor.

Meares (1993) has speculated on the ways in which the developmental processes outlined above may be disrupted. If the caregiving environment fails to provide the feeling of resonance with another, the growing individual feels unconnected. The result may be that he learns to focus solely on the outside world and attends exclusively to stimuli originating from it, particularly those that impinge upon the body. He may become preoccupied with somatic or bodily symptoms – and his attempts at conversation feel boring and dead. Hobson describes an encounter with such a patient, Freda, who is 'talking about her symptoms – as if they are "out there". She is treating herself as if she were only a thing, and talking at me as if I were a thing, not talking with me as a person' (Hobson, 1985: 21–8).

Alternatively, the growth toward 'myself' may be disrupted by repeated traumas, which may not even be remembered. These might include threats of abandonment, shaming, ridiculing, or simply failing to acknowledge the child. In adult life, some patients who have experienced such traumata will live with an enduring and profound inner emptiness.

The therapeutic conversation attempts to address these deficiencies by the creation of a relationship within which the patient and therapist, alone and together, can discover the 'myself' who was lost or submerged. In and between the therapeutic space, the symbolic language of play is reinvented, in order to access the inner world which has been stunted. The key to this world lies in metaphor, 'understanding and experiencing one thing in terms of another' (Lakoff and Johnson, 1980: 5) for it can only be reached indirectly. The conversational therapist does not know the appropriate language beforehand, but has to learn it in a collaborative process with each patient, proceeding tentatively and making continual corrections and adjustments, so that a harmony develops and patient and therapist are truly conversing.

Practice and clinical issues

The goal of the approach is to promote personal problem solving. It is assumed that the patient will have been using inappropriate or maladaptive ways of avoiding pain, especially that of loss or separation. The aim is to create a situation in which the problem will be directly presented in the relationship with the therapist, rather than merely talked about. It may then be identified, explored and modified within the context of the therapeutic conversation. This is a reciprocal and creative process. Despite its multi-dimensional theoretical underpinnings, the Conversational Model lends itself quite readily to a teaching package, which can be learned relatively quickly by trainee therapists. Its essential elements are as follows:

1. The therapist's style.
2. Specific actions by the therapist during sessions.
3. Using metaphor.
4. Developing the conversation.
5. Setting and structure.

Style

The therapist aims to help the patient feel understood not only by appearing friendly and interested, but also by using more specific techniques, with scrupulous attention to the 'how' rather than the 'what'.

'I' AND 'WE'   Whenever possible, the therapist refers to herself and to the patient in the first person. This emphasizes the importance and immediacy of a dialogue between two separate yet related persons.

USING STATEMENTS   The therapist uses statements rather than questions. If questioned, the patient may feel interrogated and under pressure to provide some sort of answer. Statements give him the space and freedom to develop and explore themes.

NEGOTIATING   Statements should be made tentatively rather than dogmatically, to allow the patient to correct or modify therapist interventions. The therapist does not need to get everything right first time. If the patient sees that he is being encouraged to help the therapist with the process of trying to get it right, they can establish an atmosphere of collaboration – a true conversation. This promotes both a sense of autonomy and a feeling of really being understood in a deeper way than if the therapist were to behave as though she were the infallible source of all wisdom. The patient is also less likely to feel intruded upon by an all-knowing other.

Hobson writes: 'A personal conversation is a movement; it progresses not by comfortable agreement but by correction of mistakes. In intimate relationships we constantly miss the mark and it is out of the gap that new possibilities emerge. Then it is possible to explore jointly the nature of the misunderstanding' (Hobson, 1985: 197).

Specific therapist actions

STAYING WITH THE 'HERE AND NOW'   Although the therapist's statements are tentatively put, she is not passive. She should direct the patient repeatedly to focus on what is being experienced at that moment, during the interview. This technique attempts to enable the patient to recreate past feelings and to express and explore them in the immediate therapeutic environment.

PICKING UP CUES   A therapist's task is to listen and to observe the minute particulars of the patient's words, tone of voice and behaviour. These are cues – verbal, vocal and non-verbal – which the therapist must first register and then find a way to feed back to the patient so that they may work together on whatever theme the cue has attempted to communicate.

Some cues arise from the therapist herself. She may become aware of strong feelings toward a patient during a session, or notice that she is behaving somewhat unusually. If she reflects upon these types of cues she may discover that they are pointers to how the patient is feeling. The idea is similar to psychodynamic concepts of 'countertransference', where the patient may unconsciously be influencing the therapist to respond in certain ways that are characteristic of the patient's interpersonal relationships. Sometimes the patient's feelings are so intolerably uncomfortable that they are projected or deposited into the therapist, who then experiences them on the patient's behalf. Supervision is extremely important to enable the therapist to understand and manage this aspect of therapeutic practice.

GENERATING HYPOTHESES   Like many everyday English words, 'hypothesis' has a specific meaning in the Conversational Model. Hobson has defined hypotheses as 'ways of promoting the exploration and organisation of feeling' (Hobson, 1985: 198). Despite some similarity to 'interpretations' in analytical psychotherapy, hypotheses differ in several important respects. 'They are not the goal of therapy, nor are they essential for "insight"' (p. 198). They are also offered by the therapist in a manner that carries less certainty and conviction and conveyed in more subtle language. There are three types of hypothesis: understanding hypotheses; linking hypotheses; explanatory hypotheses.

1 *Understanding hypotheses*. This type of hypothesis leads most directly from cues given by the patient and picked up by the therapist. It is a statement of empathy, but it attempts to go beyond mere empathic reflection of the patient's feelings. The therapist tries to express empathy in a way that communicates a desire to understand. The aim is to elicit a response that can build a dialogue within which the patient's feelings can be further explored.
2 *The linking hypothesis* is a statement that relates feelings which emerge during therapy sessions with other feelings both inside and outside the therapy. It identifies a parallel between the patient–therapist relationship and other important relationships in the patient's life and therefore draws on the psychodynamic concept of transference.
3 *An explanatory hypothesis* approaches most closely the concept of the interpretation. It is the most complex of the three kinds of hypothesis and the therapist should refrain from offering it until she has been able to accumulate sufficient knowledge of the patient for it to make sense to both of them. Hobson distinguishes between 'reasons for' and 'causes of ' disturbances in interpersonal relationships. An explanatory hypothesis attempts to put forward a reason, which may or may not be a cause. In its most complete form, the explanatory hypothesis puts together three 'because' clauses, for example, 'I shrink back into my overcoat because I am scared of getting too close to you because, then, you would cruelly reject me' (Hobson, 1985: 198.) This is a particularly concise example and often the explanatory hypothesis will extend over a much longer verbal exchange in the session.

The reason for the difficulties in interpersonal relationships usually lies in a repeated pattern of maladaptive behaviour. With the explanatory hypothesis the therapist is trying to link this behaviour to an underlying conflict or fear. If the hypothesis is offered in a way that feels acceptable to the patient, he can acknowledge and own the conflict, begin to explore it with the therapist and perhaps find alternative and more healthy ways of dealing with the difficulties.

Metaphor

Metaphor may be simply defined as 'understanding and experiencing one thing in terms of another' (Lakoff and Johnson, 1980: 5). It is usually viewed as a linguistic concept, but 'it is pervasive in every day life, not just in language but in thought and action' (p. 3.) Language, then, functions as a source of evidence for the nature of our conceptual system, or how we define the world and ourselves. Unsurprisingly, therefore, metaphor has been invaluable to psychotherapists as a means of enriching emotional communication with patients and deepening the mutual understanding of experiences.

Metaphor is a particularly vital component of the Conversational Model, being especially relevant to promoting what Hobson terms a symbolical attitude. By this, he means a willingness to value and confront the 'living symbol' as an important message to be explored. Living symbols may take many forms: they may be words, pictures, everyday physical objects or dreams. As he points out, a symbol 'throws together' (sym, bole) what is known and what is (as yet) unknown (Hobson 1985: 110). It can form a bridge between the external and internal worlds and so illuminate hidden depths of the individual psyche. 'The growth of a personal conversation means discovering living symbols that can be shared, stayed with and developed' (p. 112). This kind of 'imaginative elaboration of feeling' is essential to the process of 'personal problem solving' (p. 112).

Developing the conversation

The process of personal problem solving is the central activity of the Conversational Model. This is a creative, shared activity wherein patient and therapist work together to discover a language of feeling. The patient's interpersonal problems are located as they manifest themselves within the therapeutic conversation. This will reveal ways in which the patient has habitually avoided pain, which may mean acknowledging actions that were formerly denied or disclaimed. Hobson's notion of disclaimed actions has something in common with the psychodynamic concept of the unconscious, but the process by which the patient comes to own his actions is more gradual than via the traditional psychoanalytic interpretation.

Using the specific techniques described above, the therapist aims to build a relationship with the patient which is mutual yet asymmetrical. The therapist is not 'opaque' like the psychoanalyst; she is perceived as a human being rather than a blank screen. But she does not burden the patient with information about her own life and its problems.

Similarly she must find a balance between empathy and collaboration. Like the person-centred therapist, she aims to empower the patient, but this model emphasizes a more active method of engagement, which goes beyond providing 'facilitating conditions' for the client to reach his human potential.

The overall balance to be sought is an even subtler one. The conversational therapist must strive to be both artist and technician. It is essential to be open to the nuances of symbolic imagery when it is presented in a psychotherapeutic session and to work with the patient in a sincere, genuine and spontaneous way. But it is equally essential to be attentive to learning, practising, evaluating and refining the skills that are necessary to achieve this end. 'Neither imagination nor sincerity are enough without style and technical skill. If sincerity or candour is absent, art is corrupt; if the technique or mode of expression is inadequate then art is poor. Psychotherapy can be corrupt and it can be poor' (Collingwood, 1963 cited in Hobson, 1985: 93). 'There can be poor art and poor psychotherapy which, although not corrupt, fail owing to inadequate technique' (p. 94). Hobson recommends learning and self-monitoring via 'the disciplined use' of tape recorders and videos.

Setting and structure

As with other models of psychotherapy, regularity and predictability of time and place are important boundaries to contain the patient in an often difficult and painful endeavour. A typical session will take place on the same day each week, the room will remain constant, and the furniture will be arranged so that patient and therapist can sit on identical chairs set at an angle, so that each can look at each other or look away.

A therapeutic contract is discussed and agreed at the beginning of therapy and will include details of time and place for appointments, the expected duration of therapy and agreement, if necessary, over certain 'conditions', for example, that the patient is expected not to self-harm or take recreational drugs during the period of the therapy. (Whether or not such conditions need to be negotiated will vary from individual to individual, but it is important to be clear about this from the outset when particular problems can be easily predicted from the formulation.) Therapy may be open ended or time limited, short term or long, but the essential point is that both parties agree upon an appropriate plan before therapy starts.

At the start of a first session, the therapist may acknowledge the patient's anxiety by making some remark about the unfamiliarity of the situation, for example, 'I suppose you might be feeling a bit strange, coming to see someone like me'. This should have the effect of making the patient feel a little more at ease and encourages him to express feelings from the first few moments of the therapy. On subsequent occasions the patient will usually make the opening remark.

The start of a session is also the time at which to communicate any anticipated changes to the routine of therapy, for example, if the therapist is going to have to cancel or rearrange a session. The therapist must ensure that there is time to discuss and explore such issues, both in terms of maintaining the therapeutic alliance and also because changes and interruptions may throw up important personal material for the patient.

Through the middle part of a session the therapist should listen attentively and with interest to the patient, mindful all the while of cues that can be picked up and worked with. She uses the specific techniques and strategies already outlined, to build a conversation and to deepen rapport. When the time seems right, hypotheses are offered and the patient is given the opportunity to accept, reject or modify them and to work with what they suggest to him about himself.

If the patient has become distressed, the therapist should help him to gather and prepare himself for the end of the session by saying how much time is remaining. Clearly, her manner and tone of voice are crucial factors that can make this feel helpful for the patient rather than like an abrupt dismissal.

Indications and contraindications

Unlike, for example, cognitive therapy, the Conversational Model is not symptom specific and can therefore be useful to a variety of patients and problems. There is good evidence that it is effective for patients with mild to moderate depressive disorders (for example, Shapiro and Firth, 1987) and probably for the more enduring state of low mood known as 'dysthymia'. It is not incompatible with concurrent pharmacological treatment by antidepressants, although often it will follow a course of drug treatment rather than coincide with it. As with other forms of psychological treatment, this type of therapy by itself is not sufficient for people going through a more severe form of depression, when they are too ill to make use of an explorative approach, but a 'conversational' approach can be part of a multi-dimensional treatment package and can attempt to reach out to the depressed patient in his terrible loneliness and despair.

The Conversational Model has been used with in-patients on psychiatric wards who are suffering from the more severe forms of 'mental illness' such as bipolar affective disorder (or 'manic depression') and schizophrenia. Again, and particularly if the patient is acutely psychotic, it forms just one part of a treatment package that may include psychotropic drugs and other forms of therapy. This approach challenges some conventional thinking of the modern 'biological' approach in psychiatry in that it attempts, through the conversation, to assist the patient in finding personal meaning in apparently bizarre and incomprehensible psychological experiences. In that sense, it harks back to an earlier era in psychiatry, predating the advent of antipsychotic drugs in the 1950s, but by no means rejects the importance of pharmacotherapy.

Another example of the more 'difficult' patient in psychotherapy terms is the person who somatizes, or expresses personal problems in bodily terms. This kind of patient is traditionally regarded as 'unsuitable' for psychotherapy because of a lack of 'psychological mindedness'. He thinks and speaks in concrete terms and has particular difficulty with symbol formation. In more severe instances, these patients may have no words for emotional feelings. The term 'alexithymia' (Nemiah and Sifneos, 1970) has been used to describe this phenomenon. With its emphasis on interpersonal communication by means of metaphor, the Conversational Model can be particularly helpful for these people (see also Guthrie et al., 1991).

The principles of the Conversational Model have also been used to inform group, couple and family practice. In all these situations the principles of developing a common feeling language are followed.

It is important to mention that, just as medicinal drugs can have undesirable side effects, any form of psychotherapy has the potential to do harm. In a classic paper, 'The Persecutory Therapist', Meares and Hobson (1977) examined the characteristics of a damaging situation where therapy can become a reciprocal, mounting attack. Though this is more likely to arise with certain types of client, they warn that it can be exacerbated or even created by the therapist, particularly if the therapist has a 'blind spot' about particular emotional themes.

Case study

The patient

Louise was a 38-year-old woman seen by one of us (JM) for a total of 25 weekly therapy sessions in the setting of a specialized NHS outpatient psychotherapy department. She had presented to her general practitioner with depression following the serious illness of her husband, who had developed cancer when their baby daughter was six months old. The child was three years old when I began seeing Louise and was undergoing investigations for epilepsy. Louise's depressive symptoms had improved with antidepressants, but she herself believed that psychological therapy was required in order for her to understand more fully the roots of her depression. She had had a hard life, but had always 'coped' with adversity in the past and was dismayed to find that she could no longer do so. In her assessment session (with FM) she was able to identify that her 'coping' had consisted of a tendency to compartmentalize her problems, which she had then been able to solve using her intellect and practical skills, while denying her emotional distress.

Louise was the only child of a mother who seems to have had mental health difficulties that resulted in unpredictably aggressive behaviour, which was usually directed at her daughter. Memories of childhood consisted largely of repeated attempts to placate mother, which only failed and resulted in further emotional neglect and physical cruelty. Father, who was much older than mother, had died four years previously of cancer. Louise remembered him with great affection, but recalled that he had 'kept his head down' when mother went on the rampage. From an early age, therefore, Louise had learned to look out for herself and to sort out her own problems. She left home at 17 and had lived independently until the age of 35, when she married an older man who had been in good health until his recent illness.

The therapy

At our first meeting, Louise stated that she wanted two results from therapy: first, to avoid repeating the same 'cycle of abuse' with her own daughter; second, to be able to 'feel good about myself'. It was clear that she was devoted to her child and she recognized that she was a good mother, but it was equally clear that exhausting amounts of energy were dedicated to trying to be as *unlike* her own mother as possible. She told me that she would 'comfort eat' and then feel bad about herself, but that her obesity served to 'give me a reason for why people won't like me. Now, if I was *thin* . . . !'

In our early sessions, it was difficult to get the *conversation* going. Louise always attended punctually and scrupulously observed the other structural boundaries of the treatment alliance, but she frequently expressed bewilderment about what she was 'supposed to do' and stated that she could not always understand the things I said and did. (In response to this I felt a strong urge to soothe, reassure and explain.) It all felt rather awkward until after I had had to cancel a session unexpectedly. Over the next few weeks we were able to begin to explore the effect on Louise of my sudden 'abandonment' of her. While she insisted angrily that it had been of no great importance, the material she brought was all about people in her life who had let her down by leaving her. She was so distressed at the end of one session that I found myself guiding her out of my room to ensure that she was alright before leaving the building. Gradually we were able to look at the split between her angry dismissal of me and her more hidden plea for care and guidance. Her formerly denied neediness was present in the here-and-now relationship between us and its emotional impact was available to us, to be explored in a deepening *conversation*.

EXTRACT FROM EARLY SESSION
> L: I don't feel very well today. Nearly didn't come. [*Pause*] Mind if I keep my coat on? I'm feeling a bit shivery.
> JM: [*Nods and gestures assent.*]
> L: I didn't want to cancel, in case you thought I wasn't bothered about the therapy. [*Pause*]
> JM: Mmm. And I might . . . ?
> L: Mmm. Well . . . [*avoids addressing the possibility that **I** might not be bothered about **her**.*] Last week's session [*the session after a break*] I don't think it went very well. It was like starting all over again.

JM: After I cancelled on you. [*addressing her avoidance of the pain of my abandonment of her*]

L: Yeah. And then you seemed to be telling me I was angry about it. And I *wasn't* angry [*sounding angry*] – I was *disappointed*. And I thought, *you* don't know me; *you* don't know what I'm feeling. [*Pause*] And I was ready to talk about my dad that week [*sounding sad*] and now the moment's passed. [*Here I had probably failed to pick up an important cue, 'You don't know what I'm feeling' and had allowed 'the moment' to pass.*]

L: [*has gone on to talk about her disappointment at a friend's plans to move away*] So it's not worth getting close to people, is it?

JM: [*bringing us back to the here and now*] And I guess *I'm* going to move away from you, next September. [*the expected end date for our therapeutic contract*]

L: Yes, but I don't have any expectations of you, in an emotional sense.

JM: Perhaps it almost feels like it's not worth it, if I'm going to leave you anyway.

L: Mmm. [*Pause*] You know, my mum used to forget my birthday. And when I said anything she used to say *she* never had any birthday cards, so, it was like, you know, why should it matter to *me*?

JM: Sort of, maybe, like telling you how you were feeling. [*picking up on the cue previously given and missed, which is here being offered again*]

L: Yeah. Maybe. [*Pause*]

JM: And just now you said you felt like *I* was telling you how you were feeling, last week [*a linking hypothesis*]

L: Yeah, it's sort of similar, I suppose, isn't it? [*Pause*] I've always felt stupid, and wrong. What I want is to be treated with respect. [*Pause*] It's funny, my dad's dead and my mum's still alive, but sometimes I feel as if she's died too.

JM: As if you're having to grieve for her too.

L: Yeah. [*tearful*] It's like an open wound . . .

JM: . . . that won't heal [*picking up her metaphor*]

L: [*cries*] No, it won't.

Now that we were beginning to speak the same language, we could start to make links between Louise's feelings towards me and her earlier experiences, in particular her relationship with her mother. The essential task for us in this therapy was the emotional re-creation of a maternal relationship which, however, should not merely recapitulate the old abusive dynamics. For example, Louise was later able to tell me how fearful she had been of my possible hostile retaliation when she had plucked up the courage to tell me of her anger towards me and how, when I did not launch a counter-attack, she had felt safe enough to explore showing her feelings more openly, not only with me but also in other contexts outside the therapy.

By extracting the foregoing details from the early sessions of this therapy, I have attempted to illustrate some of the components of the Conversational Model, namely the importance of: staying with the here and now; picking up cues (both in the patient and in oneself); generating hypotheses; and metaphor.

I understood Louise's depression as the result of her having internalized a sense of a cruel chastiser (in psychoanalytic terms she could be thought of as having developed a particularly punishing superego). For Louise I represented both such an unpredictably critical and abusive figure and also potentially a 'fairy godmother' rescuer. But I think it was the tentative, negotiating style of the therapy that made it possible for Louise to work with me in the transference and to understand the experience, without feeling overwhelmed. This process was facilitated by the use of *metaphor* in which the therapy was particularly rich. We were able to work together in a symbolical way, developing our own therapeutic language.

An example of the kinds of metaphor that developed between us was the humorous use of the word 'Utopia' to refer to a small, drab Lancashire mill-town that is hardly famous for its utopian qualities. Louise had often considered moving to live there, so as to be close to her in-laws, whom she tended to idealize as being a 'normal' family. Over the weeks and months, the metaphor was extended until it had become a kind of mutually acceptable shorthand for all that Louise had yearned for in her life. Gradually she was able to recognize how her idealization of people and places operated to defend her against her despair at her feelings of being inadequately 'mothered'. Further than this, she struggled to acknowledge her feelings of disappointment in my failure to provide her with the longed for perfect mothering. She accurately compared the therapy to a process of grieving, where she passed through stages of denial, followed by anger, bargaining, searching, sorrow (she became more depressed for a while) and finally a sense of peace.

At the end of the therapy Louise reported that she could delight in her husband and daughter, no longer constantly fearing that they were going to be snatched away from her. She had started a weight-reducing diet and was enrolling for adult education classes with a view to moving on to paid employment again. Her angry despair about her mother had mutated into a more integrated mixture of compassion and regret and she had (symbolically) begun to wear a ring her mother had once given her.

Some months later she demonstrated how far she was continuing to be able to utilize the metaphorical language of the therapy. When I wrote to her for permission to use this material, I added a postscript to let her know that a potted plant she had given me at our final session was 'thriving'. In her written reply she added that she too was 'thriving'.

Wider implications and applications

Just as it may be used for working with a wide variety of clients and clinical problems, so the model lends itself flexibly to a range of settings. It has been used principally in the context of the British National Health Service until now, but is also used in independent practice. Within the NHS, it was first developed in hospital settings, with both outpatients and inpatients. When Dr Hobson first returned from London to Manchester in 1974 he developed the Conversational Model as a practical application of psychotherapy which could be utilized across a range of services, both specialized and more general psychiatric centres. He established a psychotherapy service at Gaskell House in Central Manchester. The use of a coherent model of psychodynamic interpersonal therapy, even with acutely ill inpatients, has influenced a generation of psychiatrists, psychologists, nurses, occupational therapists and social workers working in that setting. Hobson has been equally influential in forging academic links between psychotherapy and psychiatry, which have led on to a programme of research and development between Manchester, Sheffield and Leeds and with North America and Australia (see Barkham et al., in press). The research developments have focused on three main areas:

1. There have been six randomized controlled studies of the model in patients with depression, long-term psychiatric illness and somatization. All have shown that the Conversational Model is effective and in comparisons with cognitive behavioural therapy the two methods are similar in their effectiveness. Therapy can be very short, for example, in the '3 + 1 sessions model' or very long term.
2. The process underlying therapeutic change has focused on the therapeutic alliance and a model of assimilating problems. A key aspect of the model was the use of metaphor in a study of effective therapies where the client reported new insights.
3. The third theme has been the development of new teaching methods using video teaching tapes, supervision and role play with doctors, nurses, psychologists and counsellors. The research on the teaching methods suggests that the basic principles are easy to acquire and are remembered well.

Future developments

The Conversational Model is by far the most intensively researched psychodynamic model in the UK. There is an active research programme trying to gather more knowledge about how people are helped to change, with whom the model is most helpful and how therapists can become more skilled in recognizing therapeutic dilemmas and dealing with them. This has led to more attention being paid to the underlying skills (or 'competencies' in modern terminology) and how the can be taught more effectively. The early research work focused on depression and somatic problems. Recently the model has been used to help staff on inpatient wards to develop a team formulation and to withstand the powerful dynamics of splitting and projection which occur in working with psychosis, especially where there has been sexual abuse (Davenport, 1997). In a sense this is the model returning to its roots as Hobson originally described it in an intensive therapeutic milieu.

Psychotherapy is in a strange situation at the turn of this century: the imperative of evidence practice is pushing health service practitioners into a critical scrutiny of their own effectiveness. The work on the Conversational Model has shown that therapists can stand and be counted in terms of evaluating their own practice. Concurrent research on the underlying therapeutic processes supports the idea that change can occur through many different pathways. The evidence that metaphor is used as a foundation stone in effective therapies has validated the insistence of Conversational Model therapists that we pay attention to the 'minute particulars' of language and develop a 'shared feeling language'.

It is striking that these research discoveries are not only congruent with what therapists believe, but are also consonant with the other pressures on practitioners: to be self-reflexive, aware of subtle cultural nuances, meeting the patient or client as equal while retaining responsibility for ethical practice, and finally in meeting the user-led demand for therapies to deal with the meaning of underlying symptoms.

The focus on the Conversational Model from the outset has been to live in the rich but uncomfortable zone where psychotherapy should be evaluated at least as rigorously as physical treatments while also developing a conversation between persons. The current research on the Conversational Model has been extending the role of therapy for patients who had previously been excluded. We have been working with patients who have attended as psychiatric outpatients for long periods with no benefit and shown that even brief therapy can reduce symptoms and also reduce the overall cost of treatment. Other work led by Dr Else Guthrie has been with patients who present with physical symptoms such as irritable bowel syndrome. Recently, we have started work with counsellors in primary care, trying to impart the basic Conversational Model skills to help their work with clients who have significant difficulties like somatization or intense suicidal thoughts. We have developed a teaching package including videotapes, role plays and a treatment guide to help keep the key therapeutic issues in focus.

Notes

In an attempt to address the perennial dilemma of the English language's gender-specific pronouns, 'she' has been used throughout to denote caregiver and therapist, while 'he' has been used for the child and the patient.

The Conversational Model was developed by a doctor and has grown up in the context of the National Health Service. The authors are both doctors and are therefore most familiar with the term 'patient' rather than 'client'. The application of this term in no way implies that other practitioners using this model in other settings should adopt our medical language. In the true spirit of the Conversational Model we believe that therapist and client/patient should feel free to use the language which feels most appropriate to them both.

References

Barkham, M., Guthrie, E., Hardy, G., Margison, F. and Shapiro, D. (in press) *Psychodynamic-Interpersonal Therapy*. London: Sage.

Collingwood, R.G. (1963) *The Principles of Art*. London: Oxford University Press.

Davenport, S. (1997) 'Psychological interactions between psychosis and childhood sexual abuse in in-patient settings: their dynamics, consequences and management', in C. Mace and F. Margison (eds), *Psychotherapy of Psychosis*. London: Gaskell.

Guthrie, E., Creed, F., Dawson, D. and Tomenson, B. (1991) 'A controlled trial of psychological treatment for the irritable bowel syndrome', *Gastroenterology*, 100: 450–7.

Hobson, R.F. (1979) 'The Messianic Community', in R.D. Hinshelwood and N. Manning (eds), *Therapeutic Communities*. London: Boston and Henley.

Hobson, R.F. (1985) *Forms of Feeling: The Heart of Psychotherapy*. London: Tavistock/Routledge.

James, W. (1962) *Psychology: Briefer Course*. London and New York: Collier.

Lakoff, G. and Johnson, M. (1980) *Metaphors We Live By*. Chicago and London: University of Chicago Press.

Margison, F.R. (1984) *A Conversational Model of Psychotherapy: A Teaching Model*. London: Tavistock. (Now available from Technical Manager, University Dept. of Psychiatry, Withington Hospital, West Didsbury, Manchester M20 8LR.)

Meares, R. (1993) *The Metaphor of Play: Disruption and Restoration in the Borderline Experience*. Northvale, NJ: Jason Aronson.

Meares, R. and Hobson, R.F. (1977) 'The persecutory therapist', *British Journal of Medical Psychology*, 50: 349–59.

Nemiah, J. and Sifneos, P. (1970) 'Affect and fantasy in patients with psychosomatic disorders', in O.W. Hill (ed.), *Modern Trends in Psychosomatic Medicine: 2*. London: Butterworth.

Shapiro, D.A. and Firth, J. (1987) 'Prescriptive vs. exploratory psychotherapy: outcomes of the Sheffield Psychotherapy Project', *British Journal of Psychiatry*, 151: 790–9.

4
INTEGRATING SYSTEMIC THINKING IN COUNSELLING AND PSYCHOTHERAPY

David Bott

Systemic thinking in counselling and psychotherapy is perhaps best defined by distinguishing it from the psychological theories and models which preceded it. While there are fundamental differences between the way in which psychodynamic, cognitive-behavioural and humanistic approaches view the etiology of problems and how intervention should proceed, they share a common emphasis on intrapsychic processes. These are described variously as: unresolved conflicts related to developmental experience; faulty and inadequate learning; or a self-concept that is restrictive of actualization. Psychological approaches, while often recognizing the centrality of family experience, focus primarily on the family in its internalized form and intervention is directed towards changing the way in which the client deals with internal experience. This usually takes place within an exclusive therapeutic relationship with a view to working through transference phenomena; enhancing and reinforcing learning; or offering the core conditions for growth.

Systemic thinking has been described as a shift in paradigm (Kuhn, 1962) in that primacy is given to the context or environment within which problems concerning an individual emerge with particular attention to the living family group. Symptoms are understood as arising from inherent tensions and contradictions within family life and intervention is directed towards changing relationships rather than the intrapsychic functioning of the individual who is identified as having a problem.

This is not to suggest that psychological and systemic thinking are mutually exclusive. The polarization that was, until recently, a feature of the relationship between systemic and individual approaches is giving way to rapprochement (Bott, 1994). Indeed, while integration across paradigms is not a simple matter of eclectic addition, the two approaches have the potential to complement one another and the same practitioner who focuses intrapsychically on the internalized family can, at the same time, give attention to the externals of family life (Bott, 1990). Further, thinking and intervening systemically no longer requires that whole families attend and additions to the literature have looked at the potential for working systemically with individuals (Allen, 1988; Jenkins, 1989; Jenkins and Asen, 1992; Bott, 1992; Bott, 1994). A new flexibility of approach is most apparent in the opportunities presented by post-modern ideas and the impact of social constructionism upon systemic practice (Pocock, 1995a, 1995b). This chapter will explore the way in which family systems theory may be applied outside the formal arrangements and technology that have characterized work with family groups. Possibilities for integration both within a systemic framework and in relation to other theories and models will be examined.

Development of the therapy

The origins of the central principles which underpin the therapeutic application of systems thinking are to be found within developments in mathematics and physics during the late 1940s and 1950s and the attempt to model mechanically aspects of human thinking (Guttman, 1991). The project for general systems theory was to arrive at functional and structural rules which could describe all systems. In this process Norbert Wiener (1954) recognized the importance of self-regulation as an aspect of systemic functioning, focusing on the way in which information on past performance is fed back into the system influencing future behaviour. He coined the term 'cybernetics' for the study of this self-correcting feedback process.

Gregory Bateson, working as an anthropologist in the 1950s, is to be credited with recognizing the significance of these ideas for the realm of human activity, noting the way in which self-correcting patterns of behaviour were manifest in cultural activities and ceremony. He went on to develop these ideas within the Palo Alto group (Haley, 1976) which was funded to study communication with particular attention to families with a schizophrenic member. In applying principles from cybernetics to human communication and organization, this group had enormous influence on the development of family therapy as not just a new mode of treatment but a radically distinct way of thinking and intervening. Bateson himself, although regarded by many as the founding figure in the development of family systems theory and family therapy, was not primarily interested in therapeutic intervention and subsequently moved on to study communication in porpoises.

Pocock (1995b), drawing on Hegel's notion that the historical development of ideas proceeds by a process of the antithetical rejection of an initial thesis followed by synthesis, has recently drawn attention to the way in which the development of family therapy has been characterized by radical leaping at the expense of consolidation and synthesis. While there is common ground in the view that symptomatic behaviour in an individual is best understood within the context of that person's significant relationships, the short history of family systems thinking and practice has been complex and diverse with a number of distinct schools emerging.

Theory and basic concepts

Feedback, circularity and immanent mind

The critical idea that sets family systems theory apart from other therapeutic approaches is Bateson's notion of 'immanent mind' in that it locates thinking not within the individual's brain but as part of larger systems residing in balance with the environment:

> The basic rule of systems theory is that, if you want to understand some phenomenon or appearance, you must consider that phenomenon within the context of all *completed* circuits which are relevant to it. The emphasis is on the concept of the completed communicational circuit and implicit in the theory is the expectation that all units containing completed circuits will show mental characteristics. The mind, in other words, is immanent in the circuitry. We are accustomed to thinking of the mind as somehow contained within the skin of the organism, but the circuitry is not contained within the skin. (Bateson, 1971: 224)

This enables Keeney (1979: 120) to postulate the following generalizations:

1 Difficulties in any part of the relationship system may give rise to symptomatic expression in other parts of the system.
2 Symptomatic relief at one part of the system may result in the transfer of symptomatic expression to another site.
3 Significant change . . . in any part of the system may result in changes in other parts of the system.

The implications of this are that symptoms presented in an individual cannot be understood outside the context in which they emerge and causality is viewed as circular rather than linear.

The family life cycle

Although family process is to be understood in terms of circularity, families exist in the linear dimension of time and family stress is most likely to occur around life-cycle transition points (Carter and McGoldrick, 1989). Within the family it is necessary to manage the dual functions of providing security and stability while accommodating the developmental needs of all family members. Thus, the family must, by its nature, make significant changes over time and the tension between stability and change is worked through in a series of discontinuous crises interspersed with periods of comparative calm. This is a complex process since family interrelatedness means that the developmental achievement of each person is dependent upon the support and success of all other members. The emergence of symptoms in a family member may be understood as a function of the failure of the family to negotiate sufficiently the upheavals required to accommodate the changing needs of its members. Carter and McGoldrick take the view that a particularly fraught time leading to symptom formation will be when the 'horizontal stressors' of both predictable and unpredictable life changes combine with 'vertical stressors' inherited from past generations in the form of family history, patterns and myths. In this way, a difficulty presented by a family member may be understood as providing solution to a developmental problem which appears intractable for the family.

An example of this is offered by Haley who argues (1976, 1980) that the point where a young person is leaving home can be such a time of multiple crisis with all generations of family members facing challenging transitions. At the same time that the young person faces the challenges of independence, the parent generation have to re-establish a relationship as a pair and pick up new responsibilities for the grandparent generation who, themselves, may be facing failing health, dependency and death. The situation will be exacerbated if tension in the spouse relationship has been mediated through parenting or where there has been a separation and the young person has assumed a pseudo-spouse role. If transgenerational vertical themes of loss and separation also feature, an intolerable family crisis may be avoided at the expense of the young person concerned through failure or emotional breakdown. In systems terminology (Guttman, 1991) deviation amplifying events activate feedback mechanisms which have the potential to affect family life and organization in one of two ways: either the basic rules and equilibrium of the system are maintained in homeostasis or there is a dramatic overall change in the rules of the system and a fundamental rearrangement in the relationship between the elements of the system. In this case, the threat to the family status quo presented by the young person's departure can either introduce positive feedback to the family system, taking it forward into a new set of rules and a rearrangement of relationships, or result in negative feedback that serves to keep the family frozen and unable to move on. It follows that systemic intervention is directed towards introducing new information into the system with a view to promoting deviance amplification in such a way that it cannot be ignored or disqualified.

In response to this challenge a number of schools have emerged. These can be defined as systemic in that they share a common basis in the view that interactional patterns between people contribute significantly to the difficulties experienced by individuals (Jones, 1993). At the same time, there are differences in the way that therapeutic goals are defined and in the interventions used to achieve these. Further, family systems approaches differ in the manner in which they draw explicitly or implicitly upon other social and psychological theories and models.

Family systems approaches

An attempt to account fully for the wide range of developments in the field would occupy several volumes in its own right. At the risk of over-simplification, brief summaries of significant movements and schools will be provided as a basis for establishing their potential for integration within the broad field of counselling and psychotherapy. Taking up Pocock's comments mentioned earlier, three core movements can be identified within which separate schools or approaches may be located.

THE PSYCHODYNAMIC IMPETUS   Given the tensions that are often present between psychodynamic and systemic practitioners, it is interesting to note that the initial impetus for contextual family work came from psychodynamically oriented individual therapists. Examples of this are to be found in the work of: Nathan Ackerman, Murray Bowen, Lyman Wynne, Carl Whitaker, Ivan Boszormenyi-Nagy and James Framo in the USA. Robin Skynner (A.C.R. Skynner) and John Byng-Hall are British examples of the same movement. Here, the attempt was made to link intrapsychic and systemic ideas. For these theoreticians and practitioners, the focus on the present of systems theory is combined with a concern for how the system has developed over time through the identification and examination of transgenerational issues. Problems are understood in terms of repeated patterns in relating (Framo, 1976) perpetuated by family myths or scripts (Byng-Hall, 1973) and as failure in the process of separation and individuation from the family of origin (Bowen, 1978). Intervention is aimed at insight and understanding combined with changing actual behaviours with current intimates. Until very recently, the psychodynamic transgenerational contribution has been relatively neglected with the pre-eminence of the communication theories developed at Palo Alto and the subsequent development of the structural, strategic and early Milan models.

STRUCTURAL, STRATEGIC AND EARLY MILAN MODELS   Structural therapy followed from the work of Salvador Minuchin (1976) combining systemic thinking with sociological principles to delineate a structural functional model of the family, giving attention to the appropriateness of: the boundaries around activities in the family and around the family as a whole; the alignment of family members; and hierarchies of decision making. Problems are viewed as a function of poor or inappropriate family organization and change is directed towards realigning family relationships in such a way that symptomatic behaviour becomes redundant. Although often linked with the structural approach, strategic models (Haley, 1976; Madanes, 1981; Fisch et al., 1983) are less concerned with form and structure than with a close examination of communication processes. The hypnotic techniques of Milton Erikson have also been very influential (Haley, 1973) and the strategic model can be viewed more accurately as a theory of resistance and change rather than a model family functioning.

Problems follow from mismanagement of family life-cycle imperatives and change is introduced through the use of indirect tactics utilizing paradox and metaphor usually as an aspect of task setting. The early Milan approach (Selvini Palazzoli et al., 1978) set out to adhere closely to Bateson's original ideas and the subsequent work of the Palo Alto team on communication (Watzlawick et al., 1967). The central principles of the approach are: the formulation of hypotheses which attempt to encompass the family relational system and the meaning of the symptomatic behaviour within it; the use of circular questions (Tomm, 1987a, 1987b, 1988) about relationships within the family, operationalizing Bateson's notions of feedback and circularity by introducing information about difference; and holding a neutral position in relation to individual family member's views. Assuming the homeostatic tendency of systems, paradoxical interventions are a feature of the approach. These are considered to be counterparadoxical in that they are intended to 'counter' the paradoxical double-bind that is a feature of dysfunctional family communication (Watzlawick et al., 1967; Selvini Palazzoli et al., 1978).

In the late 1980s disquiet was beginning to be expressed about the excesses of what has come to be called 'modernist' systemic theorizing (Lask, 1987; Speed, 1987) and the appropriateness of developments within the systemic practice as a response to human pain and distress. Nichols (1987) reminded practitioners that to say the family is *like* a system as a way of conveying the rich inter-connectedness between family members is quite different from the dehumanizing reification of treating the family as a *system*: 'Family therapy has taught us to see a wife's nagging and a husband's withdrawing as circular, it sometimes fails to see the pain behind this behaviour' (Nichols, 1987: 20).

POST-MODERNISM AND SECOND ORDER CYBERNETICS   Most recently, partly in a response to these concerns, there has been considerable enthusiasm for a post-modern narrative position which seeks to replace the cybernetic metaphor with a linguistic one (Anderson and Goolishian, 1988; Hoffman, 1990; White and Epston, 1990). The project of these recent developments has been to reject what is viewed as the potential for oppressive practice in the therapeutic certainty of modernist approaches in favour of a more respectful collaborative approach. Here, family systems practitioners have rediscovered social constructionism (McNamee and Gergen, 1992) and this has been combined with a widened focus extending to the social and political drawing on Foucalt's (1980) ideas about power and discourse. As family experience is organized in the form of narratives or stories, the social construction of meaning through language becomes the focus for understanding difficulties and the therapeutic task is to create the conditions where new more productive stories become a possibility. The experience of family members is validated through the recognition that all views are valid and therapist power is challenged as representative of a dominant discourse. A full exposition of philosophical, theoretical and practical implications of these developments is beyond the scope of this account, but the introduction of a post-modern social constructionist view has important implications in terms of the objectives of this book. If the extreme relativity of some interpretations of this position is put on one side, it not only provides us with a useful critique of the potential for oppressive practice which follows from the 'expert position' of modernist certainty, but also creates the philosophical conditions where integration across theories and models is possible. As Pocock argues: 'All serious theories of individual, family and societal processes, whatever their origin, can have a place since none is true' (1995b: 48).

> One challenge for family therapists is to risk the insecurity and disloyalty of de-identifying from any major theoretical approach and instead to see them all as possible perspectives from which to look at and think about any therapy situation. (Pocock, 1997: 295)

Practice and clinical issues

It will have become clear from the preceding section that, with perhaps the exception of the early Milan approach, there is no such thing as a pure systems approach to therapy. The Milan approach itself has now been superseded by what has been termed 'second order cybernetics' which is closely linked to post-modern narrative approaches to therapy (Jones, 1993). In applying the systemic metaphor to the therapeutic process, practitioners and theorists have found it necessary to draw on the contribution of other approaches and disciplines. However, there remains a perspective that may be viewed primarily as systemic in that it emphasizes reciprocity or circularity, understands symptomatic behaviour in context and intervenes at that level of relationship. A framework is now suggested for practice which is informed by integrated systems thinking. Here, the reader may chose to interpret integration in either or both of two ways. It is possible to remain primarily 'systemic' in focus and, in that case, integration is achieved by drawing upon a range of family systems models at different stages of the therapeutic process. Equally, integration may be viewed in broader terms, crossing the systemic and psychological paradigms referred to earlier and integrated practice may involve the selective use of systemically informed models while working predominantly from a psychological perspective. Both of these possibilities are in keeping with the new freedoms we allow ourselves in a post-modern era which, while recognizing knowledge, is less certain about truth (Pocock, 1995).

The therapeutic relationship

The considerable attention given to the nature of the therapeutic relationship in the family systems literature of late and the case for a more 'user friendly' approach (Reimers and Treacher, 1995) requires only limited comment here given a readership which is likely to regard it as axiomatic that the notion of respect for persons should underpin all therapeutic activity. Individually oriented counsellors and psychotherapists may be puzzled by the conclusions for practice arising out of the social constructionist approach since they appear to replicate many aspects of Rogers's (1990) 'core conditions'. This is not to suggest that empathy was every absent from much of family systems practice, but rather that it did not necessarily follow from the application of cybernetics and the possibility was left open for mechanistic and oppressive practice.

A number of papers have appeared in the systemic literature which address this issue (Wilkinson, 1992; Perry, 1993; Pocock, 1997). Given a systemic view, empathy also takes on an additional aspect (Bott, 1994). In common with other approaches, empathy directed towards the client is essential for engagement and maintaining the therapeutic relationship. Additionally, as intervention is primarily concerned with real relationships in the present, the experience of receiving an empathetic response provides the client with a model which can be transferred to their own dealings with other family members and a method for engaging with them in a non-threatening manner with a view to changing transactional patterns (Bott, 1992).

An integrated family systems framework

Throughout work with a client, in keeping with both social constructionist and humanistic approaches, the therapeutic relationship will be characterized by collaboration and respect for the uniqueness and validity of the client's story about themselves. At the same time the client's narrative will be located within the relational context in which it has been constructed. Over the therapeutic process of engagement, intervention and change, different systems approaches suggest themselves at particular stages of the work (Bott, 1994).

Referral, assessment and engagement

The family life cycle has a significant contribution to make at the initial stages of intervention. In order to bring a contextual perspective to bear on client referral, the first question asked by a systemically informed practitioner is 'why now?'. The client's symptoms will be viewed in relation to the developmental challenges being negotiated by all family members and the attempt to distinguish between problems which are a manifestation of the 'normal' crises generated at times of life-cycle upheaval and more chronic difficulties requiring intervention will be central to assessment. This is to avoid becoming part of the problem by unintentionally acting as a stabilizing influence at a time when change is indicated. As Haley (1976: 3) argues: 'When a therapeutic problem is defined as the social relationships of clients, a therapist must include himself [sic] in the issue since he helps define the problem. . . . The way one labels a human dilemma can crystallise a problem and make it chronic.'

For example, a child experiencing difficulties in going to school may be unintentionally resolving a life-cycle related dilemma for other family members thrown up by the tangible indication of separation from the family. Defining the presenting problem as a psychological symptom and thus legitimizing the child remaining at home will have very different consequences from a label of school refusal. It should be added that a systemic approach would require investigation of the school 'system' with a view to uncovering circumstances that might equally account for the symptomatic behaviour. If these emerged then intervention could be directed at the level of the school.

The structural approach (Minuchin, 1976) also has a particularly useful part to play at the opening stages of intervention. Minuchin proposes a normative model for healthy family functioning which requires that the family system as a whole, and the subsystems contained within it, are surrounded by clearly marked but permeable boundaries and that relationships are organized hierarchically with parents taking charge of children while treating them in an age-appropriate way. Symptoms are understood as a function of inappropriate or poor organization and intervention is guided by an examination of: boundary arrangements; alignments between family members; and the way in which authority is exercised. Thus in the example of school refusal above, a structural formulation might be: that there are rigid impermeable boundaries around the family system and a close alliance between one parent and the child is undermining effectiveness of the other parent.

Within a traditional family systems model, therapy would require that the whole family attend and the therapist would note how the process was acted out in the therapy room. Arguably, this is still indicated where the person identified as having the problem is a child. Children do not have the power to make changes in their relationships with other family members. However, when an adult comes for individual counselling or psychotherapy, issues concerning boundaries, alignment and hierarchy can be addressed by asking the following questions:

1 What was the function of the client's role in their family of origin at critical transitions in the family life cycle?
2 How differentiated is the client from her or his family of origin?
3 How functional is the structure of the client's family of marriage or partnership.

In this way structural principles can guide both assessment and treatment planning (Bott, 1994). An important caveat here is that it is essential to keep in mind cultural and ethnic variations (Bott and Hodes, 1989).

Intervention

The circular questioning of the Milan School, which uses feedback to gather information about relationships and thus about the family system, provides a means by which the systemically informed individual practitioner can 'bring the family into the room'. This combines the gathering of information with an intervention in itself as the client increasingly 'notices' the context of the perceptions, attitudes and beliefs within which the symptomatic behaviour occurs. As Jenkins and Asen (1992: 7) point out: 'The therapist's questioning is intended to help the client view himself as having options for change, examine his beliefs about others' imagined beliefs about him, and see himself and others as part of a wider interactional system'.

Circular questioning will address the past, present and future in relation to the problem and potential blocks for change can be identified and addressed by inviting the client to imagine the consequences of change for those with whom she or he is in a significant relationship.

Geneogram construction, an approach associated with transgenerational family systems models (Bowen, 1978; Lieberman, 1979), provides another way of bringing the family into the room. As with circular questioning, it feeds back to the client information about the family system in a way that it is less likely to be ignored or disqualified. The geneogram constitutes a visual representation which not only provides facts concerning events over the history of the family and its cultural influences, but also has the potential to indicate repetitive transgenerational patterns and provide clues about family myths that may have been incorporated into a 'script' (Byng-Hall, 1985). In this way individualistic assumptions can be challenged as the client's difficulties are understood contextually both in terms of the 'horizontal' challenges of the family life cycle and the 'vertical' replication of transgenerational family issues.

Minuchin (1976) has coined the term 'family dance' capturing the implications of interconnectedness of family membership and the need for everyone to move in order to accommodate change in one member. As intervention proceeds and the client becomes increasingly aware of the 'dance' in which they are engaged, the focus will be directed increasingly towards helping them actively to change the part they play in the family system. At this stage the client and therapist will identify and negotiate tasks which involve the client changing an aspect of their communication or behaviour and holding that change against pressures to conform to predictable patterns by other family members. For example, a familiar issue in couple work is where a poor boundary around the couple relationship prevents a renegotiation of roles with either or both partners remaining 'children' within their family of origin. Here, a task might be agreed which functions to define the new arrangements by reducing or changing the nature of communication with the parent generation. Strategic interventions (Haley, 1976; Madanes, 1981; Fisch et al., 1983) may also have a part to play at this stage. The use of paradoxical techniques may be regarded as questionable by some practitioners, but other aspects of the approach like reframing, positive connotation and the introduction of play can be helpful in changing the meaning of relational patterns, thus destabilizing rigid arrangements and creating a climate where the unpredictable is possible.

Change – returning home in order to leave

Where family systems intervention has taken the form of work with an individual, the closing stage is directed towards helping the client to control and change the part that they play in the system of their family of origin (Bott, 1992). Here, intervention is informed by the approach of Murray Bowen (1978). The central principle of this work is Bowen's view that the relationship between the self and the system is characterized by a variable degree of differentiation in relation to fusion which, in the absence of intervention, remains broadly constant throughout an individual's life. Psychological well-being is a function of the extent to which an individual can differentiate a 'solid self', characterized by clearly defined principles and autonomous choices, from the 'pseudo self' that is an expression of failure to separate from the emotional enmeshment of his or her family of origin. Therapeutic intervention is guided by two principles. The first is that of triangulation: the recognition that two-person relationships are inherently unstable and that, when there is stress, a third person will be drawn in to divert anxiety leading to stability without resolution. Second, there is the notion of 'reactive distance'. This describes the tendency for an individual to react to a strong pull towards fusion by cutting off entirely from family contact. Ironically, distance only serves to intensify lack of resolution and leads to a re-enactment of the family dilemma in new relationships. Therapeutic intervention aims to help the client re-enter the family system in order to establish a person-to-person relationship with each family member and thus to interrupt triangulation. With this, the therapist supports the client in holding a differentiated position against the pressure to conform to previous family patterns.

Allen (1988) has taken up these ideas while also introducing the notions of 'empathic discussion' and 'metacommunication'. Empathic discussion provides the client with a way of approaching family members which is likely to reduce resistance. The client is encouraged to understand other family members' feelings and actions and to communicate that understanding instead of attacking and blaming them. Metacommunication is a central principle in all systemic work describing the process of communicating about communication (Watzlawick et al., 1967). Family stuckness is maintained by an unspoken rule that members do not communicate about their communication with one another, or, put another way, they do not talk about what is going on between them. The therapist helps the client introduce metacommunication moving from a discussion of past events to the current family predicament. Thus, in the latter part of the therapeutic process the therapist sets out to help the client to help the family to help them change (Bott, 1992). Here, it is no longer necessary to bring an imaginary family into the room since there are real family members available with whom it is possible to make direct contact. Overall, the intention is for the client to establish a differentiated position in relation to other family members and to hold that position while introducing information to create a 'difference that makes a difference' (Bateson, 1971).

Combining systemic and psychological approaches

In keeping with the emphasis of this chapter and, in the interests of coherence, a model for integration within the systems paradigm has been presented. This does not preclude the possibility of practitioners who work predominantly from a psychological perspective from drawing eclectically from any of the stages presented above providing that the fundamental distinctions of levels of explanation and intervention are kept in mind (Bott, 1990).

One possibility within an integrated humanistic approach is to conduct therapeutic intervention in such a way as to shift the emphasis from psyche to system as therapy progresses. Thus, the experience of the core conditions (Rogers, 1990) at the opening stages of intervention not only provides the client with an opportunity to identify unhelpful introjects acquired in childhood in the form of a restricting self-concept but also models the skills the client will need later to deal with family members in the present. Similarly, the next stage characteristic of an integrated model where the focus shifts to themes and patterns and the way these are acted out in the therapeutic relationship provides the experience of metacommunication as therapist and client give attention to the way they are dealing with each other. As has been outlined above, the ability to empathize and metacommunicate while holding an individuated position are means by which the client can unlock the family dilemma and change patterns of relating.

Indications and contraindications

The view taken here is that it is both appropriate and effective to view problems within the context of family arrangements and to intervene by engaging with or having an individual client engage with actual family members. While, arguably, a systemic perspective is always useful, direct relationship work is contra-indicated where there has been a history of sexual or severe physical abuse. Here, intervention should be directed towards supporting the client in building support systems as an alternative to destructive family experiences. Also, strategic interventions have no part to play where there are issues of safety for the client or others with whom they are in contact.

Case study

The client

John was referred for individual therapy by a colleague who had been working with him and his partner Jane as a couple. John and Jane had originally sought help because of John's ambivalence in making a commitment to Jane and difficulties in their sexual relationship. In terms of systemic thinking, the couple therapy had had the unfortunate consequence of defining John as the problem. However, as individual work had been requested and as both John and Jane felt that couple therapy had proceeded as far as it could without John making a fundamental shift, I agreed to offer one-to-one work with John while retaining a systemic focus and leaving it open that couple work might be introduced at a later stage. This willingness to work flexibly from the clients' perceptions of the problem and how they would like to be helped rather than imposing a particular mode of intervention is consistent with the shift in systemic work towards 'user friendliness' (Reimers and Treacher, 1995).

John, a teacher in his late twenties, had originally come to the south of England from the Midlands to attend university and had subsequently stayed on. Even as a student, he had had very little contact with his family, choosing to spend vacations working locally. Now contact was limited to the occasional letter from his mother and brief attendances at major family events where John would leave at the earliest possible opportunity. John recounted how he had had a row with his father when he was 16 and had never had a proper conversation with him since. His relationships with women, prior to meeting Jane, had been casual and brief. Interestingly, in terms of the presenting problem, he reported having experienced no difficulties in sexual performance before his relationship with Jane. Now, for the first time, he had met someone for whom he had deep feelings and to whom he felt he wished to make a commitment, yet at the same time he experienced severe doubts which were exacerbated by difficulties in obtaining and sustaining an erection.

The therapy

Initial speculation around life-cycle issues suggested that John had not negotiated the necessary upheavals and rearrangements around leaving home, acting in a manner consistent with Bowen's notion of reactive distance. It appeared that the challenge of managing a committed relationship with Jane was contaminated by this unresolved family dilemma. In short, John needed to separate satisfactorily before he could try to reattach.

Therapeutic intervention proceeded by addressing the structural questions suggested above. It transpired that John had grown up in a rural area where his father owned a large farm. John was the eldest of four children, having a brother three years younger than him and, then, two younger sisters at two-year intervals. He described his father as distant and controlling. His mother by contrast looked to John for the emotional support she was unable to obtain from his father, with John also taking on the responsibilities for his younger siblings which were more appropriate to a parental rather than a sibling relationship. A tentative structural formulation at this stage suggested that: there had been a very poor spouse relationship; John and his mother had been in a close alliance with John acting as a spouse-child; John had taken on some inappropriate parental functions; and the family had been geographically and socially isolated showing tendencies towards enmeshment. The hypothesis of enmeshment was supported by the information that John's brother and one of his sisters still lived in the family home and his youngest sister lived close by, spending much of her time there.

Systemically, the process of information gathering can be viewed as an intervention in itself. As John began to answer questions about relationships between himself and family members and family members' relationships with one another, information about his family system was being 'fed back' to him as he noticed what I was noticing. The same process was apparent in geneogram construction which yielded among other things a history of a proud and independent family arranged along patriarchal lines. An interesting feature of this was the way in which the family tended to absorb marriage partners at the expense of contact with their own families of origin.

As John's understanding of the family context within which he had grown up developed, attention was given to preparation for returning home. This aspect of systemic work has been described as 'coaching' (Carter and McGoldrick, 1976) and techniques of assertiveness, role play and role reversal were employed to support John in his attempt to re-enter his family while retaining a differentiated position. It was decided that he would approach his family in two stages. First, he would meet with his siblings and, though apparently surprised by being contacted by John after so many years, a time-limited get-together was arranged at his youngest sister's house. Sadly, his brother was unwilling to attend. It should be emphasized here that, from a systemic perspective, it is the process of changing patterns of relating that is critical. Family of origin work does not entail the cathartic unloading of past resentments which is a feature of some individual therapies. Instead it requires that, on the basis of an understanding of their family system achieved at the earlier stages of intervention, the client deals sensitively with actual living family members. This is achieved by communicating understanding about the feelings and actions of other family members while respecting their ability to face the emotions thrown up by this process.

Encouraged by what had turned out to be a surprisingly positive experience, John prepared to return to the family home. This was initiated by writing a letter to his father stating the wish to visit, in itself a change to the predictable family pattern, as was a letter from his father suggesting possible times. There is insufficient space to go into detail but the outcome of the visit was that, to his great satisfaction, John had actually managed to have independent contact with both his mother and father. It is worth mentioning here that clients are often surprised by the way in which, contrary to their expectations, family members are willing to meet them half-way and even appear relieved that an impasse has been broken. John reported that he was struck by a 'little world very closed in with nothing impinging'. In a direct but not aggressive manner John had told his father about his new relationship and that he was considering marriage. His father was clearly unhappy with what he had been told but instead of escalating the conflict, John had expressed understanding of his father's position while making it clear that he would decide for himself. John, while realistic about the extent to which things could change, was nonetheless pleased that he had been able to have some direct contact with his father as a grown man rather than remaining emotionally 'stuck' in the position of an angry and confused adolescent. He reported being 'glad he went'.

The next task was to address John's current relationship. Here, a return to couple work was proposed. This needed to be carefully handled because of the unbalancing effect of John's relationship with me and particular attention needed to be given to engaging with Jane (Boddington, 1993). The complications thrown up by moving from individual to couple work or vice versa are mitigated within a systemic approach by the non-transferential emphasis of the therapeutic relationship. The systemic practitioner seeks to put the transference back where it belongs by giving primary attention to actual family relationships rather than focusing on distortions in the therapist–client relationship. Thus, at the outset of the couple phase of therapy, attention was given to exploring the replication of family of origin patterns in John and Jane's relationship (Framo, 1982).

It was unsurprising to learn that Jane had held a triangulated position in her own family. As a child she had attempted to provide emotional support for both her parents through a long and acrimonious marriage break-up. It seemed reasonable to speculate that from John's relationship with his mother intimacy had become confused with intrusion where, for Jane, John may have represented something of the father she could not reach out to. It emerged that Jane's mother now lived a few streets away from her and her sister had come to live in the same town. John's ambivalence might also be explained by the potential for exchanging one enmeshed family with another. Structural intervention was directed towards encouraging John and Jane to place a boundary around their relationship, controlling Jane's availability in response to the continuing emotional demands of her mother and sister. A combination of behavioural and strategic principles informed work on the sexual issues. Central to this process were 'homework' tasks which, while requiring sensual sharing, forbade genital contact or intercourse.[1] This paradoxical injunction served to relieve performance anxiety while speaking to aspects of John's rebellious character forged by his experiences of being over-controlled as a child.

Just prior to completing therapy John took Jane on a visit to his parental home announcing their engagement while making it clear that they would be having a simple wedding close to their home in the south. They are now married.

Wider implications and applications

As has been demonstrated, the systemic approach lends itself to individual, couple and family work. This also extends to the level of the community and systemic responses to juvenile crime are being developed in the USA (Henggeler et al., 1996). Further, practitioners working in other approaches will benefit by incorporating systemic thinking and taking a contextual view of problems presented in an individual.

Future developments

The systems approach grew out of a combination of frustration with the efficacy of one-to-one psychodynamically informed work and an enthusiasm for the conceptual elegance of a comprehensive explanation of human relatedness. Over its life family systems therapy has had to negotiate the developmental challenges of separation and individuation. It managed the exit from its early confusion of identity with its psychoanalytic parent by defining itself in terms of what it was not: an approach giving attention to individual experience. New found confidence made it possible for rapprochement and models for working systemically with individuals began to be developed. Most recently the considerable interest in social constructionism has challenged the mechanistic tendencies which can follow from a systemic metaphor, reintroducing individual experience. This can be taken too far. As Nichols (1987: 85) argues: 'Attempting to do therapy without transforming the context may at best be slow, at worst futile' and Whitaker (1982) goes so far as to suggest that individual therapy only works to the extent that the clients are able to change their intimate relationships. Philosophical developments have provided the conditions for a new flexibility and the future for both contextual and individual approaches lies in a synthesis which recognizes what each has to offer the other.

Note

1 It should be noted that practitioners who have not had a formal training in sex therapy would need to refer on for this aspect of the work.

References

Allen, D. (1988) *Unifying Individual and Family Therapies*. San Francisco: Jossey-Bass.
Anderson, H. and Goolishian, H. (1988) 'Human systems as linguistic systems: preliminary and evolving ideas about the implications for clinical theory', *Family Process*, 27 (4): 371–93.
Bateson, G. (1971) 'A systems approach', *International Journal of Psychiatry*, 9: 242–4.
Boddington, D. (1993) 'Limitations of personal counselling: the case for couple therapy', *Journal of the British Association for Counselling*, 4: 33–5.
Bott, D. (1990) 'Epistemology: the place of systems theory in an integrated model of counselling', *Journal of the British Association for Counselling*, 1 (1): 23–5.
Bott, D. (1992) '"Can I help you help me change?" Systemic intervention in an integrated model of counselling', *Journal of the British Association for Counselling*, 3 (1): 31–3.
Bott, D. (1994) 'A family systems framework for intervention with individuals', *Counselling Psychology Quarterly*, 7 (2): 105–15.
Bott, D. and Hodes, M. (1989) 'Structural therapy with a West African family', *Journal of Family Therapy*, 11: 169–79.
Bowen, M. (1978) *Family Therapy in Clinical Practice*. New York: Jason Aronson.
Byng-Hall, J. (1973) 'Family myths used as a defence in conjoint family therapy', *British Journal of Medical Psychology*, 46: 239–50.
Byng-Hall, J. (1985) 'The family script: a useful bridge between theory and practice', *Journal of Family Therapy*, 7: 301–5.
Byng-Hall, J. (1995) 'Creating a secure family base: implication of attachment theory for family therapy', *Family Process*, 34: 45–58.

Carter, E. and McGoldrick, M. (1976) 'Family therapy with one person and the family therapists own family, in P.J. Guerin (ed.), *Family Therapy: Theory and Practice*. New York: Gardner Press.

Carter, E. and McGoldrick, M. (1989) *The Changing Family Life Cycle*. Boston: Allyn Bacon.

Fisch, R., Weakland, J.H. and Segal, L. (1983) *The Tactics of Change*. San Francisco: Jossey-Bass.

Foucalt, M. (1980) *Power/Knowledge: Selected Interviews and Writings*. New York: Pantheon Books.

Framo, J. (1976) 'Family of origin as a therapeutic resource for adults in marital and family therapy: you can and should go home again', *Family Process*, 15: 193–210.

Framo, J.L. (1982) *Explorations in Marital and Family Therapy: Selected Papers of James Framo, Ph.D.* New York: Springer.

Guttman, H. (1991) 'Systems theory, cybernetics and epistemology', A. Gurman and D. Kniskern (eds), *Handbook of Family Therapy*, vol. 2. New York: Brunner/Mazel.

Haley, J. (1973) *Uncommon Therapy*. New York: W.W. Norton.

Haley, J. (1976) *Problem-solving Therapy*. San Francisco: Jossey-Bass.

Haley, J. (1980) *Leaving Home*. New York: McGraw-Hill.

Henggeler, S.W., Cunninghan, P.B., Pickrel, S.G., Schoenwald, S.K. and Brondino, M.J. (1996) 'Multisystemic therapy: an effective violence prevention approach for serious juvenile offenders', *Journal of Adolescence*, 19: 47–61.

Hoffman, L. (1990) 'Constructing realities: an art of lenses', *Family Process*, 29 (1): 1–12.

Jenkins, H. (1989) 'Family therapy with one person: a systemic framework for treating individuals', *Psihoterapija*, 19: 61–73.

Jenkins, H. and Asen, K. (1992) 'Family therapy without the family: a framework for systemic practice', *Journal of Family Therapy*, 14: 1–14.

Jones, E. (1993) *Family Systems Therapy*. New York: Wiley.

Keeney, B. (1979) 'Ecosystemic epistemology: an alternative paradigm for diagnosis', *Family Process*, 18: 117–27.

Kuhn, T. (1962) *The Structure of Scientific Revolutions*. Chicago: University of Chicago Press.

Lask, B. (1987) 'Cybernetico-epistobabble, the emperor's new clothes and other sacred cows', *Journal of Family Therapy*, 9: 207–15.

Lieberman, S. (1979) *Transgenerational Family Therapy*. London: Croom-Helm.

McNamee, S. and Gergen, K. (eds) (1992) *Therapy as Social Construction*. London: Sage.

Madanes, C. (1981) *Strategic Family Therapy*. San Francisco: Jossey-Bass.

Minuchin, S. (1976) *Families and Family Therapy*. Cambridge, MA: Harvard University Press.

Nichols, M. (1987) *The Self in the System*. New York: Brunner/Mazel.

Perry, R. (1993) 'Empathy – still at the heart of therapy. The interplay of context and empathy', *Australian and New Zealand Journal of Family Therapy*, 14 (2): 63–74.

Pocock, D. (1995a) 'Searching for a better story: harnessing modern and postmodern positions in family therapy', *Journal of Family Therapy*, 17: 149–73.

Pocock, D. (1995b) 'Postmodern chic: postmodern critique', *Context*, 24: 46–8.

Pocock, D. (1997) 'Feeling understood in family therapy', *Journal of Family Therapy*, 19 (3): 283–302.

Reimers, S. and Treacher, A. (1995) *Introducing User-friendly Family Therapy*. London: Routledge.

Rogers, C. (1990) 'The necessary and sufficient conditions of therapeutic personality change', in H. Kirschenbaum and V. Henderson (eds), *The Carl Rogers Reader*. London: Constable.

Selvini Palazzoli, M., Boscolo, L., Cecchin, G. and Prata, G. (1978) *Paradox and Counterparadox: A New Model in the Therapy of the Family in Schizophrenic Transaction*. New York: Jason Aronson.

Speed, B. (1987) 'Over the top in the theory and practice of family therapy', *Journal of Family Therapy*, 9: 231–40.

Tomm, K. (1987a) 'Interventive interviewing: Part I. Strategizing as a fourth guideline for the therapist', *Family Process*, 26: 3–13.

Tomm, K. (1987b) 'Interventive interviewing: Part II. Reflexive questioning as a means to self-healing', *Family Process*, 26: 167–83.

Tomm, K. (1988) 'Interventive interviewing: Part III. Intending to ask lineal, circular, strategic or reflexive questions?', *Family Process*, 27: 1–15.

Watzlawick, P., Beavin, J., Jackson, D. (1967) *Pragmatics of Human Communication: A Study of Interactional Patterns, Pathologies, and Paradoxes*. New York: W.W. Norton.

Whitaker, C. (1982) 'My philosophy in psychotherapy', in J.R. Neil and D.P. Kniskern (eds), *From Psyche to System: The Evolving Therapy of Carl Whitaker*. New York: Guilford Press. pp. 31–6.

White, M. and Epston, D. (1990) *Narrative Means to Therapeutic Ends*. New York: W.W. Norton.

Wiener, N. (1954) *Cybernetics or Control and Communication in the Animal and the Machine*, 2nd edn. Cambridge, MA: Massachusetts Institute of Technology Press.

Wilkinson, M. (1992) 'How do we understand empathy systemically?' *Journal of Family Therapy*, 14: 193–205.

5
A SYSTEMATIC INTEGRATIVE RELATIONAL MODEL FOR COUNSELLING AND PSYCHOTHERAPY

Katherine Murphy and Maria Gilbert

The systematic integrative relational model of therapy as presented in this chapter is derived from the assumption that each of us has an internal belief system, the 'core interpersonal schema' (Beitman, 1992) that is shaped by our unique developmental and family history and our unique responses to these influences. Essentially this is an interactive relational model focused on the interpersonal and intrapsychic dimensions of a person's experience. It is based on an interactive developmental model that stresses the primacy of relationship as a motivational force and as the medium in which core beliefs about self and others are forged.

In therapy the practitioner is actively choosing interpersonal styles that throw some light on the client's repetitive interactive patterns and characteristic styles of relating to people and the world around them. The model draws from the range of humanistic, behavioural, systemic and psychoanalytic traditions which share a common conceptualization of repetitive defensive strategies developed early in life in the interests of survival. In his search for a common language for integration, Goldfried has formulated a schema for analysing recurrences of aspects of functioning, 'typically a distorted/antiquated/maladaptive reaction pattern' or 'vicious cycle' of interaction between people that results in predictable self-limiting outcomes (Goldfried, 1995: 231). This concept, couched in various terminologies, is common to all four traditions of psychotherapy mentioned above.

Development of the therapy

We are linking two concepts: the concept of an internalized representational world of internal dialogue and a concept of repetitive, non-problem-solving strategies that result from unsatisfactory resolution of interpersonal needs and the inner conflict related to this experience. If parents are not able to adapt and respond to a growing child's needs, then that child will suppress those needs and experience an inner conflict whenever a 'forbidden' need threatens to surface. The 'internal dialogue' of a client often represents the point of fixation or 'impasse' that reflects the unresolved developmental dilemma that the person is still struggling to resolve in the present. Because these concepts are common to all four traditions listed above, varied approaches to therapy have evolved in each of these traditions with different emphases but focused on dealing with such repetitive self-defeating rigidity that forecloses on options for being in the world.

Therapists in all four traditions will attempt to analyse the elements that make up the repetitive cycle and the beliefs that underpin these nonproblem-solving outdated behaviour patterns. The purpose of such an analysis is to help clients understand how they get 'stuck' in a vicious repetitive cycle and support them to change what they do, to reassess the unhelpful beliefs that underpin their behaviour and to get in touch with basic needs and feelings which may lie buried out of their immediate awareness. In this way clients gradually learn new patterns of interaction that lead to more satisfactory outcomes – whether by insight, by direct behavioural practice, by identifying and expressing underlying feelings and needs, by changing their outdated irrational beliefs or by any combination of the above, depending on the stress in the particular approach to therapy. From an integrative perspective, we hold that all these methods of change are equally valid and draw on the accumulated wisdom embodied in the different schools of therapy.

Theory and basic concepts

People are relationship seeking

Our approach to therapy is a relational approach that regards the therapeutic relationship as the fundamental vehicle for change by providing a new experience that challenges the beliefs embedded in the 'core interpersonal schema' (Beitman, 1992) carried by the client. We believe that people are primarily relationship seeking and are interactive by nature from the moment of conception. The quality of the responses from significant others in the person's early environment will consequently shape subsequent relationship patterns for better or for worse.

The psychoanalyst John Bowlby maintained that the attachment between mother and child is a psychological bond in its own right and is as great as the child's hunger for food (Holmes, 1993). Donald Fairbairn, a psychoanalyst and one of the early object relations theorists, talked of people as 'primarily object-seeking' (Fairbairn, 1952: 82). He stressed the importance of the bonds of love between the child and significant others in his early life in the shaping of the child's internal object world. Winnicott's famous quotation 'there is no baby without a mother' again stresses the significance he placed on early bonding with the mother (Winnicott, 1992). It is Daniel Stern, however, who has more recently drawn together much of the information from infant studies to show that social relatedness is present from birth as a need in its own right. In *The Interpersonal World of the Infant* he describes the sensitive and delicate attention of the well-attuned mother to the baby's responses and developmental needs (Stern, 1985). This intersubjective 'dance' is the material of relationship and forms the prototype for subsequent interactions with people in adult life and so also for the client–therapist relationship.

Internalized relationship patterns

We work from the assumption that all individuals internalize significant early relationship experiences that become part of their internal representational world and shape their subsequent experience. The growing child will internalize its own version of events, which will be coloured both by the actual experiences and by its understanding of them relative to its stage of development. Fantasy may also play a significant part in this process of constructing the child's 'world view' and 'relationship map'. Each person develops a pattern of internalized beliefs about the nature of the self in relation to others which includes their own reactions, the reactions of others towards them and the presence of an emotional tone which can be pleasant or unpleasant. The core interpersonal schema represents our own unique view of the world. This belief system, developed over time, has both life-enhancing and self-limiting aspects directly related to the choices available in the formative experience and influenced by subsequent significant events.

People tend to act to reinforce their beliefs so that the core interpersonal schema is a mechanism for ensuring predictability and renders the world 'safe' and familiar, if uncomfortable and unsatisfactory. 'The basic elements of the core interpersonal schema are two figures in relationship to each other. Usually one of the two figures is dominant and the other is submissive' (Beitman, 1992: 207). The process of shaping and reshaping this internal relationship 'map' spans the person's lifetime and many events may provide the opportunities to reinforce or change the existing patterns of belief. We believe that therapy constitutes, at its best, one such experience. (See Figure 5.1.)

In discussion of child development, Stern (1985) describes how a child builds up over time from repeated similar experiences with a primary carer a representation of interactions that becomes a generalized assumption about a particular kind of experience (RIG). Such RIGs then create certain expectations for future experiences and often operate below the level of awareness: for example, 'people will respond if you let them know what you want' or 'people are not to be trusted to take care of you, so look after yourself'. The various RIGs we develop in interaction with others will gradually converge to shape our core interpersonal schema and guide our

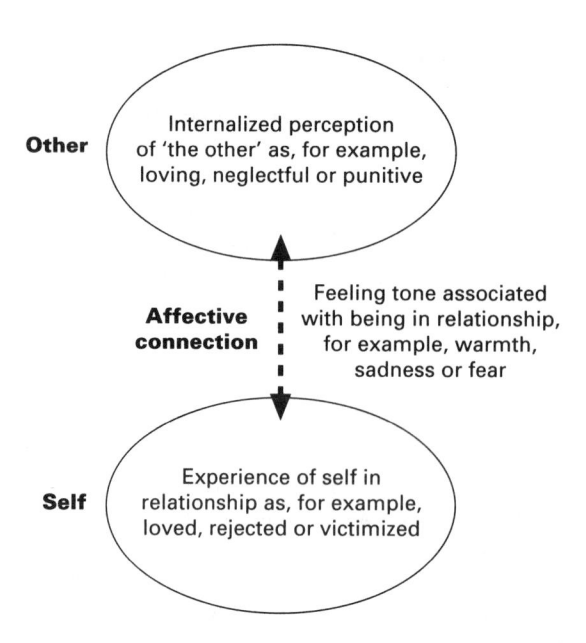

```
Other  ( Internalized perception
         of 'the other' as, for example,
         loving, neglectful or punitive )

                Feeling tone associated
  Affective    with being in relationship,
  connection   for example, warmth,
                sadness or fear

Self   ( Experience of self in
         relationship as, for example,
         loved, rejected or victimized )
```

Figure 5.1 *Core interpersonal schema (based on Beitman, 1992)*

subsequent behaviour. For example, a child may conclude from the way in which she is repeatedly treated that it is 'worthless', that 'others are too busy to be interested or available' and consequently that 'life is an empty and pointless struggle'. A bleak view of life of this kind will probably lead the child to withdraw and mistrust people, resulting in a reinforced belief that the world is a lonely and unrewarding place.

This 'self-fulfilling prophecy' (Merton, 1948 quoted in Norcross and Goldfried, 1992) is the result of the child's attempt to survive in a situation in which her basic needs were not attuned or attended to and represents the best means of survival in that context. As an adult, this strategy may be outmoded since circumstances are generally different and there are more choices available, but the fear of being hurt and rejected may lead to a clinging to the original survival strategy. Of course, if we begin to have experiences that contradict the beliefs we have formed, we may gradually change these as we build up new RIGs that create different expectations. This is the process that takes place in effective therapy. The rigidity of the core interpersonal schema will affect the ease with which people are prepared to take on new information and change their frame of reference.

The tenacity with which people cling to their outdated belief systems is often governed by the extent of the threat they experienced to their psychological or physical survival in the formative context. This will constitute a challenge to the therapist whose provision of a safe and boundaried relationship offers an alternative context in which change can take place.

Repetitive patterns

Following on from the above, it is commonly accepted across traditions that in the developmental process when certain needs are not met by parents and/or are regarded as unacceptable by them, the child will wall these off and guard against letting such needs surface in current relationships. In this way the child will more or less severely restrict the range of its interactions with others and the rewards that come from closeness and intimacy. 'If parents cannot adapt themselves to the changing needs of their developing child, then the child will adapt itself to what is available in order to maintain the required ties' (Stolorow et al., 1987: 90). This process results in an internal conflict between different parts of the self which leads to repetitive non-problem-solving behaviour patterns in a misdirected attempt to get the need met while not showing any vulnerability. The repetitive patterns form part of the defence system developed to protect people from the pain of the original deficit. In fact, the person is likely to experience fear or anxiety when a suppressed need of this kind emerges into awareness; at which point the person will move into a characteristic defence as a way of protecting himself from pain. If the defence fails to cope with the anxiety generated by the conflict between the underlying need and the perceived threats associated with letting it surface, then the person may develop a 'symptom' that becomes part of the repetitive, non-creative pattern of relating to the world around him.

For example, if a child was punished for crying or displaying signs of distress, then the child may make a decision not to show any vulnerability in future interactions with parents. This strategy 'solves' the immediate dilemma in that the child protects herself from hurt. However, in this protective process she also gives up on her need for warm supportive comfort in times of upset. Whenever she feels the need for comfort or is about to cry, she will suppress these needs and sensations and put on a brave front. She will then show the world her 'brave' face for which she will probably be praised, but this independent stance obscures a need for closeness and comfort. This 'brave' behaviour thus disguises the underlying need. In response to this pattern others are likely to leave the child alone while all the while she longs and hopes that someone may understand her need and 'see through' to the person crying underneath. The fact that the child gets praise for her protective strategy means that this pattern will become reinforced and form a regular part of her behavioural repertoire. At a certain point in life she may develop anxiety symptoms which may even turn into a generalized anxiety disorder, at which point she may present for therapy.

Such a 'disguised' behaviour pattern tends to lead to disappointment since it often evokes the old unsatisfactory response from others rather than leading to a new experience of satisfaction. Our work as therapists is to help clients understand the nature of these 'vicious cycles' of interaction

(Goldfried, 1995), also known as the 'games' of transactional analysis (Berne, 1961), in order to find creative alternatives to them.

The process of change

Change involves the individual moving from fixed patterns of rigidity to fluidity, spontaneity and the choice between a variety of options. The experience of a relationship in the present both confronts and confounds the fixed core interpersonal schema and offers the possibility of the co-construction of a new relationship and an expanded relational field. The client will present with self object needs, particularly for being mirrored by the other (Kohut, 1984), which arise from the early deficit. Rogers (1951) many years ago realized the crucial importance for the process of healing of providing accurate empathy and understanding to facilitate the person's own growth potential. The therapist provides a new experience for the client in striving to understand the original parental failures and the person's response to these painful events which have resulted in self-limiting behaviours in the present. In the safety of the therapeutic relationship the person can explore new options in the present.

A sample strategy for analysing the core interpersonal schema

Listen for and identify a recurrent pattern of interaction that the client experiences and reports as problematic. This pattern may also be manifest in the therapeutic relationship. By encouraging the client to reconnect with a typical incident and re-experience the sensations, feelings and behaviours associated with it, the therapist can facilitate the client to uncover the internal dialogue (self-talk) that supports the pattern of response. By encouraging the client to verbalize his responses to the internal 'messages', he can begin to identify the conclusion he has drawn as a result of these and which shape his core interpersonal schema. The core interpersonal schema, following Beitman (1992) and Goldfried (1995) can be analysed with the client as shown in Figure 5.2.

The following example demonstrates how this process can be analysed in working with a client to show both the circular nature of the process and its self-defeating consequences for the person.

John's colleague was promoted to a position which John himself turned down. At the same time John is full of reproachful envy of the colleague for 'getting ahead' and feels despair. John revisits decisions he has made in the past that undermined his chances and begins to feel 'on the scrap heap' just as he once felt at school where his unrecognized dyslexia did result in his being called 'stupid' and where he was denied ordinary educational help that would have allowed him to flourish. Consequently, he began to avoid taking any opportunities that might show up his disability and at the

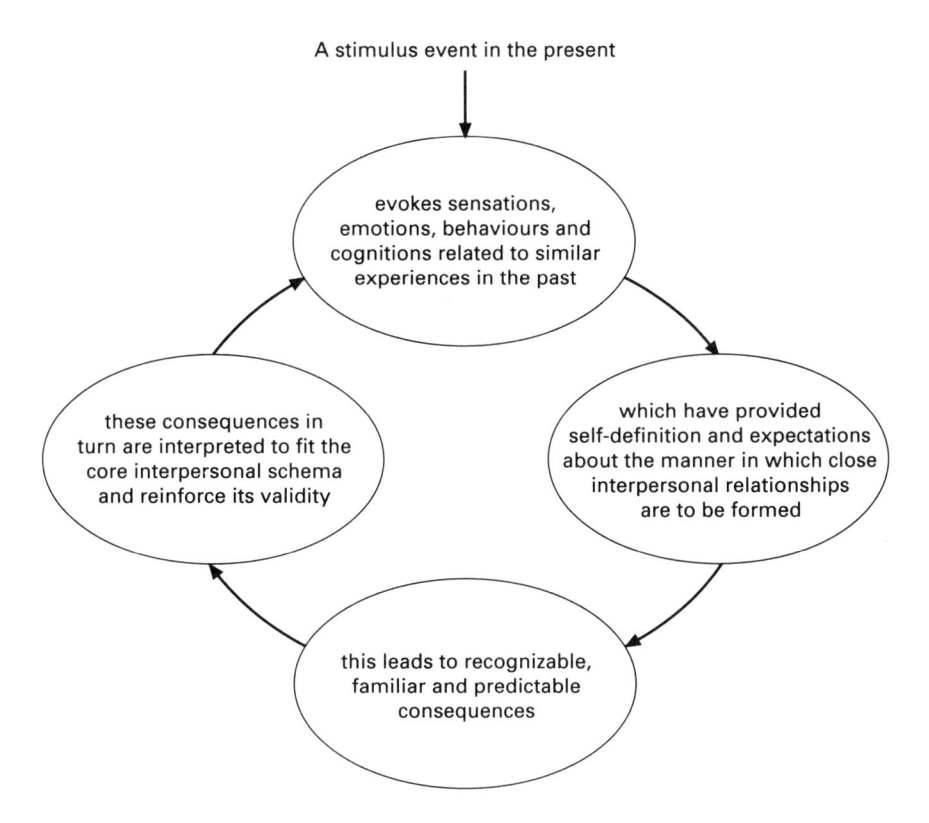

```
                    A stimulus event in the present
                                   │
                                   ▼
                    ┌─────────────────────────┐
                    │   evokes sensations,    │
                    │  emotions, behaviours   │
                    │  and cognitions related │
                    │  to similar experiences │
                    │        in the past      │
                    └─────────────────────────┘
```

Figure 5.2 *Reinforcing the core interpersonal schema*

- evokes sensations, emotions, behaviours and cognitions related to similar experiences in the past
- which have provided self-definition and expectations about the manner in which close interpersonal relationships are to be formed
- this leads to recognizable, familiar and predictable consequences
- these consequences in turn are interpreted to fit the core interpersonal schema and reinforce its validity

same time he would feel a resentment for 'being penalized'. The self-definition he carries is of someone who is flawed, stupid and 'a piece of useless scrap'. His expectations of relationship are that he will not be recognized for his talents and that other people despise him. This internal process results in a familiar, lonely and dissatisfied state when his colleague is promoted.

Practice and clinical issues

We believe that every therapeutic encounter is unique and unfolds in its particular idiosyncratic way, and in a way each practitioner and client co-create their own system of psychotherapy. At the same time, the work is typical in that it is bounded in space and time and is structured by the practitioner's therapeutic ritual and rationale (Frank, 1961). The thrust of this work is to establish a healing setting (Frank, 1961), physically and psychically, in which client and practitioner feel safe to explore, understand and experience what is of distress to the client. The aims of therapy in our model are to help the client to experience and understand the current and historic implications of the core interpersonal schema in terms of self and others; to review and therefore reframe this rigid, closed system in order to increase openness, spontaneity, options and choice; and thence to experiment living from this different intrapsychic and interpersonal perspective.

The direction of this working relationship is toward changing an outdated way of being-in-the-world to a responsive and responsible way of being in the present. This is balanced by our belief that fixed patterns in the present are outdated relics of necessary survival strategies for the past and therefore need to be treated with respect and care. They are there for a purpose that we believed was essential for our survival and we do not yet accept that it is safe to give them up. Second, we also subscribe to the central paradox of change (Rogers, 1951) that it is only when I accept myself fully as I am that change becomes possible. As practitioners we believe in the change process, yet we are not pushing for change. We are co-constructing the conditions whereby change may become inevitable.

This way of working stresses the nature and style of the interpersonal encounter between client and practitioner and in particular the centrality of the three relationship stances described by Gelso and Carter (1985): the working alliance, the real relationship and the transference relationship with primary emphasis on the working alliance and the real relationship.

Stages of therapy

There is no typical format to a session in this model since the shape of the session will be co-created by both therapist and client each time they meet. With each client a particular format may evolve over time that meets the needs of that person. This will be determined in part by the learning style of the client. For example, Jane may first need to analyse her interactions from the previous week in order to contact her underlying feelings and then give expression to them. Whereas Fred may typically start with an explosive outburst of angry emotion related to his frustrations, before settling down to reflect on how he may have contributed to the situations. However, each session will generally involve some moving through and integration of thinking, sensation, feeling and behaviour related to new choices. The therapist may end each session with a summarizing or anchoring statement of the process that has occurred in addition to grounding the client in their present reality.

Therapy, however, often progresses through a number of easily recognizable stages. Although we list these in a linear fashion in line with their customary occurrence, we are the first to acknowledge that stages are often recycled and/or may overlap. Most approaches to psychotherapy have some sense of the direction of therapy from a beginning stage, to a working through stage, to a termination stage. We have further elaborated these broad stages as follows, drawing particularly on input from Prochashka and Diclemente (1992), Pulleyblank and McCormick (1985) and Elton Wilson (1996).

Stage 1   Is it possible for us to work together?

This is an initial exploration which may even be done on the telephone to establish that it is ethical and/or appropriate for the therapist to engage with the prospective client, even for an initial assessment. This will involve a brief discussion to establish whether psychotherapy seems to be a possible treatment of choice. Sometimes at first contact it emerges that the client's problem is outside the therapist's limits of competence or that there is a conflict of interest and an onward referral is required.

Stage 2   The first meeting and assessment

At this point the therapist is interested in hearing the client's explanation of why they are currently seeking this type of help. The client's expectations of what the therapist might do for them are explored in order to establish the client's hopes and desires of the process. The therapist is listening 'with all their senses' to the client's presentation as this gives clues to the underlying core interpersonal schema. It is important at this stage that the therapist seeks to understand the client's subjective world by asking clarifying questions and by the use of empathic responses.

The primary purpose of this beginning assessment process is:

- to clarify the client's motivation;
- to explore the elements of the presenting problem;
- to establish some relational basis for working together.

The client needs to have an experience right from the start of the type of interaction that will form the basis of the work.

Stage 3   Establishing trust: the working alliance

At this stage the client receives an experience of the therapist as a reliable professional and a concerned human being through the therapist's careful attention both to practical arrangements and to the scope of the client's expressed problem. This stage will involve a discussion of whether the client wishes to receive help for an immediate life crisis or whether the concern also includes understanding and changing deep-seated patterns of response (the repetitive patterns discussed above). This stage will involve the client identifying and experiencing the internal dialogue between parts of self and noticing how these may be acted out with others, including the therapist.

As the client develops this level of awareness, motivation may shift from a specific behavioural solution to a desire to resolve the conflict underpinning the problem in the present. This process will give rise to the therapist and client formulating a therapeutic 'contract' or setting specified goals. If the client decides to focus on the solution to a particular behavioural or relationship issue, this is an equally valid option for therapy. The work is to help the client to decide at what level to engage. Whatever the decision of the client, the theoretical model outlined above can usefully inform the therapist's conceptualization of the issue and inform his interventions.

Stage 4   Moving through: the process of exploration and change

At this stage there is a deepening of trust as the therapist begins to demonstrate an understanding of the origin and function of the client's stereotypical ways of relating and solving problems, without requiring the client to change these except insofar as there is a wish to exercise new choices. The therapist's capacity for empathy and acceptance, even in the face of provocation to confirm the self-fulfilling prophecy, supports the client to re-examine beliefs about self and others. This forms the heart of the healing process in this model. The combination of careful analysis and understanding of self-defeating behaviour alongside the opportunity for experiencing and practising new responses is the essence of the change process. The client will also come up against the early disappointments and failures of his parents (or significant others) to meet his needs in certain respects. The therapist's task is to facilitate the client to grieve for these losses in order to move forward, rather than continuing to search in the present for the aspects of parenting that he missed in the past and that are irrecoverable because they relate to children not adults. This disinvestment from the past releases energy for creative relating and fulfilling choices in the present context. The client will not necessarily thank the therapist for being part of this process of disillusionment, grieving and letting go of the desire for a 'magical' outcome.

Stage 5   Experimenting in the present and living new choices

At this point the clients have changed their old negative internal dialogues for more supportive, flexible internal self-talk that encourages a variety of choices where before they were limited to one restricted response. This can be both exciting and frightening and requires the therapist's ongoing support as the client no longer has the 'comfortable' if self-limiting assurance of 'predictability'. Sometimes clients are tempted to leave therapy at the end of Stage 4, thus depriving themselves of the therapist's backing as they take their new learning out into the world.

Stage 6   Saying goodbye

This was always a time-limited relationship whose function it is to act as a bridge for the clients back into their everyday lives. In this last stage, the gains of therapy are evaluated and both parties to the relationship will review key moments of the process. This may be a tender time for both therapist and client since both have invested emotional energy and have developed an attachment in different ways through the therapeutic encounter.

Indications and contraindications

This approach is contraindicated for people who have suffered and survived severe early physical and/or psychological abuse, traumatic privations or primary relationship deficits in the early years. Such people often have a fragmented sense of self which requires the gradual building up of trust and a reparative relationship that provides a medium for the restoration of the self over an extended period of time. An approach that focuses too early or too directly on their defence systems may undermine their fragile hold on reality and lead to a decompensation of the personality.

This approach is particularly indicated for people with a fairly consistent and reliable sense of self and a degree of ego strength that can support them through the process of challenging their belief systems. We are assuming that people will be able to stand back and reflect on their own repetitive non-problem-solving patterns of interaction while retaining the coherence of self-structures. Such an approach is less appropriate for people with heavily shame-based systems of internal dialogue who may experience a sense of exposure by this kind of challenge rather than be helped in a constructive process of change.

Using this model would, however, be appropriate at the working through phase of longer term therapy when the working alliance is well established and the client and therapist can work together on transference phenomena which this model is eminently suited to illuminate. We also think that it is particularly suitable for brief term therapy where the client has some ego strength and presents with a current life, interpersonal or work-related difficulty. Changing the components of the core interpersonal schema can lead to a satisfactory inroad into the problem area so that the person is enabled to continue the process of change after the end of the intervention.

Case study

Sheila contacted me via her previous therapist, a colleague of mine. They had had a planned ending due to the therapist's pregnancy and Sheila wished to continue the work. The woman I met on the telephone was softly spoken, clear about what she wanted and thoughtful. There was no obvious ethical impediment to us meeting for an initial assessment and we found a mutually convenient time without difficulty. I felt interested to meet her.

Sheila, is a single, Anglo-Saxon, professional woman in her early thirties, living in her own flat with the company of her cat. She works as an accountant in a large successful firm and is also studying with the Open University. She has many friends with whom, she stays on weekends. She has not had a sexual relationship for several years and feels 'odd' because of this and some shame. She is overweight for her height and build and wears drab and shapeless clothes to 'try and blot this out'. I see her as a very pretty, large, woman. She sees herself in critical terms. She feels flat, listless, guilt that she 'isn't doing enough' and resentful towards her employers in particular. I experience her as sluggish and yet she sometimes has a lively twinkle in her eyes and occasionally a wicked sense of humour slips out, in spite of herself. There is promise of a playful, vital woman lurking in the wings.

She wants to stop the 'internal nagging' by which she feels browbeaten and to become kind towards herself, to feel comfortable inside. She wants to stand on her own two feet, to be assertive in her job, with her parents and with her friends. She wants to have fun in her life and to be open to any kind of positive relationship, including sexual. She said, 'I want confidence . . . to feel I am valid and there is someone called me . . . and I don't have to make sacrifices to keep everyone happy.'

We agreed to work together on a weekly basis and decided to review, and perhaps refocus, after six sessions when we had more of a sense of each other and the kind of working relationship that we were developing. Sheila was exquisitely aware of the sharp, critical internal nagging that she felt harassed by, and the internalized judgement that she was not good enough. She has a driven sense that the only way to appease this 'judge' is to work very hard and do very good works. She often talked about needing to know what the rules were so that she could keep the rules. We spent our initial sessions with Sheila feeling her way into a working relationship with me and mourning her previous relationship. She talked a lot about the details of her life, how hard she worked, her quiet fury with her boss, her 'well-balanced family'. She experienced a lot of internal conflict and guilt about not doing more and was resentful for having to do so much. I continued also to 'see' a feisty, lively, bright-eyed and playful self who seemed hidden, but not lost. I found that humour was a way of making contact with Sheila and by which I could support her in reflecting on her internal judge, who was later named 'Old Grizzle'.

We established a reliable working alliance and, as well as examining the content of her external and internal world, we gently explored our relationship in the sense of what it was like for her if I did not have a rigid set of rules for her to obey, over and above our business agreements regarding time, fees, cancellations and so forth. This became an important focus of our work together and provided the opportunities for us to elaborate Sheila's core interpersonal schema, with its historical origins.

Sheila had a strong internal critic and seemed quite flattened by the persistence of this internal tirade. Yet she was beginning to bristle with anger, but seemed stuck in between these conflicting energies. She did want to stand on her own two feet, she did want to move. She did want to experience and express her feelings and she did want to talk about sex. This movement, this kind of self-expression, would provoke a damning internal tirade so that she would feel guilty in response, get depressed and then withdraw.

Sheila began to talk of this conflict as a battle and we began exploring the nature and strategies of both sides. She had a lot of energy for this and began, with humour, to describe how she would want to take on 'the judge – Old Grizzle'. We play-acted what she would want to say and she would swagger around my room ridiculing the judge and telling her off. As the judge became an obvious other, Sheila began to talk painfully and haltingly about what living in this 'well-balanced family' had felt like for her. She felt that expressing energetic feelings was unacceptable, that it would be frowned on to make a fuss, that being assertive was dangerous and that sexual feelings and desires were disgusting. She began to peel back the layers of her early experiences and talked of her loneliness and her feelings of isolation. She talked of the various moves before she was 13, her shyness at new schools, the sternness of her rather fussy mother and the timidity of her hardworking father. She cried deeply for herself and began to feel angry about the unnecessary restrictions. The image she had was of a young child (5 or 6 years old) being sat on and stifled, yet struggling to move and get up. This became the image we worked with and 'the battle' we now addressed. Sheila was very engaged in her work. She felt the rightness of this image of her internal struggle and she wanted to free this young girl.

Sheila and I worked as thoughtful and caring 'colleagues' with the shared task of how to free this child in a way that would be safe for her and respectful of the figure sitting on her. I encouraged Sheila to think about what the/her young self would need. She began to develop the idea that what was required was an equal and opposite energy to the stifling figure, who could dislodge it and protect the child from further encroachments. She began to envisage such a figure – a counter to 'Old Grizzle'; a powerful, solid, caring figure somewhat like a neighbour she had known at that time and loved. This was a serious exercise much different from the playful skirmishings of the earlier battles. She began to build a dialogue with her child self and a robust conversation with 'Old Grizzle'. Her outward appearance began to change. She wore more colourful clothes that had shape to them. She reported saying 'no' when she would automatically have said 'yes'. For the first time in our six months of meeting she did not start her sessions by falling into the sofa and sighing woefully. She began to plan a holiday – questioning herself about what kind of holiday she really wanted.

Her internal protectors and wise woman were able to contain and counteract the 'judge' aspect of herself and had sensible opinions and observations to make about how to be in the world. The image of the sat upon young girl had changed to a child able to move and stand, protected and looked after by the internal protectors who stood between the girl and the judge. Sheila decided she wanted to go white-water rafting in India and found a reliable tour company to organize it. She was applying for a job that sounded interesting and exciting. We were now in the 'experimenting in the present' phase. She got the job and went on holiday.

While she was away I occasionally wondered how she was and re-experienced my enjoyment in working with her and an anticipatory pang about the inevitable goodbye. Sheila returned refreshed, happy and lively. She had enjoyed herself, made friends and had fun. She was stimulated in her new job. She began to talk about her body with shy curiosity and some tenderness. On holiday she had felt big, but she had also experienced herself as agile and graceful – words she had never ascribed to herself before. She continued to experiment with her clothes. Her internal image of herself was holding. She raised the question of us stopping. As we reflected back to what she had wanted for herself when we agreed to work a year ago, Sheila's assessment was that she was standing on her own two feet. She was making her own rules for living and these were negotiable. She was assertive in ways that were different and new and most of all she had a tender attitude towards herself, body and soul. We agreed that there were more stages to this journey and it was important she choose for herself how she wanted to proceed at this stage. Sheila chose to stop and we agreed to meet for a further six weeks to support her continuing experimentation, to consolidate what she had learned and experienced and to say goodbye. In those final weeks Sheila brought the following dream:

> I am part of a particular group, one of many who can fly using special wings that fold with the arms. I am on a practice flight and land in a clumsy, but safe, way on the roof of a building – this is OK as I am still learning. I go into a room with curtained windows and there are two people – a tired sad old woman and a wise old man. The old woman wistfully admires my wings which I lend to her thinking she won't be able to use them. The old man says she was the best flier when she was younger. Then I am the old woman with the wings, only I am not old and I fly out of the window into a clear sky. I discover I am completely in control, that I can fly and can do tricks just by willing it.

Sheila felt this was a confirmatory dream of basic changes she had made. She told it to me with both delight and poignancy and she felt that our finishing was indeed right for now. I believed Sheila was choosing well for herself and that she would seek therapy again if she wanted to.

Wider implications and applications

This approach lends itself both to private practice settings and to organizational contexts where the offer of therapy may be time limited due to constraints on resources. Many employee assistance programmes offer clients a focused therapeutic response involving four to six sessions. This approach is equally applicable to other settings such as GP practices, student counselling services, crisis intervention services and couples counselling where a shorter intervention may be required. We consider that this approach may be increasingly used in brief term therapy because it offers a method for focusing and prioritizing issues. It can also work well with clients who come with a particular focus to therapy and can supply the therapist with a very pragmatic and usable frame of reference for intervention.

An approach that enables the therapist to identify fairly rapidly nonproductive interpersonal processes and work with these in the present is well suited to this kind of strategic work. The format suggested here supports the therapist to intervene at a cognitive, an emotional and/or a behavioural level with a client in the present context of the therapeutic alliance. This model adapts well to incremental change which may be initiated in the course of the six-session intervention and may then continue over a period of time as the client reflects on his own progress. In a brief term therapy context, the role of the therapist is to act as the stimulator of a change process begun in the therapy context and continued by the client long after the therapy has ended. The client has the knowledge and resources to build on a process started in the therapy.

However, as we have pointed out earlier, this model is also of particular use in the working through stages of a longer term therapy. It is appropriate once the client has learnt to support herself better and has established a trusting relationship with the therapist. The conceptual framework can be helpful to all therapists, including couples therapists, since it offers an accessible model for exploring intrapsychic and interpersonal patterns of relating to self and others.

Future developments

The nature of the current 'marketplace' and people's life styles are progressively requiring a counselling/therapy service that offers a time-limited intervention for which this model provides a helpful framework. We anticipate that future developments will favour an approach that is eclectically based and incorporates common elements from different theories of psychotherapy. Such an approach is open, flexible and able to incorporate new elements and interventions from the different schools of psychology and psychotherapy. This approach is available to updating as new knowledge of human processes becomes available. It is also open to re-evaluating its own interpersonal schema.

This approach encourages the practitioner and the client to make links between what is happening in the present, what is happening in the therapeutic encounter and what happened in the past without giving special weight to any of these dimensions, but rather using the links as a way of making a difference in the client's present context.

This approach is also compatible with the current emphasis on the central importance of the therapeutic relationship in therapy and allows for the use of different relationship modalities as required. We see growing attention being given to this area of development in therapy. Importantly, we think that there will be a greater emphasis on the person of the therapist – who this person is culturally, politically, socially, sexually, racially – as well as their capacity for ordinary human relating.

References

Beitman, B.D. (1992) 'Integration through fundamental similarities and useful differences among the schools', in J.C. Norcross and M.R. Goldfried (eds), *Handbook of Psychotherapy Intergration*. New York: Basic Books.

Berne, E. (1961) *Transactional Analysis in Psychotherapy*. New York: Ballantine Books.

Elton Wilson, J. (1996) *Time-conscious Psychotherapy – A Life Stage to Go Through*. London: Routledge.
Fairbairn, W.R.D. (1952) *Psychoanalytic Studies of the Personality*. London: Routledge.
Frank, J.D. (1961) *Persuasion and Healing*. Baltimore: Johns Hopkins University Press.
Gelso, C.J. and Carter, J.A. (1985) 'The relationship in counselling and psychotherapy: components, consequences and theoretical antecedents', *Counseling Psychologist*, 13 (2): 153–243.
Goldfried, M.R. (1995) 'Toward a common language for case formulation', *Journal of Psychotherapy Integration*, 5 (3): 221–44.
Holmes, J. (1993) *John Bowlby and Attachment Theory*. London: Routledge.
Kohut, H. (1984) *How Does Analysis Cure?* Chicago: University of Chicago Press.
Norcross, J.C. and Goldfried, M.R. (1992) *Handbook of Psychotherapy Integration*. New York: Basic Books.
Prochaska, J.O. and Diclemente, C.C. 'The transtheoretical approach', in J.C. Norcross and M.R. Goldfried (eds), *Handbook of Psychotherapy Integration*. New York: Basic Books.
Pulleyblank, E. and McCormick, P. (1985) 'The stages of redecision therapy', in L.B. Kadis (ed.), *Redecision Therapy: Expanded Perspectives*. Watsonville, CA: WIGFT.
Rogers, C.R. (1951) *Client-Centered Therapy*. Boston: Houghton Mifflin.
Stern, D.N. (1985) *The Interpersonal World of the Infant*. New York: Basic Books.
Stolorow, R.D., Brandchaft, B. and Atwood, G.E. (1987) *Psychoanalytic Treatment: An Intersubjective Approach*. Hillsdale, NJ: Analytic Press.
Winnicott, D.W. (1992) *Through Paediatrics to Psychoanalysis: Collected Papers*. London: Karnac Books and the Institute of Psychoanalysis.

6
A RELATIONAL APPROACH TO THERAPY

Stephen Paul and Geoff Pelham

The relational approach has one central defining assumption:

Relations between people are the basis of social and individual life and relational concepts are used to understand human life in all its complexity.

Relationships are of fundamental importance in:

- the development of personality and a sense of self;
- the difficulty clients bring to therapy (relations with the self and relations with other people);
- the therapeutic process (the therapy relationship is the heart of the process).

The relational approach to therapy focuses on the relationship in therapeutic encounter. This therapeutic relationship is considered central to change.

The model draws from the major theoretical traditions in order to provide as full as possible understanding of the relational components of individual psychological problems. It also provides a common framework for therapists from different therapeutic roots or persuasions to make sense of the therapeutic relationship from an integrated perspective.

Development of the theory

Broadly speaking, traditional psychotherapy theories are based upon what can be described as 'one person psychologies' (Modell, 1984). There is a person and there is an environment. The focus is on the innate structure, dynamics and potential of the individual. Human beings are *pre-wired*, the mind evolves through predetermined structures. The external world is an environment in which the innate potential is expressed, repressed, conditioned, and so forth. For example, in classical Freudian theory the mind is based upon instincts of sex and aggression. The external world is the site for the possible expression or repression of these instincts. The humanistic theories postulate innate drives for self-actualization. The external world provides the conditions that either facilitate or inhibit this self-actualization. The horticultural metaphor is expressed in the common usage of the concept of *organism* in referring to individuals and *environment* as setting the possibilities of growth (Goldstein, 1939). For example, in the person-centred approach, self-actualization is dependent upon experiencing the *core conditions* as the required facilitating environment. In these approaches the humanness of this environment is either not strictly necessary, or only implied.

Although theoretically these approaches are based upon one-person psychologies, the actual practice of psychotherapy and counselling confronts practitioners with the day-to-day reality that our clients' difficulties are rooted in relationships with other people. As soon as one speaks of relationship, then there is a movement toward two-person psychologies, where the existence and identity of two or more people are inextricably linked. This clinical reality has to be dealt with both in practice and in theory. For example, psychodynamic theorists gradually introduced the concepts of *object relations theory* (Greenberg and Mitchell, 1983) to understand the relational nature of human experience. Person-centred theory introduced the notion of *congruence* to conceptualize the fact that therapy happens between two (or more) people (Lietaer, 1993). Across the board, theories that are basically one-person psychologies have had to accommodate the relational nature of human existence.

The past decade has seen the development of a new paradigm that puts the relational nature of human existence at the heart of the theory and practice of therapy. It is an approach based in 'two-person psychologies' that seek to understand the dyadic, dialogic and mutual nature of relationships. It is an integrative approach as its central theoretical assumptions catch the clinical reality of practitioners from differing traditions. It can be described as a paradigm as it is not a unified theory, more a set of basic assumptions that allow for a variety of concepts and practices (Clarkson, 1995). This paradigm will develop largely through discussion and disputes between those who accept its basic assumptions.

The stimulus for the authors to develop the relational approach was being members of a team of trainers collaboratively developing counselling training at Park Lane College and Leeds Metropolitan University. For a number of years the trainers struggled to define a shared framework. The staff group felt that although individual trainers came from differing backgrounds (person-centred, existential, psychodynamic) the areas of agreement outweighed the differences. It seemed that frequently it was language that separated our discussions. Our own background learning had been in schools that did not share any common means of exploration. As soon as we tried to be specific, we had to use the concepts of particular traditions (e.g. congruence or countertransference to talk about the therapist's awareness of self in the counselling relationship). The challenge was to find the approach that offers an integration of our common ground. It is apparent that many experienced therapists trained in a uni-theoretical core model seek, in their professional development, to develop and maximize their practice by drawing from other paradigms (Feltham, 1997). There is an ongoing debate about the efficacy of this (Wheeler, 1998).

It was through debating Mitchell's work (Greenberg and Mitchell, 1983; Mitchell, 1988, 1993) on the relational paradigm in the psychoanalytic tradition that we found our way through to a shared framework. Mitchell distinguishes between the classical Freudian 'drive' paradigm and the more recent forms of the relational paradigm (such as object relations, interpersonal and self-psychology) as a way of clarifying the fundamental differences and order in the multiplicity of psychodynamic theories.

We believe that a relational approach is apparent not just in the psychoanalytic tradition but is the common ground of our different perspectives, offering a genuine integration. We felt that the relational paradigm caught the essence of our therapeutic work, not only for psychodynamic aspects but also of other traditions, especially humanistic approaches (Kahn, 1991). There are many common links:

- Existential-humanistic thinking (May, 1939; Rogers, 1961; Buber, 1970) emphasizes the centrality of the relationship.
- In the psychodynamic tradition, the relationship between client and therapist is central as in humanistic and existential approaches. Kohut (1984) emphasized the importance of the human, empathic being of the therapist in the psychodynamic relationship.
- Interpersonal therapy (Sullivan, 1953) indicates that a person's subjective sense of self arises from past interpersonal experience.
- In recent times, much psychotherapy research has emphasized the importance of the relationship between therapist and client regardless of therapeutic model used (Orlinsky et al., 1994).

An explicit focus on the relational and the relationship is becoming more apparent in counselling and psychotherapy. For example, in the psychodynamic tradition is the relatively new journal *Psychoanalytic Dialogues. A Journal of Relational Perspectives*. A further example is Clarkson (1995), who identifies five kinds of therapeutic relationship which provide an integrating framework for the theory and practice of counselling and psychotherapy.

Theory and basic concepts

Assumptions about human nature

Relationships are central to the human condition (Clarkson, 1995). The human being is inextricably bound in relationships to others, as much as the interdependence of individual cells of the body. A person is born with natural potential which develops through relations with other people (Rogers, 1961; Maslow, 1973; Brazelton and Cramer, 1991). Physical and psychological dependency in infancy and childhood ensure the crucial importance of caregivers (Stern, 1985; Bowlby, 1988). Paradoxically, it is through relations with others that the person develops, maintains, and changes a sense of self (Rogers, 1961; Winnicott, 1965). Infancy and childhood are enormously important, but throughout life there are experiences and challenges that profoundly affect the person (Sullivan, 1953).

Power is often unequally distributed in relationships. However, both (or all) parties in relationships contribute to and co-create the relationship. For example, the parent has far more power than the newborn child. Yet the parent becomes a parent through the existence of the child and the parent's sense of identity, of being 'good enough', is dependent upon the 'performance' of the child (feeding well, sleeping at night, not unduly crying, being 'clever' or 'slow', etc.). Research has shown that infants come into the world as active partners in the infant–parent relationship, with differing constitutions that impact upon that relationship (Brazelton and Cramer, 1991). With the development of self comes the process of interpreting the meaning and nature of the world including, crucially, relations with other people. The person generates internal 'working models' (Fairbairn, 1952; Stern, 1985, 1995; Bowlby, 1988) of these relations with others which form the basis for interpersonal action. Each person, therefore, through actions that flow from his/her interpretation of relationships, co-creates the relationships of which s/he is a participant.

The self is fluid and changing through life experiences. People have the opportunity, through relations with others, to maximize their own unique potential and achieve fulfilment. This will be achieved in direct relation to congruity in their interpersonal relations. A person who is able to experience fulfilment in interpersonal relations with others will be functioning more fully and therefore will experience a deeper and enhanced sense of self (Maslow, 1973).

Relatedness with others is a primary state of being. Heidegger (1962) noted that being-in-the-world with others is central to and inseparable from the human condition.

How psychological disturbance is acquired and perpetuated

The fact that identities are intertwined (that my sense of self comes through my relations with others, and the other's sense of self comes through their relations with me) has enormous implications for psychological health and disturbance. 'Significant others' (parents, siblings, friends, teachers, etc.) do not exist simply to provide optimal experience for the self. Each has his/her own personal agendas through which they relate to others. For example, a parent experiences a newborn child through a cultural and personal history that significantly determines how s/he 'meets' and experiences the child (Bowlby, 1988). Parental fantasies, hopes, fears, conflicts and needs are expressed in the relationship and profoundly influence the developing sense of self of the child (Sameroff and Emde, 1989; Brazelton and Cramer, 1991; Stern, 1995). The interpersonal dynamic will be assimilated and become part of the self. Emotional states that were not attuned to or were forbidden can be lost or disavowed (Stern, 1985). Needs that were not met or distained (e.g. for closeness or separation) can be repressed and projected (Bowlby, 1988). Emotional states, behaviours and achievements that are 'required' (being a 'good' child, academic success, etc.) may produce a 'false self' (Winnicott, 1965). If love is conditional, then the child will strive to meet those conditions (Rogers, 1951).

The difficulties and disturbances which a person experiences can easily be reduced to 'bad parenting'. Such a reduction misses the struggles and conflicts that are deeply embedded in the very nature of relationships: these include jealousy/envy of siblings and others; managing simultaneous love and hate; attachment and separateness; the experience of relations of power; the 'existential' challenges of death, freedom, responsibility, meaning and choice (Yalom, 1980; Deurzen-Smith, 1996; Cohn, 1997); the possibly conflicting desires and risks of intimacy, lust and security (Sullivan, 1953). In some sense it is through the experiencing of such deep fundamental concerns about being-in-the world that the individual comes to terms with his/her existence (Binswanger, 1963).

There are also deep social and cultural sources of identity, opportunity and risk, as in forms of oppression based upon race, gender, sexuality, disability and class (Davies and Neal, 1996; Lago and Thompson, 1996). The individual experiences such forms of oppression on a daily basis. Throughout a person's life events occur that can cause trauma. This trauma may be exacerbated by previous life experiences or may be focused around the traumatic event itself: examples include the death of a relative or experience of redundancy. Oppressive and traumatic experiences can trigger distortions in a person's perceptions of self and others.

The developing person has to find ways of managing the difficulties and conflicts s/he experiences while still retaining psychological contact with important others. The deepest catastrophe would be psychological abandonment, an absolute rupture of relationships, an experience of utter loneliness (Fairbairn, 1952; Mitchell, 1988, 1993). The various psychological traditions have described a host of ways in which the person protects him/herself from psychological distress, trauma and unmet needs. These have been described as defence mechanisms or 'security operations' (Sullivan, 1953). They include such strategies as repression, displacement, splitting, denial, use of drugs and alcohol, and so forth. The breakdown of these defensive/protective manoeuvres leads to pain, anxiety and depression.

These security operations are adopted to protect the self while maintaining a form of connection to others. At the same time they generate their own difficulties and distress through the distortions and limitations created for the self and relations with others. For example, a person may use food, drugs or drink to ward off painful feelings despite the fact that these substances create their own problems.

The person develops patterns of relating to others based upon his/her sense of self, which tend to ensure that the world conforms to preconceived expectations and defensive strategies. For example, the person expecting rejection tends to be very vigilant for signs of rejection from others, interprets ambiguous situations to meet expectations and acts in ways that generate rejection by others (Rogers, 1951; Casement, 1985; Bowlby, 1988). A self-fulfilling cycle is set in place. Interpersonal dynamics tend to perpetuate the problem. It is as if the person has his or her own unconscious 'drama' or 'script' that s/he repetitively recreates. It frequently happens that a person enters into relationships with others that embody and recreate the familiar disturbed dynamics. Thus, the person expecting rejection enters a relationship with a partner who is rejecting. In this way, it can be said, the person recreates at a deeply unconscious level a psychological connection with the original familial relations (Fairbairn, 1952). The current relationship may be deeply unsatisfying, even destructive, but somehow it feels right. This recreation is particularly resistant to change because of the unconscious ties to earlier (usually parental) relations including the person's fantasies and expectations about close relationships which are borne out by current experience.

Movement toward psychological health

The movement toward psychological health is a process of exploring, challenging and modifying the defensive/protective strategies that a person employs, the repetitive and unsatisfying forms of relating s/he has developed and the familiar (familial) 'drama' s/he seeks to recreate. The aim is to enable the person to develop a more positive sense of self, the recognition of self-chosen life choices and the ability to establish freely chosen forms of relating to others, including intimate relations (if so desired).

Practice and clinical issues

Mitchell (1988) offers the story of Penelope in Homer's *Odyssey* as a metaphor for understanding the tension between the desires to change yet holding firm to familiar relational ties. Still loyal to the missing Odysseus, not willing to enter a world of new relational possibilities, Penelope tells suitors she cannot marry until she has woven a shroud for Laertes, her father-in-law. She weaves the shroud during the day and unpicks it at night.

> One might regard the relational matrix within which each of us lives as a tapestry woven on Penelope's loom, a tapestry whose design is rich with interacting figures. Some represent images and metaphors around which one's self is experienced; some represent images and phantoms of others, whom one endlessly

pursues, or escapes, in a complex choreography of movements, gestures, and arrangements woven together from fragments of experience and a cast of characters in one's early interpersonal world. Like Penelope, each of us weaves and unravels, constructing our relational world to maintain the same dramatic tensions, perpetuating – with many different people as vehicles – the same longing, suspense, revenge, surprise, and struggles. Like Penelope in the seeming purposiveness of her daytime labors, we experience our lives as directional and linear; we are trying to get somewhere, to do things, to define ourselves in some fashion. Yet like Penelope in her nighttime sabotage, we unconsciously counterbalance our efforts, complicate our intended goals, seek out and construct the very restraints and obstacles we struggle against. Psychopathology in its infinite variations reflects our unconscious commitment to stasis, to embeddedness in deep loyalty to the familiar. (Mitchell, 1988: 272–3)

The client brings his own tapestry into the therapeutic relationship (it is, after all just another form of relationship). Consciously seeking to change, the client unconsciously reproduces the loyalty to the familiar. The challenge in the therapy to is loosen the familiar ties and enter a world of new possibilities.

As one might expect in this approach, the relationship between the therapist and client is seen as the heart of the therapeutic process. It is a relationship jointly created by both participants. While the overt focus, especially in the early stages of the work, is likely to be on the client's relational experience in the outside world, this exploration takes place within a counselling relationship offering a canvas for potential relational themes. The organization of the therapeutic setting creates rich possibilities for these themes to be expressed: issues of acceptance/rejection, asymmetry of role and power, the acknowledgement of positive and negative feelings and thoughts, the necessity for and frustration of boundaries, social and cultural differences. This will be a challenge to the therapist as well as to the client, for the therapist brings his own tapestry into the relationship. The work is not primarily 'technical' (the implementation of skills and strategies), rather a human enterprise. The challenge will be whether the participants can work through the relational barriers and inhibitions and genuinely meet each other in a way that is functional to therapeutic change.

The therapeutic frame

The initial task for the therapist on first meeting a client is to seek to provide a space for the client to explore his/herself, a 'secure base' (Bowlby, 1988). One aspect of creating the frame for this self-exploration is in the initial contracting over time, place, arrangements for missed sessions, confidentiality, fees, and so on. This contracting establishes the 'therapeutic frame' (Langs, 1992; Casement, 1985; Gray, 1994). At one level this agreement can be seen as purely 'administrative', creating the necessary arrangements for the work. It is an agreement entered into freely by both parties which respects and enhances the autonomy of the client. The client clearly knows and can negotiate the arrangements and can take an informed judgement as to whether or not to enter therapy. Clear 'administrative' arrangements and respect for the autonomy of the client are essential elements of the therapeutic relationship (an aspect of the 'purposeful daytime labours'). At another level the frame can become the site for the experiencing and expression of important and relatively unconscious relational themes. By unconscious we mean out of everyday awareness. It can become the structure within/against which previous experience and expectations around issues of power, authority, safety, containment, desire, attachment/separation and anxiety are evoked. The therapist needs to develop awareness of the relational dynamics being expressed around the frame and the relational implications of managing frame issues (e.g. to change/not change an appointment time).

A further aspect of this frame is the therapist offering a non-judgemental, respectful attitude in which there is a genuine intention to understand the issues which the client wishes to discuss. The therapist hears and explores the client's 'story', bringing to this task the fundamental therapeutic skills. The presence, authenticity and self-awareness of the therapist facilitate the client's self-exploration. The core conditions of the person-centred approach provide the essential foundation for this relationship, as they do for relationships in everyday life (Mearns and Thorne, 1988). The therapist seeks to embody empathy in reaching out to the world of the other, aiming to be totally congruent in her relation to the client. She aims to be present in the here and now and embody a genuine human helping relationship. The therapist aims to be as accepting of the client as it is possible to be. The totality of being that the therapist brings to the encounter, through personal exploration and self-development, through full and thorough understanding of psychological theory, and through reflective practice can all be embodied in the therapist's presence with the client.

For change to take place, the therapist and the client must be not only in psychological contact (Rogers, 1951) but the client must be motivated to change. The client must to some degree be willing to trust the therapist and sense that the therapist is in a position to maintain a helpful relationship with the client.

The therapist will seek to work with empathy, congruence and acceptance in being with the client as fully as possible and will challenge and question perceived inconsistencies in the client's expressions. As the client talks, the therapist organizes her listening and interventions around the client's past and current relational experience while working very much in the here and now. This may include, for example, listening to and wondering about family and cultural experience (such as early death of the mother; being an only child; strongly religious family; being lesbian; having a disfiguring birthmark).

The experience of being accepted and heard by the therapist and having the opportunity to explore thoughts, fantasies, feelings and behaviours deeply can be immensely helpful and healing for the client (though such attitudes and actions by the therapist will always be experienced through the client's 'tapestry'). This work can be taken further by identifying characteristic patterns and themes in the client's work and, where helpful, linking this to earlier relational experience. Sometimes the client may not need more than this to get what s/he needs from therapy. The client can use the work to reconsider and change specific aspects of his/her life.

A relational understanding of the dynamics of the therapeutic relationship

Like an overture to an opera, all the client's relational themes are likely to be present at the first meeting, though usually not in a form that can be readily understood. In short term work the client is most likely to focus on specific and particular aspects of life, as indicated above. Over the longer term the client's relational tapestry is likely to become more evident. This tapestry can be understood as the client's own 'dance' in which the familiar relational themes are replayed in the counselling. This enactment of the client's 'dance' in the therapeutic relationship is the relational understanding of the concept of transference.

If the therapist is emotionally open to the client (an essential attribute for working therapeutically) then it is inevitable that the therapist will be responsive to the client's relational field. The therapist will be co-opted and prompted to incarnate themes and roles from the client's drama. There are many ways in which this can happen, such as through projective identification, creating therapeutic conflicts and dilemmas (e.g. the client repeatedly arriving late for 'good' reasons), 'identification with the aggressor', and so forth (Casement, 1985; Maroda, 1991). In this process the client is not meeting the therapist as a separate person in her/his own right, but rather as a pre-existing personification (Sullivan, 1953) from the client's internal relational world.

If the therapist accepts the projection from the client (and the interpersonal pressure can make it hard to resist) then s/he may have a disturbing/discomforting 'me, yet not-me' experience in the presence of the client. For example, as the therapist I may feel bored (or irritated, excited, aroused, hopeless, etc.) and this is definitely my feeling. Yet at the same time I do not quite understand or 'own' the feeling; I cannot quite pinpoint its source. Somehow I am being treated or prompted by the client to 'be' someone other than I am. In the therapeutic situation this 'me, yet not-me' experience can also be called 'countertransference'. The 'countertransference' is the response evoked in the therapist by the relational pressure from the client to play a pre-assigned role in his 'dance'.

Though the 'me, yet not-me' experience may be discomforting and disconcerting, it is important that it should happen. It signals the enactment of the client's dance in the therapeutic relationship, an entry into his tapestry, into relational dynamics that are often unconscious and inaccessible to the conscious awareness of the client. Moreover these dynamics will be experienced with a cognitive, emotional and behavioural intensity that creates the possibility for fundamental transformation. The challenge for therapist and client is to work with the repetitive, restrictive, relational disabling drama, to loosen its hold and create the possibility of more flexibility and choice.

Though it is inevitable and necessary that the therapist is responsive to the client's relational world, it is important that the client's dance is not simply replayed. This outcome would reinforce and confirm precisely what needs to change. If the work is to have therapeutic value the client needs to experience deeply both the familiar drama and a different outcome. The exact nature of this 'different outcome' is specific to the client's particular tapestry (Casement, 1985, 1990) and not reducible to simple notions such as the provision of 'better parenting' by the therapist, or the client taking responsibility for his life.

The heart of the process of challenging the client's drama is through the self-awareness of the therapist (Maroda, 1991). The 'me, not-me' experience offers the therapist the deepest understanding and therapeutic 'leverage'. The therapist at first allows herself fully to experience her personification in the client's drama. This process may in some sense involve 'losses' of individual sense of self in this process. The therapist then seeks authentically to engage with the client and thus challenges the client's personifications, reasserting his or her own sense of reality and challenges the assigned position as a figure in the client's archaic but ever-present drama. The therapist in effect says 'I respectfully insist on the right to meet you as the person I am, not the person you seek to make me into'. For example, a therapist with a critical client is likely to feel criticized, deeply inadequate, inept, and so forth. It is likely that anxiety and fear will be felt at the prospect of meeting the client. In turn, the therapist may be too critical of the client. The therapeutic path is first the acknowledgement of the depth and power of these feelings, then their gradual exploration and working through in supervision and in the therapeutic relationship. The pre-formed drama will have lost its hold when the therapist is able to restore a sense of competence and acceptance of the client, for this will go hand in hand with the client's own sense of acceptance of self and others.

This approach places great emphasis on the presence, authenticity, self-awareness and congruence of the therapist. Martin Buber (1970) explained the nature of the I–Thou relationship. I, the subject of my experiencing world encounter You, the subject of your experiencing world. The therapist does not relate to the client as a person with a diagnostic condition or work with objectifying conceptualizations in the encounter.

The I–Thou relationship, in which the therapist responds to the client as another subjectively experiencing and accepting human being who is here to help the client with all of his capabilities without therapeutic judgement or compartmentalization, is central to the therapeutic relationship. The therapist experiences the client as another unique person.

The challenges to the therapist are likely to be greatest when the 'role being assigned' by the client is one that is familiar and comfortable for the therapist (e.g. a therapist who likes ideas being drawn into academic discussion) or where it resonates with the therapist's unresolved conflicts and defensiveness.

There is not a prescribed set of interventions in this approach to counselling. The interventions that the therapist uses will depend upon their 'personal equation'. This will include prior training, experience, theoretical understanding and preferences for ways of working (Heron, 1990). The authenticity of the therapist, so fundamental to the process, invites the therapist to draw on her own (clinically informed) intuitive sense of how to be in the moment. At the same time the therapist should always be wondering about the relational meaning of her interventions. What is happening in the relationship at this moment that I am being challenging/empathic/self-disclosing, and what are the relational implications of using this or that intervention?

Indications and contraindications

This approach can be used for time-limited work (Strupp and Binder, 1984; Levenson, 1995) and in-depth psychotherapy and counselling. It is appropriate for one-to-one counselling, couple counselling and group work. It is clearly suitable for people with relationship issues as well as long-standing, non-specific existential or generalized problems. Persons experiencing repeating patterns of difficulty may similarly benefit.

The approach may be less successful with those seeking behavioural change without insight. Those seeking more pragmatic problem solving may also find this approach less suited to their needs. Those not motivated to change may find this approach unhelpful.

The quality of psychological contact that the client is able to make may have a direct influence on the depth of work possible, the length of therapy and the potential outcome.

Case study

In this example an aspect of a therapeutic relationship will be explored to bring out important features of the relational approach. The relational dynamics are described in rather broad brush strokes. The subtlety and intricacy of the relational themes of any therapeutic encounter are more complex than outlined below. To protect the confidentiality of clients the example is fictitious.

The client, Nicola, first made contact by phone saying she urgently needed to see a therapist. The therapist felt a strong pressure to respond to the urgency and offered an appointment the following day. She arrived for the first meeting in an agitated state, keeping her coat on throughout the hour. She said she was constantly anxious and frequently crying. Her present relationship was in crisis, primarily because of her own critical and hostile behaviour to her partner. She was also intensely jealous of her partner's relationships with other people. Nicola said that coming to therapy was an act of desperation. She had had therapy before for a brief period, but it had not been very helpful. She questioned the therapist about his qualifications and experience and asked how he could help her. The therapist was quite defensive, feeling a need to prove himself yet with a sense of hopelessness about being able help.

Over the next few sessions Nicola spoke of her familiar pattern in relationships that was repeating itself with her present partner. Once out of a relationship she would feel a profound loneliness. She would then become infatuated with someone and quickly enter an intense relationship. Nicola would then be consumed with hostility and jealousy which would wreck the relationship.

Nicola would frequently comment that she did not feel she was benefiting from therapy. The therapist's experience was of feeling 'not good enough'. He constantly expected her to say she had decided to leave. He realized that he both looked forward to and dreaded meeting her. Through supervision he gained some clarity about his experience. He also regained his underlying self-belief that in fact he was a 'good enough' therapist and that the constellation of negative self-experience arose through contact with Nicola. In supervision he discussed how he might communicate his experience to Nicola in such a way that it could be received as an invitation to explore what was happening in their relationship (as against an attack or retaliation by the therapist).

The therapist waited until the familiar negative feelings were real again in the therapy and what he wished to communicate was relevant to the material Nicola was working through. He shared the experience of not feeling good enough and waiting to be left. This enabled Nicola to bring to awareness her underlying belief that she was not good enough, not wanted and the expectation that those upon whom she was emotionally dependent would leave her. She spoke emotionally of her childhood. She was the first-born child and her parents had made it clear (through 'jokes') that they had wanted a boy. They had planned to call the boy Nicolas, changing this to Nicola when she was born. She had two younger brothers and always believed her parents favoured them, indeed believed that she was not wanted.

Throughout life she had tried to be acceptable, but this was in fact hopeless, she was a girl not a boy. Nicola reflected on how she played out her distress in relationships. As a form of self-protection she induced in others the sense of being not good enough. Rather than risk the despair of waiting to be left, she provoked the separation.

This mutual exploration of the therapeutic relationship and Nicola's heartfelt account of her past and present relationships engendered a sense of closeness and intimacy that was new. The therapist was able to share that he genuinely looked forward to their meetings. He was aware that such statements could be experienced as a form of seduction, but the emotional contact seemed such that Nicola was likely to hear it as a genuine statement. It felt important to the therapist that Nicola heard this aspect of his experience of knowing her.

This meeting was a crucial moment in the therapy. The therapist had demonstrated that he could be deeply in touch with the aspects of the underlying distress in Nocola's life (not being good enough, waiting to be left, hopelessness) and that he was not overwhelmed by it. He had also demonstrated he could withstand the attacks she made upon him (which mirrored her experience of being attacked) and reconnect with his own sense of being good enough. Nicola felt deeply understood and accepted.

The themes experienced in this session were revisited many times over in the therapy. The very intimacy experienced in the relationship heightened the relational dynamics. As the therapist became a more important figure in Nicola's life, the same 'dance' was experienced with greater intensity. The new understanding of herself that arose from the emotionally real re-experiencing of her issues in the therapeutic relationship gave her some perspective on the current relationships in her life, enabling her to acknowledge the genuine valuing and caring that others offered. A crucial factor here was the experience that the therapist truly knew her and genuinely valued her.

Wider implications and applications

The relational approach is by its very nature a broad, integrative approach that can be used in many settings (private practice, voluntary and statutory agencies) and with a variety of clients (individuals, groups, families).

Though it offers a coherent theoretical and practical framework, the relational paradigm generates rich and vigorous discussion and debate about fundamental issues. Clarkson (1995), for example, explores five forms of the therapeutic relationship. Within each of these forms are issues of theory and practice, exploration of which will enhance the effectiveness of practitioners. At a more fundamental level are the choices between the various forms of relating. For example, does the therapist believe that the client who is experiencing deep distress requires a reparative/developmentally needed response (perhaps physical holding), transference interpretation ('you experience me as the mother/father who did not care for you') or an I–Thou acknowledgement of the depth of the client's distress and hopelessness.

The therapeutic relationship develops from, is permeated by and embedded within social processes that have to be understood and addressed. For example, the relational approach acknowledges the concept of attachment. It can be argued, however, that the importance of this concept is not so much as a reflection of 'human nature', but more a product of present-day social arrangements that 'separate' individuals. In Eurocentric culture it is common for infants and children to sleep separately from parents and for children to be with childminders and nurseries, often from a very young age. Likewise, concepts of self-actualization may reflect a society which stresses individual advancement and achievement.

The relational approach has the potential to challenge forms of understanding based on fixed views of human nature and stages of development (Cushman, 1991). The relational approach also invites us to consider the interaction between the inner and outer worlds, social/political relations and their implication for therapy (Samuels, 1993; Pilgrim, 1997). It is an approach that offers a framework for understanding theoretically and practically challenging the forms of oppression inherent in class, sexuality, race, gender, disability, ageism and so forth.

By the very nature of the approach each relationship is different and issues of difference must be acknowledged by the therapist.

Future developments

The understanding of the social and political in counselling is a major area for development of the relational approach. Psychological theories are clearly influenced by social influences – hence the continual revisions, reworking and debunking of approaches using outdated metaphors (such as Freud's 'hydraulic' approach). The relational approach therefore is potentially radical. It is very much based in the here-and-now of human interaction which is in constant interplay with both internal and external forces. By its very nature, a relational approach invites us to consider wider social/political relations and their implications for theory and therapy.

Another underdeveloped and challenging aspect is the understanding of the mutuality and reciprocity of the therapeutic relationship. In this chapter the focus has been on the client's tapestry, with occasional references to the therapist's relational world. The 'working assumption' has been that somehow therapists can sufficiently set aside or bracket their tapestry to enable the focus to be on the client's issues and that a genuine person-to-person relationship can be established as the client works through and resolves his compulsive adherence to archaic forms of relating. From a relational perspective, this one-sided approach is serviceable but ultimately untenable. A relationship is irreducibly intersubjective, created by both parties. Various writers have tried to address this mutuality and reciprocity (Maroda, 1991; Natterson, 1991; Lomas, 1993; Ogden, 1994; Rucker and Lombardi, 1998). Searles (1975), for example, believed that the client needs to know she has genuinely affected, indeed been healing to the therapist (in a way she was never able to heal her parents). At present this area of mutuality is unclear (witness the two meanings of the concept of countertransference: therapist's unresolved pathology and affect of client on the therapist). Clarification of these fundamental issues will be a key area for development.

Groups are central to human relationships. Many individual personal psychopathologies are replayed in group social interactions. Foulkes (Foulkes and Anthony, 1965; Pines, 1992), Bion (1961), Rogers (1970), Yalom (1985), Sullivan (Barton Evans, 1996) and others have all contributed to the field of group psychotherapy. The relational approach with its focus on human relationships has much potential in the field of group theory. It offers the possibility of an integrative understanding of the therapeutic dynamics of the healing process in groups in a way that is not bound by limiting conceptual frameworks. Most of the work on the relational approach has been developed in the field of individual therapy and has yet to be applied to group work. The application of relational theory to groups is now a prime focus for development.

References

Barton Evans, F. (1996) *Harry Stack Sullivan: Interpersonal Theory and Psychotherapy*. London and New York: Routledge.
Binswanger, L. (1963) *Being-in-the-World: Selected Papers of Ludwig Bingswanger*. New York: Basic Books.
Bion, W.R. (1961) *Experiences in Groups*. London: Tavistock.
Bowlby, J. (1988) *A Secure Base*. London: Routledge.
Brazelton, B.T. and Cramer, B.G. (1991) *The Earliest Relationship*. London: Karnac Books.
Buber, M. (1970) *I And Thou*. Edinburgh: T. & T. Clarke.
Casement, P. (1985) *On Learning from the Patient*. London: Tavistock/Routledge.
Casement, P. (1990) *Further Learning from the Patient*. London: Tavistock/Routledge.
Clarkson, P. (1995) *The Therapeutic Relationship*. London: Whurr.
Cohn, H.W. (1997) *Existential Thought and Therapeutic Practice*. London: Sage.
Cushman, P. (1991) 'Ideology obscured. Political uses of the self in Daniel Stern's infant', *American Psychologist*, 46, (3): 206–19.
Davies, D and Neal, C. (1996) *Pink Therapy*. Buckingham: Open University Press.

Deurzen-Smith, E. van (1996) *Everyday Mysteries. Existential Dimensions of Psychotherapy*. London: Routledge.
Fairbairn, W.R.D. (1952) *An Object Relations Theory of the Personality*. New York: Basic Books.
Feltham, C. (1997) 'Challenging the core theoretical model', *Counselling*, 8 (2): 121–5.
Foulkes, S.H. and Anthony, E.J. (1965) *Group Psychotherapy*. London: Maresfield Library.
Goldstein, K. (1939) *The Organism*. New York: American Book.
Gray, A. (1994) *An Introduction to the Therapeutic Frame*. London and New York: Routledge.
Greenberg, J. and Mitchell, S. (1983) *Object Relations in Psychoanalytic Theory*. Cambridge MA: Harvard University Press.
Heidegger, M. (1962) *Being and Time*. New York: Harper and Row.
Heron, J. (1990) *Helping the Client*. London: Sage.
Kahn, M. (1991) *Between Therapist and Client*. New York: W.H. Freeman.
Kohut, H. (1984) *How does Analysis Cure?* Chicago: University of Chicago Press.
Lago, C. and Thompson, J. (1996) *Race, Culture and Counselling*. Buckingham: Open University Press.
Langs, R. (1992) *Psychotherapy: A Basic Text*. New York: Jason Aronson.
Levenson, H. (1995) *Time-Limited Dynamic Psychotherapy*. New York: Basic Books.
Lietaer, G. (1993) 'Authenticity, congruence and transparency', in D. Brazier (ed.), *Beyond Carl Rogers*. London: Constable.
Lomas, P. (1993) *The Psychotherapy of Everyday Life*. New Brunswick: Transaction Publishers.
Maroda, J. (1991) *The Power of Countertransference*. New York: Wiley.
Maslow, A.H. (1973) *The Farther Reaches of Human Nature*. Harmondsworth: Penguin.
May, R. (1939) *The Art of Counseling*. Nashville: Abingdon-Cokesbury.
Mearns, D. and Thorne, B. (1988) *Person Centred Counselling in Action*. London: Sage.
Mitchell, S.A. (1988) *Relational Concepts in Psychoanalysis*. Cambridge, MA: Harvard University Press.
Mitchell, S.A. (1993) *Hope and Dread in Psychoanalysis*. New York: Basic Books.
Modell, A.H. (1984) *Psychoanalysis in a New Context*. New York: International Universities Press.
Natterson, J. (1991) *Beyond Countertransference*. Northvale, NJ: Jason Aronson.
Ogden, T.H. (1994) *Subjects of Analysis*. London: Karnac Books.
Orlinsky, D., Grauwe, K. and Parks, B.K. (1994) Chapter 8 in A. Bergin and S. Garfield (eds), *Handbook of Psychotherapy and Behavior Change*. New York: Wiley.
Pilgrim, D. (1997) *Psychotherapy and Society*. London: Sage.
Pines, M. (ed.) (1992) *Bion and Group Psychotherapy*. London: Routledge.
Psychoanalytic Dialogues. A Journal Of Relational Perspectives. Hillsdale, NJ: Analytic Press.
Rogers, C.R. (1951) *Client-Centered Therapy: Its Current Practice, Implications and Theory*. Boston: Houghton Mifflin.
Rogers, C.R. (1961) *On Becoming a Person*. Boston: Houghton Mifflin.
Rogers, C.R. (1970) *Encounter Groups*. New York: Harper and Row.
Rucker, N.G. and Lombardi, K.L. (1998) *Subject Relations: Unconscious Experience and Relational Psychoanalysis*. New York and London: Routledge.

Sameroff, A.J. and Emde, R.N. (1989) *Relationship Disturbances in Early Childhood*. New York: Basic Books.
Samuels, A. (1993) *The Political Psyche*. London: Routledge.
Searles, H.F. (1975) 'The patient as therapist to the analyst', in R. Langs (ed.), *Classics in Psychoanalytic Technique*. New York: Jason Aronson.
Stern, D. (1985) *The Interpersonal World of the Infant*. New York: Basic Books.
Stern, D. (1995) *The Motherhood Constellation*. New York: Basic Books.
Strupp, H.H. and Binder, J.L. (1984) *Psychotherapy in a New Key*. New York: Basic Books.
Sullivan, H.S. (1953) *The Interpersonal Theory of Psychiatry*. New York: W.W. Norton.
Wheeler, S. (1998) 'Challenging the core theoretical model: a reply to Colin Feltham, *Counselling*, 9 (2): 134–8.
Winnicott, D.W. (1965) *Maturational Processes and the Facilitating Environment*. London: Hogarth Press.
Yalom, I.D. (1980) *Existential Psychotherapy*. New York: Basic Books.
Yalom, I.D. (1985) *The Theory and Practice of Group Psychotherapy*. New York: Basic Books.

7
INTEGRATED ECLECTICISM
A therapeutic synthesis

Clare Austen

Eclectic practitioners are continually making decisions as to which approach they will apply, with which clients and under which circumstances. Such a variety of factors has raised understandable difficulties in terms of cohesion of ideas and consistency of application. This model grew out of my work as a family and individual therapist and draws on a variety of sources, including Stiles (1990), Pinsof (1994) and Holmes (1985). It suggests an approach which is based on the proposition that individuals pass through similar stages of conceptual organization in all psychological therapies and that therapies may differ not only in their emphases on the stages of this process, but also in the depth of cognitive and affective processing they access. It is argued that a decision about treatment of choice may be made by assessing not only the client's stage of problem conceptualization but also the depth of processing required to solve the presenting problem. Further, assessment is viewed as an interactive, developing process which allows for a change in therapeutic orientation as the therapy evolves.

Theory and basic concepts

The need to integrate the eclectic approach

The benefits of an eclectic approach to psychological therapy have been variously described by Dimond et al. (1978), Ryle (1978), Clarkson (1992), Dryden (1992), Pinsof (1994) and Garfield (1995). It is recognized that no one approach is suitable for all clients, problems and situations. However, some researchers (Luborsky, 1984; Messer, 1986) have argued that treatment purity is essential. Therefore, if different approaches are to be used with a client, each should be used discretely and in a planned sequence. To avoid an unplanned, ad hoc approach, it is necessary to develop an integrated eclecticism. This requires a model which maintains a theoretical coherence and posits specific principles of application.

Philosophical assumptions

Eclecticism by its very nature requires a resolution of the underlying contradictions inherent in the different therapeutic approaches. How, for instance, can the idea of the person as a collection of biological drives, many of them destructive, who is held in check by social controls, be equated with the view of human beings as basically 'OK', needing only the right conditions to achieve self-actualization?

In drawing on a variety of models and approaches, it is acknowledged that no one approach contains an objective 'truth'. Any therapeutic approach necessarily involves assumptions about the nature of reality, in terms of basic beliefs about human nature, the origins of disorder and the nature of change. Of necessity, these beliefs will reflect an underlying assumption concerning the nature of knowledge and whether or not we consider that there is an objective, knowable reality. On the one hand, scientific positivism supposes that an objective truth exists and can be understood through the use of reason. Psychological disturbance will thus be viewed in terms of linear causality, as evidenced in the work of Freud. Such an approach would necessarily exclude eclecticism, which by definition draws on many different therapeutic approaches with differing beliefs and assumptions concerning human nature.

In contrast, post-modern approaches postulate that meaning is created by ourselves and influenced by social and cultural factors (Berger and Lindeman, 1966). For instance, family therapists will consider not only how meaning is constructed by the individual within the family context, but also how the family's reality is co-constructed in relation to wider social and cultural beliefs and values. This social constructionist approach therefore allows for a wider inclusion of therapeutic approaches, since meaning is constantly reconstructed both inside and outside the therapeutic encounter. Taken to its extremes, however, by validating all interpretations of reality equally, this view would completely deny the possibility of relative knowledge and thus the proposition that one view of reality may be more accurate or knowledgeable than another. This view was modified by Heron (1988) who suggested that there is an objective reality, but that our understanding of it is only partial and is limited by our social and cultural circumstances. Thus, our knowledge and understanding increases over time and may become more vericidal. The integrated eclecticism model adopts this position and is what Pinsof (1994: 131) describes as an 'interactive constructivist' approach. Knowledge of a client's reality and difficulties is ever-evolving and never fully revealed. Assessment is therefore an ongoing process. We learn more about our clients as we interact with them over time.

This inevitably has implications for practice in that, since we do not have the certainty of fully knowing an objective truth, there will not be a definitive diagnosis of our clients, but rather our assessment will evolve as our knowledge of them gradually increases. This gives freedom also to alter our therapeutic approach as necessary, drawing on the theory or therapeutic application we find most appropriate.

The underlying theoretical framework of the model is based on systemic theory, in that clients are viewed not only as interactive parts of wider systems, such as partners and families, but also as systems in themselves. Clients are thus seen to have internal, interactive psychological systems of cognition, affect and behaviour. The framework can therefore comfortably accommodate various family therapies and experiential approaches, as well as psychodynamic approaches such as object relations theory.

Kleinian theory, for example, which describes how parts of the self may be split or cut off, is see as analogous to the way in which the family system may fragment. Such an interactive approach necessarily explains theory in terms of circular rather than linear causality and would therefore exclude therapeutic approaches described in such terms, for example, Freudian theory.

The process of conceptual reorganization in psychological therapies

It is evident that therapists working to a particular model of therapy base their work on differing theories as to the origins of disorder, how they should be treated and how change is brought about. For instance, psychodynamic therapists view problems in terms of core conflicts and developmental deficits which are treated within a transferential relationship. Person-centred therapists would construe problems in terms of false self versus organismic self with change achieved through personal growth within an I–Thou relationship. However, despite these theoretical differences, Stiles (1990) has argued that a similar process occurs in all psychological therapies. Based on the work of Piaget (1958) this theory has at its heart the concept of the development of mental schemas in the adaptation of problematic experiences. Schemas involve the conceptual reorganization through which the individual gives meaning to the environment. Experiences are viewed in the individual's frame of understanding, which is constructed of a series of associations. These series of associations are formed in two processes of interaction between the individual and the environment, assimilation and accommodation. Accommodation refers to the modification of each schema that occurs as assimilation takes place. These processes are concurrent, complementary and occur at all levels of the processing and understanding of problematic experiences. Thus, a problematic experience will be experienced as alien to the idea of the self or self-schema and will therefore be unassimilated. Stiles (1990) usefully describes how assimilation occurs in a continuum from warded off, painful feelings, through unwanted thoughts, to vague awareness, to problem statement, to understanding insight, to application, working through, to problem solution and mastery. Initially, the client experiences psychological discomfort as feelings which were warded off are drawn into consciousness through unwanted thoughts. Gradually, the client starts to identify what s/he is feeling as vague awareness grows to problem statement. The client is then able clearly to conceptualize the painful material in terms of what is needed to bring about change. As the client moves towards insight, s/he starts to make new connections in terms of him/her self, either intrapsychically or interpersonally. Finally, the client is able to apply this knowledge to a plan of action for problem solution.

Relating this process to different therapeutic approaches, Stiles (1990) suggests that the psychodynamic and experiential therapies tend to work along the earlier part of the continuum, dealing with warded off, painful feelings, with an end goal of insight or understanding. Cognitive behavioural therapies, on the other hand, tend to begin in the middle of the continuum at problem statement and culminate in mastery of the problem. It can thus be argued that different therapies give different parts of the process of conceptual reorganization the main emphasis.

Depth of processing

While assimilation takes place in all therapies, some therapists have argued that change can occur at different levels according to the depth of processing accessed by the therapy used. Holmes (1985) argues that different approaches to therapy may bring about two different levels of change, which involve different levels of processing and awareness. Holmes posits that family therapy, for example, can deal quickly and effectively with issues such as relationship problems, but underlying and long-standing difficulties are not addressed. There is, therefore, no change in underlying mental structures. Deeper change is created in therapies which promote insight and understanding to bring about intrapsychic reconstruction. Dimond et al. (1978: 241) also suggest that change may take place at the 'environmental' or interactional level, which involves wider parts of the system, such as family or partner, or at the level of personality change. The latter is differentiated into behavioural, phenomenological and intrapsychic levels, which can be easily transposed onto the assimilation continuum, in terms of behavioural, experiential and psychodynamic therapies, respectively. Pinsof (1994) developed this further and provides a comprehensive analysis of therapeutic approaches appropriate to each level of treatment, ranging from behavioural-interactional approaches to experiential, including cognitive, affective and interpersonal therapies as well as psychodynamic and psychoanalytic treatments. Inherent in his approach is the idea that intrapsychic change may take place at different levels. He differentiates between experiential therapies, which address primarily the client's present experience, and psychodynamic and psychoanalytic therapies which give emphasis to the historical determinants of the problem. Thus, within second order change there may be further differentiation between the depth of processing achieved by different approaches.

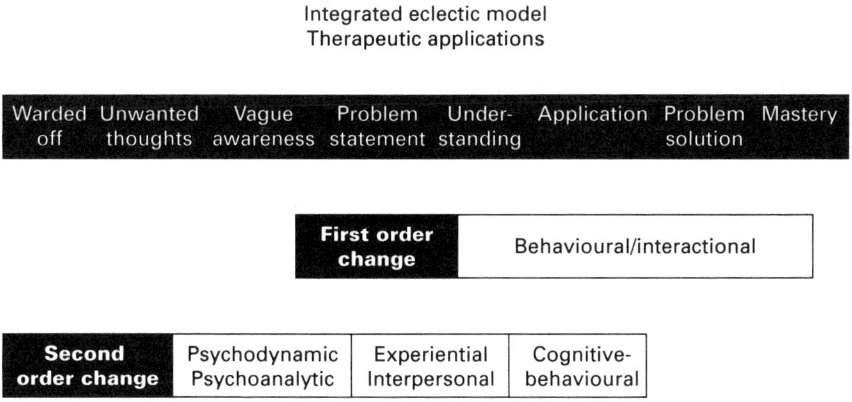

Integrated eclectic model
Therapeutic applications

| Warded off | Unwanted thoughts | Vague awareness | Problem statement | Under-standing | Application | Problem solution | Mastery |

| | First order change | Behavioural/interactional |

| Second order change | Psychodynamic Psychoanalytic | Experiential Interpersonal | Cognitive-behavioural |

Figure 7.1 *Assimilation continuum (adapted from Stiles, 1990)*

If we relate the concept of different levels of change to Stiles's assimilation continuum (Figure 7.1), it is evident that first order change will tend to occur in the area from problem statement to mastery. Second order change will entail the accessing and integration of warded off, painful emotion, leading to understanding and insight as well as problem solution.

Application

It has therefore been argued that:

1 Clients pass through similar stages of conceptual organization in all psychological therapies.
2 Different therapies focus on different levels of awareness in the reorganization process.
3 Different therapies work to bring about different levels of change.

Based on these assumptions, it is possible to argue that therapy of choice can be selected by deciding first at what level change is required and second by assessing the client's level of processing of the problematic experience. Thus, first order change will aim to increase understanding and communication within relationships and behavioural change, rather than to promote profound change in underlying mental structures. Indicators for first order change requiring a systemic approach include a problem defined as in a relationship, such as when a client continually 'includes' an absent family member in the session material; waiting room syndrome, when the client is constantly accompanied to the session by another person; or situations when a family is undergoing dramatic change, such as an adolescent leaving home.

Should second order change be indicated, an assessment is made of the client's conceptualization of the problem to define treatment strategy.

Using Pinsof's therapeutic classifications, clients with warded off, painful feelings indicate a psychodynamic approach. Clients showing vague awareness indicate an experiential approach. Clients further along the continuum, showing a clear conceptualization of the problem, will be worked with using cognitive-behavioural methods. It is possible to adapt the approach as necessary and move between approaches as required. For instance, a client from whom experiential work has clarified vague emotion may then be worked with using cognitive-behavioural methods. Alternatively, if after working cognitively it becomes evident that intrapsychic issues are blocking the process, a psychodynamic approach may be used until the assimilation of warded off, painful feelings is achieved.

There are thus two questions that the therapist needs to address in assessing which therapeutic approach is treatment of choice:

1 What is the level of change required to resolve the problematic experience?
2 Where is the client in terms of the assimilation of the problematic experience?

Case studies

First order change

EXAMPLE 1: ANNIE   Annie, a 59-year-old woman suffering from rheumatoid arthritis, was referred by her GP with mild depression, anxiety and panic attacks. Despite the physical limitations imposed by her illness, she maintained an attractive, well-groomed appearance with stylish blond hair and a good complexion. Previously an active and gregarious woman, Annie had run her own small hotel until forced into retirement by the increasing restrictions of her physical condition.

Annie attended the first session with Derek, her husband, maintaining that he accompanied her on all her appointments. He was, she explained, her chief carer. In accordance with the model, I accepted the client's definition of the problem in that by bringing him she was demonstrating that he was involved in the difficulty to be addressed. I therefore included him in the session. This, together with a clearly defined problem, indicated a behavioural/interactional approach. The session proved to be a very moving one. By using systemic methods such as circular questioning to improve communication, I enabled Annie to express her experience to Derek.

She talked of her sadness at the loss of independence and freedom involved in her illness and the panic and fear she felt when he left her alone. She feared how she would cope without his being there and consequently worried about his safety when he left the house. They were able to talk through these fears together and Derek explained his need for these periods of personal space in his life as her carer. He also expressed his love and care for her openly and tenderly.

The couple talked through ways of helping her to increase her independence including contacting relevant agencies, which she had previously been reluctant to do. I also introduced some anxiety management techniques to them both, treating the panic attacks as a shared problem, in accordance with systemic theory. Two follow-up sessions were used to consolidate the anxiety management work although the incidence of panic attacks had greatly reduced following the first session.

This relatively brief intervention using interactional and behavioural methods demonstrates first order change in the alleviation of a clearly defined problem.

EXAMPLE 2: SADIE Sadie, a 42-year-old homemaker, was referred by her GP with depression. She explained that she had been married for 20 years to Tim, a carpenter. The couple had two children, 19-year-old Max and 12-year-old Freddie. At the age of 17, Max had been diagnosed as suffering from schizophrenia and the family had experienced great difficulty in adjusting to the diagnosis and its implications. Gradually, the situation had deteriorated and Max's behaviour had become increasingly difficult. Arguments between Max and Tim were frequent and had on occasion resulted in violence. The strain of the situation was extracting its toll and Sadie was depressed and tearful.

As Sadie had 'included' several family members in the session by explaining the difficulty in inclusive terms and since the presenting problem, Max's illness, affected the whole family, I suggested a family session. In this session, Tim explained that Max was truculent and difficult, refusing to get up in the morning and also not attending his course at the local college. Max also stayed out too late in the evening and was, in Tim's view, disobedient and unco-operative. Tim's anger was palpable, while Max remained silent and withdrawn. By using systemic techniques, such as reframing and circular questioning, the communication within the family was opened up. Tim was able to express his concern over Max's future and Max expressed his frustration at the restrictions imposed on him by his parents. Some of his difficulties were then understood in terms of a young adult seeking autonomy and independence rather than in terms of his illness. The interactive sequences within the family were examined and they began to understand how each person's behaviour was linked interactively. Tim realized that the more angry he became with Max, the more Max withdrew and became unco-operative, thus increasing Tim's anger. Subsequent sessions addressed the impact of Max's diagnosis on the family, as well as increasing their understanding of the illness and how they as a family could manage it. We thus worked through problem statement to an understanding of Max's illness in the context of the family, allowing Max and his parents to apply this understanding to their own problem solution.

Second order change

EXAMPLE 3: JOHN   John was a slender young man, 28 years old, with a slightly stooped gait, who cultivated a masculine appearance with his sombre clothes, 'biker' leather jacket and bushy moustache. His employment history was sporadic as periods of casual labouring work had been interspersed with bouts of mental ill health.

John was referred for psychological therapy following a hospital admission for a depression which had culminated in an overdose. This had been his third admission for depression in the previous two-year period. There had also been some self-harm. He described a total lack of any feeling since his early teens, when he had decided that his experience of emotion had been so painful that it was preferable to feel nothing. He was pervaded by a feeling of emptiness and lack of personal identity. This demonstrated itself in interpersonal relationships by a lack of trust in others and an inability to sustain intimate relationships. John thus appeared to be functioning at the early end of the assimilation continuum as his feelings were warded off, with some vague awareness. He was also seeking insight, understanding and self-knowledge rather than behavioural change so I found psychodynamic concepts applicable in my work with him. Change was therefore indicated at second order level, since a change in intrapsychic structures was required.

At the start of our work, John described himself as a rudderless boat, adrift in an ocean of fog. His denial of any emotion was evident when he described painful events such as family bereavement in a flat, almost cynical way. At these times I was aware of experiencing almost overwhelming feelings of sadness, loneliness and loss, which I understood in terms of projective identification. I was thus feeling for John the emotion he was unable to experience. As work progressed, it was evident that the intensity of John's experience indicated very early traumatic events as we began to understand his difficulties in terms of his developmental experience. An extremely sensitive and vulnerable child, John had been raised in a large, chaotic family with a culture of aggression and submerged anger. His own feelings of vulnerability, fear of abandonment and need for containment of his anxieties had been denied and his experience had been invalidated. Additionally, there had also been some sexual abuse by a maternal uncle in early childhood. In understanding John's difficulties, the work of psychodynamic writers such as Lang et al. (1987) and Higgitt and Fonaghy (1992) were most appropriate.

Using this psychodynamic thinking, and as John became more aware of his feelings, I worked experientially with John, paying attention to the interaction between us in the therapy. I was aware of his acute need for containment and desperate fear of abandonment in providing a safe and secure relationship base where he could build trust. Using the knowledge of child development and early needs, John began to make sense of his experience. We used some of the thinking in transactional analysis to help John understand his own mixed responses in terms, for instance, of abandoned child and punitive parent. He thus progressed through vague awareness of his feelings to problem statement.

As John became more aware of his feelings and began to understand them, we started to address some of the difficulties he was experiencing in his life external to the therapy room. In essence, the focus shifted and since John was now seeking behavioural change we used some of the ideas within the cognitive-behavioural approach to help him view both himself and others more productively by questioning faulty cognitions and working with him to find alternative views. On a practical level, we addressed issues such as social skills and assertiveness. Thus, as John became aware of and was able to process and understand his feelings, he was able to move to a problem statement, understanding and direct application of this knowledge to work on specific areas of concern in his life.

EXAMPLE 4: THE SOAMES FAMILY   Ten-year-old Melanie was referred because of behavioural difficulties. She attended with her mother, Brenda, a quiet, nervous and unassertive woman. Brenda explained that Melanie was difficult to handle, disobedient and prone to temper outbursts. Melanie, a sturdy child with a grave expression, said little during the session, despite attempts to encourage her participation. On exploring the family situation, I found that Brenda had been living with her partner, Dennis, for the past six years and the couple had a young son, Michael, aged two. When asked about Melanie's father, Brenda became uncomfortable and embarrassed and said she did not talk about him.

As the presenting problem was Melanie's behaviour, this clearly stated problem indicated first order change at a behavioural/interactional level. A session was arranged to include Dennis and Michael. During this session it became clear that Dennis and Brenda were unable to provide a united approach with clear guidelines for Melanie. Brenda accused Dennis of being too harsh in his dealings with the child and Melanie observed this disagreement. Her refusal to obey Dennis began an argument between her parents as Brenda remonstrated on her daughter's behalf. Observing this interaction, I asked Brenda and Dennis to agree on set boundaries of behaviour for Melanie and each to support the other.

At the next session the couple reported that they had been unable to carry out the agreed tasks. Their animosity with each other was evident. It was obvious that difficulties in the relationship were impeding the execution of the behavioural task agreed. We agreed to spend a few sessions working on the issues in their relationship. During these sessions, it emerged that Dennis was attempting to set boundaries for Melanie but Brenda always intervened. Dennis saw his attempts to provide structure for Melanie as a way of showing his affection for the child and his concern for Brenda, whom he often found withdrawn and uncommunicative. Brenda explained that she often felt depressed and she feared Dennis's relationship with Melanie might replicate her own experience of harsh treatment in childhood. She also felt angry and resentful with Melanie's birth father. He had abandoned her shortly after Melanie's birth, following an abusive two-year relationship. After several joint sessions, Dennis was increasingly insightful of the situation, but Brenda was still angry, depressed and withdrawn and it was evident that her own issues were impeding progress. As the problem had not been resolved by first order change, it was necessary to move to second order level and allow Brenda time to work on intrapsychic issues on an individual basis. There was thus a change in emphasis in that we were now working at the earlier part of the assimilation continuum. By focusing on Brenda's experience, the task was to enable her to assimilate her own problematic experiences, which appeared to be blocking the resolution of the presenting problem.

Subsequent sessions allowed Brenda to come to terms with the previously warded off issues of anger and resentment from previous relationships as well as the lack of self-worth originating in an abusive childhood. As Brenda became more self-accepting, her relationship with Dennis improved. She no longer experienced Dennis's implementation of the parental role with Melanie as abusive. Both she and Dennis were able to provide firm boundaries and affection for the child, whose behaviour subsequently improved.

EXAMPLE 5: BILL, Bill, a 34-year-old industrial chemist, was referred with depression and anxiety. He reported two main areas of concern: his highly pressurized job and his worry over his wife who had been ill with chronic fatigue syndrome for two of their three years of marriage. He sought to understand his feelings of depression and stress in the context of his home and working life. Bill's main focus was therefore on gaining insight into his own reactions and feelings. He was not expressing the problem in terms of his relationship with his wife, but felt that he needed space and time to understand his own issues and the ways that these were affecting his interactions with others. This indicated the need for change at a second order level. Since there was no clear problem statement and Bill's feelings were only partially experienced, exploratory work was indicated. I began to work using an experiential approach. Gradually, Bill became aware of the anger he felt at his marital situation, which had been blighted by his wife's illness. He began to understand how self-blame was his way of understanding his situation, owing to early developmental experience from a strict, withdrawn father and undemonstrative mother. Bill was thus moving through the stages of vague awareness of his feelings to a conceptualization of the problem. Gradually, as he reached the stage of insight and understanding, he realized that his lack of awareness of his own needs was impeding his ability to assert himself both at home and at work. With the knowledge and insight gained in this work, Bill felt better equipped to cope in both his home and work situations.

Practice and clinical issues

These examples demonstrate that the assessment of the client's situation is made in terms of the client's view of the problem. Although Sadie (Example 2) was the identified patient, it became clear that she viewed her problem in terms of her family situation and her son's illness, not in terms of her own intrapsychic processes. In accepting her view of the problem, it was possible to move from an individual to a systemic approach. Conversely, the Soames family (Example 4) construed their difficulties in terms of Melanie's behaviour. By accepting this and working with the family, we began a process of mutually gained insight and understanding of the problem as the focus shifted from Melanie to the couple relationship and finally to Brenda's own experience. Again, although Bill (Example 5) realized that his wife's illness was affecting him, he was not expressing his problem in terms of his relationship with her and wished to concentrate on his own experience.

The approach is therefore client led; it does not attempt to fit the client into a preconceived ideology in terms of the therapeutic approach. By taking an interactive constructivist approach, the therapist acknowledges that our knowledge is ever partial and will evolve and expand over time. It is therefore not possible for the therapist to know the 'truth' of the client's situation. The therapist needs to track the client carefully as the story unfolds, so that the most appropriate therapeutic approach can be adopted. There may, of course, be many other issues in our client's lives which we as therapists may consider important, but these would be addressed only if the client identified them as significant. In other words, we do only the work required to solve the presenting problem.

The therapeutic relationship

The importance of the therapeutic relationship in the application of this model cannot be overemphasized. It requires great sensitivity on the part of the therapist; first, to assess client readiness in terms of the assimilation continuum; second, to move to a different approach if required. Any such change must necessarily be instigated only if the client is comfortable with the change and the therapeutic alliance must always take priority. Essentially, a change in approach is not to suggest a change in the therapist's 'being with' the client, but rather that the conceptual approach utilized may be informed by different therapeutic approaches. Thus, in my work with John (Example 3), although I drew heavily on psychodynamic thinking to understand his experience and my own responses, I did not alter my usual way of relating to my clients. As my approach is widely humanistic I did not, for instance, aim to work through and encourage any transferential feelings, nor to change my practice of transparency in the therapeutic encounter. Neither did I become patently didactic when using cognitive-behavioural ideas: rather, these were introduced in the atmosphere of openness and trust which had developed over the course of the therapy in a spirit of open enquiry. Each therapist will, therefore, find their own fine-grained ways of working within the overall framework of the model, while maintaining the therapeutic alliance.

Indications and contraindications

This model is extremely flexible since it relies neither on clients' psychological mindedness nor on degree of client psychological health or pathology. Rather, it addresses the problem as presented and by positing two levels of change recognizes that change may be possible even in clients who are extremely disturbed. For instance, clients who are incapable of the insight brought about by some therapeutic work by nature of an illness such as schizophrenia or a severe personality disturbance, may still be helped to overcome the problems of day-to-day living in terms of behaviour and relationships by means of a behavioural/interactional approach. It is a very client-centred approach in that it is trusting of the client's view of the problem and seeks to work with the client on the problem as stated in the client's terms. There is thus less likelihood of using an approach that is damaging to the client or incongruent with the client's needs. The limitations of the model lie mainly with the therapist's expertise in applying the ideas inherent in the various therapeutic approaches. However, should practitioners not feel competent in using all of the approaches available to the model, it provides a useful rule of thumb guide for referral.

Wider implications and applications

The model may be used in any setting in which an eclectic approach is deemed appropriate, such as primary care, private practice and both child and adult psychiatry. Its cohesive framework also provides a blueprint for trainers in the eclectic approach as it suggests a rationale for the application of the different therapeutic orientations.

Conclusion

This model has several advantages for the eclectic practitioner. First, it begins where the client is, at the client's understanding of the problem, and treats the problem in terms that are congruent with the client's views. Second, it is economical, since work at deeper levels proceeds only as necessary. If it is possible to achieve a resolution of the presenting problem at first order level, this can be achieved speedily and effectively. If not, work can proceed to deeper levels as required. Third, it provides a systematic plan for the application of different approaches. It has provided a useful overall guide in my work as an eclectic practitioner and will, I hope, contribute to the debate on eclectic practice.

References

Berger, P. and Lindeman, T. (1966) *The Social Construction of Reality: A Treatise on the Sociology of Knowledge*. London: Penguin.
Clarkson, P. (1992) *Transactional Analysis Psychotherapy: An Integrated Approach*. London: Routledge.
Dimond, R., Havens, R. and Jones, A. (1978) 'A conceptual framework for the practice of prescriptive eclecticism in psychotherapy', *American Psychologist*, March: 239–47.

Dryden, W. (ed.) (1992) *Integrative and Eclectic Therapy*. Buckingham: Open University Press.

Garfield, S. (1995) *Psychotherapy: An Eclectic Integrative Approach*. Chichester: Wiley.

Heron, J. (1988) 'Validity in co-operative inquiry', in P. Reason, (ed.), *Human Inquiry in Action*. Chichester: Wiley.

Higgitt, A. and Fonaghy, P. (1992) 'Psychotherapy in borderline and narcissistic personality disorder', *British Journal of Psychiatry*, 161: 23–43.

Holmes, J. (1985) 'Family and individual therapy: comparisons and contrasts', *British Journal of Psychiatry*, 147: 668–76.

Lang, J.A., Grotstein, J.S. and Soloman, M.F. (1987) *Convergence and Controversy: 1 Theory of the Borderline in the Borderline Patient; Emerging Concepts in Diagnosis, Psychodynamics and Treatment*. Hillsdale, NJ: The Analytic Press, pp. 187–200.

Luborsky, L. (1984) *Principles of Psychoanalytic Therapy: A Manual for Supportive-Expressive Treatment*. New York: Basic Books.

Messer, S.B. (1986) 'Eclecticism in psychotherapy: underlying assumptions, problems and tradeoffs', in J.C. Norcross (ed.), *Handbook of Eclectic Psychotherapy*. New York: Brunner/Mazel.

Piaget, J. (1958) *The Growth of Logical Thinking from Childhood to Adolescence*. London: Routledge and Kegan Paul.

Pinsof, W. (1994) 'An overview of integrative problem centred therapy: a synthesis of family and individual psychotherapies', *Journal of Family Therapy*, 16 (1): 123–39.

Ryle, A. (1978) 'A common language for all psychotherapies?', *British Journal of Psychiatry*, 132: 585–94.

Stiles, W. (1990) 'Assimilation of problematic experiences by clients in psychotherapy', *Psychotherapy*, 27 (3): 411–19.

8
MULTIMODAL THERAPY

Stephen Palmer

Multimodal therapy is a systematic and technically eclectic psychotherapeutic approach. Techniques and interventions are applied systematically, based on data from client qualities, the counsellor's clinical skills and specific techniques. The approach is technically eclectic as it uses techniques taken from many different psychological theories and systems, without necessarily being concerned with the validity of the theoretical principles that underpin the different approaches from which it takes its techniques and methods (Palmer and Dryden, 1995).

The multimodal orientation transcends the behavioural tradition by adding unique assessment procedures and focusing on seven different aspects or dimensions (known as modalities) of human personality (Lazarus, 1995a). Not only is a serious attempt made to tailor the therapy to each client's unique requirements but the counsellor also endeavours to match his or her interpersonal style and interaction to the individual needs of each client, thereby maximizing the therapeutic outcome.

Development of the therapy

During the 1950s Arnold Lazarus, a clinical psychologist, undertook his formal training in South Africa. The main focus of this training was underpinned by Freudian, Rogerian and Sullivanian theories and methods. He attended seminars by Joseph Wolpe about conditioning therapies and reciprocal inhibition. During 1957 he spent several months as an intern at the Marlborough Day Hospital in London, where he learned about the Adlerian orientation. He believed that no one system of therapy could provide a complete understanding of either human development or condition. In 1958 he became the first psychologist to use the terms 'behavior therapist' and 'behavior therapy' in an academic article (Lazarus, 1958).

Lazarus conducted follow-up inquiries into clients who had received behaviour therapy and found that many had relapsed. However, when clients had used both behaviour and cognitive techniques more durable results were obtained. In the early 1970s he started advocating a broad but systematic range of cognitive-behavioural techniques and his follow-up inquiries indicated the importance of breadth if therapeutic gains were to be maintained. This led to the development of multimodal therapy which places emphasis on seven discrete but interactive dimensions or modalities which encompass all aspects of human personality.

During the 1990s in Britain, Stephen Palmer, a psychologist, has developed multimodal therapy and applied it to the field of stress management and counselling (Palmer and Dryden, 1991, 1995; Palmer, 1992).

Theory and basic concepts

Multimodal therapy is underpinned on the theoretical base of social learning theory (Bandura, 1969, 1977, 1986). It also draws from general systems theory (Bertalanffy, 1974; Buckley, 1967) and group and communications theory (Watzlawick et al., 1974). According to Lazarus (1995a: 323) 'These diverse theories blend harmoniously into a congruent framework.' However, multimodal therapists do not inflexibly adhere to any one theory in a rigid manner (Lazarus, 1989). Although multimodal therapy uses many techniques and strategies taken from behaviour therapy, cognitive therapy and rational emotive behaviour therapy, it has six distinctive features which set it apart from all the other approaches (adapted from Lazarus, 1995a: 323).

1. The specific and comprehensive attention given to the entire seven modalities (known as BASIC I.D.).
2. The use of second-order BASIC I.D. assessments.
3. The use of modality profiles.
4. The use of structural profiles.
5. Deliberate bridging procedures.
6. Tracking the modality firing order.

These features will be examined in either this section or under Practice and Clinical Issues.

Modalities

Individuals are essentially biological organisms (neurophysiological/biochemical entities) who behave (act and react), emote (experience affective responses), sense (respond to olfactory, tactile, gustatory, visual and auditory stimuli), imagine (conjure up sights, sounds and other events in the mind's eye), think (hold beliefs, opinions, attitudes and values), and interact with one another (tolerate, enjoy or endure various interpersonal relationships). These seven aspects or dimensions of human personality are known as modalities. By referring to these seven modalities as Behaviour, Affect, Sensations, Images, Cognitions, Interpersonal and

Drugs/biology, the useful acronym and aide memoire BASIC I.D. arises from the first letter of each (Lazarus, 1989).

From the multimodal perspective these seven modalities may interact with each other; for example, a negative thought or an unpleasant image may trigger a negative emotion such as guilt or shame. The multimodal approach rests on the assumption that unless the seven modalities are assessed, therapy is likely to overlook significant concerns. Clients are usually troubled by a multitude of specific problems which should be dealt with by a similar multitude of specific interventions or techniques (Lazarus, 1991). For example, a client may suffer from poor time management, guilt about being a 'useless' parent, physical tension and a poor diet. Each problem will probably need a specific intervention to help the client improve his or her condition.

Arnold Lazarus found that individuals tend to prefer some of the BASIC I.D. modalities to others. They are referred to as 'cognitive reactors' or 'sensory reactors' or 'imagery reactors' depending upon which modality they favour (Lazarus, 1989).

Thresholds

A basic premise made in multimodal therapy is that people have different thresholds for pain, stress, frustration, external and internal stimuli in the form of sound, light, touch, taste and smell. Psychological interventions can be applied by individuals to help modify these thresholds but often the genetic diathesis or predisposition usually prevails in the final analysis (Lazarus, 1995a). For example, a client with a low tolerance to stress may be able to use stress management techniques to deal with many difficult situations, yet may still become clinically anxious and depressed during periods of relatively high workloads.

Principle of parity

In multimodal therapy the therapist and client are considered equal in their humanity (the principle of parity). Politicians, royalty, pop stars and heads of large organizations are all equal. However, the therapist may be more skilled in certain areas in which the client has particular deficits. Therefore, it is not automatically assumed that clients know how to deal with their problems and have requisite skills. The therapist may need to model or teach the client various skills and strategies to help overcome his or her problem(s) or clinical disorders.

The development of problems and how they are maintained

Problems develop and are maintained for a variety of reasons and social learning, systems and communication theories usually provide possible answers. A key role is played by association (Lazarus, 1995a). Events that occur either close together, simultaneously or sometimes just frequently may become temporally linked or associated. Therefore individuals' feelings, thinking, images and behaviours may arise due to conditioning. Aversions and phobias that may occur are usually maintained by avoidance. Fortunately, these may be modified by using appropriate techniques and strategies. However, not all clients necessarily respond successfully to classical or operant conditioning, modelling and vicarious procedures. Not only do their perceptions, appraisals, beliefs, misunderstandings and attitudes help to maintain a particular problem, but they may also affect the therapeutic outcome. Finally the biological and genetic dimensions can have an overriding affect on acquisition, maintenance and possible therapeutic outcome. In this section additional key factors will be discussed.

Defensive reactions

Individuals may avoid or defend against pain, discomfort, frustration, or negative emotions such as anxiety, guilt, shame and depression. They may intellectualize, rationalize or project their own feelings onto others as a form of defence. Unfortunately, these defensive reactions do not teach individuals how to cope adaptively with their fears and difficulties.

Metacommunications

Interactions involving two people or more include communications and metacommunications (i.e. communications about their communication). Communication can disintegrate when individuals are unable to stand back from the transaction, thereby failing to examine the content and process of ongoing relationships. This helps to trigger and then subsequently maintain conflict and difficulties for the individuals involved.

Non-conscious processes

Non-conscious processes are often involved in learning. Unrecognized (subliminal) stimuli can influence feelings, conscious thoughts/images and behaviours and may go unrecognized by the individual concerned. In addition, individuals have different degrees and levels of self-awareness (Lazarus, 1987). (The term 'non-conscious' should not be confused with the more familiar psychodynamic term 'unconscious'.)

Misinformation

Over a period of time people may learn incorrect assumptions and beliefs about life. For example, the beliefs 'I can't stand frustrating situations', 'I must perform well otherwise I'm worthless', 'I'm useless if my partner leaves me' or 'Life's awful' may be imbibed by listening to significant others such as parents, siblings, teachers or peers. On many occasions, these beliefs may be largely responsible for considerable distress when external life events challenge them. Couples may also hold on to unhelpful beliefs or myths such as 'If you feel guilty, confess' or 'Total honesty is the best policy' (see Lazarus, 1985a; Lazarus et al., 1993). Misinformation also applies when individuals have misunderstood health and medically related issues such as treatment of heart disease or cancer. Unless the health professionals correct these errors, then patient compliance to medical procedures may be hindered or even non-existent.

Missing information

Unlike misinformation, with missing information people have not learnt the necessary skills, knowledge or methods to either understand or undertake particular activities or recognize specific problems. For example, people may not have in their repertoire of behaviour presentation skills, friendship skills, communication skills, assertiveness skills or know how to open a bank account. They may not realize that a pain in their chest could signify heart disease and that it may be strongly advisable to have a medical check-up. These types of issues may be raised during counselling and are dealt with accordingly.

Lack of self-acceptance

Individuals tend to link their behaviour skills deficits and/or personality traits directly to their totality as a human being. Depending upon the particular belief the individual holds, this tends to lead to anxiety, depression, shame or anger. For example, an individual may believe, 'If I fail my driving test, therefore I'm a failure as a person.' A more helpful, realistic and logical way of looking at the situation could be, 'If I fail my driving test all it proves is that I've got driving skills deficits. It would not mean that I'm a failure as a person'. The unhelpful beliefs may have been imbibed from parents and other significant people in the child's life but they may be reinforced and perpetuated by the person constantly re-indoctrinating him or herself on a regular basis throughout adulthood. In multimodal therapy the contents of self-defeating or unrealistic beliefs are examined and replaced by more self-helping and realistic beliefs. Clients are taught self-acceptance as opposed to enhancing self-esteem (see Lazarus, 1977; Palmer, 1997b).

From psychological disturbance to psychological health

The issues discussed in the previous sections and the path to psychological health can be expressed in the form of the BASIC I.D. modalities below:

1 *Behaviour*: ceasing unhelpful behaviours; performing wanted behaviours; stop unnecessary or irrational avoidances; take effective behaviours to achieve realistic goals.
2 *Affect*: admitting, clarifying and accepting feelings; coping or managing unpleasant feelings and enhancing positive feelings; abreaction (i.e. living and recounting painful experiences and emotions).

3 *Sensation*: tension release; sensory pleasuring; awareness of positive and negative sensations; improve threshold tolerance to pain and other stimuli.
4 *Imagery*: developing helpful coping images; improving self-image; getting in touch with one's imagination.
5 *Cognition*: greater awareness of cognitions; improve problem-solving skills; modify self-defeating and rigid beliefs; enhance flexible and realistic thinking; increase self-acceptance; modify beliefs that exacerbate low thresholds to frustration or pain (e.g. 'I can't stand it' to 'I don't like it but I'm living proof that I can stand it'). Correct misinformation and provide accurate missing information.
6 *Interpersonal*: non-judgemental acceptance of others; model useful interpersonal skills; dispersing unhealthy collusions; improve assertiveness, communication, social and friendship skills.
7 *Drugs/biology*: better nutrition and exercise; substance abuse cessation; drink alcohol in moderation; medication when indicated for mental or physical disorders.

Practice and clinical issues

Goals of multimodal therapy

The goals of multimodal therapy are to help clients to have a happier life and achieve their own realistic goals. Therefore the goals are tailored to each client. A philosophy of long-term hedonism is advocated whereby the client may need to decide how much pleasure they may want in the present compared to the sacrifices they may have to make to attain their desires and wishes.

Relationship between the therapist and client

The relationship is underpinned by core therapeutic conditions suggested by Carl Rogers: empathy, congruence and unconditional positive regard (see Raskin and Rogers, 1995). Although a good therapeutic relationship, a constructive working alliance and adequate rapport are usually necessary, multimodal therapists consider that they are often insufficient for effective therapy (Fay and Lazarus, 1993). The counsellor–client relationship is considered as the soil that enables the strategies and techniques to take root. The experienced multimodal counsellor hopes to offer a lot more by assessing and treating the client's BASIC I.D., endeavouring to 'leave no stone (or modality) unturned' (Palmer, 1997a: 156).

Multimodal therapists often see themselves in a teacher–student or coach/trainer–trainee relationship as opposed to a doctor–patient relationship, thereby encouraging self-change rather than dependency. Therefore the usual approach taken is active-directive where the counsellor provides information and suggests possible strategies and interventions to help the client manage or resolve specific problems. However, this would depend upon the issues being discussed and the personality characteristics of the client.

Flexible interpersonal styles of the counsellor which match client needs can reduce attrition (i.e. premature termination of therapy) and help the therapeutic relationship and alliance. This approach is known in multimodal therapy as being an 'authentic chameleon' (Lazarus, 1993). For example, if a client states that she wants a 'tough, no nonsense approach' she is likely to find a 'warm, gentle' approach not helpful or conducive to client disclosure (Palmer and Dryden, 1995). Other clients may ask for a therapist who will 'listen to my problems and be supportive'. These clients may consider an active-directive approach as intrusive, whereas a client who states, 'I would value your comments and opinions on my problems' may become very irritated by a counsellor who only reflects back the client's opinions and sentiments. This flexibility in the therapist's interpersonal therapeutic style underpins effective multimodal therapy. Therapists are expected to exhibit different aspects of their own personality to help the therapeutic relationship and clients to reach their goals such as being formal or informal, willing to self-disclose and share experiences (if appropriate), and the use of humour. The term 'bespoke therapy' has been used to describe the custom-made emphasis of the approach (Zilbergeld, 1982).

The process of change

The process of change may start prior to the first therapy session as clients are usually sent details about the approach with some explanation of the key techniques such as coping imagery, thinking skills or relaxation (e.g. Palmer and Strickland, 1996). Often the client has already started using these self-help techniques before the therapy formally commences. In Britain at the Centre for Multimodal Therapy, included with the details is a client checklist of issues to discuss with the counsellor at the first meeting (Palmer and Szymanska, 1994). This checklist encourages the client to ask the counsellor relevant questions about the approach, the therapist's qualifications and training and contractual issues, thereby giving the client more control of the session and therapy.

During the course of therapy, the client's problems are expressed in terms of the seven BASIC I.D. modalities and client change occurs as the major different problems are managed or resolved across the entire BASIC I.D. Initially, sessions are often held weekly. (Very anxious or depressed clients, especially those with suicidal ideation, may be seen more frequently.) As client gains are made then the sessions are held with longer intervals in between, such as fortnightly or monthly. Termination of counselling usually occurs when clients have dealt with the major problems on their modality profile or feel that they can cope with the remaining problems.

Initial assessment

Assessment helps both the client and therapist to understand the client's presenting problems and their degree of severity. The assessment procedure then leads on to the development of a therapy programme focusing on dealing with each presenting problem. In multimodal therapy, the first or second counselling sessions are used to place the client's problems within the BASIC I.D. framework (see later). The therapist uses the initial interview to derive a number of determinations (adapted from Lazarus, 1987; Palmer and Dryden, 1995):

1. Are there any signs of 'psychosis'?
2. Are there any signs of organicity, organic pathology or any disturbed motor activity?
3. Is there any evidence of depression, suicidal or homicidal tendencies?
4. What are the persisting complaints and their main precipitating events?
5. What appear to be some important antecedent events?
6. Who or what appears to be maintaining the client's overt or covert problems?
7. What does the client wish to derive from therapy?
8. Are there clear indications or contraindications for the adoption of a particular therapeutic style (e.g. is there a preference for a directive or a non-directive style)?
9. Are there any indications as to whether it would be in the client's interests to be seen as part of dyad, triad, family unit and/or in a group?
10. Can a mutually satisfying relationship ensue, or should the client be referred elsewhere?
11. Has the client previous experience of therapy or relevant training? If yes, what was the outcome? Were any difficulties encountered? Was it a positive, negative or neutral experience, and why?
12. Why is the client seeking therapy at this time and not last week, last month or last year?
13. What are some of the client's positive attributes and strengths?

During the beginning phase of therapy the multimodal therapist is collecting information and looking for underlying themes and problems. Additionally, the therapist endeavours to ascertain whether a judicious referral may be necessary to a medical practitioner, psychiatrist or other professional. During the first session the client is usually asked to give details about his or her problem(s) near the start of the session and often within only 20 minutes the client has provided information about a large majority of the 13 determinations. Further questioning will normally fill in any gaps without appearing too intrusive. Then the therapist would usually explain that it is useful to investigate the client's problems in terms of the BASIC I.D. modalities. This can be undertaken fairly easily in the session by using a whiteboard or paper that the client can see. With the therapist's assistance, the client decides which Behaviours he or she would like to stop, introduce or modify. This is written on the whiteboard and then the next BASIC I.D. modality is assessed which is Affect. This process is continued until all of the seven modalities have been assessed. Table 8.1 is a BASIC I.D. chart, more commonly known as a Modality Profile, which in this example illustrates John's problems (see case study later). If appropriate, during the first session the therapist will make a therapeutic intervention such as using an imagery or relaxation technique, to help the client cope with his or her most pressing problem(s) and instil some hope into the situation.

Table 8.1 *John's Modality Profile (or BASIC I.D. chart)*

Modality	Problem
Behaviour	Eats/walks fast, always in a rush, hostile, competitive: indicative of Type A Avoidance of giving presentations Accident-proneness
Affect	Anxious when giving presentations Guilt when work targets not achieved Frequent angry outbursts at work
Sensation	Tension in shoulders Palpitations Frequent headaches Sleeping difficulties
Imagery	Negative images of not performing well Images of losing control Poor self-image
Cognition	I must perform well otherwise it will be awful and I couldn't stand it. I must be in control. Significant others should recognize my work. If I fail then I am a total failure
Interpersonal	Passive/aggressive in relationships Manipulative tendencies at work Always put self first Few supportive friends
Drugs/biology	Feeling inexplicably tired Takes aspirins for headaches Consumes ten cups of coffee a day Poor nutrition and little exercise

Source: Palmer (1997c)

Depending upon the time left in the session either the counsellor and client can negotiate a counselling programme or postpone this to the following session. If the client reads an article or book about techniques and interventions that are used in multimodal therapy between sessions one and two, then he or she is more likely to be constructively involved in negotiating a comprehensive counselling programme in the next session. Bibliotherapy is an important part of multimodal therapy and includes the use of books, articles, handouts and audio-visual material. In addition, the client may be asked to complete a Multimodal Life History Inventory (MLHI) (Lazarus and Lazarus, 1991) at home. This is a 15-page questionnaire which can aid assessment and the development of a therapeutic programme. It has sections covering each modality and includes routine history taking and expectations regarding therapy. Therefore the therapist has less need to ask too many questions during the first session.

In a subsequent session an additional assessment tool is used. To obtain more clinical information and also general goals for counselling, a Structural Profile is drawn (Lazarus, 1989). This can be derived from the MLHI or by asking clients to rate subjectively, on a scale of 1 to 7, how they perceive themselves in relation to the seven modalities. The counsellor can ask a number of different questions that focus on the seven modalities:

- *Behaviour*: How much of a 'doer' are you?
- *Affect*: How emotional are you?
- *Sensation:* How 'tuned in' are you to your bodily sensations?
- *Imagery*: How imaginative are you?
- *Cognition*: How much of a 'thinker' are you?
- *Interpersonal*: How much of a 'social being' are you?
- *Drugs/biology*: To what extent are you health conscious?

Then in the session the counsellor can illustrate these scores graphically by representing them in the form of a bar chart on paper. Figure 8.1 illustrates John's Structural Profile (discussed later in the case study). Then clients are asked in what way they would like to change their profiles during the course of counselling. Once again the client is asked to rate subjectively each modality on a score from 1 to 7. Figure 8.2 illustrates John's Desired Structural Profile.

From assessment to an individual counselling programme

Multimodal therapists counsellors take Gordon Paul's (1967: 111) mandate very seriously: 'What treatment, by *whom*, is most effective for *this* individual with *that* specific problem and under *which* set of circumstances?' In addition the *relationships of choice* is also considered. After the initial therapy or assessment session, assuming that the therapist believes that he or she can offer the right type of help and approach to the client, they then negotiate a therapeutic programme.

As multimodal therapy is technically eclectic, it will use techniques and interventions from a variety of different therapies. Table 8.2 (adapted from Palmer, 1992) highlights the main techniques used. Although these are

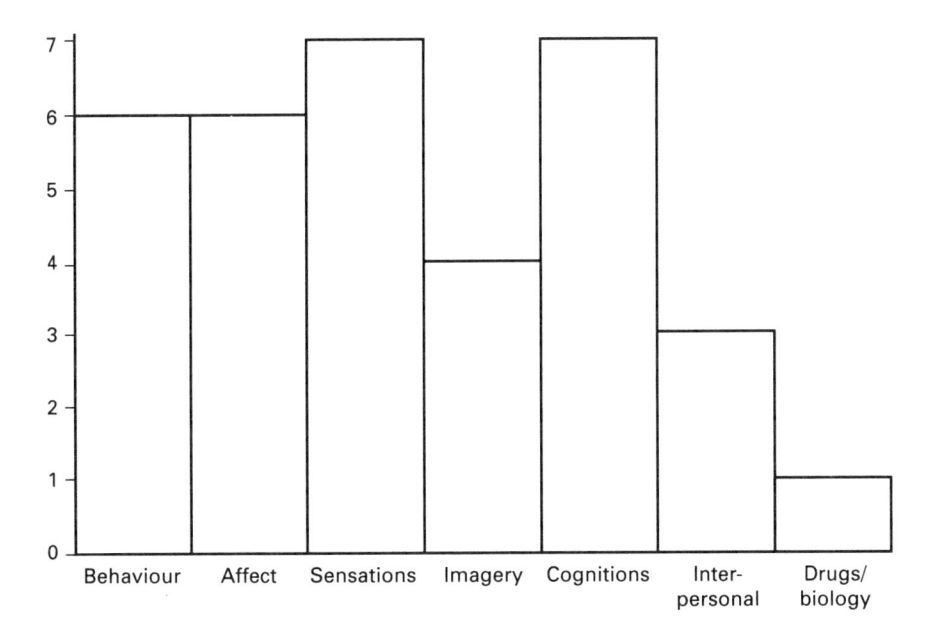

Figure 8.1 *John's Structural Profile (Palmer, 1997c)*

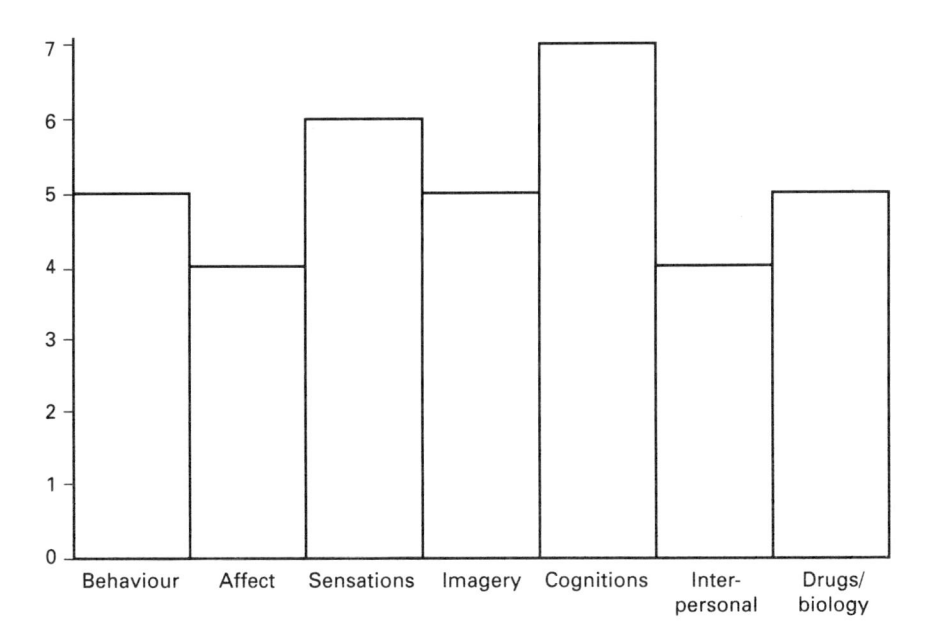

Figure 8.2 *John's Desired Structural Profile (Palmer, 1997c)*

largely based on behaviour therapy, rational emotive behaviour therapy and cognitive therapy, techniques are also taken from other approaches too such as Gestalt and psychodynamic therapy. The next section will focus on techniques and strategies which are used more exclusively in multimodal therapy.

Table 8.2 *Frequently used techniques in multimodal therapy and training*

Modality	Techniques/interventions
Behaviour	Behaviour rehearsal
	Empty chair
	Exposure programme
	Fixed role therapy
	Modelling
	Paradoxical intention
	Psychodrama
	Reinforcement programmes
	Response prevention/cost
	Risk-taking exercises
	Self-monitoring and recording
	Stimulus control
	Shame-attacking
Affect	Anger expression
	Anxiety management
	Feeling identification
Sensation	Biofeedback
	Hypnosis
	Meditation
	Relaxation training
	Sensate focus training
	Threshold training
Imagery	Anti-future shock imagery
	Associated imagery
	Aversive imagery
	Coping imagery
	Implosion and imaginal exposure
	Positive imagery
	Rational emotive imagery
	Time projection and motivation imagery
Cognition	Bibliotherapy
	Challenging faulty inferences
	Cognitive rehearsal
	Coping statements
	Correcting misinfomation/providing missing infomation
	Disputing irrational beliefs
	Focusing
	Positive self-statements
	Problem-solving training
	Rational proselytizing
	Self-acceptance training
	Thought-stopping

Modality	Techniques/interventions
Interpersonal	Assertion training
	Communication training
	Contracting
	Fixed role therapy
	Friendship/intimacy training
	Graded sexual approaches
	Paradoxical intentions
	Role play
	Social skills training
Drugs/biology	Alcohol reduction programme
	Lifestyle changes, e.g., exercise, nutrition, etc.
	Referral to physicians or other specialists
	Stop smoking programme
	Weight reduction and maintenance programme

Source: Adapted from Palmer (1992)

A full Modality Profile

Once the Modality Profile consisting of the problem list divided into each modality has been noted down, then the therapist and client negotiate techniques and interventions that can be used to help deal with each problem. Table 8.3 (Palmer, 1997c) is John's full Modality Profile which will be discussed later in the case study. The Modality Profile guides the course of therapy, keeping the therapist and client focused on the particular problems and the specific interventions. During the course of therapy, the profile is modified as new relevant information is obtained. It is important for clients to be involved with developing the therapeutic programme to ensure that they understand the rationale for each intervention recommended and take ownership of their own programme. Often clients will suggest interventions that might be helpful, such as enrolling on to an adult education class in aerobics, assertiveness, self-hypnosis or meditation. Others suggest joining self-help groups such as stop smoking or weight control. The counsellor will always take these ideas seriously as they may well be beneficial.

Second-order BASIC I.D.

When selecting techniques and strategies, a multimodal axiom is: 'Begin with the most obvious and logical procedures' (Lazarus, 1985b: 11). According to Lazarus, this avoids the penchant for making straightforward problems needlessly complicated. However, when an impasse is reached further assessment may be required. A second-order BASIC I.D. is undertaken when the interventions or techniques applied to help a specific problem do not appear to have resolved it. This is a modality profile which solely focuses on the different aspects of a resistant or recalcitrant problem,

Table 8.3 John's full Modality Profile (or BASIC I.D. chart)

Modality	Problem	Proposed counselling programme
Behaviour	Eats/walks fast, always in a rush, hostile, competitive: indicative of Type A Avoidance of giving presentations Accident-proneness	Discuss advantages of slowing down; disadvantages of rushing and being hostile; teach relaxation exercise; dispute self-defeating beliefs Exposure programme; teach necessary skills; dispute self-defeating beliefs Discuss advantages of slowing down
Affect	Anxious when giving presentations Guilt when work targets not achieved Frequent angry outbursts at work	Anxiety management Dispute self-defeating thinking Anger management; dispute irrational beliefs; empathic imagery
Sensation	Tension in shoulders Palpitations Frequent headaches Sleeping difficulties	Self-massage; muscle relaxation exercises Anxiety management, e.g. breathing relaxation technique, dispute catastrophic thinking Relaxation exercise and biofeedback Relaxation or self-hypnosis tape for bedtime use; behavioural retraining; possibly reduce caffeine intake
Imagery	Negative images of not performing well Images of losing control Poor self-image	Coping imagery focusing on giving adequate presentations Coping imagery of dealing with difficult work situations and with presentations; 'step-up' imagery (Palmer and Dryden, 1995) Positive imagery (Lazarus, 1984)
Cognition	I must perform well otherwise it will be awful and I couldn't stand it. I must be in control. Significant others should recognize my work. If I fail then I am a total failure	Dispute self-defeating and irrational beliefs; coping statements; cognitive restructuring; ABCDE paradigm (Ellis et al. 1997); bibliotherapy; coping imagery (Palmer and Dryden, 1995)
Interpersonal	Passive/aggressive in relationships Manipulative tendencies at work Always put self first Few supportive friends	Assertiveness training; coping and motivation imagery Discuss pros and cons of behaviour Discuss pros and cons of behaviour; empathic imagery Friendship training (Palmer and Dryden, 1995)
Drugs/biology	Feeling inexplicably tired Takes aspirins for headaches Consumes ten cups of coffee a day Poor nutrition and little exercise	Improve sleeping and reassess; refer to GP Refer to GP; relaxation exercises Discuss benefits of reducing caffeine intake Nutrition and exercise programme

Source: Adapted from Palmer (1997c)

as opposed to the initial assessment which looks more at the overview or 'big picture'.

Tracking

Tracking is another procedure regularly used in multimodal therapy in which the 'firing order' of the different modalities is noted for a specific problem. Therapeutic interventions are linked to the sequence of the firing order of the modalities. This procedure usually short circuits the undesired response and helps the therapist to select the most effective technique(s) for the particular client with his or her specific problem. For example, Peter wanted promotion at work. However, he never applied for the job as manager as it would involve giving presentations. When he last attempted to speak to a group of people he encountered difficulties and since that occasion he has refused to speak publicly again. On analysing the sequence of the modalities the therapist found an imagery-sensation-cognition-behaviour firing order (Palmer and Dryden, 1995: 35).

1 *Imagery*: self-image of being unable to speak.
2 *Sensation*: rapid heart beat, clammy hands, shallow breathing, dry mouth.
3 *Cognition*: 'This is awful. What's wrong with me? I'm going to really mess this up and look stupid.'
4 *Behaviour*: escape.

The firing order is usually written in its annotated form, in this case I-S-C-B. Peter agreed with his therapist to take up the next offer of making a presentation. The subsequent therapeutic programme was linked to the sequence of the firing order of the modalities. Initially, to counter the negative self-image (I) Peter used a coping image of performing well and simultaneously used a relaxation exercise (S). If he still felt very anxious he would counter his negative cognitions with a coping statement (C). Lastly, the rationale was explained why it is preferable to stay in the anxiety provoking situation as opposed to avoidance (B). Peter practised these techniques daily before making the presentation. This procedure helped Peter successfully to give a presentation to a group of colleagues (see Palmer and Dryden, 1995 for further information about this case example).

Bridging

Clients often have a favoured modality which they may use to communicate with the therapist; for example, talking about the cognitions, sensations or images they may experience. This corresponds with the type of 'reactor' they are; for example, 'sensory reactors', etc. The highest scores on their Structural Profiles often reflect the modality reactor. Multimodal therapists deliberately use a 'bridging' procedure initially to 'key into' a client's preferred modality, before gently exploring a modality that the client may be intentionally or unintentionally avoiding such as the affect modality. For example, a therapist may ask a client how she or he feels (affect modality) about an event and the client responds by describing what actually happened (cognitive) and not how she or he felt. The therapist would 'key into' the client's preferred modality (in this example, cognitive) and 'bridge' into another modality such as imagery before returning to the modality under examination, in this example, affect. This method avoids direct confrontation and therefore does not threaten the therapeutic alliance by repetitively asking the client how she or he felt about the event in question.

Format of a typical session

The formats of sessions are adapted to what would enable the client to reach their therapeutic goals. However, it is often advantageous to use a recognizable structure similar to that used in behaviour or cognitive therapy. This could include setting an agenda of therapeutic topics or issues the client and therapist wish to discuss in the session. The agenda would usually include reviewing the client's homework assignments from the previous session; agreeing topics to be covered in the present session; negotiating further relevant homework assignments; eliciting client feedback about the session and tackling any problems that may have arisen during the session (see Palmer and Dryden, 1995).

Indications and contraindications

As multimodal therapy uses cognitive-behavioural techniques and strategies, the approach can be used with clients suffering from anxiety and stress-related disorders, substance abuse, depression, anorexia nervosa and obesity. It has also been used for airsickness, schizophrenia, and career education. As therapists are expected to adjust their interpersonal style to each client, they may encounter less relationship difficulties when compared to other less flexible approaches. This flexible approach leads to a reduced rate of attrition and, to a certain extent, the limitations of the multimodal orientation rest in the particular proclivities of each therapist. However, as with all therapies, multimodal therapy has its failures. Some clients are not prepared to face their fears, use coping imagery, challenge their unhelpful thinking, practise relaxation techniques, become assertive with significant others, or cease self-destructive behaviours, etc. Individuals who have psychiatric disorders or other difficulties that may prevent them from engaging in therapy would not necessarily find the approach suitable. Likewise clients who are in the pre-contemplative stage and have not made up their minds to change or attempt to resolve their problems may find the approach unsuitable.

Case study

The client

John was a 43-year-old married man with no children. He worked as a manager of a large national supermarket chain. He was referred by his doctor for therapy suffering from occupational stress. He had been under pressure at work to reach new targets which he believed were unrealistic and unattainable. This was leading to angry outbursts at work which were causing interpersonal difficulties. For the past couple of months he had experienced sleeping difficulties, palpitations, tension and headaches. He was concerned that 'my performance at work is suffering and I just seem to be losing control'. His employers were concerned about the profitability of his branch and had become aware of his angry outbursts. They were willing to fund an initial six sessions of counselling.

The therapy

John was sent an administration letter giving a time for the therapy session, details about the location, a client checklist (Palmer and Szymanska, 1994) and a self-help book, *Stress Management: A Quick Guide* (Palmer and Strickland, 1996).

At the beginning of the first session John was asked if he had any questions about the therapy or about the therapist. He had read the pre-therapy material about the approach and enquired about the therapist's training and qualifications. He understood the benefits of recording the therapy sessions: he could listen to the tapes at home and go over any sections he had not fully grasped; the therapist could listen to the sessions with his supervisor in confidence, to ensure that he had not overlooked any important issues and to receive useful guidance.

John spent the next 15 minutes explaining his difficulties while the therapist took a few notes of the key problems. The counsellor interjected occasionally to clarify any points he did not understand. The therapist then described the BASIC I.D. assessment procedure:

> *Therapist*: In this approach to ensure that we have correctly understood the client's problems we usually focus on seven key areas or modalities. I'll use this whiteboard so we can both go through the different issues together. The first area to look at is Behaviour. [*Therapist writes Behaviour at the top left-hand corner of the whiteboard.*] You mentioned that you are 'always in a rush'. [*Therapist writes this in central part of the whiteboard.*] Can you give me some specific examples?

John: I eat and walk fast. My wife always tells me to 'slow down'!
Therapist: You mentioned that you are 'hostile' and 'competitive'.
John: Yes. Mainly at work although I can be outside of work too.
Therapist: [*Therapist writes 'hostile' and 'competitive' on the whiteboard.*] It sounds to me as if you have what is often known as 'Type A' behaviour.
John: You're right. I read an article about it once in a magazine.
Therapist: [*Therapist writes 'Type A' behaviour on the whiteboard.*] You mentioned that you avoid giving presentations at work and you've become accident prone. [*Therapist writes these on the whiteboard.*] Are there any other behavioural problems that you would like to add to this list?
John: No. They are the main ones.
Therapist: Okay. The next area we can examine is what is known as Affect or your Emotions. [*Therapist writes Affect/emotions on left-hand side of the whiteboard.*] You mentioned that you are 'anxious when giving presentations' and 'guilty when work targets not achieved'. [*Therapist writes these on the whiteboard.*] Are there any other emotional problems you want to deal with?

This process was continued until each modality had been assessed. Table 8.1 (Palmer, 1997c) is John's Modality Profile (see earlier section). As John had read the self-help book (Palmer and Strickland, 1996) prior to the session he was in a position to negotiate with his therapist his own therapeutic programme. Table 8.3 (Palmer, 1997c) is John's completed Modality Profile. The techniques and interventions were written on the right-hand side of the whiteboard corresponding to each particular problem. It was explained that the Modality Profile serves as 'working hypotheses' which can be modified or revised as new information arises. Before the end of the session John was introduced to the MLHI.

Therapist: I have found it very useful if my clients complete this questionnaire at home. [*Therapist showed John the MLHI.*] It saves me taking up a lot of your time asking questions about different aspects of your life. It will not only focus on your anxiety and job performance, but may provide us with information that would help us deal with your other problems too.
John: Sounds like a good idea.
Therapist: You can either bring it to the next session or send it to me beforehand to give me time to read it.
John: I'll pop it in the post.
Therapist: In that case do make sure you mark it private and confidential.

Careful analysis of John's full Modality Profile indicated that teaching him a suitable relaxation technique would help him deal or cope with a number of different problems. This was brought to his attention and he agreed to listen to a commercially manufactured relaxation tape once a day before his evening dinner.

The next session was seven days later. An agenda for the session was set which included looking at how he had got on with the relaxation tape; queries regarding the MLHI; drawing his Structural Profiles; modifying his self-defeating beliefs, and new homework assignment. Figures 8.1 and 8.2 were John's Structural Profiles. It is worth noting that his Structural Profile (Figure 8.1) had scores of 7 in sensation and cognitive modalities. When high Structural Profile scores occur in a particular modality, often the person is responsive to techniques used from that modality. John found the sensation and cognitive techniques were very helpful. John was both a 'sensory and cognitive reactor'. It was agreed that session three would be a fortnight later.

Over the remaining sessions John found that attempting to slow down, modifying his beliefs, relaxation exercises, and coping imagery were very beneficial. He reduced his caffeine intake and found that his sleeping improved. The intervals between the last two sessions were increased to four weekly to give him the opportunity to apply the range of techniques he had learnt in counselling. Tracking was used to assess the firing order of the modalities when he had to face giving a presentation.

By the last session John had learnt to slow down and had reduced his feelings of guilt and anxiety; although he was still prone under extremes of pressure to become angry, at least it was more controlled. Physically he was feeling much better and more relaxed with less headaches and better sleeping patterns. In addition he had modified his self-defeating beliefs although he still needed more self-acceptance training. It was agreed that he would undertake further bibliotherapy and read material and self-help books on this subject.

The interpersonal modality required more attention. As he was feeling less stressed he had become less hostile and aggressive although his manipulative tendencies had not abated. John and the therapist agreed that he would attend a follow-up session three months later to review progress and monitor how he was getting on using assertiveness skills. The therapist decided that if the problem proved difficult to resolve, then later in the year he and John could develop a second-order BASIC I.D. focusing on this particular issue.

Wider implications and applications

Similar to other therapies, YAVIS clients, in other words, Young, Active, Verbal, Intelligent and Successful, tend to do well in therapy. However, multimodal therapy has been shown to benefit children, adults and older client groups from different backgrounds with a range of abilities, experiencing a wide range of problems or disorders. It has been used in a variety of settings including private practice, hospital, residential and educational establishments. In addition, its technically eclectic and problem-focused approach has been applied to industrial stress management workshops.

Training is available in the USA and at the Centre for Multimodal Therapy in London. The Centre is associated with the Centre for Stress Management and shares the same accommodation. The Centre's programme is modular and students can attend introductory two-day courses or an Advanced Certificate/Diploma in Multimodal Psychotherapy and Counselling. Suitably qualified graduates have become accredited through the British Association for Behavioural and Cognitive Psychotherapies and registered with the United Kingdom Council for Psychotherapy (UKCP).

Future developments

The integration of different forms of psychotherapy will continue to interest practitioners. However, on analysis, the successful integration of therapies may prove elusive for those that are fundamentally different and underpinned by conflicting theories (see Lazarus, 1995b). With the thrust within the National Health Service and private healthcare for brief and effective therapy (see Lazarus, 1997), more research is likely to be undertaken over the next couple of decades which may highlight the problems associated with the idiosyncratic application by therapists of integrative approaches. It is likely that specific techniques for particular problems such as traumatic flashbacks, etc., will be shown to be more effective than the actual therapeutic approach from which they are taken. Therefore, multimodal therapy which focuses on the application of appropriate techniques for specific problems may become more popular with practitioners.

References

Bandura, A. (1969) *Principles of Behavior Modification*. New York: Holt, Rinehart and Winston.
Bandura, A. (1977) *Social Learning Theory*. Englewood Cliffs, NJ: Prentice-Hall.
Bandura, A. (1986) *Social Foundations of Thought and Action: A Social Cognitive Theory*. Englewood Cliffs, NJ: Prentice-Hall.

Bertalanffy, L. von (1974) 'General systems theory and psychiatry', in S. Ariety (ed.), *American Handbook of Psychiatry*, vol. 1. New York: Basic Books, pp. 1095–117.
Buckley, W. (1967) *Modern Systems Research for the Behavioral Scientist*. Chicago: Aldine.
Ellis, A., Gordon, J., Neenan, M. and Palmer, S. (1997) *Stress Counselling: A Rational Emotive Behaviour Approach*. London: Cassell.
Fay, A. and Lazarus, A.A. (1993) 'On necessity and sufficiency in psychotherapy', *Psychotherapy in Private Practice*, 12: 33–9.
Lazarus, A.A. (1958) 'New methods in psychotherapy: a case study', *South African Medical Journal*, 32: 660–4.
Lazarus, A.A. (1977) 'Toward an egoless state of being', in A. Ellis and R. Grieger (eds), *Handbook of Rational-Emotive Therapy*. New York: Springer.
Lazarus, A.A. (1984) *In the Mind's Eye*. New York: Guilford Press.
Lazarus, A.A. (1985a) *Marital Myths*. San Luis Obispo: Impact Publishers.
Lazarus, A.A. (1985b) 'A brief overview of multimodal therapy', in A.A. Lazarus (ed.), *Casebook of Multimodal Therapy*. New York: Guilford Press.
Lazarus, A.A. (1987) 'The multimodal approach with adult outpatients', in N.S. Jacobson (ed.), *Psychotherapists in Clinical Practice*. New York: Guilford Press.
Lazarus, A.A. (1989) *The Practice of Multimodal Therapy: Systematic, Comprehensive, and Effective Psychotherapy*. Baltimore: Johns Hopkins University Press.
Lazarus, A.A. (1991) 'The multimodal approach with adult outpatients', in W. Dryden (ed.), *The Essential Arnold Lazarus*. London: Whurr.
Lazarus, A.A. (1993) 'Tailoring the therapeutic relationship or being an authentic chameleon', *Psychotherapy*, 30: 404–7.
Lazarus, A.A. (1995a) 'Multimodal therapy', in R.J. Corsini and W. Wedding (eds), *Current Psychotherapies*, 5th edn. Itasca, IL: F.E. Peacock.
Lazarus, A.A. (1995b) 'Different types of eclecticism and integration: let's be aware of the dangers', *Journal of Psychotherapy Integration*, 5 (1): 27–39.
Lazarus, A.A. (1997) *Brief But Comprehensive Psychotherapy: The Multimodal Way*. New York: Springer.
Lazarus, A.A. and Lazarus, C.N. (1991) *Multimodal Life History Inventory*. Champaign, IL: Research Press.
Lazarus, A.A., Lazarus, C.N. and Fay, A. (1993) *Don't Believe It For A Minute*. San Luis Obispo: Impact Publishers.
Palmer, S. (1992) 'Multimodal assessment and therapy: a systematic, technically eclectic approach to counselling, psychotherapy and stress management', *Counselling*, 3 (4): 220–4.
Palmer, S. (1997a) 'Multimodal therapy', in C. Feltham (ed.), *Which Psychotherapy*. London: Sage.
Palmer, S. (1997b) 'Self-acceptance: concept, techniques and interventions', *The Rational Emotive Behaviour Therapist*, 5 (1): 4–30.
Palmer, S. (1997c) 'Modality assessment', in S. Palmer and G. McMahon (eds), *Client Assessment*. London: Sage.
Palmer, S. and Dryden, W. (1991) 'A multimodal approach to stress management', *Stress News*, 3 (1): 2–10.
Palmer, S. and Dryden, W. (1995) *Counselling for Stress Problems*. London: Sage.
Palmer, S. and Strickland, L. (1996) *Stress Management: A Quick Guide*. Dunstable: Folens Publishers.
Palmer, S. and Szymanska, K. (1994) 'A checklist for clients interested in receiving counselling, psychotherapy or hypnosis', *The Rational Emotive Behaviour Therapist*, 2 (1): 25–7.

Paul, G.L. (1967) 'Strategy of outcome research in psychotherapy', *Journal of Consulting Psychology*, 331: 109–18.

Raskin, N.J. and Rogers, C.R. (1995) 'Person-centered therapy', in R.J. Corsini and W. Wedding (eds), *Current Psychotherapies*, 5th edn. Itasca, IL: F.E. Peacock.

Watzlawick, P., Weakland, J. and Fish, R. (1974) *Change: Principles of Problem Formulation and Problem Resolution*. New York: W.W. Norton.

Zilbergeld, B. (1982) 'Bespoke therapy', *Psychology Today*, 16: 85–6.

9
GERARD EGAN'S SKILLED HELPER MODEL

Peter Jenkins

The skills-based model of therapy developed by Gerard Egan is an active, collaborative and integrative approach to client problem management. It shares some characteristics of the cognitive-behavioural school and is firmly grounded in the core conditions of the person-centred approach. Widely taught on counselling courses, the model was first introduced by its author as a 'practical model for *doing* counselling' (1975: v). The model is pragmatic, change oriented and specifies the appropriate skills available to the helper at different stages of the counselling process. This problem-management model is restless and dynamic, undergoing significant refinements over the last 25 years. Egan's style is relentless in incorporating new approaches, optimistic in its emphasis on the innate potential of human beings to move forward, to work with and resolve intrapersonal and interpersonal problems, using the essentially flexible 'map' on which the model is based. The emphasis on skills has helped to demystify counsellor training for a generation of trainers and trainees alike. Combining exploration of the client's feeling, thinking and behaviour, the model establishes a bridge between the human potential movement of the 1960s, more recent concepts of client empowerment and managerial approaches to organizational change and restructuring in the 1990s.

Development of the therapy

Gerard Egan is currently Professor of Organization Studies and Psychology and Programme Director for the Centre for Organization Development (CORD) at the Loyola University of Chicago. He describes the three main influences upon the development of the model as being skills-training approaches to counselling, such as those advanced by Truax and Carkhuff (1967), the social influence theory associated with Strong (1968) and behavioural theories of learning and change. His model is an explicit attempt to weld these strands together, in a way that makes their respective contributions more readily accessible to practitioners. Behavioural techniques are proposed as an essential requirement for any counsellor's 'toolkit' of responses, given their proven value in assisting clients to plan and carry out change in their own behaviour. Social influence theory recognizes the *power* held by the counsellor to influence client change, to the extent that the former is seen to be expert, attractive and trustworthy by the client.

Skills training builds on the work of those researchers following Rogers, who sought to identify the specific responses and qualities which contributed most to client change. More personal influences on Egan have clearly been his own training as a Jesuit, with its emphasis on goals and achievement and its role as the probable inspiration for the three-stage model as 'Think. Judge. Act' (Egan, 1975: 2; Coles, 1996). The approach has had a major influence on counselling practice in the UK, particularly through its adoption as a training model by organizations such as Relate, its influence in nursing training, and the impact of summer schools held at York over the last ten years. *The Skilled Helper* has gone through six editions since 1975, with supporting exercise manuals, training videos, audio-tapes and trainer handbooks. Egan's interests have encompassed group work, communication skills, wider social systems and counselling. More recently they have moved towards the direction of management consultancy and facilitating organizational change (Egan, 1970, 1973, 1976, 1977, 1993a, 1994b, 1998; Egan and Cowan, 1979).

Theory and basic concepts

The model consists of three components. First, Egan describes the value base of the approach as including pragmatism, competence, respect, genuineness and client self-responsibility. Values provide the criteria for making decisions in the process of helping clients, for example, in shaping the respective contributions to be made by client and helper, or in determining the optimum number of sessions on offer. Pragmatism provides the justification for the model's integrative flavour: or, as he puts it bluntly, 'do whatever is ethical and works' (1990: 62). Egan's style is ultimately based on an authentic American can-do optimism, of the kind that puts 'psychology' under the 'self-help' section in most US bookstores.

Three-stage model

The other, better known elements of the approach are the three-stage model and his emphasis on specific skills in the helping process. The three-stage model is illustrated by a series of changing and sometimes confusing sets of graphics. Essentially, the model moves from the initial stage of exploring the client's current problem situation, through a stage

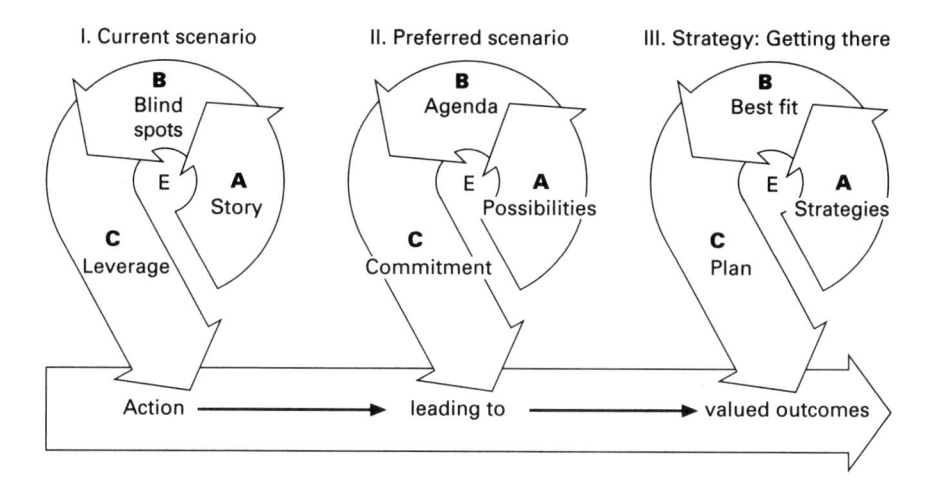

```
   I. Current scenario          II. Preferred scenario       III. Strategy: Getting there
              B                            B                              B
          Blind                         Agenda                         Best fit
          spots
           E    A                        E    A                         E    A
              Story                        Possibilities                   Strategies
           C                             C                              C
         Leverage                    Commitment                        Plan


       Action    ─────────▶   leading to   ─────────▶   valued outcomes
```

Figure 9.1 *The Skilled Helper model (Egan, 1998). Copyright ©1998, 1994, 1990, 1986, 1982, 1975 Brooks/Cole Publishing Company, Pacific Grove, CA 93950, a division of International Thomson Publishing Inc. By permission of the publisher*

of imagining possible alternative preferred futures, to a final stage of planning and implementing action to achieve agreed goals for change. Egan argues that this template for change, or cognitive map for client and helper, embodies universal principles of resolving problems and is therefore transferable across cultures (Sugarman, 1995: 276). Each of the three stages consists of sub-stages, so the initial stage of focusing on the current scenario includes helping the client to tell their story, exploring possible 'blind spots' and in gaining momentum or leverage to move on to more proactive problem-managing outcomes.

Far from presenting a model which is rigid and strictly linear, Egan emphasizes the *fluidity* of the actual process of helping, where the stages and sub-stages merely represent the potential gain of certain ways of relating to, and working with, the client. In practice, it is often necessary to loop backwards and forwards within the various stages. One presenting client issue, such as low self-esteem, may give way to another more pressing one, such as resolving an immediate conflict over financial support from a previous marital partner, requiring more urgent attention from the client and helper (Figure 9.1).

The model has been subject to development and changes over time, such as the reversal of steps 1B and 1C between the third and fourth editions. There have been chances of emphasis throughout the six editions, replacing problem solving with problem management, with the recognition that some problems, such as terminal illness, can only be *managed*, not solved as such. The model has moved more recently to emphasize evaluation and the messier, arational 'shadow side' of the helping process (Sugarman, 1995: 276–9).

The third component of the model consists of Egan's identification of the key skills which are, at the same time, appropriate, effective and consistent with the values espoused by the helper. These are essentially divided into basic communication skills, such as attending and developing empathic understanding, and those more advanced skills which involve presenting a greater degree of challenge towards the client. (These skills are outlined in more detail in the later section 'Practice and Clinical Issues'.)

Basic assumptions of the model

In terms of its basic assumptions about human nature, the model presents a somewhat contradictory picture. On the one hand, people are seen as active, lifelong learners, adapting to change, acquiring new skills and meeting challenges presented at different life stages in differing contexts, such as within relationships, at work and in their communities; on the other, human beings are also 'bottomless pits' of shadow side or self-defeating activities, often swayed from pursuing their goals by a lack of self-confidence, by using unsuitable strategies, or by negative self-talk. Where *choosing* to change is involved, human beings have a somewhat poor track record of success, according to Egan, given the all too powerful countervailing pressures of entropy and inertia. In common with other problem-focused approaches (Pentony, 1981), Egan places stress on the unused and unrecognized resources held by the client, on the careful elaboration of achievable goals and on practising those skills and behaviours which will help the client to move in their desired direction.

'People in systems'

The individual focus of the Skilled Helper underplays a wider sociological concern evident in Egan's published work – namely that clients and helpers need to be understood in terms of their social context. The 'people in systems' framework presented in his pivotal text (Egan and Cowan, 1979) provides an underpinning analysis of stages of human development and of the problematic tasks confronting individuals at different points of their lives. Helpers need to understand the specific developmental tasks confronting their clients, for example, in adapting to a full-time role as a student in college, or in coping with the loss of a key supportive relationship. They also need to grasp the context in which the client lives and moves, in terms of their family, neighbourhood and workplace (Egan and Cowan, 1979, 1980; Egan, 1984). Thus, the counsellor's role is to help the client who faces difficulties in making a transition, as from moving from work to unemployment; or in working through a developmental task, as in making meaningful and satisfying personal relationships; or in managing a stressful situation in the workplace, by becoming more assertive. The key focus is on the client developing new and more effective competencies. This may be expressed as a need to learn new life skills, related to the tasks required by the interaction of the particular developmental stage and the level of social setting. These skills might be related to self-management, interpersonal communication, to the process of becoming lifelong learners, to the issue of decision making, or to acquiring skills in small group work.

Psychological disturbance is produced, in this model, through problems in adapting to *change*, whether these difficulties are personal/developmental, organizational or social. Distress and confusion are maintained largely through a lack of the life skills needed to work through and resolve these tasks. However, it is also recognized that a lack of skills may simply be a contributory factor rather than the sole reason for the problems experienced. For example, a person with learning disabilities may well face a range of problems in adapting to independent living after leaving residential care. They will inevitably confront wider social constraints and prejudices, in addition perhaps to needing to develop greater confidence in their own assertiveness or social skills. The client's problems need to be understood in their wider social context and not simply laid at the feet of the individual concerned.

Towards psychological health

Egan's model of psychology is basically an optimistic one, expressing the potential for healthy adaptation to change, rather than one rooted in the extremes of individual pathology (Inskipp, 1993b: 92). The individual moves from psychological disturbance to psychological health primarily through changes in *behaviour*. The processes of emotional experiencing and cognitive 'reframing' within therapy are, to paraphrase Rogers, necessary but not sufficient conditions of longer lasting change in the external world. For Egan, learning, change and adaptation come about through *action*: 'The heart of the problem-solving process is the client's action itself' (Egan, 1975: 227). This is expressed in the often kinetic, muscular quality of his prose and use of metaphor. He writes about the client 'whistling in the wind', 'spinning his wheels', stopping 'dead in the water' or of 'dragging her feet', and of the heart-stopping 'trapeze effect' of leaping to clutch out at new, untested behaviour, while at the same time letting go of old, familiar but disabling patterns.

The change process for the client involves, initially, their 'telling the story' to a skilled and empathic listener. This may lead to the discovery and application of unused potential resources. The client may then begin to reframe her experience in terms of being a resourceful *survivor* of abuse, rather than simply perceiving herself as a passive victim. Instead of feeling totally isolated, another client's existing support systems of friends or family may come to be recognized and valued as a source of help. If the client's difficulties arise essentially from problems in negotiating change, or in resolving crucial developmental tasks, the key to adaptation is through action, reflection and new learning. Insight, however, valuable and powerful, is not enough on its own to produce or maintain lasting change. New insight needs to be tested out, to be expressed in new forms of behaviour, if it is to make an enduring difference in work or key personal relationships. Hence, for Egan, 'constructive change is always the bottom line' (1990: 207). This approach also sets out the standard by which the effectiveness of the counsellor and of the help on offer can best be judged. 'Helpers are successful to the degree that their clients – because of client–helper interactions – are in a better position to manage specific problem situations and develop specific unused resources and opportunities more effectively' (Egan, 1998: 7).

Practice and clinical issues

The goals of the Skilled Helper model are to assist clients to develop their understanding of key problems and to build the skills which will enable them to manage their situation in a more satisfactory and effective manner. For the counsellor, therefore, the goals of therapy are:

- to build an empathic and accepting relationship with the client;
- to assist the client in exploring key feelings, experiences and behaviours;
- to identify with the client future realistic goals for change;
- to support the client in taking the practical steps which will achieve the goals of their own plan for action;
- to evaluate this change process together with the client, in order to realize the gains and learning which come out of this process.

Some of the practice issues which need to be considered are the counsellor's use of the model itself, the ability to respond to the client in a skilled and effective way, the nature and purpose of the change process itself and the form taken by the therapeutic relationship.

Counsellor's use of the model

To use the Skilled Helper model, the counsellor needs both an understanding of the three-stage model and the confidence to adapt it to the client's needs as the work unfolds. Far from being rigid and prescriptive, the model is intended to set out how to *be* with the client, according to varying needs of the therapeutic process. Hence, the counsellor may be silent at points, listening intently to the client's story. She may be challenging, through the use of immediate 'here and now' talk, or she may be supportive in helping the client to evaluate the success or otherwise of a first attempt at trying out new behaviours in a difficult work relationship. Part of the process of using the model is for the counsellor to be able to identify and use the appropriate skills, either as her own 'internal supervisor' or for later evaluation. At the very simplest level, this may involve the ability to convey basic attending skills, through awareness and use of the mnemonic SOLER (Squarely; Open; Lean; Eye; Relaxed) for appropriate non-verbal communication.

A more difficult facility is that of using the model as a template for change or as a cognitive 'map' of the therapeutic process. This can involve the counsellor being able to use the three-stage model as a guide to how best to work with and respond to the client's needs. A client with a ready-made issue, for example, anxiety attacks when flying, may want to move quickly into the third stage of elaborating action for change, rather than dwell on telling their story at length. Another client, with an extensive history of abuse, may need to spend much longer periods telling and retelling their story and connecting with buried feelings, rather than moving abruptly to the stage of goal setting. The client's willingness to change acts as a brake on a directive and over-hasty counsellor: clients, by and large, cannot be made to move faster through the change process than they are actually ready and willing to do.

Part of using the model will involve using assessment skills, or an external frame of reference on the client's issues. Is the degree of depression experienced by the client likely to get in the way of achieving their desired change in mood and improved social relationships? In the case of working with grief, does the client appear 'stuck' or willing to move on? Informed judgements on the client, however provisional, provide at least some basis for trying to gear the therapeutic work to the client's perceived ability to work within the model. The hardest parts of the model to convey are skills of *sensitivity and timing*. The model can be used crassly or inappropriately in much the same way as any other therapeutic approach, as in the case of the counsellor brightly asking the grieving client 'and how would you like it to be, then?' As with any approach, simple reliance on the model is in itself no guarantor of therapeutic success.

The use of a contract is a key feature of the work done with the client, setting out the focus of the work, the nature and frequency of contact, any limits to confidentiality and including provision for review and evaluation. Evaluation should be a continuing aspect of work done with the client, in order for the counsellor to learn, session by session, what the client's experience and reflections are concerning the counselling, as in identifying the most helpful or least helpful aspects of counselling during the current session.

Use of skills

The Skilled Helper model places a particular ethical and professional responsibility on counsellors to be just that – highly skilled and reflective practitioners, alert to the development of new techniques and research findings and able to be critical of their own practice. The use of the model rests on the counsellor's ability to *engage* with the client through basic communication skills. These include attending, active listening, establishing and conveying empathy and the use of probes or questions. In addition, the counsellor needs to be confident in using more challenging skills, such as the use of intuition or advanced empathy, immediacy, helper self-disclosure and sharing relevant information with the client. Unlike the basic communication skills, the more advanced challenging skills necessarily operate *outside* the client's frame of reference and hence carry a greater degree not only of risk, but also of potential client gain.

The technique of brainstorming is closely identified with the Egan model as a powerful, primarily cognitive, means of helping the client to generate new perspectives on the situation. When the client's issues have been accurately summarized and checked out by the counsellor, it becomes possible to move forward by asking the client 'what do you really want *for yourself* in this situation?' Any other suitable form of prompt can be effective at this stage, including those akin to the 'miracle question' used in brief therapy, or 'blank wall' visualization from neuro-linguistic programming (De Shazar, 1988; O'Connor and McDermott, 1996). At an affective or feeling level, the purpose of brainstorming possible futures is to generate the *hope* that things could be different. The emotional energy released provides the dynamic force for helping the client to move forward into creatively working with what may seem, at first, to be overwhelming problems. In common with behavioural and cognitive approaches, the model places a particular value on the shared process of goal setting and review. The client's hopes need to be translated into goals that are SMART, namely specific, measurable, achievable, realistic and time-limited. Failure to work at the detail of setting and achieving basic goals leaves the work of client and counsellor at the point of rumination, rather than engaging with more lasting change in the real world.

Change process

Egan's perception of the change process 'owes a clear debt to the behavioural approach' (Woolfe et al., 1989: 11). It stresses the primacy of behavioural change over both cognitive change such as insight and over emotional experiencing. Egan acknowledges that change may be internal (a client's goal may be 'not to feel this bad'), but this attitudinal change ultimately needs to find some expression in changed *behaviour* (Egan, 1990: 28; Sugarman, 1995: 278). The model's insistence on behavioural 'markers' or outcomes might be accused by critics of betraying a crude and simplistic reliance on behaviourism, at the expense of the counsellor engaging with the client's underlying feelings. This is to undervalue the real therapeutic potential of the model. Certainly, the counsellor needs the skill of conveying empathy to building a strong working alliance with the client, through the exploration of feelings and 'core messages'. However, the client's expressing feelings within therapy may only be one essential aspect of their achieving overall change. In a key article, Karasu refers to 'three therapeutic change agents: affective experiencing, cognitive mastery and behavioural regulation' (1986: 690). All three features are central to the effective use of the Skilled Helper model. Counselling which is limited to cognitive reframing alone, or to the discharge of powerful feelings, may not help the client to transfer their new insight or emotional experiencing to the world outside of therapy: 'While the affective experiencing may prepare the patient for cognitive learning, the latter requires gradual assimilation and behavioural application of new input if therapeutic effects are to endure' (Karasu, 1986: 692).

Nature of therapeutic relationship

It flows from this that the therapeutic relationship is seen as *instrumental* rather than necessarily of determining importance to the counselling work undertaken (see Table 9.1). It is therefore 'a relationship of service, not an end in itself' (Egan, 1990: 57). The role of the counsellor is to act as a change consultant to the client, working to achieve shared goals within agreed time limits, rather than offering open-ended support. Seeing the therapeutic alliance in very pragmatic terms may require the counsellor trying to 'match' their style of experiencing and communication to that of the client's, in terms of the relative value given to thinking, feeling and doing (Hutchins, 1990). From an integrative perspective, the counsellor may take on the role of 'translator' of wider research or outside knowledge for the client. The counsellor thus has permission to bring in other techniques, such as the use of the 'empty chair' from Gestalt, or fresh perspectives, as from transactional analysis, where this might be helpful to the client. The therapeutic relationship provides the *foundation* for the work to be done but is, in the end, simply a form of support and a means to the client achieving greater control over an important aspect of life.

The subordinate value placed on the therapeutic relationship marks the Skilled Helper model as being distinct from the person-centred tradition. Egan has described himself as 'standing on Rogers' shoulders' at one of the York summer schools and clearly acknowledges the debt owed to the core conditions in the development of his own approach. Whereas Rogers' focus was on the *person* as a whole being, Egan's primary interest is in the perceived *problem* or issue. Other differences of emphasis are suggested in Table 9.1

Table 9.1 *Comparison of non-specific factors in Egan's and Rogers's models of counselling (adapted from Corey, 1991: 424–47)*

Key aspects of counselling		Egan	Rogers
Support	Role of therapist	Change consultant	Facilitator
	Therapist–client relationship	Instrumental	Expressive
Learning	Focus of diagnosis/assessment	Client resources	Client self-diagnosis
	Techniques	Skill-based/integrative	Communication of core conditions
Action	Goals of therapy	Task-centred/problem management	Person-centred/client self-actualization
	Evaluation criteria	Behavioural outcomes	Client-led evaluation

The Skilled Helper model, while resting on the acknowledged importance of the core conditions, marks a clear point of departure from person-centred approaches in its emphasis on counsellor *skills* rather than on qualities and on behavioural *change* rather than self-actualization as the purpose of the therapy.

Format for a typical session

There is no set format for individual sessions, according to the Skilled Helper model. The format will depend upon where the client has reached in the change process. In the case of a single session, it is possible to work through the three main stages of the model on an issue, but this would not apply in most cases.

Indications and contraindications

Contraindications for this therapy are broadly similar to those of most cognitive and behavioural approaches. It is unlikely to be suitable for clients who are actively psychotic, experiencing serious, untreated clinical depression or who possess a major personality disorder. The use of the model relies crucially on the *client's motivation to change* and, ultimately, to test out changes in feeling and perception in new behaviours outside of therapy. Clients who are in the 'pre-contemplative' stage, namely 'thinking about thinking about change' may not be ready for the more active client role assumed by this approach (Prochaska and DiClemente, 1986).

The model is applicable to a wide range of clients and situations, including depression (Mynors-Wallis et al., 1995; Seeley et al., 1996), sexual abuse and eating disorders (Perry, 1993) and fertility problems (Read, 1995). It can also be used in working with young people (Mabey and Sorensen, 1995). The three-stage model bears some similarities to Worden's tasks of grieving and can be used in situations of bereavement and in working with death following a terminal illness (Lugton, 1989; Worden, 1991). Although the model has been described as eclectic in the past (Inskipp and Johns, 1984), it is more accurately defined as *integrative*, in that it provides a basic framework for incorporating other techniques at different stages of the work with the client.

The strengths and limitations of the model are, according to McLeod (1998), those held by cognitive-behavioural approaches in general: namely an undervaluing of the therapeutic relationship as a key dynamic factor in producing change and a failure to acknowledge the role of unconscious processes deriving from the psychodynamic tradition. Nelson-Jones (1982, 1995) also points to the model as being somewhat inflexible and to its weakness in dealing with the 'repetition phenomenon', where clients have deep-seated problems which limit their skills across a wide range of social situations. For others, the model is not sufficiently person centred and is in danger of elevating the counsellor into the role of 'expert' on the client's problems (Frankland and Sanders, 1995).

The model can be criticized as being overly rational, perhaps betraying an unconscious gender bias in its rush to focus on task, cognition and behaviour, rather than on process and feelings (Atkinson et al., 1991). This argument might suggest that the model legitimates an avoidance of less easily quantifiable aspects of therapy in its harsh insistence on measurable outcomes, rather than on less tangible variables such as the quality of the client–helper relationship and possible transference issues. This may be so, although in practice acknowledgement and exploration of feeling are absolutely crucial aspects of the model. The model's points of difference with other more affective styles of counselling, such as the person-centred approach, may in the end be less to do with gender than with right or left brain dominance, with a preference for structure over form and for evidence over intuition.

Surprisingly, there is little research to validate the three-stage model as a specific construct or to distinguish between the effectiveness of different versions. However, there is evidence on the effectiveness of generic problem-solving approaches, which are comparable to the model (Catalan et al., 1991). In one small sample, clients experienced a sequence of exploratory counselling followed by more proactive problem solving as more fluent and productive than counselling where the sequence was reversed (Shapiro and Firth, 1987; Barkham, 1992: 259). This would appear to endorse the underlying logic of the three-stage model as a process moving from the exploration of current issues, through preferred futures, to the achievement of agreed goals for improved problem management.

Case study

The following case study describes the use of the Skilled Helper model with a young man aged 21 who was experiencing a number of interrelated problems affecting work, career choices, relationships, coping with past losses and, more generally, making decisions about where to go with his life.

The client

Sandy was a young man who had no prior experience of being counselled, referred by his mother who knew my preferred way of counselling was based on the Skilled Helper model. At the first session the presenting problems seemed to me quite daunting. His immediate concern was that he felt 'queasy' when going into work as a salesperson and that this 'sick feeling' was now beginning to interfere with his social life as well, but without there being any clear medical cause. He felt under pressure to 'perform' in his sales work in ways which did not feel right or acceptable to him. In brief, he found dealing with the public face to face quite stressful and did not really enjoy his job, but could see no other realistic alternative.

Other issues which were important for him were that he had lived with his girlfriend for three years, but this had not worked out and he had then returned home to live with his mother and stepfather. The relationship still continued, but he was now unsure whether he wanted to built a long-term commitment with his girlfriend. Overall, he felt he was lacking in both direction and energy, finding it difficult to make decisions for himself. He was hoping that counselling might help him to sort out his goals for the future in some way.

The tone of this first session was comfortable, but rather 'flat' emotionally. His mood seemed to be one of defeat and disarray. The previous summer he had spent half-heartedly looking for work and lying in bed. He described, unemotionally, how his parents had split up some years before and how his father had actually committed suicide several years ago. I wondered, with some concern, if there was some underlying major depression which was the cause of his low mood and whether the feelings around his father's suicide had been worked through and resolved. However, it seemed clear from his responses that he was not keen to talk about feelings, but preferred to look at issues concerning work, alternative careers, his relationship with his girlfriend and trying to sort out his life. He specifically chose, again to my surprise, *not* to focus on his feelings of anxiety and queasiness as the main aspect of the counselling.

The therapy

We agreed to work together for ten sessions and then review the need for further work, which seemed quite likely given the range of his concerns. The verbal contract included reference to arrangements for payment, for the venue and timing of sessions and limits to confidentiality according to the BAC Code of Ethics.

The anxiety symptoms of feeling sick quickly disappeared. His job situation changed quite rapidly, with Sandy immediately deciding to leave his current job and then going through a period of looking for part-time work while considering the possibility of retraining for a complete change of career. We used brainstorming as a technique to look at possible alternative careers, his personal assets and the kinds of training courses which might be suitable. Despite feeling rather awkward for both of us, this session proved to be useful in generating ideas and mental 'lists' of things he could pursue over the following week.

More issues emerged, predictably, during the subsequent sessions. The anniversary of his father's suicide seemed to present a worrying time for him, prompting exploration of the circumstances of his death, their relationship and the feelings of loss, which remained very strong. The legacy of the suicide seemed to have left him with doubts about his own status as a man. It became important for him to establish his own masculinity, in one respect at least, by getting a motorbike and wearing the 'leathers' that were an essential part of the biker's uniform and identity. Again, any deeper issues about the longer term impact of his father's loss or on his own sense of self or sexual identity were not subjects that he felt any keenness to discuss.

What the suicide had also left unresolved was a set of problems of a more practical kind. Although he had taken on adult responsibility in helping to arrange the funeral, the question of the will had been left unresolved for almost three years. He felt he was being 'fobbed off' by the solicitor, but seemed unable to take charge of things and get the money owing to him from his father's estate. There was also a valuable stamp collection, which he now owned in theory, scattered among a number of other collectors and valuers who were in no rush to hand back to him either the stamps or their equivalent value.

What was evident from the second session was a sense of the work moving forward, despite the weight of interlocking problems Sandy was facing. He quickly made progress on the 'tasky' side of things, such as finding part-time work and choosing a suitable training course to pursue at college. However, his difficulty in making life decisions would reappear in the actual sessions. When offered a choice of areas to look at in more depth, he would back off and find the process of choosing difficult to manage. Exploring feelings was never an appealing area for him to engage in, although he talked a lot about his relationship with his late father and how much he had valued it.

The issues around the will seemed to me to be a possible key, linked both to his unresolved feelings about the suicide and to his own sense of feeling 'blocked', in emotional terms, and in relation to 'getting things sorted out'. He continually referred to the will as 'the money' which was owed to him. I challenged him, fairly gently, and suggested he look at it as *'his* money', which the solicitor, rightly or wrongly, was keeping back from him. The effect of this reframing was very powerful. He set himself a goal of phoning the solicitor during the next week. Within a matter of weeks, he had received the full amount owing to him, to our shared amazement.

Somehow, the actual process of engaging with the counselling was releasing the energy that he felt was blocked off to him. From what had seemed initially to me as a fairly unpromising start, Sandy quickly began to gain confidence in a growing range of areas in his own life. He passed his motorbike test, started a new part-time job and enrolled for a college course. He decided to end his relationship with his girlfriend, or at least to make it clear that he did not see a long-term future for it. This in turn freed him to look at other possible relationships, rather than continuing to feel trapped by a sense of outworn obligation. Sessions came to focus increasingly on how to tackle the remaining problems, particularly that of the stamp collection now scattered to the four corners of the county. Again, once having decided what he wanted to achieve, he worked at a 'second best' solution which, while not perfect, brought him back the ownership of key parts of the collection (an inheritance from his father) and, more importantly, a sense of being back in control of his own life.

The pace of change was dramatic and exhilarating for both of us. Underlying issues about loss and identity were dealt with in his own preferred way, rather than in the way *I* would have seen as 'better', namely by exploring and expressing the feelings concerned within the actual therapy sessions. In evaluating the effect of the counselling, Sandy described the most useful aspects as having been the brainstorming and flipcharting of ideas, the setting of his own goals to report back on by the following week and, initially somewhat puzzling, the 'permission' I had somehow given him to change his job. He felt that the process of setting goals and learning to have confidence in his own decisions was something that he would be able to use on his own in the future. From my own initial pessimism about the likelihood of change, I had learned how the counselling had acted as a powerful catalyst for releasing the client's own energy, drive and enthusiasm to put his life back in some sort of order.

Wider implications and applications

The Skilled Helper model is capable of being used in a wide range of settings. Its task-centred nature and skills focus makes it attractive to other professions such as nursing and social work which employ counselling skills rather than providing therapy as such. Within counselling, its emphasis on contracts, time limits and measurable outcomes gears it to work within cost-conscious arenas such as health and primary care (Andrews, 1996; NHS Executive, 1996). These features also suit it to work in student counselling centres, employment assistance programmes and those voluntary counselling agencies which are subject to audit in order to qualify for contract renewal as service providers. The value of the model in training counsellors is, by now, well established (Inskipp, 1993a; Connor, 1994).

The major area of development for the Skilled Helper model has been its successful translation into the rapidly expanding world of management consultancy (Hermansson, 1993). Egan has adapted the three-stage model to explore organizational problem solving, the skills required by managers and the more problematic shadow side of organizational culture (1985, 1988a, 1988b, 1993a, 1993b, 1994b). In this lies a clue to its success on the international scene: as has been noted, 'Egan, ahead of his time, has succeeded in capturing the emphasis of the enterprise economy of the 1980s on the acquisition of skills as a precondition for changing one's position in life' (Woolfe et al., 1989: 11).

Future developments

Egan's own stated goals for the future include producing updated editions of *The Skilled Helper*, a primer on communication skills for the twenty-first century, and further developing the application of the model to organizational settings (Coles, 1996). The model's adept linkage to a wider contract and business culture will ensure its continued use into the next century. However, despite the growing general popularity of skills-based and problem-focused counselling approaches (Nelson-Jones, 1988, 1995; Culley, 1991), there is little evidence of the emergence of a recognized 'school' or movement based on the Skilled Helper model. As with all counselling approaches which centre around a key individual, the model's ultimate survival will depend on the emergence of others to continue the process of refining and adapting it to changing circumstances over the coming decades.

References

Andrews, G. (1996) 'Talk that works: the rise of cognitive behaviour therapy', *British Medical Journal*, 313: 1501–2.

Atkinson, D.R., Worthington, R.L., Dana, D.M. and Good, G.E. (1991) 'Etiology beliefs, preferences for counseling orientations, and counseling effectiveness', *Journal of Counseling Psychology*, 38 (3): 258–64.

Barkham, M. (1992) 'Research on integrative and eclectic therapy', in W. Dryden (ed.), *Integrative and Eclectic Therapy: A Handbook*. Buckingham: Open University Press. pp. 239–68.

Catalan, J., Gath, D.H., Anastasiades, P., Bond, A.K., Day, A. and Hall, L. (1991) 'Evaluation of a brief psychological treatment for emotional disorders in primary care', *Psychological Medicine*, 21: 1013–18.

Coles, A. (1996) 'From priesthood to management consultancy: Adrian Coles interviews Gerard Egan', *Counselling*, 7 (3): 194–7.

Connor, M. (1994) *Training the Counsellor: An Integrative Model*. London: Routledge.

Corey, G. (1991) *Theory and Practice of Counseling and Psychotherapy*, 4th edn. Pacific Grove, CA: Brooks/Cole.

Culley, S. (1991) *Integrative Counselling Skills in Action*. London: Sage.

De Shazer, S. (1988) *Clues: Investigating Solutions in Brief Therapy*. New York: W.W. Norton.

Egan, G. (1970) *Encounter: Group Processes for Interpersonal Growth*. Monterery, CA: Brooks/Cole.

Egan, G. (1973) *Face to Face: The Small Group Experience and Interpersonal Growth*. Monterey, CA: Brooks/Cole.

Egan, G. (1975, 1982, 1986, 1990, 1994a, 1998) *The Skilled Helper*, 2nd–6th edns. Pacific Grove, CA: Brooks/Cole.

Egan, G. (1976) *Interpersonal Living: A Skills-Contract Approach to Human Relations Training in Groups*. Monterey, CA: Brooks/Cole.

Egan, G. (1977) *You and Me: The Skills of Communicating and Relating to Others*. Monterey, CA: Brooks/Cole.

Egan, G. (1984) 'People in systems: a comprehensive model for psychosocial education and training', in D. Larson (ed.), *Teaching Psychological Skills: Models for Giving Psychology Away*. Monterey, CA: Brooks/Cole.

Egan, G. (1985) *Change Agent Skills in Helping and Human Service Settings*. Monterey, CA: Brooks/Cole.

Egan, G. (1988a) *Change Agent Skills A: Assessing and Designing Excellence*. San Diego: University Associates.

Egan, G. (1988b) *Change Agent Skills B: Managing Innovation and Change*. San Diego: University Associates.

Egan, G. (1993a) *Adding Value. A Systematic Guide to Business-Driven Management and Leadership*. San Francisco: Jossey-Bass.

Egan, G. (1993b) 'The shadow side', *Management Today*, September, 33–8.

Egan, G. (1994b) *Working the Shadow Side: A Guide to Positive Behind-the-scenes Management*. San Francisco: Jossey-Bass.
Egan, G. and Cowan, M. (1979) *People in Systems: A Model for Development in the Human-Service Professions and Education*. Monterey, CA: Brooks/Cole.
Egan, G. and Cowan, M. (1980) *Moving into Adulthood: Themes and Variations in Self-directed Development for Effective Living*. Monterey, CA: Brooks/Cole.
Frankland, A. and Sanders, P. (1995) *Next Steps in Counselling*. Manchester: PCCS.
Hermansson, G.L. (1993) 'Counsellors and organisational change: Egan's systems model as a tool in organisational consulting', *British Journal of Guidance and Counselling*, 21 (2): 133–44.
Hutchins, D.E. (1990) 'Improving the counselling relationship, in W. Dryden (ed.), *Key Issues for Counselling in Action*. London: Sage. pp. 53–62.
Inskipp, H. (1993a) *Counselling: The Trainer's Handbook*. Cambridge: National Extension College.
Inskipp, H. (1993b) 'Beyond Egan', in W. Dryden (ed.), *Questions and Answers on Counselling in Action*. London: Sage. pp. 90–4.
Inskipp, F. and Johns, H. (1984) 'Developmental eclecticism: Egan's skills model of helping', in W. Dryden (ed.), *Individual Therapy in Britain*. London: Harper and Row. pp. 364–89.
Karasu, T. (1986) 'The specificity versus non-specificity dilemma: towards identifying therapeutic change agents', *American Journal of Psychiatry*, 143 (6): 687–95.
Lugton, J. (1989) 'Making plans', *Nursing Times*, 85 (18): 44–5.
Mabey, J. and Sorensen, B. (1995) *Counselling for Young People*. Buckingham: Open University Press.
McLeod, J. (1998) *An Introduction to Counselling*, 2nd edn. Buckingham: Open University Press.
Mynors-Wallis, L.M., Gath, D.H., Lloyd-Thomas, A.R. and Tomlinson, D. (1995) 'Randomised controlled trial comparing problem solving treatment with amitriptyline and placebo for major depression in primary care', *British Medical Journal*, 310: 441–5.
NHS Executive (1996) *Review of Strategic Policy on NHS Psychotherapy Services in England and Wales*. London: Department of Health.
Nelson-Jones, R. (1982) *The Theory and Practice of Counselling Psychology*. London: Cassell.
Nelson-Jones, R. (1988) *Practical Counselling and Helping Skills*, 2nd edn. London: Cassell.
Nelson-Jones, R. (1995) *The Theory and Practice of Counselling*. London: Cassell.
O'Connor, J. and McDermott, I. (1996) *Thorson's Principles of NLP*. London: Thorsons.
Pentony, P. (1981) *Models of Influence in Psychotherapy*. New York: Free Press.
Perry, J. (1993) *Counselling for Women*. Buckingham: Open University Press.
Prochaska, J. and DiClemente, C. (1986) 'The transtheoretical approach', in J. Norcross (ed.), *Handbook of Eclectic Psychotherapy*. New York: Brunner/Mazel.
Read, J. (1995) *Counselling for Fertility Problems*. London: Sage.
Seeley, S., Murray, L. and Cooper, P. (1996) 'The outcome for mothers and babies of health visitor intervention', *Health Visitor*, 69 (4): 135–8.
Shapiro, D.A. and Firth, J. (1987) 'Prescriptive v. exploratory psychotherapy: outcomes of the Sheffield Psychotherapy project', *British Journal of Psychiatry*, 151: 790–9.

Strong, S. (1968) 'Counseling: an interpersonal influence process', *Journal of Counseling Psychology*, 15: 215–24.
Sugarman, L. (1995) 'Action Man: an interview with Gerard Egan', *British Journal of Guidance and Counselling*, 23 (2): 275–86.
Truax, C. and Carkhuff, R. (1967) *Toward Effective Counselling and Psychotherapy*. Chicago: Aldine.
Woolfe, R., Dryden, W. and Charles-Edwards, D. (1989) 'The nature and range of counselling practice', in *Handbook of Counselling in Britain*. London: Tavistock/Routledge. pp. 3–27.
Worden, W. (1991) *Grief Counselling and Grief Therapy*, 2nd edn. London: Tavistock/Routledge.

10
PROBLEM-FOCUSED COUNSELLING AND PSYCHOTHERAPY

Stephen Palmer and Michael Neenan

Problem-focused therapy is a method of counselling, coaching or teaching individuals to deal with current problems in a structured, systematic manner. Although these problems can be of a practical nature, such as giving a presentation, and may not involve any overlapping emotional dilemmas such as anxiety about giving a presentation, frequently these two components, the practical and the emotional, are found together in clients' presenting problems (see Neenan and Palmer, 1996; in press, a, b). Problem-focused counselling and psychotherapy can be considered as a dual-systems approach: initially dealing with the emotional aspects of a problem and subsequently dealing with its practical aspects. However, occasionally on initial presentation, as the client is not emotionally disturbed about a particular problem, the focus during counselling is on dealing with the practical side of the problem.

The problem-focused approach described in this chapter is cognitive-behavioural as it helps the clients to examine how their thinking affects their emotions and behaviour. The approach integrates rational emotive behaviour therapy (Ellis, 1994, 1996) with traditional problem-solving methods (e.g. D'Zurilla, 1986).

Development of the therapy

Problem-focused counselling or coaching has largely evolved as a psychoeducational method of teaching clients or trainees new coping skills or strategies (Ellis, 1994). A number of different problem-solving methods have been developed by psychologists (e.g. Wasik, 1984; Meichenbaum, 1985; D'Zurilla, 1986; Hawton and Kirk, 1989). They are all structured in their approach and share a similar, although not always identical, sequence of problem-solving steps for both counsellor and client to follow (see later).

Although skills acquisition is considered an important part of the problem-solving method, helping clients to learn cognitive coping strategies is often necessary too.

The problem-focused approach we describe in this chapter integrates rational emotive behaviour therapy (REBT) (Ellis, 1994) with traditional problem-solving methods (e.g. D'Zurilla, 1986). Albert Ellis founded REBT in 1955. He was influenced by Greek philosophers such as the first century AD Stoic philosopher, Epictetus who stated: 'People are disturbed not by things, but by views they take of them.' In other words, reactions to stressors or life events are largely determined by an individual's perceptions, meanings and evaluations of these events rather than by the events themselves (see Woods, 1987).

The integration of REBT and problem-solving models has been recently developed in Britain by Palmer and Neenan due to their interest in brief and time-limited stress counselling (see Palmer and Burton, 1996; Palmer, 1997a, 1997b; Milner and Palmer, 1998; Neenan and Palmer, in press, a, b).

Theory and basic concepts

Lazarus (1981) identified two key forms of coping: (a) emotion-focused coping (which regulates distressing emotions); (b) problem-focused coping (which attempts to alter the person–environment relationship causing the distress (see D'Zurilla, 1986). When a problematic situation is accurately perceived as changeable, then problem-focused coping strategies which attempt to alter the situation and emotion-focused coping strategies which help to modify the client's reactions to the situation may both be adaptive. If it is not possible to alter the situation then the only adaptive approach may be emotion-focused coping (see Lazarus and Folkman, 1984; D'Zurilla, 1986). In this section the seven-step sequential model of problem solving and REBT will be described.

Seven-step, sequential model of practical problem solving

On initial presentation, if the client is not overly emotionally disturbed about a particular problem, the counsellor may decide, after assessment, to focus on practical problem solving. However, if the client is very distressed about the problem or life event then the counsellor will normally choose to focus on using the REBT model to alleviate the emotional disturbance before looking at the practical side of the problem.

A typical seven-step, problem-solving sequence and the corresponding questions than an individual or the counsellor can ask at each step are shown in Table 10.1.

Table 10.1 *Typical seven-step, problem-solving sequence with questions/actions*

Step	Stages	Questions/Actions
1	Identifying the problem	What is the problem?
2	Selecting goals	What outcome(s) do I want?
3	Exploring options	How do I reach these goals?
4	Considering the consequences	Weigh up the pros and cons?
5	Taking decisions	Choosing the most feasible solution?
6	Agreeing actions	Plan approach step by step and then act.
7	Evaluating the strategy	What happened? How successful was it? What can be learnt?

STEP 1   At Step 1 the client is asked for a problem or concern that he or she wishes to resolve. At this stage the client's response or reaction to a stressor can also be defined as a problem that needs solving, for example, anxiety about a forthcoming job interview (Palmer, 1994). Very stressful events may need to be reduced to smaller, more manageable stressors. A problem list can be drawn up if the client has a multitude of difficulties that need addressing. At this stage it is useful to assess the client's existing skills, personal assets, strengths and supports.

STEP 2   Step 2 involves selecting realistic and precise goals. This usually involves negotiation between the client and the counsellor. It is useful if the goals are stated in behavioural and emotional terms. The counsellor needs gently to challenge unrealistic or unattainable goals to avoid later disappointment (see D'Zurilla, 1986).

STEP 3   The counsellor encourages the client to think of as many options and alternatives as possible to reach his/her realistic goals. At this stage the counsellor and client need to keep an open mind as potential solutions may need plenty of creativity (Palmer, 1997a). An important skill at this stage is brainstorming, whereby all possible solutions are written down on a large sheet of paper, initially without criticism by the counsellor or the client. Some of the most absurd ideas may be the embryo of a good alternative. Osborn (1963) recommends three principles: (a) the quantity principle; (b) the deferment-of-judgement principle; (c) the variety principle. Adhering to these three principles will generally lead to the largest and most diverse number of potential options and alternatives.

STEP 4   At Step 4 the client considers the advantages and disadvantages of the different solutions to his or her problems which were developed during the brainstorming session. It is useful at this stage to assess the possible consequences of undertaking the more desirable options. For example, if one option involves acting in an assertive manner, how would the other person react? Would the person become violent? Would the client lose her/his job? This list of options could initially be divided into three groups (adapted from D'Zurilla, 1986): unacceptable (due to high likelihood of negative consequences); not feasible (lack of resources); feasible. This process helps to reduce the number of options quite rapidly in the majority of cases. Options can also be rated on a plausibility scale of 0–10 where 0 is least plausible and 10 is most plausible.

STEP 5   The client now chooses which solution is the most feasible and most likely to succeed, with the least negative consequences for the greatest gain (Palmer, 1997a).

STEP 6   This involves breaking down the chosen solution into manageable steps and the client rehearsing in the counselling session the behaviour he or she is going to undertake in vivo. The counsellor prepares the client for any setbacks that may occur and considers how they can be dealt with.

STEP 7   In the next session, assuming the client has carried out the agreed solution, the counsellor and client evaluate its outcome. (This is sometimes undertaken in a telephone counselling session when necessary.) The two key questions are:

1   Have the goals stated at the outset been achieved?
2   Has the problem stated at the outset been resolved or managed?

The client is taught that problem-solving is a process of trial and error. If the problem has not been satisfactorily dealt with, the counsellor and client should go back to the drawing board. If the proposed solution has been successful then the client either leaves counselling or chooses another problem from her list and starts the process again at Step 1.

Sometimes while going through Steps 1 to 6, the client may experience a high level of emotional disturbance (e.g. anxiety, depression, shame) about tackling the selected problem or lack of progress. In this case it is usually necessary for the counsellor to use the ABCDE emotional problem-solving method before returning to the practical problem-solving, seven-step method.

ABCDE model of emotional disturbance and change

REBT provides a five-stage model which explains how an individual's thinking can largely contribute to emotional disturbance such as anxiety and depression and how to modify the disturbance-producing thinking (Table 10.2).

Table 10.2 *ABCDE model of emotional disturbance and change*

A = Activating Events	Stressors or problematic situations (actual or inferred past, present or future occurrences): e.g. meeting an important deadline.
B = Beliefs	Rigid and unqualified demands in the form of musts, shoulds, have to's, got to's and oughts, which are involved with the appraisal of the event: e.g. 'I must meet the deadline. If I don't meet it, it would prove that I'm a failure.'
C = Consequences	Emotional, behavioural and physiological disturbances largely determined by the individual's beliefs about the event, resulting in reduced productivity, performance and problem solving: e.g. feels anxious about failing, procrastinates, and starts to experience palpitations.
D = Disputing	Cognitive, emotive, behavioural or imaginal challenging of, problem-interfering beliefs: e.g. 'Although it's strongly preferable to reach the deadline, I don't have too. If I don't, all it proves is that I failed to reach it. This does not make me a failure.'
E = Effective	Efficient, flexible outlook that is problem-solving and therefore reverses the decline noted at C: e.g. Feels concerned about reaching the deadline but not overwhelmingly anxious. Starts to work towards achieving the goal and stops procrastinating. Physiological symptoms of anxiety will have disappeared.

REBT asserts that absolute, rigid and evaluative beliefs in the form of musts, shoulds, have to's, got to's and oughts are normally found at the core of human emotional disturbance. These demanding beliefs that individuals place upon themselves, others and the world may lead to unnecessary distress and emotional disturbance, for example, 'I must perform well.' Derived from the evaluative beliefs or premise are evaluative conclusions or derivatives:

1 *Low frustration tolerance*: an individual's perceived inability to endure frustration or discomfort in life, e.g. 'I can't stand not performing well.'
2 *Awfulizing*: the defining of stressors or negative events as so awful that they should not happen and are beyond human understanding, e.g. 'This should not be happening to me. It's really awful.'
3 *Damnation of self, others or world conditions*: assigning a global negative rating on a particular stressor, life event or characteristic, e.g. 'Performing badly confirms that I'm a failure as a human being.'

These inflexible beliefs are called problem interfering or self-defeating because they are seen as unrealistic or illogical. They interfere with attempts at practical problem resolution, thereby impeding goal attainment, and create emotional disturbance. In mainstream REBT literature they are also referred to as irrational beliefs. However, this can lead to misunderstandings by the client. Therefore, in problem-focused counselling this term is seldom used. REBT asserts that all humans have an innate tendency to think in a self-defeating manner. Ellis (1976, 1994) based this finding on his observation that so many humans are able to distress themselves over adverse stressors, life events or environmental conditions, for example, divorce, poor job conditions or queues in shops. Although these external activating events may trigger or contribute to emotional disturbance, they are not considered sufficient in themselves to explain the level of distress experienced by the individual.

REBT asserts that to attain emotional health individuals need to develop a belief system based on non-absolute and flexible preferences, wants, wishes and desires, for example, 'I strongly prefer to perform well, but realistically, I don't have to. I'll do the best I can within the circumstances.' These beliefs are problem focused and self-helping because they are seen as realistic, logical and problem facilitating, thereby aiding goal attainment and reducing emotional distress. Derived from these preferences, wishes, wants and desires are three major evaluative conclusions or derivatives and constructive alternatives to those listed above:

1 *High frustration tolerance*: the ability to tolerate or withstand frustration or discomfort in life, e.g. 'Even though I don't like it, I can stand not performing well.'
2 *Anti-awfulizing*: stressors or negative events are evaluated on a scale of badness that lies within human understanding, e.g. 'Whether I like it or not, unpleasant things do happen to me. They may be bad but hardly awful.'
3 *Acceptance of self, others and the world*: human beings are seen as imperfect and fallible. As they are in a constant state of flux and change they are too complex to be assigned a single global rating, e.g. 'Even if I do fail to perform well, this would not make me a failure as a person.'

REBT also asserts that humans have a second innate tendency to regard their thinking in a self-helping manner, thereby reducing the potential negative effects of their self-defeating thinking. By developing a functional philosophy of living, individuals can learn to moderate their levels of distress as well as increase their striving for self-actualization.

Once clients have dealt with their self-defeating and problem-interfering beliefs and applied appropriate problem-solving and coping-skills strategies, they will normally move from psychological disturbance to psychological health.

Practice and clinical issues

The goals of problem-focused counselling are to help clients to achieve the following:

- to challenge their disturbance-producing, problem-interfering and self-defeating thinking;

- to develop problem-focused and self-helping beliefs;
- to select appropriate goals and act in goal-directed ways;
- to feel less emotionally disturbed;
- to learn new emotion- and problem-focused skills, strategies and techniques;
- to become their own counsellors for present and future problem solving.

The dual systems approach to problem solving or management helps individuals to deal with their practical and emotional problems in order for them to lead healthier, happier and more fulfilling lives.

Socializing clients into problem-focused counselling

From the outset, clients are shown what is expected of them, both inside and outside the therapeutic hour. This enables them to participate effectively in this approach, thereby getting the most out of counselling. This procedure may be postponed if the client is, initially, too disturbed to digest this information. In this case clients are shown two forms of responsibility:

1. *Emotional*: that their emotional disturbance is largely (but not totally) self-induced.
2. *Therapeutic*: that if they want to overcome or moderate this emotional disturbance, they need to undertake a number of tasks or homework assignments, sometimes on a lifelong basis, if they wish to maintain their counselling gains.

To accelerate the learning process, problem-focused counsellors use an active-directive style to teach clients these responsibilities by separating their presenting problems into their constituent parts: A (stressors, events or problematic situations); B (beliefs); C (emotions, behaviours and physiological response). Clients are discouraged from A–C thinking (e.g. 'My manager's comments make me feel guilty') to B–C thinking (e.g. 'I make myself feel guilty about my manager's comments?'). The counsellor uses B–C language to reinforce emotional responsibility.

Therapeutic relationship

Similar to REBT therapists, problem-focused counsellors agree that the core conditions of therapy are necessary for the development of a working alliance. However, they are concerned about exhibiting behaviours that could be counterproductive. These include displaying too much warmth, as this may strengthen some clients dire needs for approval and love which could then lead to overdependency on the counsellor rather than facing their problems head on. Working together in collaboration to solve the client's problems is the major focus of the therapeutic alliance.

Assessment

It is important to assess whether the client's presenting problem is either largely practical or emotional in its nature or a combination of both as this determines which method the counsellor will initially apply. For example, if a client wishes to tell his manager that he is being overloaded with work but feels very anxious about stating his case and avoiding the subsequent discussion, this would indicate that the most suitable initial intervention would be focused on emotional problem solving. If, on the other hand, the client did not feel anxious about stating his case but was unsure about what to say and how to present it this might indicate a practical problem-solving method which would probably include role play in the counselling session. If the client was very anxious and was also unsure what to say and how to present himself, then this would indicate:

1. Initially focusing on reducing the emotional disturbance by using the ABCDE method.
2. Then applying the seven-step, problem-solving sequence to help him with the practical aspects of the problem.

In this case if the counsellor initially applied the ABCDE model, A would involve *telling the manager about being overloaded with work*. However, at this stage the counsellor and the client may not be fully aware of what the latter is most anxious about. To uncover this, the counsellor usually needs to 'delve deeper' by using a procedure known as inference chaining in which the client's personally significant assumptions about this situation are linked through a series of 'Let's assume . . . then what?' questions. The aim of inference chaining is to pinpoint which inference the client is most disturbed about (known as the critical A). The process usually starts as follows:

Client: I'm anxious about telling my manager that I'm overloaded with work.
Counsellor: Can you imagine you are telling your manager that you are overloaded with work. I'll give you a few moments to imagine that. . . . What would be anxiety provoking in your mind about you telling her?
Client: She might become angry.
Counsellor: Let's assume for the moment that she does become angry. Then what?
Client: She might think I'm no good or she might sack me?
Counsellor: What are you most anxious about? Her thinking you're 'no good' or her sacking you? [*Counsellor clarifying which issue is most relevant.*]
Client: She probably wouldn't sack me and if she did I could get another job. But I really wouldn't like her thinking that I'm 'no good'.
Counsellor: Okay. If she did say that you are 'no good', would you agree with her?

Client: She's a very experienced manager. Of course I would agree with her.
Counsellor: So what is more important for you: being 'no good' in her eyes or in your eyes?
Client: You see, she would have found me out and confirmed what I already know; that 'I'm 'no good'. I suppose that it's in my eyes what I'm really upset about.
Counsellor: So you are most anxious about confirmation that in your eyes you are 'no good'. [*The critical A.*] Therefore you are reluctant to tell your manager that you are overloaded with work.
Client: Yes, that's it.

The next step would be to elicit from the client the demands being made about the critical A, for example, 'I must cope with my workload otherwise this confirms that I'm no good' (B). The counsellor could employ a wide range of emotive, imaginal, cognitive and behavioural techniques to dispute (D) this belief (and other relevant self-defeating beliefs that the client needs to modify). Once this process has been undertaken, then the client would focus on how to develop a new and effective approach to the problem (E). In the example given the client may still need to use the seven-step model to decide what to say and how to present himself.

Techniques used in conjunction with the ABCDE model

Cognitive techniques

These techniques help clients to think about their thinking in a more problem-focused and self-helping way.

QUESTIONING   Clients are taught to examine the evidence for and against their self-defeating beliefs by using three major criteria:

1 *Empiricism*. Where is it written that you must attain what you desire? Where is the evidence that the universe must obey your demands? Although it's strongly preferable to cope with your workload, why must you cope with it? Apart from inside your head, where is the evidence that you are 'no good' if you are unable to deal with your workload?
2 *Logic*. Just because you would greatly prefer to cope with your workload, how does it logically follow that you must cope with it? Does it logically follow that you are 'no good' if you do not cope with your workload?
3 *Pragmatism*. Is it helpful holding on to this belief? Where is it going to get you as long as you hold on to the belief that you must cope otherwise you are no good?

COST-BENEFIT ANALYSIS OF BELIEFS   This is a pragmatic approach to help the client assess the pros and cons of holding a self-defeating belief (see Palmer and Burton, 1996; Ellis et al., 1997). The client, with the counsellor's help, writes down in two columns the advantages and disadvantages of the particular belief. After this is completed a new problem-focused and self-helping belief is developed and the process is repeated again but this time for the new functional belief.

TESTING OUT THE VALIDITY   Having modified their self-defeating belief with a self-helping one, clients are encouraged to test out their thoughts in the form of behavioural experiments.

ALTERNATIVE PERSPECTIVES   The client is encouraged to look at the situation from a different perspective, e.g. how their closest friend would view it. Usually the friend's perspective is more realistic.

Behavioural techniques

Behavioural techniques and strategies have a variety of purposes. They may help clients to challenge their self-defeating beliefs. Depressed clients may be encouraged to undertake small tasks that previously gave them pleasure or simply to counter withdrawal.

Behavioural assignments are negotiated with the client on the basis of challenging, but not overwhelming, to promote therapeutic change but not so formidable as to prevent clients from attempting them.

EXPOSURE   Clients are encouraged to face their fears and phobias in vivo and thereby reality test or challenge their self-defeating beliefs. These assignments may be graded, starting with the least anxiety-provoking step first. However, for the sake of efficiency, clients are encouraged whenever possible to face their main fears without graded exposure.

SCHEDULING ACTIVITIES   With withdrawn, depressed clients the counsellor negotiates a schedule of activities which are slotted into the day in order to increase pleasure and encourage positive social contact.

RELAXATION TECHNIQUES   These techniques are used to reduce the negative physiological aspects of anxiety if the client could possibly feel overwhelmed by undertaking a particular assignment (see Palmer and Dryden, 1995).

EMOTIVE TECHNIQUES   These involve fully engaging clients' emotions while they forcefully dispute their self-defeating ideas.

FAILURE ATTACKING   Clients who believe that they are total failures are encouraged to spend five to ten minutes acting as if they really are total failures. The counsellor would remind them that a total failure would be unable to leave the counselling room, put on their jacket, leave the building, walk, etc. This would not be suggested to a client with suicidal ideation.

SHAME ATTACKING   Clients are encouraged to act in what they perceive as a 'shameful' way in order to attract public disapproval or ridicule and at the same time powerfully striving for self-acceptance with self-helping beliefs as 'Just because I'm acting in an idiotic manner doesn't make me an idiot. If people wish to reject me because of my behaviour, then tough, too bad!' Clients can learn not to rate themselves globally or to condemn themselves on the reactions of others to their behaviours.

Imagery techniques

Imagery techniques are used for a number of purposes. They can help clients to face their fears in imagination, to practise how to cope with specific feared situations and to look forward in time beyond the current crisis.

INACTION VERSUS ACTION IMAGERY (MOTIVATION IMAGERY)   Clients are encouraged to imagine the rest of their lives without tackling their particular problem (inaction imagery). Following this, clients imagine their future without the particular problem as they have learnt to deal with it through hard work and practice (action imagery). This double imagery procedure is used to motivate clients into action and subsequently to undertake their assignments.

COPING IMAGERY   Clients are encouraged to envision themselves coping with a situation they are anxious about. The exercise would include them seeing how they would deal constructively with difficulties they believe might arise.

Practical problem-solving section of counselling

Once the client's emotional distress has diminished, the focus of the counselling session shifts towards addressing the practical aspects of the problem(s) by using the seven-step model previously described. This section will cover a number of key strategies or techniques that can be applied at the different steps.

Techniques and strategies

Step 1

EXTERNALIZING AND VISUALIZING   This involves displaying information visually to help free the client and counsellor's mind from having to retain and understand data so that they can focus on the more crucial activities of interpretation and evaluation. Flip-charts, notepads and whiteboards may be used for this purpose.

STRESS MAPPING OR PLANOGRAMS   If a client presents a 'messy' problem which needs further analysis, stress mapping (Palmer, 1990) or planograms (Palmer and Burton, 1996) are used to aid assessment and problem definition. With these visual techniques different aspects or components of the problem such as a difficult manager, work overload, etc., are drawn on a whiteboard or notepad. These are connected with lines to the problem owner (the client) who is placed in the centre of the diagram. This usually enables the client and counsellor to get a clearer picture of the problem.

Step 2

'WHY?' QUESTIONS   Although 'Why?' questions are often avoided in counselling it is useful at Step 2 to ask why the client wishes to achieve specific goals. Sometimes by asking this question the counsellor may discover the underlying problem that needs resolving.

Step 3

HOW WOULD OTHERS COPE?   Once a selection of options has been noted after the brainstorming session, the list of available alternatives can be increased further by asking the client to imagine what her/his friend or somebody she/he admires would do in a similar situation.

Step 4

TIME PROJECTION IMAGERY   Time projection imagery is a technique in which the client visualizes a future event or situation (Palmer and Dryden, 1995). The client can use this technique to assess and imagine what may happen in the future if she or he applied a specific option.

Step 5

SOLUTION PLANS   D'Zurilla (1986) emphasizes that any solution plan should aim to:

- resolve the problem;
- maximize personal and emotional well-being;
- minimize time and effort.

The plan could take two forms. A simple plan will focus on one single solution or course of action. This is desirable if one option is likely to have a clear positive outcome. A complex plan can take two forms:

- pursuing several solutions at the same time;
- following a series of solutions: initially A, and if this does not work then B; then if B does not work then C.

The complex plan takes a trouble-shooting approach as it gives the client a variety of prepared solutions if setbacks occur.

Step 6

ROLE PLAY   If the agreed solution involves the client interacting with others, the client may often benefit from practising in the counselling session what he or she is going to say and how to behave. In role play the counsellor acts out the role of the other party involved and the client can practise his or her part. The counsellor gives constructive feedback and the exercise is repeated until the client can give an adequate performance.

Step 7

FAILURE IS IN THE EYES OF THE BEHOLDER   It is important for counsellors to show clients that even if they fail to succeed at a particular assignment, it does not mean that they are a failure in themselves. In addition, each task undertaken provides more useful information for the next attempt. During this stage the counsellor may need to be supportive and encouraging.

The process of therapeutic change

This involves a number of steps for clients to learn and these include:

1. That individuals largely (but not totally) create their own emotional disturbances about stressors, life events or practical problems through their problem interfering and self-defeating thinking.
2. That individuals have the ability to minimize or remove these disturbances by identifying, challenging and changing their inflexible thinking styles. Once this has been achieved, individuals can focus their energies on practical problem solving.
3. In order to acquire a flexible style of thinking, individuals need to think, feel and act against their problem interfering and self-defeating beliefs. This is usually on a lifelong basis, if they wish to remain emotionally healthy and problem orientated.
4. Problem solving usually involves learning a combination of both emotion and problem-focused skills. Skills deficits are usually remedied by regular hard work and practice.

The seven-step and ABCDE models provide the frameworks in which this process of therapeutic change can occur.

Format of a typical session

The session normally starts with the counsellor and client negotiating an agenda which focuses on the latter's practical and emotional problem(s). The agenda would include reviewing the client's homework assignments from the previous week; agreeing the topics to be discussed in the present session; negotiating further assignments that arise from the work done in the session; and eliciting client feedback about the session.

Indications and contraindications

Problem-solving and rational emotive behaviour therapy and training has been shown to be effective for a wide range of problems and disorders when used with children, adults and couples (see Coche and Flick, 1975; DiGiuseppe and Miller, 1977; Intagliatia, 1978; Karol and Richards, 1978; Richards and Perri, 1978; Jannoum et al., 1980; Robin, 1981; Schinke et al., 1981; Black and Scherba, 1983; Falloon et al., 1984; Jacobson, 1984; Nezu, 1986; Hawton and Catalan, 1987; Hawton and Kirk, 1989; Silverman et al., 1992; Ellis et al., 1997).

Hawton and Kirk (1989) refer to a number of possible contraindications and reasons for failure. Three key areas are:

1 Client's problems cannot be specified.
2 Client's goals seem unrealistic.
3 Severe acute psychiatric illness.

The approach is also contraindicated with very deluded clients with schizophrenia, or very retarded or agitated depressed clients who will not necessarily be able to focus on the tasks.

Case Study

The client

Sara was a 30-year-old single woman. She worked within a large organization and held a middle management position in marketing. She was very anxious about giving a presentation to the board of directors. Whenever possible she had always avoided giving presentations and was relatively inexperienced in this area. A course of five counselling sessions was agreed with the possibility of extending therapy if necessary. (This would be renegotiated.)

The therapy

In the first session the counsellor gathered more background information on Sara and her problem. The process of socializing her into counselling began by establishing her goal(s) for change. Sara's chosen goal was to feel less anxious about giving her presentation. However, a difficulty arose when she qualified her goal as she wanted to give a 'stunning presentation to the board of directors'. The counsellor decided that it would be beneficial to use an analogy to demonstrate the possible problems that could be encountered.

> *Counsellor*: I just want to consider other learning experiences you've had and then return to the presentation. Is that okay?
> *Sara*: Yes.
> *Counsellor*: Can you describe the first driving lesson you had?
> *Sara*: I remember it well! As soon as I started to drive I stalled the car. I was glad when it was over.
> *Counsellor*: How long did it take you to pass your test?
> *Sara*: About eight months of driving lessons.
> *Counsellor*: Do you remember after passing the test, that very first drive by yourself?
> *Sara*: Yes, it really felt strange.
> *Counsellor*: And parking the car by yourself?
> *Sara*: [*Laughs*] I still have difficulties now!
> *Counsellor*: I just want to return to your goal. Do you really believe you are being realistic when you want to give a stunning presentation next month yet you've never given any presentations before and lack the practice? Like most people, you found learning to drive difficult initially.
> *Sara*: Well, when you put it like that and considering what I was like learning to drive, perhaps I am being unrealistic.
> *Counsellor*: Considering how nervous you are about presentations and how you've spent years avoiding giving them, it's likely that you may literally stall at your first attempt, especially if it was to a very important audience. Perhaps we should reconsider this goal and break it down into smaller steps. Any ideas?
> *Sara*: Perhaps first I could do a short presentation to my staff and then gradually build up to the board presentation.
> *Counsellor*: Makes sense to me. Let's now focus on the presentation to your staff.

The analogy was used to remind the client that learning new skills is not necessarily straightforward or easy for anybody. The counsellor was then able to renegotiate a more realistic goal of giving a satisfactory presentation (see Palmer, 1997a).

As Sara was still anxious about the practice run with her staff the counsellor decided to use the ABCDE model of emotional problem solving. The A was giving the presentation and the C was anxiety, procrastination and palpitations. To uncover what she was most anxious about in giving the presentation, the counsellor used inference chaining (described earlier).

Counsellor: What is anxiety [C] provoking about not giving a good presentation?
Sara: My colleagues may laugh.
Counsellor: Let's assume for the moment that they do laugh. What is anxiety provoking about that?
Sara: I'll be discredited. They might think I'm stupid.
Counsellor: For the moment let's assume you are discredited and are seen as stupid. What's anxiety provoking about that?
Sara: My boss may get to hear about it and I could lose my job.
Counsellor: If you did lose your job, what would you be anxious about?
Sara: Well, I suppose I might lose my flat and end up on the streets.
Counsellor: I'd just like to review what we've covered. You are possibly anxious about a number of issues: (1) your colleagues laughing; (2) being discredited and being seen as stupid; (3) you could lose your job; (4) you could lose your flat and end up on the street. . . . When you are getting anxious what do you think you are most anxious about?
Sara: I very much doubt I'll lose my flat and end up on the street. But my job means so much to me. I wouldn't want to lose it. It's what I've always wanted.
Counsellor: Are you saying that it's not so much the presentation you're anxious about but that the real fear is losing the job you treasure?
Sara: Yeah.
Counsellor: Does this also apply to you being anxious about the presentation to the board?
Sara: It most certainly does.

Once the critical A is uncovered then the counsellor elicits the problem-interfering beliefs:

Counsellor: I want to really imagine you have lost your job . . . the job you've always wanted. Remember, you've spent years striving to get this job and you've lost it. Can you see this in your mind's eye?
Sara: [upset] I can.
Counsellor: What are you telling yourself at this very moment?
Sara: I must not lose this job.

Counsellor: And if you did lose it?
Sara: I couldn't stand it. Life would be awful.
Counsellor: How would you see yourself as a person?
Sara: A failure!

The client's self-defeating beliefs were noted down and became the focus for disputation. Sara's beliefs were:

B = I must not lose this job, and if I did
I couldn't stand it
Life would be awful
I would be a failure.

Once sufficient challenging of the beliefs had occurred then the counsellor and client developed more helpful, flexible and problem-focused beliefs: 'It's strongly preferable not to lose my job, but if I do, I could stand it, it may be bad but hardly awful, and it would not prove that I'm a failure – only that I failed to keep my job.' The first homework task was for Sara to read an REBT self-help book on performance anxiety (Robin and Balter, 1995).

The course of therapy

In the following two sessions the counsellor continued to challenge Sara's self-defeating beliefs using a variety of different cognitive methods. Sara found that the belief cost-benefit analysis was most persuasive in reinforcing the strength of her newly emerging self-helping beliefs. Other homework tasks included using coping imagery.

As Sara's anxiety was gradually improving, in session four the seven-step model was introduced to focus on the practical aspect of her problem. The starting point was giving the first presentation to her staff.

STEP 1 IDENTIFYING THE PROBLEM   Presentation skills deficits.

STEP 2 SELECTING GOAL(S)   To give an acceptable presentation to my staff.

STEP 3 EXPLORING OPTIONS

(a) 'Just do it'.
(b) 'Read books about giving talks.'
(c) 'Forget it.'
(d) 'Observe others giving presentations.'
(e) 'Ask colleagues for tips about giving presentations.'

(f) 'Practise using an overhead projector.'

STEP 4 CONSIDERING THE CONSEQUENCES   Sara wrote her comments:

(a) 'This is a mistake. Preparation is important.'
(b) 'This is a good idea. Obtain the book from Dillons.'
(c) 'If I give up now I'll never improve my job prospects.'
(d) 'This sounds good. There's one next week I can attend.'
(e) 'John always seems to give a polished presentation. I'll have a chat with him.'
(f) 'This would be excellent. I can use acetates to jog my memory in case I forget what I want to say.'

STEP 5 TAKING DECISIONS   'This is straightforward. I'll choose options (b), (d), (e) and (f). I'll do this before our next counselling session.'

STEP 6 AGREEING ACTIONS   In the counselling session Sara rehearsed her presentation. This included practising having a confident body posture and maintaining eye contact. She used coping imagery to help her imagine how she would deal with her worst fears, i.e. being asked difficult questions, her mind going blank and her nervous cough returning.

STEP 7 EVALUATION   The feedback from her staff and a trusted colleague whose views she valued was positive. Her colleague suggested a number of minor improvements.

The therapy was extended for another two sessions held monthly. In this time she gave three more presentations and finally she gave a short presentation to the board. It was agreed that if she suffered any great setbacks or started to avoid giving presentations she could return for a booster session.

Wider implications and applications

Problem-focused counselling as described in this chapter can be used in a range of settings. One of the major limitations are the skills or skills deficits of the counsellor or psychologist applying the approach. Due to its inherently brief and time-limited focus it is well suited to general practice or employee assistance programmes (EAPs) whether it is used for stress, anxiety or depression. It is suitable for college counselling services and is of particular relevance to helping students manage exam anxiety or cope with difficult relationships and new situations. It has been used within the community to help families cope with a member who suffers from schizophrenia (see Falloon et al., 1984) as well as in psychiatric units.

Over the past 20 years much research has been published on the application of problem-solving approaches and methods to a variety of different problems (see 'Indications'). Its use within individual, family or group settings is well documented. It is suitable for use within private practice.

Future developments

Due to managed care in the USA and the demand for brief or time-limited counselling within Britain's NHS and EAP services, well-researched approaches that have been shown to be effective with a range of problems and disorders and can be used in a number of different settings and modalities are going to become very popular (Ellis, 1996). With increasing client–therapist litigation in the USA and more recently in Britain, offering the client the most effective form of therapy may become an important issue. We may see problem-solving forms of therapy being used more frequently and replacing more traditional therapies.

There is some slight evidence to support this prediction. The most recent Delphi poll (see Neimeyer and Norcross, 1997) predicted that present-centred, structured and directive techniques were expected to increase markedly in the forthcoming decade. Self-change, problem-solving and homework assignments were expected to lead the way. By contrast, historically oriented, relatively passive and unstructured procedures were predicted to decline.

References

Black, D.R. and Scherba, D.S. (1983) 'Contracting to problem solve versus contracting to practice behavioural weight loss skills', *Behavior Therapy*, 14: 100–9.

Coche, E. and Flick, A. (1975) 'Problem-solving training groups for hospitalized psychiatric patients', *Journal of Psychology*, 91: 19–29.

DiGiuseppe, R.A. and Miller, N.J. (1977) 'A review of outcome studies on rational-emotive therapy', in A. Ellis and R. Grieger (eds), *Handbook of Rational-Emotive Therapy*. New York: Springer.

D'Zurilla, T.J. (1986) *Problem-Solving Therapy: A Social Competence Approach to Clinical Intervention*. New York: Springer.

Ellis, A. (1976) 'The biological basis of human irrationality', *Journal of Individual Psychology*, 32: 145–68.

Ellis, A. (1994) *Reason and Emotion in Psychotherapy*, 2nd edn. New York: Carol Publishing.

Ellis, A. (1996) *Better, Deeper and More Enduring Brief Therapy: The Rational Emotive Behavior Approach*. New York: Brunner/Mazel.

Ellis, A., Gordon, J., Neenan, N. and Palmer, S. (1997) *Stress Counselling: A Rational Emotive Behaviour Approach*. London: Sage.

Falloon, I.R.H., Boyd, J.L. and McGill, C. (1984) 'Problem-solving training', in *Family Care of Schizophrenia*. New York: Guilford Press.

Hawton, K. and Catalan, J. (1987) *Attempted Suicide: A Practical Guide to its Nature and Management*, 2nd edn. Oxford: Oxford University Press.

Hawton, K. and Kirk, J. (1989) 'Problem-solving', in K. Hawton, P. Salkovskis, J. Kirk and D. Clarke (eds), *Cognitive Behaviour Therapy for Psychiatric Problems: A Practical Guide*. Oxford: Oxford University Press.

Intagliatia, J.C. (1978) 'Increasing the interpersonal problem solving skills of an alcoholic population', *Journal of Consulting and Clinical Psychology*, 46: 489–98.

Jacobson, N.S. (1984) 'A component analysis of marital behavior therapy: the relative effectiveness of behavior exchange and communication/problem-solving training', *Journal of Consulting and Clinical Psychology*, 52: 295–305.

Jannoum, L., Munby, M., Catalan, J. and Gelder, M. (1980) 'A home-based treatment program for agoraphobia: replication and controlled evaluation', *Behavior Therapy*, 11: 294-305.

Karol, R.L. and Richards, C.S. (1978) 'Making treatment effects last: an investigation of maintenance strategies for smoking reduction', paper presented at the Annual Convention of the Association for the Advancement of Behavior Therapy, Chicago.

Lazarus, R.S. (1981) 'The stress coping paradigm', in C. Eisdorfer, D. Cohen, A. Kleinman and P. Maxim (eds), *Theoretical Bases for Psychopathology*. New York: Spectrum.

Lazarus, R.S. and Folkman, S. (1984) *Stress, Appraisal and Coping*. New York: Springer.

Meichenbaum, D. (1985) *Stress Inoculation Training*. New York: Pergamon.

Milner, P. and Palmer, S. (1998) *Integrative Stress Counselling: A Humanistic Problem-Focused Approach*. London: Cassell.

Neenan, M. and Palmer, S. (1996) 'Stress counselling: a cognitive-behavioural perspective', *Stress News*, 8 (4): 5–8.

Neenan, M. and Palmer, S. (in press a) 'Problem focused counselling', in S. Palmer (ed.), *An Introductory Handbook to Counselling and Psychotherapy*. London: Sage.

Neenan, M. and Palmer, S. (in press b) 'Problem solving counselling', *Counselling*.

Neimeyer G.J.and Norcross, J.C. (1997) 'The future of psychotherapy and counseling psychology in the USA: Delphi data and beyond', in S. Palmer and V. Varma (eds), *The Future of Counselling and Psychotherapy*. London: Sage.

Nezu, A.M. (1986) 'Efficacy of social problem solving therapy approach for unipolar depression', *Journal of Consulting and Clinical Psychology*, 54: 196–202.

Osborn, A. (1963) *Applied Imagination: Principles and Procedures of Creative Problem Solving*, 3rd edn. New York: Scribner.

Palmer, S. (1990) 'Stress mapping: a visual technique to aid counselling or training', *Employee Counselling Today*, 2 (2): 9–12.

Palmer, S. (1994) 'Stress management and counselling: a problem-solving approach', *Stress News*, 5 (3): 2–3.

Palmer, S. (1997a) 'Problem focused stress counselling and stress management training: an intrinsically brief integrative approach. Part 1', *Stress News*, 9 (2): 7–12.

Palmer, S. (1997b) 'Problem focused stress counselling and stress management training: an intrinsically brief integrative approach. Part 2', *Stress News*, 9 (3): 6–10.

Palmer, S. and Burton, T. (1996) *Dealing with People Problems at Work*. Maidenhead:

McGraw-Hill.

Palmer, S. and Dryden, W. (1995) *Counselling for Stress Problems*. London: Sage.

Richards, C.S. and Perri, M.G. (1978) 'Do self-control treatments last? An evaluation of behavioral problem solving and faded counselor contact as treatment maintenance strategies', *Journal of Counseling Psychology*, 25: 376–83

Robin, A.L. (1981) 'A controlled evaluation of problem-solving communication training with parent–adolescent conflict', *Behavior Therapy*, 12: 593–609.

Robin, M.W. and Balter, R. (1995) *Performance Anxiety. Overcoming Your Fear In: the Workplace, Social Situations, Interpersonal Communications, the Performing Arts*. Holbrook, MA: Adams.

Schinke, S.P., Blythe, B.J. and Gilchrist, L.D. (1981) 'Cognitive-behavioural prevention of adolescent pregnancy', *Journal of Counseling Psychology*, 28: 451–4.

Silverman, M.S., McCarthy, M. and McGovern, T. (1992) 'A review of outcome studies of rational-emotive therapy from 1982–1989', *Journal of Rational-Emotive and Cognitive-Behavior Therapy*, 10 (3): 111–86.

Wasik, B. (1984) 'Teaching parents effective problem solving: a handbook for professionals'. Unpublished manuscript. Chapel Hill: University of North Carolina.

Woods, P.J. (1987) 'Do you really want to maintain that a flat tire can upset your stomach? Using the findings of the psychophysiology of stress to bolster the arguments that are not directly disturbed by events', *Journal of Rational-Emotive Therapy*, 5 (3): 149–61.

11
COGNITIVE ANALYTIC THERAPY

David Crossley and Mark Stowell-Smith

Cognitive analytic therapy (CAT) is a form of time-limited psychotherapy that draws together a range of ideas from psychoanalytic, cognitive and personal construct theory. The origins and development of CAT are strongly associated with the work of Anthony Ryle and an overview of both its development and current theoretical position are described in Ryle's most recent texts (1995a, 1997b). The evolution of CAT theory and practice can also be traced through his earlier books (Ryle, 1982, 1990).

Both in spirit and practice CAT is best represented as a form of integrative psychotherapy. The theme of integration is expressed in Ryle's early attempts to utilize cognitive concepts as the basis for a 'common language' for psychotherapy (Ryle, 1978) and persists in CAT's continued usage of a hybrid information processing model (Procedural Sequence Object Relations Model) to both accommodate and explicate psychoanalytic ideas. Within this model psychoanalytic concepts retain a prominent position but their application is given a new twist with the formulation of the client's problems explicitly shared early on in therapy in the form of a prose and diagrammatic reformulation. As we will see later on in this chapter, this emphasis upon reformulation as a guide to problem recognition and revision is one of the hallmarks of CAT.

Development of the therapy

The rise to prominence of CAT has been rapid. From the early theoretical developments of the late 1970s it has matured over the last two decades into a coherent set of ideas and techniques.

The emergence of CAT owes much to the zeal and innovation of its creator, Anthony Ryle. Ryle initially practised psychotherapy while a general practitioner. Faced with a high incidence of emotional distress among his patient population, he developed an enduring interest in effective, time-limited therapy that might be available to all. The need for such a therapy was further underscored when he took up the post of consultant psychotherapist in an understaffed inner-city psychotherapy department.

Here he sought to resolve the dilemma of offering 'the choice of long term psychotherapy to a few or a minimum sufficient intervention for all' (Ryle, 1994a: 94) by developing a form of effective, time-limited therapy.

While the popularization of CAT clearly has much to do with the conceptual and practical innovations which Ryle and his co-workers have contributed to psychotherapy, its evolution has also been stimulated by a variety of economic and cultural influences. Recent years, for example, have witnessed a growing movement in the public mental health sector towards the implementation of forms of brief psychotherapy. The greater degree of financial accountability brought about by the transition of NHS hospitals to trust status has meant that briefer forms of psychotherapy (which are comparatively less expensive and easier to audit, than, for example, longer term psychodynamic therapy) have increasingly become the treatment of choice for purchasers. Van Schoor (1996) has also noted the way in which technique-oriented forms of brief therapy appear to have taken root in a technologically saturated culture of the late twentieth century. According to Van Schoor, this culture involves 'regimentation, specialisation and standardisation': qualities that are reflected in brief psychotherapy's use of standardized procedure, its manipulation of time and its use of technical procedure.

Theory and basic concepts

CAT aims to combine within a single framework what is most useful in psychoanalytical and cognitive therapy theories, especially for the many people whose difficulties are not easily understood in other models of psychotherapy and have therefore often been excluded. Although derived from cognitive and analytical traditions, the CAT framework is based on an innovative and unitary model – the Procedural Sequence Object Relations Model (PSORM) – which aims to provide a coherent and distinctive approach to the understanding of clients' problems (Leiman, 1994).

Prior to examining the model, it will be useful to look at its theoretical antecedents in more depth. A major 'parental' influence on CAT is from cognitive psychology and personal construct theory (Marzillier and Butler, 1995). Here CAT picks up the assumption – from personal construct theory (Kelly, 1955) – that people actively 'construct' their realities. We are as it were always in dialogue with our world. The dialogue and questioning may only become explicit when change is afoot, for example, when the old system of assumptions ('constructs') is starting to fail because of overwhelming life events. Or it may never have been put together very well, for example, in people with personality difficulties. The realities we construct may sometimes limit our ability to learn from experience depending on the framework we have made (or been given) in which to frame the questions. The constructs fashion the experience by having implied expectations. If another person fails to fulfil our implicit expectations of them there could be conflict. Therapy is, in part, about making expectations explicit and therefore open to change.

The development of role behaviour is a key idea for CAT which is in part underpinned by its analytic (i.e. object relations) perspective. CAT theory envisages a developmental psychology compatible with certain aspects of object relations theory but is significantly different in other ways (Ryle, 1990; Leighton and Ryle, 1995). In common with object relations theory is the assumption that we not only make relationships but relationships are the making of us. CAT accepts that the development of our sense of who we are, as distinct from who we are not, is brought about by a process of both internalizing aspects of others (e.g. attachment figures) and also (potentially) disowning aspects of ourselves which then may be seen as located in others. In consequence the self is reflexive – in dialogue with itself as it were (Leiman, 1997). If we think about ourselves there is an I relating to a me and what began as an external dialogue (I and you) has become an internal dialogue. Our sense of self is achieved by this joint activity – the external dialogue and signs of relationship – as we learn to relate to/think about ourselves in the way we have been related to by significant others. The signs that mediate relationship – our words, gestures, transactions – not only bring the relationship into effect, as it were, but also point beyond it to its wider cultural origins into a network of relationships not in immediate proximity. Thus even private thought has interpersonal origins and a dialogical structure (I think about myself). CAT gains these perspectives from the Russian psychologists Bakhtin and Vygotsky (Leiman, 1997; Ryle, 1997b). Where CAT leaves earlier versions of object relations theory behind is therefore in giving emphasis to what is historically accessible in terms of our relationship with others, rather than suggesting that emotional difficulties are the result of constitutionally conflict-prone inner drives and impulses at war with each other.

Thus the self is made up of a set of interrelating roles that effect both internal and external relationships (Stiles, 1997). As I care for and control myself, the roles (the I and the me) get enacted internally together with the expectations and feelings that go with them. I may have an angry demanding part which relates to a resentfully submissive aspect of myself. The former may be derived from, say, the experience of my mother; the latter from myself as her child. These aspects of me are not necessarily my entire self but important parts of me. CAT terms these 'self-states' – states of feeling, behaviour and cognition that reflect important inner patterns of relationships that may get split off from other parts – for example, the parts where I can nurture and look after myself. Therapy is then about integrating the parts into a whole, putting all the self-states on the same map by developing a capacity to reflect on oneself from a different observational stance collaboratively achieved in the relationship with the therapist.

The CAT therapist is always going to try and provide in a collaborative explicit way an 'overview' function and anticipate how she and the client will get drawn into the client's pattern of relating. CAT does this at a theoretical and practical level. This is how CAT brings together its analytic and cognitive inheritance into something new – the PSORM. CAT describes intentional action as 'procedures': sequences which may be cyclical that begin with an aim, then an appraisal of the situation, then the action itself and any evaluation after the action. Procedures may be hierarchical as some aims are part of wider ones (e.g. the aim of reading this book may be within the wider aim of training as a psychotherapist).

Thinking about the steps necessary for training as a psychotherapist is one thing, but procedures to do with relationship are different. Relating is not possible without role behaviour. A particular situation or perception may determine this. If you are my mother – or just seem to be a bit like her – I will have certain expectations about my role and yours. I will have to have an idea about two roles – yours and mine – and I will seek to establish what is termed a 'reciprocal role procedure' (RRP), or complementarity. If I am six months old I may play a 'hungry infant' role to your 'providing mother'. This is where object relations theory is embedded at a cognitive level within CAT and how the therapists understand their transference relationship with the client (Ryle, 1995b). Indeed, CAT sees the personality concept as a particular repertoire of reciprocal role procedures and the concept of projective identification can be considered as a form of reciprocal role procedure – not therefore as something necessarily pathological and entirely unconscious but a key process in the formation of any relationship (Ryle, 1994b). A client expects a certain role from the therapist and indeed my elicit it (e.g. a needy client to a providing therapist) but not always, because the therapist may choose not to play the role if it exemplifies the client's difficulties. For example, if a powerless, dependent-like client induces feelings of all-knowingness in a therapist, the situation would require comment and understanding, not enactment on the part of the therapist. Empathy on its own may not help therapy and may even hinder it.

CAT understands our activity (including thinking) in procedure terms and our relating activity in reciprocal role procedure terms. Procedures that are faulty follow recognizable patterns – patterns of thought, feeling and behaviour linked in some recurrent sequence that end up in some emotional difficulty. CAT describes this psychological disturbance in terms of three patterns called traps, dilemmas and snags. Therapy is about first learning to recognize and then change these patterns and so moving towards psychological health. A trap is a vicious circle in which an action reinforces the problem. For example, I may fear leaving my house but in not leaving it I never give myself the opportunity to find out that it may not be frightening and thus my avoidance feeds my fear. A dilemma is a false or narrow choice. Past experience may suggest to me that I have no real choices – both options or neither may seem to be the correct one. For example, I act as if either I stick up for myself (but get attacked) or I give in (but get put upon). A snag is when an action or choice seems unavailable as if forbidden. For example, we may sabotage our success as if success is a problem to ourselves (eliciting guilt) or others (I anticipate their envy). A child may feel disloyal and guilty if she does better than her parents and therefore she does not.

CAT has an interpersonal focus but the therapist does not proceed by making interpretations about the client's unconscious. Rather the emphasis is cognitive in the sense of making accurate descriptions to enable clients to observe themselves in new ways and see how they can integrate different problematic procedures.

Practice and clinical issues

The goal of therapy is to enhance the clients' ability to recognize their unhelpful procedures and then enable them to adopt an active problem-solving stance. Usually CAT is conducted within a sixteen-week time frame with sessions lasting an hour. Therapy consists of three phases. The introductory sessions are primarily concerned with assessing the client's problems and background and forming a shared understanding. The fourth session is the point at which the therapist gathers all the strands together and offers his or her understanding of the client's distress in the form of a 'reformulation' letter. This aims to promote mutual understanding of and agreement about the major issues with which the therapy will then concern itself. The remaining sessions are devoted to recognizing how these issues (the target problem procedures) operate in the client's daily life and working towards change. The ending of therapy may be anticipated as early as the reformulation letter and its meaning for the individual client is a crucial consideration for CAT which has to be addressed in good time. Attachment and separation can be addressed in microcosm since CAT is both time limited and allows therapist and client alike to reflect on the relationship of care.

The introductory session

There is no one style of therapeutic relationship prescribed for the therapist in CAT but it is likely that the therapist will remain less hidden or inactive in comparison to less structured therapies. From early on clients are encouraged to be active in relation to their problems – as active enquirer, active learner, active experimenter. The therapist's assessment will be oriented towards the writing of the reformulation letter. To this end information is harvested from many sources through the unstructured interview process, the therapist's critical evaluation of the relationship they have with the client (the transference and countertransference) and from pen and paper self-report tasks.

A therapist's focus of attention during the unstructured interview will be to help identify the sequences of assumptions, predictions, actions and evaluations that the client uses repeatedly despite having negative outcomes, i.e. the possible range of target problem procedures. This process involves hearing the client's account of their early years, key relationships and significant life events. It may be highly relevant for the therapist to observe their own responses to the account given as this may give valuable insight into how the client looks after themselves and the range of reciprocal role relationships that may be elicited. The therapist tries to get a sense of the chronically endured distress that the client brings and attempts to understand their inability to discover effective escape routes from it. In addition to the unstructured interviewing and the therapist's self-reflection, the client is also asked to become an active observer by the use of pen and paper techniques. These can be used with a degree of flexibility although one questionnaire – the psychotherapy file – is always given. This offers the client examples of patterns of thought, feelings and behaviour that are failing to help the client, yet are hard to break. These are characterized as 'traps', 'dilemmas' and 'snags' (see above). This file is generally given in the first session in the hope that clients will be enabled to recognize aspects of themselves in a non-judgemental way. Ideally clients find their own words for these patterns (the problem procedures). Self-monitoring in the form of a diary of mood shifts and symptoms can be used for diagnostic purposes (for example, by getting clients to keep a diary of event-thought-feeling links) but it can also promote confidence in solving problems and be targeted at specific problem procedures. Other methods of self-observation can be used such as writing a self-portrait as if by a friend.

Reformulation

This is the key task in CAT. By the third or fourth session the therapist comes to a provisional view about the origins and central features of the client's core problems as defined in terms of traps, dilemmas and snags. This is committed to paper and shared and revised with the client. The style is usually in the form of a letter from therapist to client but other approaches may be used. Some CAT therapists use the client's own voice if this is not overly intrusive. The reformulation should validate the client's experience and propose what problems should be worked on. The therapist will need to gather together all the strands of information available and weave them into a coherent narrative to make sense of the client's specific emotional difficulties and why they are seeking help now. The account is likely to identify areas of emotional resilience as well as vulnerability. It may go on to predict how therapy will proceed on the basis of the client's previous experience of helping relationships. It therefore considers the repertoire of reciprocal role procedures. Commonly, a brief summary and validation of the client's experience leads to a detailed description of target problem procedures. These are succinctly and positively framed and understood as having developed through the client's attempt to cope with and master life.

After the reformulation is read out by the therapist the response is actively sought. Inaccuracies – factual or emotional – are corrected and agreement sought about the focus of therapy and the target procedures. The overall aim of therapy is related to these. For example, a target problem procedure might be 'it seems that if I feel I must then I won't' and the aim may be 'to be able to choose'. The reformulation letter is given to the patient and a copy kept by the therapist and the remaining number of sessions agreed on.

Subsequent sessions

The focus can now be directed at the mutually agreed target problems and the procedures that lead to them. There is no prescribed way in which a session goes but any homework or diaries will be reviewed. Diaries are aimed at improving the recognition of procedures and their subsequent revision (e.g. a snag diary). The client should be made aware of the session number so the end point of therapy is kept in view. Progress in recognising and revising procedures is related at the end of each session on a simple visual analogue scale. There are many techniques to promote change that can be used flexibly and are not specific to CAT. For example, behavioural interventions such as graded exposure tasks to feared situations can enable avoidance patterns to be mastered. Role play may enable clients to become aware of hidden feelings. The therapist may reflect on the way the client's reciprocal role procedures affect the relationship, with the therapist helping them to move between the here and now and the there and then.

CAT does have one technique that promotes self-observation which it may call its own. This is the use of a diagram which relates all the major target problem procedures together (the so-called Sequential Diagrammatic Reformulation). A core self-state or states is named in the middle of the diagram (the dominant reciprocal role patterns) as a place of deep long-standing distress from which the client makes failed escape attempts (the target problem procedures). The diagram can help clients see themselves more coherently and is particularly valuable for those who have unstable changes of mood, thought and behaviour as in cases of borderline personality disorder (Ryle, 1995b).

Ending therapy

Being time-limited helps CAT to remain problem focused and minimizes the risk of excessive dependency on the therapist. The ending may resonate with the client's own difficulties such as unresolved loss and provides an opportunity for therapeutic work in its own right. The therapist writes a 'Goodbye letter' and invites the client to do likewise. These letters review what has been achieved and reflect on the difficulties ahead, e.g. sustaining change. Usually they are read out in the last session. A follow-up of about three months is arranged to review progress. Occasionally further follow-up and more therapy can then be arranged.

Indications and contraindications

With some exceptions, Ryle states that CAT is a safe first therapy for all and an adequate intervention for most (1994a: 94). He suggests that although desirable, a high level of motivation is not expected of the prospective CAT client (Ryle, 1995a: 24). As we will see in the subsequent case study, the engagement of unmotivated, ambivalent or what Prochaska and DiClemente (1982) describe as 'pre-contemplative' clients can be brought about by identifying ambivalent attitudes to change in the reformulation letter. However, while CAT is presented as a suitable therapy for a wide range of neurotic and personality difficulties, there are excluding criteria. These include the existence of mental illness whose severity may undermine the client's capacity to work in therapy as well as the following categories:

1 Where the client expresses a clear preference for a different approach.
2 Serious substance abuse problems which may interfere with the process of therapy.
3 Clients who are actively suicidal and therefore best treated on an inpatient regime (Ryle, 1995a: 24).

Case study

The following case material illustrates how interpretations about the enactment of reciprocal role patterns and their related procedural loops help to facilitate the recognition of a recurrent pattern of damaging, self-limiting behaviour in a 54-year-old male client.

The patient

Phillip was referred to CAT following a series of work-related difficulties. At the initial meeting he described recurrent low mood, chronic interpersonal problems and a tendency to reproach himself for being a failure. He described a number of periods when he had 'broken down' and had been unable to continue his work as a social worker.

Philip was the older child in a sibship of two and he described being brought up in a claustrophobic, repressive, middle-class family. He experienced an early childhood dominated by an authoritarian parental grandmother and a controlling father whom he felt obliged to please by being the high achieving, perfect son. A further important feature of his early experience were recurrent feelings of emptiness, loneliness and rejection maintained by seemingly unempathic care givers. These feelings were augmented at the age of 8 when he was sent away to boarding school. He experienced this as a massive abandonment against which he sought to defend by cutting himself off emotionally from others and forming the basis of what was to be an enduring reciprocal role pattern (RRP) structured around the dimensions of 'abandoning–abandoned'. The theme of power and control, represented in his relationship to early care-giving figures, was picked up both in some of the dilemmas positively identified in the psychotherapy file and in the early transference to the therapist suggesting the operation of an RRP based around the dimensions of 'controlling–controlled'.

The therapy

The early sessions of therapy were spent obtaining a sense of Phillip's history and discussing his response to the psychotherapy file. Before the start of the third session, Phillip left in the empty waiting room some confidential files which he had brought with him from his office. He returned to the waiting room in order to collect these files. Upon re-entering the consulting room he explained that he would have to leave therapy early that night as he had more clients to visit. The unconscious meaning of this event emerged over the course of the session when he described how as a child he might resist his father's overwhelming demands to be the perfect son by covertly failing at whatever tasks were set him. With the 'controlling–controlled' RRP in mind, an interpretation was offered to Phillip that he might need to resist the anticipated demands of the therapist to be the perfect patient in covertly sabotaging therapy by making it more important to be in other places. This opened up a discussion around his anxieties regarding people's capacity to take control of him. In session four he explained how this translated into a concern that were he to comply with others' wishes or requests, then he might feel submissive, anonymous and invisible. This occurred both at work and within his family and his response was one of anger, which in turn led him to retaliate by neglecting and ignoring others – something that connected him with the 'abandoning–abandoned' RRP.

After the completion of session five, a reformulation letter was prepared. This attempted to draw together the various strands of the assessment phase, offering a tentative hypothesis about the origins of his symptomatic problems, their links with particular problem procedures and some further additional suggestions as to how these procedures might be enacted in the transference to the therapist. The reformulation letter was read out to Phillip at the beginning of the session, marking the transition from the assessment phase of therapy to an active treatment phase.

Dear Phillip

I said I would write down some of the themes that have emerged in therapy so far. You came to therapy describing recurrent feelings of failure and difficulties in being with other people. So far, we have examined these problems in relation to what you recall as an unempathic family in which you felt compelled to be the perfect son to a father whom you described as controlling and authoritarian. When you were 8 you were sent away to boarding school and this seems to have compounded your feelings of emptiness and aloneness. Perhaps at an unconscious level you have experienced this as a punishment for failing to be the perfect son that you assumed your father wanted you to be? It may be the case that these early experiences sensitized you to issues of feeling abandoned and controlled. Over the years these have become integrated into a type of dilemma in which you either felt you had to succumb to being the perfect son as required by your father, something associated with you losing your own sense of identity, or you resisted these demands and risked rejection and abandonment?

From what you have told me so far, it seems that for much of your adult life these issues have represented opposite ends of a psychological spectrum that you have sought to negotiate in an often precarious way. In relation to both your professional and personal life we have examined the need for you to remain in some way separate and different from both your family and work colleagues. With your family this seems to have taken the form of you appearing unreachable. At work it may have taken the form of what you have described as 'dropping clangers' – something that alienates and distances you from your colleagues. At one level perhaps this represents you seeking to be separate from the demanding father who wanted to create the perfect son? However, by achieving separateness you are put in touch with feelings of being cast out and rejected. In this state your self-worth is very low and you seek to restore self-esteem by working hard to regain the attention and admiration of others. Perhaps it is the sense of desperation which you experience when this cycle is at its most intense that leads you to break down?

I feel that in therapy we have begun both to explore and witness the acting out of some of these issues in your relationship with me. I wonder if this has expressed itself in a conflict about on the one hand wanting therapy, but on the other worrying about the way in which the relationship with me might compromise your sense of separateness. One way of looking at these issues would be to see them as a set of polarized choices or dilemmas. Perhaps these can be expressed as follows:

- Either I strive to feel safe from others by being in control, or I risk being compliant and controlled.
- Either I push others away, exist on my own, feel in charge but rejected, or I am with other people, feeling engulfed, invisible and taken over.

Over the course of therapy I hope we can continue to explore these issues and to look for some way out of them.

Phillip commented that the reformulation letter encapsulated many of his difficulties, but was hesitant over the wording of the target problem procedures (TPPs). He insisted that the wordings of these TPPs should be correct and between sessions six and eight continued to agonize over them. The focus during these sessions became an exploration of his anxiety regarding this issue. At session eight he arrived late for therapy and produced a copy of the rating sheet (CAT patients are required formally to rate their capacity to recognize and revise TPPs on a linear analogue scale) on which he had inscribed an edited version of the TPPs. His inscription, however, had been carried out over that part of the sheet where he was supposed to rate his continuing progress – something that prevented rating from occurring. This 'error' was taken up with Phillip as the enactment of the 'controlling–controlled' RRP in which he had again responded to the threat of the engulfing, controlling therapist/father through covert non-compliance – a response which enabled him to remain with me in therapy on his own terms and therefore at a safer distance.

The need to walk the tightrope between engulfment and abandonment became one of the major foci of the middle sessions of CAT. This conflict was represented schematically in Phillip's Sequential Diagrammatic Reformulation (SDR) (see Figure 11.1).

The creation of the SDR seemed to clarify for Phillip the manner in which anxieties about engulfment had led him defensively to push away and reject others. The SDR also served to sharpen his awareness of these issues in the reciprocal role patterns enacted with the therapist. In this respect his lateness for sessions, the struggle which he reported at the beginning of each session to get to therapy (he described a constant battle to arrive on time) and his frustration at not being able to change the time of therapy (he had previously remonstrated that the time of therapy was not convenient for him) were taken up as a type of compromise in which he was able to remain in therapy, but always at a distance maintained around conflict and rejection.

Slow, steady interpretations of the enactments of these RRPs, both within and outside therapy, appeared to enhance his level of insight, enabling him partially to disengage from their grip. Change, however, brought both anger for his childhood experience of neglect and domination and sadness due to the way in which such anxieties had led him to keep his family members at

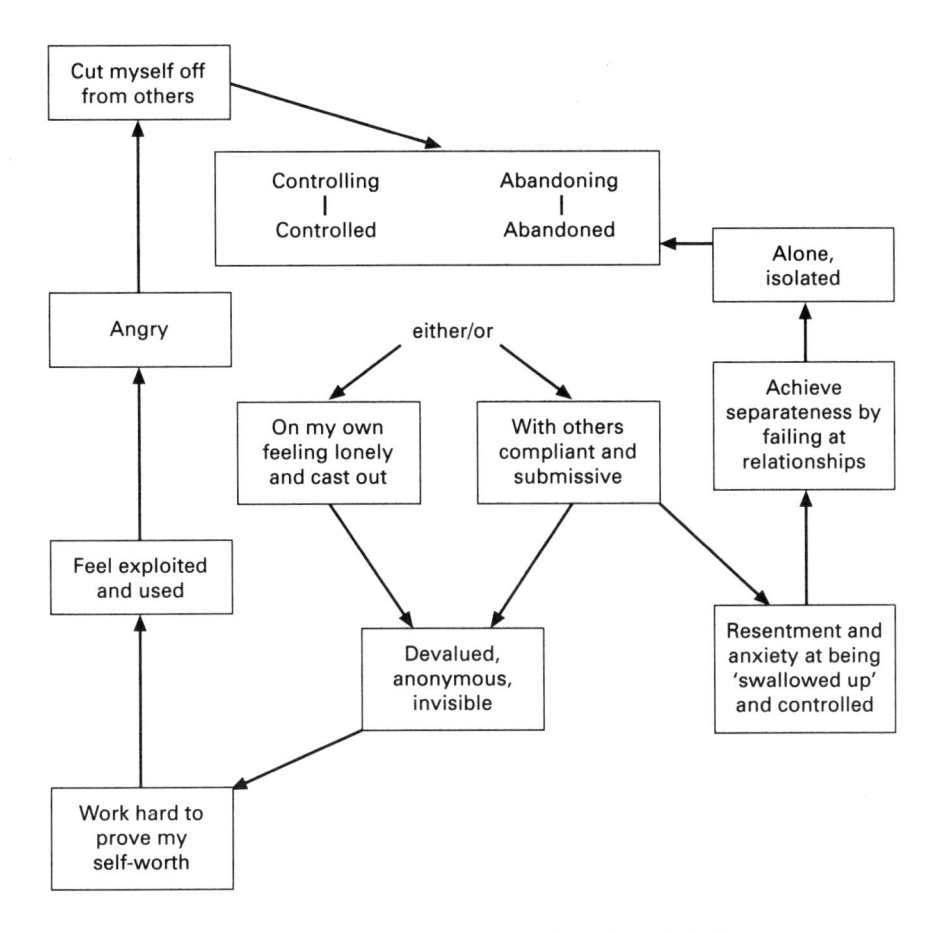

```
                                    ┌─────────────────────────────────┐
┌──────────────┐                    │ Controlling      Abandoning     │
│ Cut myself off│───────────────────▶│     │                │          │
│ from others  │                    │ Controlled       Abandoned      │                 ┌──────────┐
└──────────────┘                    └─────────────────────────────────┘◀────────────────│ Alone,   │
        ▲                                                                                │ isolated │
        │                                        either/or                              └──────────┘
┌──────────────┐                           ╱              ╲                                  ▲
│   Angry      │                          ╱                ╲                           ┌──────────────┐
└──────────────┘                         ▼                  ▼                          │   Achieve    │
        ▲                       ┌────────────────┐  ┌────────────────┐                 │ separateness by│
        │                       │  On my own     │  │  With others   │                 │  failing at  │
        │                       │ feeling lonely │  │ compliant and  │                 │ relationships│
        │                       │ and cast out   │  │   submissive   │                 └──────────────┘
┌──────────────┐                └────────────────┘  └────────────────┘                       ▲
│Feel exploited│                          ╲                ╱                                  │
│  and used    │                           ╲              ╱                         ┌──────────────┐
└──────────────┘                            ▼            ▼                          │ Resentment and│
        ▲                              ┌──────────────────┐                         │ anxiety at being│
        │                              │    Devalued,     │                         │  'swallowed up' │
        │                              │    anonymous,    │                         │  and controlled │
        │                              │    invisible     │                         └──────────────┘
┌──────────────┐                       └──────────────────┘
│ Work hard to │                                  ▲
│  prove my    │──────────────────────────────────┘
│  self-worth  │
└──────────────┘
```

Figure 11.1 *Phillip's Sequential Diagrammatic Reformulation (SDR)*

arm's length, thereby denying the possibility of a more intimate and fulfilling relationship. In session sixteen Phillip was presented with a 'goodbye letter' that brought the issues together and acknowledged his enhanced ability to recognize these repetitious procedures. At follow-up he confirmed a continuing awareness of the operation of these procedures along with a fantasy of starting his life again as though having a 'blank sheet on which I could begin to write a new diagram'. This wish was tempered, however, by a more realistic wish to repair some of the damage effected in his relationship with his wife and children by exiting from the vicious cycle of rejection and conflict which he had set up with them.

Wider implications and applications

To date, CAT has been most widely developed as a form of short-term individual therapy. In this respect its application has been described with psychotherapy outpatient populations (Brockman et al., 1987), with the clientele of social service departments (Maple, 1988), with patients in general practice (Curran, 1990) and in forensic settings (Brockman and Smith, 1990; Pollock, 1996). Its application has also been described in relation to groups (Duignan and Mitzman, 1994; Maple and Simpson, 1995) and couples (Ryle, 1990). Recently CAT's concepts have also been applied to an understanding of organizations (Walsh, 1996) and as a means for examining the dynamics between community mental health teams (Dunn and Parry, 1997) and their more damaged, long-term clients. CAT has also been promoted as a treatment approach with self-harming clients (Cowmeadow, 1994), with health issues such as poorly controlled diabetes (Fosbury, 1994) and eating disorders (Denman, 1995).

We also noted earlier how CAT has, in part, developed as a treatment approach suitable for work with those traditionally identified as either inaccessible to treatment or unmanageable. A number of theorists, for example, have argued the case for the use of CAT in the treatment and management of personality disordered clients (Beard et al., 1990). An emerging literature has developed in the application of CAT to borderline personality disorder (Marlowe, 1994; Ryle, 1995a) and has culminated in Ryle's *Cognitive Analytic Therapy and Borderline Personality Disorder* (Ryle, 1997a).

Training in CAT

Under the auspices of the Association of Cognitive Analytic Therapists (ACAT), training in CAT is now widely available at both regional and national levels. A diverse range of professionals is involved in training which is currently available at two levels.

Practitioner level training

This is a two-year course run in a number of regions throughout the UK. The course entitles therapists to practise CAT under the auspices of their own profession and comprises case supervision and theoretical lectures. Students are also required to undertake a 16-session CAT personal therapy while in training.

Psychotherapy level training

This is a three-year course held in London, the successful completion of which leads to registration as a psychotherapist within the UKCP's division of Humanistic and Integrative Psychotherapy. ACAT has also developed an 'Accreditation of Prior Learning' process, which allows trainees to attain accreditation in an individualized way both through the recognition of prior psychotherapy training and modularized learning. For those wishing to pursue enquiries regarding training, the contact address for ACAT is: Association of Cognitive Analytic Therapists, Munro Clinic, Guys Hospital, London SE1 9RT. Telephone 0171-955-2906.

Future developments

CAT has evolved over the last two decades to establish a secure niche within the infrastructure of British psychotherapy. This is reflected both in the growth and demand of training for therapy and through the establishment of a professional practice and training organization, the Association of Cognitive Analytic Therapists. Over this period of time a broad trajectory can be identified in which CAT theory and research has shifted away from more mainstream neurotic problems towards psychopathology associated with personality disorganization.

For CAT, success and the changes that accompany this success may prove a mixed blessing. Part of the difficulty for CAT may lie in the need to mark it out as a distinctive therapy that has an identity separate from those psychological therapies upon which its theoretical base is formed. The combined theoretical, professional and commercial pressures which underpin this may in turn lead to a degree of institutionalization that is at odds both with Ryle's expressed ecumenical values and the early integrationism which led to the formation of CAT as a coherent therapy.

References

Beard, H., Marlowe, M. and Ryle, A. (1990) 'The management and treatment of personality disordered patients: the use of sequential diagrammatic reformulation', *British Journal of Psychiatry*, 156: 541–5.

Brockman, B. and Smith, J. (1990) 'CAT in the forensic service', in A. Ryle, *Cognitive Analytic Therapy: Active Participation in Change*. Chichester: Wiley.

Brockman, B., Poynton, A., Ryle, A. and Watson, J. (1987) 'Effectiveness of time limited therapy carried out by trainees: comparison of two methods', *British Journal of Psychiatry*, 151: 602–10.

Cowmeadow, P. (1994) 'Deliberate self harm and cognitive analytic therapy', *International Journal of Short Term Psychotherapy*, 9: (2/3): 135–50.

Curran, A. (1990) 'CAT in general practice', in A. Ryle, *Cognitive Analytic Therapy: Active Participation in Change*. Chichester: Wiley.

Denman, F. (1995) 'Treating eating disorder using CAT: two case examples', in A. Ryle (ed.), *Cognitive Analytic Therapy: Developments in Theory and Practice*. Chichester: Wiley.

Duignan, I. and Mitzman, S. (1994) 'Change in patients receiving time limited cognitive analytic group therapy', *International Journal of Short Term Psychotherapy*, 9: 151–60.

Dunn, M. and Parry, G. (1997) 'A formulated care plan approach to caring for people with a borderline personality disorder in a community mental health service setting', *Clinical Psychology Forum*, 104: 19–22.

Fosbury, J.A. (1994) 'Cognitive analytic therapy with poorly controlled insulin dependent diabetics', in C. Coles (ed.), *Psychology and Diabetes Care*. Chichester: PMH Production.

Kelly, G. (1955) *The Psychology of Personal Constructs*. New York: Norton.

Leighton, T. and Ryle, A. (1995) 'How analytic is CAT? A discussion between Tim Leighton and Anthony Ryle', in A. Ryle (ed.), *Cognitive Analytic Therapy: Developments in Theory and Practice*. Chichester: Wiley.

Leiman, M. (1994) 'The development of cognitive analytic therapy', *International Journal of Short Term Psychotherapy*, 9 (2/3): 67–81.

Leiman, M. (1997) 'Procedures as dialogical sequences: a revised version of the fundamental concept in cognitive analytic therapy', *British Journal of Medical Psychology*, 70 (2): 193–207.

Maple, N.A. (1988) 'Cognitive analytic therapy as part of a social services team', *Social Services Research*, 2: 18–28.

Maple, N. and Simpson, I. (1995) 'CAT in groups', in A. Ryle (ed.), *Cognitive Analytic Therapy: Developments in Theory and Practice*. Chichester: Wiley.

Marlowe, M. (1994) 'CAT and borderline personality disorder: restricted reciprocal role repertoires and subpersonality organisation', *International Journal of Short Term Psychotherapy*, 9: 161–9.

Marzillier, J. and Butler, G. (1995) 'CAT in relation to cognitive therapy', in A. Ryle (ed.), *Cognitive Analytic Therapy: Developments in Theory and Practice*. Chichester: Wiley.

Pollock, P. (1996) 'Clinical issues in the cognitive analytic therapy of sexually abused women who commit violent offences against their partners', *British Journal of Medical Psychology*, 69: 117–27.

Prochaska, J.O. and DiClimente, C.C. (1982) 'Transtheoretical therapy: towards a more integrative model of change', *Psychotherapy Theory, Research and Practice*, 19: 276–8.

Ryle, A. (1978) 'A common language for the psychotherapies', *British Journal of Psychiatry*, 132: 585–94.

Ryle, A. (1982) *Psychotherapy: A Cognitive Integration of Theory and Practice*. London: Academic Press.

Ryle, A. (1990) *Cognitive Analytic Therapy: Active Participation in Change*. Chichester: Wiley.

Ryle, A. (1994a) 'Introduction to cognitive analytic therapy', *International Journal of Short Term Psychotherapy*, 9: 93–109.

Ryle, A. (1994b) 'Projective identification: a particular form of reciprocal role procedure', *British Journal of Medical Psychology*, 67 (2): 107–14.

Ryle, A. (1995a) 'The practice of CAT', in A. Ryle (ed.), *Cognitive Analytic Therapy: Developments in Theory and Practice*. Chichester: Wiley.

Ryle, A. (1995b) 'Transference and countertransference variations in the course of analytical therapy of two borderline patients. The relation to the diagrammatic reformulation of self states', *British Journal of Medical Psychology*, 68 (2): 109–24.

Ryle, A. (1997a) 'The structure and development of borderline personality disorder: a proposed model', *British Journal of Psychiatry*, 170: 82–7.

Ryle, A. (1997b) *Cognitive Analytic Therapy and Borderline Personality Disorder: The Model and the Method*. Chichester: Wiley.

Stiles, W.B. (1997) 'Signs and voices: joining a conversation in progress', *British Journal of Medical Psychology*, 70 (2): 169–76.

Van Schoor, E. (1996) 'The "technique technology" of brief psychotherapy', *Free Associations*, 6 (2): 258–75.

Walsh, S. (1996) 'Adapting cognitive analytic therapy to make sense of psychologically harmful work environments', *British Journal of Medical Psychology*, 69: 3–20.

12
ECLECTICISM AND INTEGRATION IN HUMANISTIC THERAPY

William West

Humanistic therapy is a broad term encompassing a range of practices which the individual therapist will tend to draw upon in an eclectic or integrative manner. Humanistic therapy developed as a 'third force' (Rowan, 1976) in psychology and psychotherapy in reaction to behavioural and psychoanalytic approaches. It is essentially a whole-person approach and seeks to engage with the client on physical, emotional, mental and spiritual levels of being. There is a therapeutic focus on the encounter between client and therapist in the 'here and now'. Humanistic therapy regards people as fundamentally alright and capable of change and development.

Humanistic therapy puts a great emphasis on personal experience, on respect for the client's reality and on their ability to make healthy choices and changes in their life with the support of their therapist. It is essentially an optimistic therapy embodying the American 'can do' approach to life. It can be experienced as individual or group therapy or as a mixture of both.

Development of the therapy

> Third Force Psychology, or Humanistic Psychology as it is called these days, came about because the psychologies which had become dominant in the first half of this century were felt to be oppressive. Psychoanalysis only seemed to address the question 'why?' and invalidated the patient's way of being. . . . Behaviourism . . . seemed heartless in its adherence to mechanical explanations and procedures. (Jones, 1995: 2)

Humanistic therapy developed in the USA in the 1940s onwards in reaction to the domination of academic psychology by behaviourism and of psychotherapy by psychoanalysis. Humanistic thinkers were very influenced by the European philosophical traditions of phenomenology and existentialism (McLeod, 1996). Key figures who contributed to the development of humanistic therapy include: Abraham Maslow with his theory of self-actualization (Maslow, 1970); Carl Rogers with his client-centred approach and encounter groups (Rogers, 1970, 1980); Fritz Perls with his distinctive Gestalt approach (Perls, 1969a, 1969b); Wilhelm Reich who was a major influence on humanistic therapy with his focus on body-work (Reich, 1972); and Robert Assagioli's spiritual approach, including the concept of the higher self (1980).

The development of this movement was strengthened by the founding of the American *Journal of Humanistic Psychology* in 1961 and the American Association for Humanistic Psychology in 1962. As an approach it became especially popular in California in the 1960s with the establishment of the first growth centre at Esalen in 1961. Humanistic therapy reached the UK in the late 1960s with the formation of the UK Association for Humanistic Psychology (AHP) in 1969 and the subsequent founding of its journal *Self and Society* in 1973 (Rowan, 1987). Subsequently, the AHP in the UK has 'reinvented itself on several occasions' (Jones, 1997). The focus is now less Californian. There is less emphasis placed on encounter and more on personal and professional development groups (Jones, 1997).

The humanistic tradition encompasses a number of separate approaches to therapy including person-centred, Gestalt, bioenergetics and others. In addition, existential therapy and transpersonal therapy, both of which share many of the basic humanistic tenets, are closely linked to humanistic therapy.

Humanistic therapy then is a blanket term embracing a wide range of therapeutic approaches which can give rise to a number of issues with regard to their integration. For example, do humanistic therapists touch their clients? The answer from body-based humanistic therapists might well be 'frequently' (West, 1994b), while the answer from person-centred therapists would likely be 'rarely if ever'.

Similar difficulties might arise if one considers how directive the therapist is. Person-centred therapists are non-directive or client centred (Rogers, 1970). In contrast a body-based therapist might suggest the use of bioenergetic postures or breath work (West, 1994a), or a Gestalt therapist the use of cushions (Perls, 1969b).

The work of some humanistic therapists will remain rooted within their particular school of therapy, for example, person-centred, Gestalt. Such therapists are likely to call themselves by their school rather than using the label 'humanistic'. Other humanistic therapists will draw eclectically or integratively on a range of techniques from more than one school. Indeed some training programmes are specifically labelled as 'humanistic'.

Humanistic practitioners as a group appear to be following the increasing trend towards integrative working in practice despite what they label themselves (Hollanders, 1997). In this context it is worth noting that humanistic psychotherapists within the United Kingdom Council for Psychotherapy (UKCP) form the humanistic and integrative section.

Perhaps humanistic therapy is best seen as an umbrella term for a range of overlapping but in some respects very different therapies. In the following section I will delineate some of the shared and common strands in these approaches.

Theory and basic concepts

A basic tenet of humanistic therapy is that *people are OK*. Indeed, a key transactional analysis (usually seen as a humanistic therapy) book is *I'm OK, You're OK* (Harris, 1972). Such a view of people does not deny that they are capable of violent behaviour, of acting in hurtful and selfish ways and so on. The assumption is that with the right kind of therapeutic support people will discover their innate decency and be able to live and act from that inner health.

A second basic tenet is that *people are holistic*, that is, they have a body, emotions, mind and spirit and live in interdependence with one another and all of creation. Although humanistic therapy is often seen as individualistic, a healthy outcome for anyone engaged in the therapy is inevitably holistic. From this perspective it follows that the therapy itself is concerned with working with clients at all of these four levels of their being, the exact balance varying with each client over time.

A third tenet is that *people can change and develop* and will, in a healthy environment tend, to *self-actualize*. Self-actualization is a key humanistic concept developed by Rogers (1980) and Maslow (1970). Rogers believed that with the right support people would move towards self-actualization, towards realizing their full potential. As a result, humanistic therapy centres on the growth of the client rather than on their dis-ease. This is a crucial distinction between humanistic and behavioural forms of therapy.

A fourth tenet is that *people are spiritual*, even if they do not engage with one or more of the world religions. Indeed humanistic therapy will often not consider religion at all unless that is what the client chooses to explore. There may well be a focus on experiencing the spiritual, on the common possibilities of peak or spiritual experiences, on the potential for the therapeutic encounter between client and therapist having a spiritual dimension and feel to it. Some humanistic therapists and writers on spirituality were led to form the *Journal of Transpersonal Psychology* in the USA in 1969. Transpersonal psychology became the fourth force in psychology. Many humanistic therapists embrace transpersonal ideas and practice but remain within the humanistic therapy world. For a detailed view of transpersonal therapy see Rowan (1993).

A fifth tenet is what John Rowan (1987) refers to as *abundance motivation*. By this he means that humanistic therapy does not view people as merely acting out of a deficiency, but that we also act for reasons of curiosity, creativity, a desire to achieve, to experience, and so on. Humanistic therapy is often talked of as the human potential movement, which conveys this idea of abundance motivation. Humanistic therapists regard the therapy as a process of growth.

The five basic postulates of humanistic psychology set out by Greening (1997) adopted from Bugental (1954) reflect and summarize the main strands of humanistic theory outlined above. They are as follows:

1. Human beings, as human, supersede the sum of their parts. They cannot be reduced to components.
2. Human beings have their existence in a uniquely human context, as well as in a cosmic ecology.
3. Human beings are aware and aware of being aware – i.e., they are conscious. Human consciousness always includes an awareness of oneself in the context of other people.
4. Human beings have some choice and, with that, responsibility.
5. Human beings are intentional, aim at goals, are aware that they cause future events, and seek meaning, value, and creativity. (Greening, 1997: 3)

Humanistic therapy is a *process* form of working in which the therapist engages with the client's process as it unfolds within the therapy room and outside in the client's world. There is less of a focus on intended or possible outcomes as the therapy centres on the unfolding process. It is even possible for a client to have a successful experience of the therapy and yet still remain 'uncured' of their basic problem (Totton and Edmondson, 1988). However, the therapy will almost certainly have changed their relationship to their particular problem.

Humanistic therapy is concerned with the *client's reality*. It seeks to work with how the client experiences life, with what difficulties and possibilities arise. It seeks to respect, clarify and work with the client's experience, suggesting possible ways of developing and exploring this. The therapist attempts as far as possible to bracket assumptions about the client's inner world and to be open to the client's view of their own reality, even though such bracketing is inevitably limited and partial.

Humanistic therapists very often draw their client's attention to what is happening to them physically, which may include how they are breathing. Some humanistic therapists will make use of physical contact, touching and holding their clients as a way of deepening the client's therapeutic process. However, this is a contentious area and some will never touch their clients.

Humanistic therapists will work with the sense of *contact* between themselves and their clients, focusing on the therapeutic encounter in the 'here and now', feeding back to their clients at therapeutically appropriate moments their sense of the quality of the contact made. Increasingly humanistic therapists are working with the therapeutic transference in a way somewhat akin to psychodynamic working. However, working in a very immediate way with the contact between therapist and client can change and reduce some forms of transference in contrast to the relatively more detached analytic way of working (West, 1994a).

In working with their sense of contact and with body awareness, humanistic therapists often talk in terms of energy, sometimes rather vaguely or imprecisely. Nevertheless, the energetics of the therapeutic encounter is important to humanistic therapy. Commenting on it, drawing the client's attention to it, or inviting the client's view on it often proves very valuable for the client.

Another key feature of humanistic therapy is that of *reflexivity*, that people are aware and know they are aware. One of the key features of the therapy involves working with the client's self-awareness in an holistic sense. This can include the possibility of the client being aware of more than one self, for instance the client may be aware of a transpersonal or higher self (Assagioli, 1980).

It will be apparent from the above that humanistic therapy places great value on the relationship between client and therapist. Humanistic therapists as a whole would recognize and embrace Carl Rogers's concept of the core conditions of empathy, positive unconditional regard and congruence (Rogers, 1951) as being necessary for a healthy relationship.

Humanistic therapists are as a rule relatively more active, indeed sometimes directive, with their clients, apart from those who are person-centred, and they are much more likely to introduce therapeutic structures into a therapy session. For instance, they may invite the client to make use of cushions as part of their therapy work, or employ creative visualization or guided fantasy and so on.

Psychological disturbance in general terms is seen by humanistic therapists as resulting from an upbringing and a current life situation that does not support the client in ways which allow them to grow and develop towards self-actualization. By providing such support within a safe therapeutic framework the client is enabled to begin the process of self-healing.

Practice and clinical issues

The goals of humanistic therapy, in keeping with its core philosophy of respect for the client and their reality, are a matter for the client to set in consultation with the therapist. Clearly the therapist will not agree to goals that are in contradiction to humanistic values, nor will they promise what they are unable to deliver. In general terms, the aim of humanistic therapy is for the client to be more self-aware of themselves as a person who functions at a number of levels – emotional, physical, mental and spiritual – and is able to relate to their world in a more alive, spontaneous and creative way.

I will explore the practice of humanistic therapy and clinical issues associated with it under the following headings: working with awareness; the therapeutic relationship; therapist as instrument; working holistically; bodywork and touch; groupwork; safety and ethics.

Working with awareness

Awareness is a key factor in humanistic therapy. It applies both to therapist and client. The client can gain a great deal from being invited to become more aware of what they are feeling in terms of body sensations, physical tensions, emotional states, nature of their breathing, and so on. It may also be valuable to ask them to become aware of their dreams and of how they react to their therapist and to the physical space of the consulting room. Heightening the client's awareness can have a huge impact on their therapeutic process, bringing to consciousness insights they were previously unaware of, which often results in a clearer sense of self. The therapist will use their own holistic awareness to guide the therapeutic process for the client's benefit.

The therapeutic relationship

The therapeutic relationship is a crucial element in humanistic therapy. Carl Rogers (1951), a key founding figure for humanistic therapy, insisted that if the therapist embodied the core conditions of empathy, positive unconditional regard and congruence and the client to some extent, however limited, perceived these qualities to be present, then the client would make therapeutic progress. Rogers not only insisted that the core conditions were necessary for therapeutic change, but also that they were sufficient. However, Rogers (1980) himself later questioned this conclusion with his concept of 'presence' as an extra condition. Today most humanistic therapists would take the view that the core conditions, while necessary, are not always sufficient.

Many humanistic therapists, especially those with a Gestalt (Clarkson, 1989) or Reichian bodywork orientation (West, 1994a), would talk in terms of the contact between therapist and client. The quality of this contact and the capacity the client has to make contact is explored in the 'here and now' encounter between client and therapist.

Many humanistic therapists these days work with the concept of transference and countertransference, namely that the client will at times unconsciously treat the therapist as if they are some key figure, often a parent, in the client's life. The therapist can in turn be led into a similar countertransference towards the client in which the client becomes possibly a child or some other figure from the therapist's life. The realness or congruence of the humanistic therapist may well make transference less likely to occur, or possibly harder to uncover. A useful discussion of countertransference from a person-centred perspective is provided by Wilkins (1997).

Therapist as instrument

This leads on to the notion of therapist as instrument: the humanistic therapist endeavours to be as fully present as possible for the client. In so doing, any reaction they have on any level, whether body, emotions, mind or spirit, is potential information about the client's therapeutic process. For example, I am working with a client and I have an overwhelming feeling of sadness. Is this my own sadness triggered by the client's exploring of their grief? Through my own personal therapy I am hopefully in a position to distinguish whether this is so. If not, is it a feeling of empathy with the client: am I feeling with them? Could it be that I am feeling what they do not want to feel and are pushing away? Finally, am I feeling what other significant people in the client's life feel around them? Possibly the answer is a mixture of more than one of these. In any case I need to be a clear instrument to register the feelings and/or sensations sensitively. I have painstakingly learnt over a number of years to distinguish between the above possibilities. The next step is to check out with the client in a therapeutically useful way what has been happening.

Working holistically

Humanistic therapists view people as having body, emotions, mind and spirit, existing in interdependence with one another and with the whole of creation. How this works out in practice in the therapy will vary from one client to another and between therapists. Working with the body will be explored in detail below. However, it needs to be made clear that humanistic therapy is not about cutting off one aspect of our being and focusing on that. Humanistic therapists will tend to move fluidly with the client as the focus of the therapy session shifts between body, mind, emotions and spirit. Sometimes a client will be encouraged to speak, to understand, to clarify; at other times to be quieter, breathe and listen to their body. On another occasion a guided fantasy may well yield insight into the client's spiritual state.

Bodywork and touch

With its focus on an holistic approach it is not surprising that humanistic therapists will often focus on the body, drawing their client's awareness to body sensations, muscle tensions, posture, breathing patterns, and so on. Wilhelm Reich (1897–1957) pioneered the use of a body-based approach and many of his ideas and techniques diffused into humanistic therapy via bioenergetics, radix, neo- and post-Reichian therapy (West, 1994a). In a culture that places emphasis on cognition and intellectual development, the focus on the body can prove a valuable therapeutic approach. Many of the bodywork techniques developed can provoke a strong reaction in clients and need to be used appropriately and skilfully by the therapist.

Groupwork

There is a long tradition of the use of groupwork by humanistic therapists. Carl Rogers (1970) pioneered groupwork on a client-centred basis using his core conditions in what he called encounter groups. However, there were at least two other versions of encounter groups that arose within the humanistic tradition (Rowan, 1987). The most popular, developed by Will Schutz (1973), is open encounter, where members sit on cushions and the leader works with a sense of the energy in the group and draws eclectically on a range of techniques from various humanistic approaches. A darker variation of encounter group was developed by Chuck Dederich at Synanon in his work with drug addicts and involves a high level of confrontation.

There has been a decline in the last decade or so in the number of encounter groups offered by therapists. Their place has been taken by single-school humanistic groups in, for example, Gestalt or bioenergetic therapy. Many clients can benefit from the appropriate use of humanistic groups, not only from the chance to experience directly therapeutic work within a group setting, but also from what has been called 'spectator' therapy (Bandura, 1971), namely watching someone else encountering similar problems to oneself.

Safety and ethics

It should be clear from the above that it is crucial that the therapeutic encounter occurs within a context that feels safe for the client and that the therapist behaves in a truly ethical manner. Humanistic therapy in particular needs to be conducted with the informed consent of the client and this is especially true when any use of touch or bodywork is introduced. All the training programmes for humanistic forms of therapy have clear ethical codes of practice, which clients are made aware of.

It should be apparent that there is no typical humanistic therapy session. The elements described above form the backdrop to the work and the case study presented below gives a flavour of how some of the techniques might be used in practice.

Indications and contraindications

It is important for humanistic therapists to be aware of their limitations and careful supervision of their work is necessary. Research into counselling and psychotherapy in general has shown that there is little to choose between the main orientations – that is, humanistic, cognitive-behavioural and psychodynamic – in terms of their effectiveness. However, cognitive-behavioural approaches have proved more effective with some conditions, such as phobias (McLeod, 1993). One possibility would be to use a combination of humanistic and cognitive-behavioural approaches.

A humanistic approach to therapy strongly supports the notion of consumer choice by the client and values the quality of the therapeutic relationship that is established. A humanistic therapist doubtful of being able to establish an effective working relationship with a client would not commence therapy with them and would seek instead to make an appropriate referral.

Humanistic training programmes for therapists cover assessment issues, so that they are able to recognize and refer on people too disturbed to benefit form individual or group humanistic therapy. People experiencing a psychotic episode, for instance, are not likely to benefit from the usual form of humanistic therapy offered. Likewise anyone with a heart condition or other similar physical disability would not be encouraged to use the more cathartic techniques available to the humanistic therapist.

When they first come for therapy, many humanistic clients typically report a lack of energy, a sense of not being in touch with their emotions or creativity, or of their life lacking meaning. Many humanistic therapists, perhaps those with a Gestalt or bodywork background, will attract referrals from clients who have already done some counselling and who are ready for a more deeper therapeutic exploration.

Case study

> It's always good fun to read about a therapist's clients and their sessions – as good as a novel. . . . But it is also very easy – in fact, inevitable – to over-simplify the wholeness of a person's life and struggle. (Totton and Edmondson, 1988: 3–4)

It is impossible in a short case study, and using words only, to do justice to the fine detail and complexity of the unfolding that occurs in someone's therapy. It is even harder when writing about a client whose therapy occurred over several years. However, there are aspects to this client's therapy that I find of great interest and value, which illustrate some aspects of humanistic therapy.

Richard (name and other details changed to preserve anonymity) came to me for weekly individual therapy in autumn 1990, having previously met me on a humanistic therapy group I had facilitated the previous spring. He had just completed his degree and had moved to the northern city in which I was then living. His parents were abroad in Hong Kong and he had no desire to live there with them. His main reason for moving was to get some therapy from me and to make some decisions about his future.

I felt a bit daunted by Richard's reasons for being in my home city, one of them being to seek individual therapy from me: it felt like something of a responsibility that might backfire on all concerned. Later on I was to realize the depth of the therapy work that he needed to do on himself, but also his health, his ability to cope with his therapy journey and to make a new life for himself.

Richard was fresh-faced and in his early twenties. He was personable and attractive, but a little unsteady on his feet which suggested to me a lack of grounding, probably connected with his inability to express anger and rage. Although he could feel sadness he rarely expressed this through tears. His eyes could be bright and alive, but also dull, as if he were no longer present. He said that he felt safe in his head, but not very present in his body, especially his chest and heart.

He had an aggressive, cold, opinionated father and a softer, warmer mother whose side he had learnt to take in the frequent family rows in which she always gave in to his father. His father was often absent from home because of his work.

Several issues were soon apparent: Richard's need to move out of his academic mode and into a more physical sense of himself – 'out of my head and into my body'; an overbearing father; and what the hell he was going to do with his life now he was no longer in the education system. The immediate issues he needed to address were around becoming settled in the city, making friends and seeking work.

At times in those early days of his therapy I found myself becoming overly helpful and turned into, from his point of view, an authoritarian father figure pushing him to face decisions. With his keen interest in astrology he saw this as a saturnine aspect of me. I took this countertransference on my part to supervision, recognizing that he reminded me of myself in my early twenties.

It seemed necessary for Richard to throw off such saturnine structures reflected in his overbearing father, his boarding school and university. So for him there was a time of not working, of playing music, reading, starting a computer course and quitting, and so on. These were his explorations, doing what he wanted, learning for himself and making his own mistakes.

I was well able to trust what was happening for him despite my fears about him. I felt confident that sooner or later he would bottom out. I also expected that what seemed like a deep caring impulse in him would come through to a point where he would perhaps begin some kind of caring work.

Meanwhile Richard's weekly therapy sessions had become focused for a while on the meaning of his bedwetting episodes as a child at home and at boarding school. It seemed important for him to acknowledge and then express his anger, his 'protest' as he saw it, that appeared to be at the root of this problem. Inviting him to lie down on the therapy mattress and to deepen his breathing helped him reach and express this anger emotionally and in a satisfying way.

A few months into his therapy he began work at a day centre for the mentally ill as part of a government training scheme. Here his openness to people and the comparative lack of clear boundaries between him and others was to be well tested and work with these issues became an increasingly important part of the therapy.

At this stage Richard's therapy felt to be going well. He had addressed many of the issues that had brought him to therapy and I began to feel that maybe his therapy work was over, or perhaps a new phase was about to begin. Around this time he began to drink quite seriously on occasion. It did not strike me that he was an alcoholic as such, more that he was drinking for a release of some kind. Then one Saturday morning I received a phone call from him. He was in a state. He had got very drunk the night before and various incidents had occurred, resulting eventually in a smashed window at his house, from which he sustained a gash in his arm that needed treatment at casualty.

This was in many ways a turning point for him. He felt that a hidden part of himself was communicating with him, and that the gash on his arm represented a message from that part of him. Inevitably the direction taken in this therapy was to give that part of him a voice:

> R: I just feel so frustrated. [*At this point he pounded a cushion.*] I just feel so frustrated. [*Said increasingly loudly and angrily.*]
> C: Who are you frustrated with?
> R: YOU! [*Again further rhythmic pounding on the cushion.*]
> C: Who am I?
> R: William [*expletive*] West.
> C: Who are you really angry with?
> R: I don't [*expletive*] know! Yes, my blasted father!

Again the unacceptable rage against his father: a rage that his father would not allow him to have, which if he showed any signs of expressing it would result in a beating. From then on his therapy work became even more serious and deeper, with a real and increasingly successful attempt to face himself.

This involved further challenging work that inevitably included me. In one session I found myself in a confrontation with Richard and I had the image that we were two bull elephants fighting for who was to be head of the herd. Feeling my way into the part, I said that I was afraid he would hurt and humiliate me (this was what his father had always done in fights with him). However, he said that this was not what he wanted; we locked arms and growled at each other, he with more emotion and meaning than me. We both found it exhilarating.

This seemed to me a very important session for him. It felt like part of a healthy male form of initiation, an initiation that had not been completed for him with his father. It seemed that much of his therapy at that time was in the territory of boys becoming men, with the help of their fathers and other older men.

Soon afterwards Richard landed a permanent job in a day care centre, which represented his choice, his way forward, his autonomy. His therapy work became increasingly 'here and now', focusing on how he was in the therapy room and what was happening in the therapeutic relationship with me, with occasional references to issues outside in his life. Gradually it became apparent that his therapy work was coming to a natural close and fittingly the final session seemed to have something of a ritual feel to it.

Wider implications and applications

Many therapists in private practice or employed as counsellors in the health service or at college and universities regard themselves as client centred. Perhaps only a minority of these would call themselves humanistic therapists, even though their essential therapeutic philosophy could be seen as humanistic. The Association for Humanistic Psychology (AHP) continues to thrive in the UK and has a practitioner group, the Association for Humanistic Psychology Practitioners (AHPP), which accredits humanistic practitioners under various categories including 'psychotherapist'. It is a member organization of the UK Council for Psychotherapy (UKCP). The AHP can provide details of various humanistic training courses in the UK and its journal, *Self & Society*, gives some details of groups. The Person-Centred Approach Institute (GB) can provide details of person-centred psychotherapy training in the UK.

Carl Rogers called one of his later books *A Way of Being*, and for many people the humanistic approach to therapy is also an approach to life. Rogers himself pioneered the use of his core conditions with students in student-centred learning. Many people of a humanistic persuasion have followed in his footsteps, applying his principles in educational settings both in the USA, UK and elsewhere in Europe.

Humanistic ideas have also had a tremendous impact in the sphere of work, especially in business management both in more traditional and in newer work settings including co-operatives and more informal work groups. 'Much of what is valuable in management theory today comes from humanistic psychology' (Rowan, 1987: 26).

Humanistic approaches have impacted on research into human behaviour especially of a qualitative nature, including research into counselling and psychotherapy and also management. There are a number of research approaches which reflect humanistic influences including human or co-operative inquiry (West, 1996), and heuristics (Moustakas, 1990; West, 1998a).

Carl Rogers pioneered the use of large, cross-cultural, residential groups of maybe 200 to 300 people which took place in South Africa, Russia, USA and Europe. Such groups continue on a regular basis to this day. Finally the emphasis on respecting the other person's reality and on acceptance of difficult emotions make humanistic therapy a natural part of conflict resolution and mediation programmes.

Future developments

Humanistic therapy has always been a place in which fresh therapeutic developments could occur. Indeed, the very range and scope of the so-called 'new' or 'innovative' therapies (Rowan and Dryden, 1988; Jones, 1994), which are often but not exclusively humanistic, seems at times bewildering. One danger is that: 'when a therapeutic system . . . emerges, imitators soon follow. They tend to take one small portion of the system and augment it until what was a complete therapeutic process is reduced to a fad, an emotional cliché (Rebillot, 1996: 20).

Thankfully there are now fewer new therapies being invented and the focus is more on innovation of technique along with cross-fertilization and integration, both among the various humanistic approaches and among non-humanistic therapies from the psychodynamic and cognitive-behavioural schools.

During the Thatcher years humanistic therapy seemed to be at times swimming against the tide but is now well placed to remain a significant third force in the therapy world as we move into the twenty-first century. Arguably, the requirement that the service sector prove its effectiveness, which has contributed to the focus on evaluation of therapy, has had a grounding and creative effect on the humanistic world. The huge increase in the numbers of counsellors and therapists in recent years in the UK has lead to the spread of client-centred and humanistic approaches in a way unimaginable 20 years ago. In a sense, humanistic therapy, like therapy as a whole, has come of age with all the opportunities and challenges which that brings. Humanistic therapy groups are due for a revival, perhaps with the increasing recognition that such groups provide value for money for some clients.

As qualitative approaches to research have also now become more accepted (Denzin and Lincoln, 1994), the value of humanistic approaches to human science research will probably become more widely recognized. The arts and literature have always been a natural setting for humanistic ideas and this too is likely to develop further, perhaps with growing interest shown in art therapy, psychodrama, drama therapy and biographical forms of therapy.

Many humanistic therapists welcome their clients' exploration of their spirituality (Rowan, 1993) and spirituality is expected to continue to be a key part of people's lives. Although traditional religions are in decline in the UK, the keen and ongoing interest shown by people in spirituality remains, as does the continuing phenomena of people having spiritual experiences (Hay, 1982; West, 1993, 1998a, 2000).

Perhaps because of the eclectic and integrative nature of humanistic therapy and its development as a third force in psychotherapy, it has tended not to cross-fertilize very much with psychoanalytic and cognitive-behavioural approaches. However, there is a natural link that can and is being made with cognitive approaches (McLeod, 1996), so perhaps cognitive humanistic therapy will be one of the new forms of integrative therapy in the near future.

Whatever the actual future developments turn out to be, humanistic therapy in some recognizable form will remain the third force in psychotherapy, standing alongside cognitive-behavioural and psychodynamic approaches.

Acknowledgements

My clients over the years have lived out the reality of humanistic therapy and deserve my deepest thanks. My understanding of humanistic therapy has been sustained and developed over the years by my membership of the practitioners' group of the Post Reichian Therapy Association to whose members both current and past I owe a big debt. Other people who have contributed to my understanding include: the late Brian Wade, Lyn Arnold and Peter Jones. My wife Gay has, as ever, contributed greatly to this work, not least by careful proofreading. Finally my thanks are due to my editors.

References

Assagioli, R. (1980) *Psychosynthesis*. Wellingborough: Turnstone.
Bandura, A. (1971) 'Psychotherapy based on modeling principles', in A.E. Bergin and S.L. Garfield (eds), *Handbook of Psychotherapy and Behavior Change: An Empirical Analysis*. New York: Wiley.
Bugental, J.F.T. (1954) 'The third force in psychology', *Journal of Humanistic Psychology*, 4(1): 19–25.
Clarkson, P. (1989) *Gestalt Counselling in Action*. London: Sage.
Denzin, N.K. and Lincoln, Y.S. (eds) (1994) *Handbook of Qualitative Research*. California: Sage.
Greening, T. (1997) 'Five basic postulates of humanistic psychology', *Journal of Humanistic Psychology*, 37 (3): 3.
Harris, T. (1972) *I'm OK, You're OK*. London: Pan.
Hay, D. (1982) *Exploring Inner Space, Scientists and Religious Experience*. Harmondsworth: Penguin.

Hollanders, H. (1997) 'Eclecticism/integration among counsellors in the UK in the light of Kuhn's concept of paradigm formation'. Doctoral thesis, Department of Applied Social Studies, Keele University.
Jones, D. (ed.) (1994) *Innovative Therapy: A Handbook*. Buckingham: Open University Press.
Jones, D. (1995) 'Editorial', *Self & Society*, 23 (2): 2.
Jones, D. (1997) 'Editorial', *Self & Society*, 25 (4): 2.
McLeod, J. (1993) *An Introduction to Counselling*. Buckingham: Open University Press.
McLeod, J. (1996) 'The humanistic paradigm', in R. Woolfe and W. Dryden (eds), *Handbook of Counselling Psychology*. London: Sage.
Maslow, A.H. (1970) *Religions, Values, and Peak Experiences*. New York: Viking.
Moustakas, C. (1990) *Heuristic Research, Design, Methodology, and Applications*. London: Sage.
Perls, F. (1969a) *Ego Hunger and Aggression: The Beginning of Gestalt Therapy*. New York: Random House.
Perls, F. (1969b) *Gestalt Therapy Verbatim*. California: Real People.
Rebillot, P. (1996) 'Therapeutic fads – what's popular? vs what's true?', *Self & Society*, 24 (2): 20–1.
Reich, W. (1972) *Character Analysis*. New York: Farrar, Strauss and Giroux.
Rogers, C.R. (1951) *Client-Centred Therapy: Its Current Practice, Implications, and Theory*. Boston: Houghton Mifflin.
Rogers, C.R. (1970) *Carl Rogers on Encounter Groups*. New York: Harper and Row.
Rogers, C.R. (1980) *A Way of Being*. Boston: Houghton Mifflin.
Rowan, J. (1976) *Ordinary Ecstasy: Humanistic Psychology in Action*. London: Routledge and Kegan Paul.
Rowan, J. (1987) *A Guide to Humanistic Psychology*. London: Association for Humanistic Psychology Publications.
Rowan, J. (1993) *The Transpersonal, Psychotherapy and Counselling*. London: Routledge.
Rowan, J. and Dryden, W. (1988) *Innovative Therapy in Britain*. Milton Keynes: Open University Press.
Schutz, W. (1973) *Elements of Encounter*. Harmondsworth: Penguin.
Totton, N. and Edmondson, E. (1988) *Reichian Growth Work: Melting the Blocks to Life and Love*. Dorset: Prism.
West, W. (1993) 'Spiritual experiences in therapy', *Self & Society*, 21 (5): 29–31.
West, W. (1994a) 'Post Reichian therapy', in D. Jones (ed.), *Innovative Therapy: A Handbook*. Buckingham: Open University Press.
West, W. (1994b) 'Some clients' experience of bodywork psychotherapy', *Counselling Psychology Quarterly*, 7 (3): 287–303.
West, W. (1996) 'Using human inquiry groups in counselling research', *British Journal of Guidance and Counselling*, 24 (3): 347–55.
West, W. (1998a) 'Passionate research: heuristics and the use of self in counselling research', *Changes*, 16 (1): 60–6.
West, W. (1998b) 'Therapy as a spiritual process', in C. Feltham (ed.), *Witness and Vision of Therapists*. London: Sage.
West, W. (2000) *Spirituality and Psychotherapy*. London: Sage (in press).
Wilkins, P. (1997) 'Congruence and countertransference', *Counselling*, 8 (1): 36–41.

PART III

ISSUES

13
MULTICULTURAL ISSUES IN ECLECTIC AND INTEGRATIVE COUNSELLING AND PSYCHOTHERAPY

Colin Lago and Roy Moodley

During the last decade ideas about counselling and psychotherapy in a multicultural context have been developing gradually with a consequent increase in training possibilities, research and publications becoming available to practitioners. The actual practice of therapy with clients from different ethnic origins stimulates many questions. For example, why do ethnic minorities infrequently use counselling and psychotherapy services? If they do use them what are the reasons for early termination? Are there other cultural forums providing for the mental health needs of these groups? These questions have been addressed elsewhere (see Lago and Thompson, 1996; Moodley, 1998) and so we will not go into any details here, but suffice it to say that the research context for ensuring and developing good practice is still very limited.

The process of counselling and psychotherapy is constructed and constantly being reconstructed to attempt to meet the needs of those that engage with it. Issues of 'race', culture and ethnicity should play a central role in any formulation of therapy within the available theoretical models. It is becoming clear that there are theoretical limitations in the discourse of counselling and psychotherapy with relation to cultural diversity. Pedersen (1985: 45) asserts that 'there is no well defined consistency for cross-cultural counselling and psychotherapy either as a field or as a discipline'. He suggests that the developments thus far are the result of a few interested individuals trying to develop a process from much of the scattered material gained from related disciplines. Pedersen also indicates that the existing western European models of counselling and psychotherapy have been the only resources from which perspectives on cross-cultural counselling and psychotherapy have been gained.

Multicultural therapeutic competencies are extremely difficult to acquire, as inevitably we are primarily demanding of ourselves as practitioners to attempt imaginatively to 'indwell' and thus strive to understand the 'cultural' and psychological views of the world of clients who are culturally different to ourselves. This is clearly not the same as empathically indwelling in others' psychological views of the world who are culturally similar to ourselves, for here we have some semblance of possibility of understanding their cultural perspective as we (to a greater or less extent) share that heritage. But where both the psychology and culture are different then the task becomes much more formidable. (The term 'culture' used in this paragraph relates to all the aspects of society that one is influenced by and subjected to).

Complexities of terminology

In the following discussion of multicultural issues in eclectic and integrative counselling and psychotherapy we consider how issues of 'race', culture and ethnicity engage with these therapies. The literature on this subject is also beset with its own complexity in relation to terminology and the resulting implications this has for therapeutic practice. For example, the practice is variously called: cross-cultural counselling (Pedersen, 1985), inter-cultural therapy (Kareem and Littlewood, 1992) and transcultural counselling (d'Ardenne and Mahtani, 1989; Eleftheriadou, 1994). Other hyphenated synonyms exist such as Afro-centric (Hall, 1995) and anti-racist (Moodley, 1992), as well as black feminist and politicized counselling (Pankhania, 1996). Sue and Sue (1990) discuss the same issues under a more general rubric of counselling the culturally different. There is also a tendency to discuss multicultural counselling and psychotherapy under a more sociopolitical nomenclature of 'race', ethnicity and culture. These ideas are developed in Carter (1995) and Lago and Thompson (1989, 1996).

Contemporary practice in the USA is to term the whole field as 'multicultural' which is presently being hailed as the 'fourth force' in counselling (Pedersen, 1991). Fassinger and Richie (1997: 83) suggest that in this paradigmatic change, in which the 'fourth force' is related to the 'dynamic, reciprocal relationship between intrapsychic forces and environmental influences related to one's cultural milieu' that 'counsellors are trained to think complexly, rather than categorically' (p. 84). This is refreshing given that the history of labelling ethnic minorities in the UK is problematic and beset with complexity and controversy. However much these labels may have their own unique meanings, McLeod (1993) asserts that all approaches are essentially about the race, culture and ethnic identity of the participants engaged in the counselling process. Our own intentions in writing this chapter are to encourage the reader to both critically examine their use of language and concepts within multicultural encounters and to recognize the complexity of the changes that occur in language use over time. Our overall concern is obviously to support the optimum delivery of sensitive, competent counselling practice in multicultural settings.

Assumptions, theoretical approaches and authors' limitations

Clearly it seems there are various ways in which counselling and psychotherapy with minorities is practised. In counselling the culturally different client, eclectic and integrative approaches are strongly recommended (Fassinger and Richie, 1997; Ponterotto, 1997) since potentially they offer the client a process that is broadly based and flexible. Any one 'purist' approach carries the danger of exposing the client to the hidden Eurocentric assumptions that are invariably present in conventional therapies. Another reason for advocating eclectic and integrative approaches with the culturally diverse is an understanding that members from these communities are already engaging in a form of socio-political eclecticism and so are skilled at understanding themselves in relation to different and sometimes opposing perceptions of themselves and their environment. In this chapter we have included:

- a brief review of the background and history of counselling and therapy in terms of 'race', culture and ethnicity;
- a discussion relating to issues of cultural sensitivity, world views and universal approaches.

In considering clinical issues we have focused on some specific aspects of clinical practice such as empathy, non-judgementalism, congruency and interpreting the transference. This is done through the discussion of a case study of a client in therapy with one of the authors.

A word of caution is included here for the reader in relation to the authors' views. Both authors are clinically experienced and have taught counselling. Their preferred theoretical models – person centred and psychoanalytic, do not comfortably fit into the integrative and eclectic schools. However, they remain open to many ideas but feel it incumbent to confess this 'lack' within the overall theoretical domain of this book. Their concerns, however, for sensitive informed practice in multicultural therapy are paramount and it is from this perspective and commitment that they have written this chapter.

Historical attachments

The history of counselling and psychotherapy in particular is rooted not only in its philosophical context but has been shaped very much by its social and political contexts. Sashidharan (1990: 8) reminds us of psychiatry's position that is 'rooted in colonialism and in the theories of racial differentiation'. In this sense counselling and psychotherapy are no different. This understanding has increased the development of a critique of multicultural therapy supported by theoretical ideas from post-structuralism, post-colonial and feminist theory. Some of the past ideas from 'race thinking' (Husband, 1982) still appear in the therapeutic processes today. Working with cultural diversity has always raised the objection that a single approach is problematic because its origin is located at a particular point within European culture. This can be further pinpointed as residing in particular individual people (usually men) who have developed the theoretical field, such as Freud, Jung, Adler, Klein, Lacan, Rogers, Ellis, Egan, etc. This realization begs questions of hegemonic patriarchy and negative masculinities.

During the 1980s and 1990s, the feminist movement, especially the French feminists, successfully interrogated the psychoanalytic movement for its gender bias in its theoretical formulations. The present critique through the discourses of 'race', culture and ethnicity still finds itself enveloped by themes that have repeated themselves viz. racism in the early literature of psychoanalysis (Thomas and Sillen, 1972; Dalal, 1988), cultural competence development (Pedersen, 1985; Sue and Sue, 1990) and socio-biological anthropology (Littlewood, 1990). The examples we offer below follow this pattern but offer a reminder that the background to any multicultural work in eclectic and integrative counselling and psychotherapy is made complex by this very history.

Racist theoretical underpinnings?

The initial tainting of the 'race' issue by Freud and Jung, for example, must be seen and understood in a wider historical context of the representation of 'otherness' socially, politically and medically when these authors were attempting to understand and articulate theories of human development and therapy. However, the racism that is inherent in their writing needs to be acknowledged and deconstructed. A reformulation of important and relevant concepts must be attempted and integrated in the development of the eclectic movement. For example, Jung postulated that the 'Negro has probably a whole historical layer less in the brain' (Thomas and Sillen, 1972: 239). This manifestly must be critiqued as racism but can also be seen in the light of other aspects of his awareness. At a further point in his writing he indicated that 'because the European does not know his own unconscious, he does not understand the East and projects into it everything he fears and despises in himself' (Jung, 1957: par. 8). The East here clearly being the 'other', as Jung understood it to be. Clearly Jung's position on 'race' was ambiguous and he obviously reflected more than the negative stereotyping of people from the 'Third World' than other writers of his time. According to Dalal (1988), Jung accepts stereotypes and only questions the deviation from them. Dalal offers a clear and detailed analysis of the deeply ingrained racist position that Jung took in exploring some of the major psychological processes he theorized. This useful analysis of the collected works of Jung reveals the state of thinking and the negative projections that found themselves in the analytical psychologies of this period. Although writers like Samuels (1988) and Rycroft (1988) accept the criticisms by Dalal, they nevertheless suggest that Jung's writing must be seen in the context of the thinking of his time and that value should be placed on the symbolic perception of his comments. However, valuing symbolic perceptions of those very comments is also problematic. What seems to us to be important is the possibility of using some of Jung's ideas in attempting to develop counselling and psychotherapy with minority groups and not engaging in the contradictions that have been highlighted in Eweka (1990) and the subsequent critique by Phillips (1991).

Even Freud seems to have failed to 'self-analyse' this process in himself, as his 'self' was inevitably a product of his time. Freud's contention that the unconscious was a place below – different, timeless, primordial, libidinal, separated from consciousness, unmapped, dark and without light – was said to be 'discovered' at the same time that Africa was being actively explored and exploited (Moodley, 1991). Being critical of Freud's racism is necessary but problematic if the consequences lead to a complete discounting of the theories embedded in psychoanalysis. Eclectic and integrative therapy with culturally diverse groups can benefit greatly from both analytic and humanist ideas on childhood origins of emotional problems. Psychoanalytic thought also embraces ideas on the importance of the unconscious, resistance and defences, and offers ideas on the therapeutic relationship, objective identification and splitting.

Contemporary suspicions of racist practice

Notions, indeed accusations, of racism in some areas of therapy have continued to the present day. Kennedy (1952), after treating two black women, observed that the cause of their neurosis was the result of conflicts arising from a hostile white ego ideal (cited by Carter, 1995). Sue and Sue (1990) indicated that minorities may be portrayed in professional journals as neurotic and psychotic. According to d'Ardenne and Mahtani (1989) the lack of sophistication in the host culture in understanding the impact of variables such as emigration, immigration and settlement has probably contributed to and significantly reinforced much of the racial stereotyping that already existed in the literature.

While much greater sensitivity now exists about counselling ethnic minority clients, the core processes still remain largely Eurocentric, ethnocentric and individualistic. As a way out of this dilemma and to avoid the stigmatization of this racist perception, the best option for the therapist might be seen to focus on the universal and world view models (Patterson, 1978; Pedersen, 1985; Sue and Sue, 1990).

The universal approach as problematic

A universal transculturalist model seems to place the multicultural counselling approach firmly in the realm of integrative and eclectic therapy where the clinical practice could be perceived as positively representing all things to all people. A therapeutic process that can be offered using sensitively and appropriately the ideas from different therapies to meet the needs of a heterogeneous, multi-ethnic, multiracial and multicultural group of people seems to fit the complexity of demands potentially made by clients. If this is possible at all, and indeed there are many questions raised about whether different philosophical, theoretical and practical strategies can be brought together, then we still have a situation that begs other questions. For example, McLeod (1993: 106) suggests that 'often, counsellors working in an eclectic mode may be relatively inexperienced and have limited training in the techniques they are employing'. Carter (1995) in citing Yee et al. (1993) suggests that despite the recent interest in diversity in counselling and psychotherapy the 'racial influence has not been well elaborated' (p. 23).

Clearly there are contradictions here. On the one hand, an eclectic or integrative approach appears to be best suited for multicultural work because of its flexibility and potential bringing together of the most appropriate aspects of all therapies to meet minority needs. However, such a process is likely to cause tension and suspicion among that community because it may be seen to lack direction and focus. In a situation where the counsellor appears to the client to be the 'cultural expert' (through life experience and knowledge) the counselling process could also be perceived to be problematic. Said (1978, 1993) offers a timely reminder in *Orientalism* and later in *Culture and Imperialism* by stating that 'the net effect of cultural exchange between partners conscious of inequality is that both people suffer' (p. 235). Perceived power differentials cannot be and must not be ignored within the multicultural therapeutic setting.

Pedersen (1985) suggests a process that was considered to be essentially client based rather than a counsellor generated one, called the 'cultural fit' or the conformity prescription. This asserts that the process is reformulated to fit the client. No doubt such a process as a tool in the hands of a culturally sensitive counsellor would prove to be an authentic empowering and therapeutic process. Our understanding of the 'cultural fit' model is that it would include theoretical ideas from a number of psychoanalytic, psychotherapeutic and counselling models, as well as taking account of the client's traditional practices of healing. A genuine eclectic and integrative approach where the process is altered, modified and reformulated to encompass cultural uniqueness and is conducted within the cultural norms and origins of the client's culture fits the 'cultural fit' conceptualization. If counsellors and therapists have also undergone self-exploration of their own 'race-thinking' and have a sophisticated awareness of their own cultural roots they will be in a better position to consider aspects of dissonance in their views of the client (countertransference, projections, stereotypical reactions, etc.).

Eclectic and integrative counselling and psychotherapy has an emphasis on individual autonomy and on the process of attaining optimum self-actualization. This process, however, if experienced outside the context of the social and cultural history of the client can impose additional aspects upon the client's false self (Lago and Thompson , 1997) with the danger of further exacerbating their condition, and thereby potentially increasing their anxiety and stress. Sometimes this could lead to more serious pathologies rather than ease the client's situation. Such an approach could also, through the focus on the individual rather than their collective group, separate him/her from the social and cultural archetypes which in normal times would have provided the boundaries for the ego.

A client who seeks counselling is in 'transition' (d'Ardenne and Mahtani, 1989), attempting to comprehend new realities and construct boundaries in relation to these states for a more integrated self. For some minority clients this can only be achieved through a group autonomy. Indeed this could be construed as a political enterprise. McLeod (1993), in discussing the relative merits of theoretically singular and pure approaches as against the eclectic method, suggests that there is a much larger question at stake. This relates to 'whether it is even in principle possible to create a universally acceptable framework for understanding human behaviour?' (p. 99). While it may be impossible or inappropriate for universal models to be developed, it nevertheless seems vital for counsellors to build a wide repertoire of theoretical frameworks, clinical skills and competencies to work with a culturally diverse group of people. The theory which underpins this thinking is based on the ideas that the meaning of illness for an individual is grounded in the network of meanings it has in a particular culture (see Good and Good, 1982; Littlewood, 1990). We would also wish to emphasize the suggestions made by researchers such as Doi (1963) who note that cultural ideas originating in one culture can be adapted and translated into the ideas, languages, and practices of another culture in the therapeutic process. The incorporation of cultural constructs that allow for the transferability of cultural paradigms into the therapeutic process will provide the therapist with the essential tool for effective intervention.

Cultural sensitivity

Several writers have indicated that the most important aspect of multicultural counselling and psychotherapy has to do with the levels of cultural sensitivity in the counselling process and in counsellors (Heppner and Dixon, 1981; Pomales et al., 1985; Wade and Bernstein, 1991). This has been emphasized, but not exclusively, as the acquisition of therapist skills and competence, knowledge of the cultural 'other' and an understanding of the world view of the culturally different client (Sue et al., 1992; Lago and Thompson, 1996). However, when culturally sensitive counsellors work within this broader flexible way the many implications of their knowledge and sensitivities to the issues of culture and 'race' could be anxiety producing for them. The dynamics of locating the presenting problem becomes complicated because there is no clear base line for a potential hypothesis. A multicultural trans-theoretical integrationist view on what the client shares could easily confuse and upset the therapist striving for sensitivity.

Therapist influence and power

As one example of the above point, it is not uncommon for some therapists to interpret that an Asian woman who refuses to accept an arranged marriage is experiencing a deep inner conflict living in a western European style civilization. This is a conflict between understanding the culture as an outsider on the one hand and the theoretical ideas underpinning therapy and validating individuation on the other. The therapist is potentially torn (consciously) in two directions (understanding the client's culture and constructing appropriate therapeutic responses), and influenced unconsciously in a third direction (by the implicit values underpinning Western cultural values and psychotherapeutic theory). Sometimes the therapeutic process in such cases seems to have managed these crises through the therapist's exerting an influence on finding a resolution within the therapy. Some aspects of the resolution for these clients, on hindsight, may appear to be out of context with their own ethnic cultural origins. Inevitably, the unconscious cultural hegemony of the therapist may have influenced the client's perception of various cultural characteristics such as fundamentalism and sexism.

Counselling sets out to be an open, equalizing partnership, yet the reality of such a democratic process is constrained by a number of oppressive and unequal variables for black people. Sue and Sue (1990) are critical of processes that are imbued with contradictions between the ideals of counselling and the actual practice concerning the culturally different. They maintain that while 'counseling enshrines the ideas of freedom, rational thought, tolerance of new ideas, and quality and justice for all, it can be used as an oppressive instrument by those in power to maintain the status quo' (p. 6). Counsellors and therapists (like others in society that unconsciously perpetuate prejudice and discrimination), are subject to inheriting and repeating these negative aspects of human relating within the process of counselling. It is through the subtlety of the 'countertransference' process that the projection of such unconscious inheritance is manifested, causing untold damage to the client's self by reinforcing the stereotypes of racial and cultural inferiority while at the same time espousing ideas of equality.

Is the answer a culturally matched therapist? In a study of black client perceptions by Wade and Bernstein (1991), culturally sensitive counsellors were seen to effect the process more than the 'race' of the counsellor. They point to culture and 'race' sensitivity training as the chief factor responsible for clients perceiving therapists as expert, trustworthy, attractive and empathetic. The study also found that counsellors who address cultural differences in counselling will positively affect clients' perceptions of counsellor credibility and attractiveness (also Sue, 1981), while those counsellors who lack cultural sensitivity, knowledge and awareness contribute much to the oppression of minorities (also Sue and Sue, 1990). They conclude that a humanistic process is possible if counsellors and therapists take responsibility to confront their own stereotypes and assumptions about human behaviour. Therapists also need to become aware of the client's world view and assumptions about human behaviour. In addition, therapists must take account of the historical, cultural and environmental experiences of the culturally different client. This appears to have been experienced by Phung (1995) who writes of her experience as a black client with a white male counsellor. The experience was one in which his 'openness', and his 'absence of defensiveness created a bridge of understanding'. Also his belief in 'justice', his 'interest in racism' and his acknowledgement of the 'difference in our worlds' had restored her 'faith that there were people who cared enough to want to heal the damage caused by racism' (p. 61). In addition, d'Ardenne and Mahtani (1989) recommend that counsellors examine their own cultural assumptions and develop a sensitivity to cultural variations and cultural bias of their approach when working with clients across cultures. These areas of core responsibility in multicultural therapy direct counsellors to the issues that need attention whatever their mode of practice.

Practical and clinical issues: Case study

Anna is a 26-year-old woman from North Africa who has been living in Britain for more than a decade now. As a result of experiencing bouts of depression she became withdrawn and uncommunicative at home and at work with colleagues. She decided to seek help. It was at this stage that she met with the therapist, one of the authors. The first issue confronting the therapist was whether or not to offer a handshake upon meeting. With many ethnic minority women, especially those from a Muslim background, it is taboo for men to make any physical contact, in or out of the counselling situation. The second issue that had to be faced was the building of an appropriate rapport with the client through the general opening conversation which accompanies the first contact. The development of a therapeutic relationship with some minority clients through the process of opening conversations can be anxiety producing. Clients from some ethnic minority communities, if not directly asked or invited to talk about their 'problems' and the kind of help or support they require, can tend to suspect a hidden agenda in the therapist. 'Small talk' (or light opening conversations) can be viewed as not being professional and competent. By contrast, a too direct interrogative beginning might be extremely offputting. Clients experience 'white institutional procedures' as often very formal, direct and non-humanistic procedures. How to start and how to begin to create sufficient ambience for therapy to commence can already prove problematic with culturally different clients, especially for white therapists not trained in multicultural counselling and psychotherapy.

The first session

In the first session Anna presented herself as being 'depressed in the general sense but not clinically depressed'. She was asked to clarify this self-diagnosis and how she came about understanding this. She replied that she was aware of her thinking, her behaviour and her feelings and she felt the issue was not physiological so did not warrant any medication. It was clear from subsequent sessions that she shared many of the symptoms of depression as suggested by Rowe (1983) such as feeling valueless and unacceptable to herself, which clients deem as real, absolute and an immutable truth in their lives. She talked much about her arrival in England as a post-graduate student, the isolation she felt earlier in her life in this country and the separation from her family. She felt that much had to do with issues of 'culture shock' and her own lack of understanding the specificity of the host culture. She felt that although she did not fully assimilate into the host culture she now considered that she was a 'part of society'. Indeed, her children were born here and 'spoke like a native of the land'. However, the feelings of not belonging were prevalent. She still felt 'culture shocked'. The therapist encouraged further exploration.

Counselling and psychotherapy has generally embraced the term 'culture shock' as a useful tool for understanding such a person's situation. From a cognitive-behavioural perspective, a person who is understood to be experiencing 'culture shock' may be offered help through the process of (a) identifying situations that cause anxiety in that person; (b) the therapist would then enable the client to discover new skills to reinforce stress-reducing behaviours. This approach could be perceived as 'training' people in the 'appropriate social skills'. Clearly a serious (and erroneous) assumption could be made here by a therapist considering the client's behaviour as the cause of their conflict without any reference being made to the environment which they inhabit.

Apparently, at work Anna was constantly reminded that she was different because colleagues only connected with her when the context was: 'multicultural', 'Third World', black, or when she was referred minority women students for advice and guidance. She also shared the difficulty of being the only black woman in her department.

At this point the therapist was conscious of the dilemma of whether to offer self-discourse which reflected similar or almost similar experiences. Sue et al. (1995: 723) in their review of studies that investigated therapist characteristics influencing psychotherapy conclude that 'there is some evidence to suggest that the degree of intimate self-disclosure and interest in a client's culture or race have favorable effects'. Yet therapist self-disclosure as an open-ended strategy may lead to over-identification on the part of the client. For the therapist it may also produce 'blind spots' that inhibit or prevent their full understanding of the client's perspective (Shapiro and Pinsker, 1973). Also, indiscriminate use of the strategy might produce methodological confusion in eclectic and integrative approaches.

Some implications of gender difference in transcultural therapy

Towards the end of the first interview session, the therapist and counsellor talked about the possibility of therapy in relation to the client's expectations, the therapist's method of working, times for meeting and the possible limitations on the therapy as a result of engaging in the process within the same organizational setting. She was reminded that the service offered male and female therapists and that she was free at any time to discuss a change of therapist if she wanted. The therapist explained to her that he would use a 'trans-theoretical integrationist approach' as a result of his training and experience. It was agreed that the sessions would be weekly for six weeks, each lasting about 30 to 45 minutes followed by a session to review the situation. Although the client did not seem overly anxious about these arrangements, she nevertheless pointed out at the beginning that she understood the process to be male constructed, referring to Freud, Jung and the discourse of some of the French and Anglo-Saxon feminist critiques on psychoanalysis. It transpired that Anna's research was in African women writers. In a sensitive way she also confronted the position of the process being managed by a male therapist. Clearly it seemed that the issue of gender was important to her both academically and psychologically. Counsellors and therapists have been noted, through their knowledge and impressions of the various cultures of their clients, to have changed their style of counselling to accommodate the perceived cultural qualities and differences of their clients. However, for male therapists according to Smith (1985) the problems in counselling black women are related to the counsellor's 'lack of awareness, sensitivity, and knowledge of Black women's history, culture and life concerns' (p. 185).

At a personal and reflective level the therapist noted that he felt a deep sense of awareness of such issues as Islam, ethnicity and gender, particularly the relationship of masculinities to concepts such as power and authority. He could not help thinking that such pre-countertransference must be dealt with. Dupont-Joshua (1994) cites Kareem's (1988) thoughts on pre-transference and countertransference: 'the therapist who has definite ideas about groups of people who are different from themselves, and who lives in a society which projects negative images about particular groups of people has a pre-countertransference towards clients from such groups' (p. 204). For example, when a therapist is aware than a minority client is going to arrive there has already been a countertransference reaction even before the client steps into the room. Although both therapist and client in this circumstance were apparently relatively culturally matched (both originating from the African sub-continent), it was nevertheless important for the therapist that he understood the heterogeneity of this particular therapeutic dyad. This also meant for the therapist that he understood and internalized Kareem's words personally and did not reserve it as a criticism for his white colleagues, as sometimes the theoretical debate on racism apparently allows minority groups to do.

Therapeutic approach

Rogers's (1951) 'core conditions' for therapist behaviour were seen to be essential tools for the process with Anna. Empathic understanding (perceiving and understanding the life experience of Anna by the therapist imaginatively placing himself in her experiential, psychological world), unconditional positive regard (a non-judgemental acceptance of Anna as a person), and the congruence in which the therapist engaged with Anna in the therapeutic relationship were core components of the work. They also, however, needed to be understood in the context of ethnic minority clients. For example, the concept of empathy, understood linearly as a bond of similarity between individuals, proves problematic, as Lago and Thompson (1996) point out by citing Jones (1987) who asserts that empathy defined in terms of shared qualities cannot occur. There is a need for an empathy based on differences that focuses the imagination upon transposing itself into another, rather than upon one's own feelings. In this way, 'psychotherapists might achieve a complete understanding of culturally varied predispositions, personal constructs and experience' (p. 140).

Anna's existing knowledge of counselling and psychotherapy directed the way she wanted to explore her own issues of distress and concern. She typed out her dreams and brought these to counselling for a few weeks. In a ritualistic way she would read her dreams to the therapist and try to explain the background to some of the people and images. For example, events of the day or days before, especially work scenarios, would reshape themselves into scenes that she felt were explaining racist events. Frosh (1989) in 'Psychoanalysis and racism' states that 'while racism is a social phenomenon, it operates at more than just the macro-social level. . . . [It occurs] at the level of social organisations and in encounters between individuals' (p. 229). Sometimes counsellors can feel that the issues of racism are for the social scientist.

Facilitation by the therapist of a more dense and focused nature of a few of the images brought the client realization that the unconscious works in symbolic and metaphorical ways to unearth the buried material of the past. Dreams 'may contain ineluctable truths, philosophical pronouncements, illusions, wild fantasies, memories, plans, anticipations, irrational experiences, even telepathic visions' (Jung, 1934: par. 317), and are a 'spontaneous self-portrayal, in symbolic form, of the actual situation in the unconscious' (Jung, 1945: par. 505). However, the therapist refrained from any interpretations that he felt would lead to a reductive analysis at this stage in the process remembering the words of Klein (1990: 4): 'Some people are so dominated by their pain that they cannot concentrate on much else. . . . They need to complain to us until they are sure we mind about their pain before we can educate them into taking an interest in its unconscious meaning.' She also argues that those who are not accustomed to a psychological way (European psychological) of thinking 'need time' to appreciate reflection and interpretation.

There is also the argument that psychodynamic and psychotherapeutic strategies are more conductive to western Europeans. We have come a long way from what Patterson (1978) thought about this idea:

> Westerners are more used to introspection, more ready and able to engage in self disclosure and self exploration. . . . Persons from an Oriental or some other culture, on the other hand, are more reticent, more modest about talking about themselves or personal relationships . . . psychotherapy as developed and practised in Western societies is not applicable in other societies. (Patterson, 1978: 234)

It is now becoming fairly apparent that using this argument, that the client's communication style problematizes counselling and psychotherapy with minority groups, is profoundly erroneous. We are also aware that some of the 'strait-jacket' theoretical positions held by practitioners negate any cross-cultural work. The eclectic and integrative approaches, it seems, have addressed this concern through clinical techniques which take account of what Patterson highlights, but at the same time they do not stereotype the client into universal categories.

The client's inner journey

Anna's exploration of her dreams went on for a few weeks. She seemed to like analysing her dreams through the symbols, reflecting on socio-political factors that contributed to her development, especially her childhood experiences. She was quick at deciphering the metaphors beyond the 'race' identity issue. It began to emerge that her childhood and upbringing were strictly Islamic and these values were in direct contradiction to the way she constructed her reality as an adult. Anna was aware that many of these learned childhood values infiltrated her relationship. For example, she would offer mixed messages about her role as an equal partner in the relationship and invite her partner to overindulge at her expense. At times she expected and demanded some of the 'inequalities' experienced by 'Third World' women or at other times projected a sense of dominance and matriarchy indicating that was more real for her. She explained these confusing positions as an expression of her upbringing in North Africa.

El Saadawi (1980: 13) offers an explanation of the kind of education a female child undergoes in Arab society. He states that: 'The child is trained to suppress her own desires, to empty herself of authentic, original wants and wishes linked to her own self and to fill a vacuum that results with the desires of others.' Furthermore, she states that Arab societies are 'passing through a transitional stage, and shifting over from cultural and social backwardness to a modernisim copied without any real understanding from the West. This modernization process does not prevent such societies from hanging on to many worn out traditions in the name of Islam and of Eastern moral values' (1980: 89). This seemed to be the process that Anna was undergoing within herself. Her search for the 'cultural primal scene', a return to the 'matriarchal womb' and a repositioning of her 'racial identity' were unconscious motivators in therapy. Women in Islamic societies who define an identity for themselves are struggling against the very fabric of that society. Such a process is imbued with the falsity of its construction and subsequently manifests itself in the development of the ego which is located in the imaginary. Removing the mutated layers and reaching into the depths of the real self through the images of Anna's dreams was a difficult and painful journey for her. But the 'illogicality; the indifference of the dreaming mind to convention and common sense, turned out to be of great value in forging new combinations out of seemingly incompatible contexts' (Koestler, 1964: 182). This provided Anna with the possibility of reframing her reality within the process of counselling.

The therapy sessions with Anna were generally held once a week. At the end of the contract of six weeks, a review took place and Anna continued for another eight months. Occasionally, however, the frequency was fortnightly or monthly. The sessions were also of different time durations (45, 30, 15 minutes). Here the therapist recognized and valued the fact that therapeutic moments can often occur outside Westernized, professionalized notions of conventional sessional times, particularly in multicultural therapy.

Opposing cultural values

An issue we would like to discuss before we conclude is one that confronted the therapist with the complex aspects of morality, cultural sensitivity, religious differences and human rights. The value base of clients and their cultures can confront directly and forcefully the therapists' own beliefs and truths they hold about the world. For example, in one of the therapy sessions with Anna, the 'subject' centred on the issue of clitoridectomy. Anna had undergone the operation as a child. At this stage in her life the issue was now disturbing her to the extent that she felt the culture of her childhood and her parents had collaborated to mutilate her. She talked about circumcision on both males and females in her society and within Islam. The therapist reflected to her that this might be how she felt in this society, feeling castrated in the context she found herself. She retorted back in anger that she felt that the entire culture was oppressive and managed by men to subdue women. The therapist reflected that the anger might also have something to say about their therapeutic relationship. She responded with increased anger: her voice, her vocabulary, her facial intensity and her hand gestures were staccato and strong, different to the usually composed person who sat in the chair. It was to her mum she said that she wanted to express her anger. The therapist suggested she tried the Gestalt exercise with the two chairs. She engaged with this exercise till the session finished. The therapist also suggested she might want to do some drawings but that she might choose not to bring them to therapy. The question that she posed at the end was: 'Isn't this a human rights question, really?' Then she departed. The therapist was left thinking about many other issues such as cultural sensitivity, castration complex, female corporal mutilation, masculine aggression, power and oppression. What she had said was most profound. Indeed it was a human rights issue.

As counsellors and psychotherapists we must engage with ethical issues, wrestle with objective morality and cultural sensitivity in recognizing that there is a reality in which human beings are oppressed, pained, hurt and killed and that we need to make our own stand against these oppressions (see also Lago and Thompson, 1989; Samuel, 1993). Woolfe (1995: 38) asserts that 'It would be nice if counsellors were able to work in such a way that they were able to contribute towards resisting the growth of oppressive forces rather than just deal with their consequences.'

Conclusion

Lane (1995: 38) suggests that 'it is now recognised that an interactive view of counselling is needed which approaches in a wholistic way the social, cultural, economic and emotional issues facing us'. In sharing the experience of Anna we have tried to show that issues of 'race', culture and ethnicity can be explored in a culturally sensitive and psychosocial way. The use of varying clinical strategies from different and sometimes opposing approaches in an eclectic or integrative manner is compatible with the idea of 'cultural fit'. However, we also suggest that it can become complicated and oppressive if essential aspects of therapist competencies such as cultural knowledge, 'race' awareness and tolerance of differences are not appropriately developed in the practitioner or demonstrated in clinical applications. An eclectic and integrative approach offers the opportunity for a psychotherapeutic process to engage alongside the socio-political. Clearly in a process where the cultural metaphors are interpreted alongside the psychological and politically constructed images the client is more likely to be empowered. This in turn empowers the practice, the therapeutic discourse and indeed discourse itself.

References

Carter, R.T. (1995) *The Influence of RACE and Racial Identity in Psychotherapy*. Chichester: Wiley.

d'Ardenne, P. and Mahtani, A. (1989) *Transcultural Counselling in Action*. London: Sage.

Dalal, F. (1988) 'Jung: a racist', *British Journal of Psychotherapy*, 4 (3): 263–79.

Doi, L.T. (1963) 'Some thoughts on helplessness and the desire to be loved', *Psychiatry*, 26: 266–71.

Dupont-Joshua, A. (1994) 'Intercultural therapy', *Counselling: The Journal of the British Association for Counselling*, 5 (3): 203–5.

Eleftheriadou, Z. (1994) *Transcultural Counselling*. London: Central Books.

Eweka, I. (1990) 'Counselling the ethnic minority client: pitfalls and some likely remedies', *Counselling: The Journal of the British Association for Counselling*, 1 (4): 117–19.

Fassinger, R.E. and Richie, B.S. (1997) 'Sex matters. Gender and sexual orientation in training for multicultural counselling competency', in D.B. Pope-Davis and H.L.K. Coleman (eds), *Multicultural Counselling Competency*. London: Sage.

Frosh, S. (1989) 'Psychoanalysis and racism' in B. Richards (ed.), *Crisis of the Self: Further Essays on Psychoanalysis and Politics*. London: Free Association Books.

Good, B.J. and Good, M.-J.D. (1982) 'Towards a meaning-centred analysis of popular illness categories: "fright-illness" and "heat distress" in Iran', in A.J. Marsella and G.M. White (eds), *Cultural Conceptions of Mental Health Therapy*. Dordrecht: Reidel.

Hall, W.A. (1995) 'Afro-centric counselling'. Papers presented at the Second National Black Access Conference, June, Sheffield University.

Heppner, P.P. and Dixon, D.N. (1981) 'A review of the interpersonal influence process in counselling', *Personnel and Guidance Journal*, 59: 542–50.

Husband, C. (1982) 'Introduction: "race", the continuity of a concept', in C. Husband (ed.), *'Race' in Britain: Continuity and Change*. London: Hutchinson.

Jones, E.E. (1987) 'Psychotherapy and counselling with black clients', in P. Pedersen (ed.), *Handbook of Cross-Cultural Counselling and Therapy*. New York: Praeger.

Jung, C.G. (1934) 'The practical use of dream-analysis', *Collected Works 16*, trans. R.F.C. Hull. London: Routledge and Kegan.

Jung, C.G. (1945) 'On the nature of dreams', *Collected Works 8*, trans. R.F.C. Hull. London: Routledge and Kegan.

Jung, C.G. (1957) 'Symbols and the interpretation of dreams', *Collected Works 18*, trans. R.F.C. Hull. London: Routledge and Kegan.

Kareem, J. (1988) 'Outside in . . . inside out . . . some considerations in inter-cultural psychotherapy', *Social Work Practice*, 3 (3): 57–77.

Kareem, J. and Littlewood, R. (eds) (1992) *Intercultural Therapy Themes, Interpretations and Practice*. London: Blackwell.

Kennedy, J. (1952) 'Problems posed in the analysis of black patients', *Psychiatry*, 15: 313–27.

Klein, J. (1990) 'Patients who are not ready for interpretation', *British Journal of Psychotherapy*, 7 (1): 38–49.

Koestler, A. (1964) *The Act of Creation*. London: Hutchinson.

Lago, C. and Thompson, J. (1989) 'Counselling and race', in W. Dryden, D. Charles-Edwards and R. Woolfe (eds), *Handbook of Counselling in Britain*. London: Tavistock/Routledge.

Lago, C. and Thompson, J. (1996) *Race, Culture and Counselling*. Buckingham: Open University Press.

Lago, C. and Thompson, J. (1997) 'The triangle with curved sides: issues of race and culture in counselling supervision', in G. Shipton (ed.), *Supervision of Psychotherapy and Counselling: Making a Place to Think*. Buckingham: Open University Press.

Lane, D. (1995) 'New directions in counselling: a roundtable', *Counselling: The Journal of the British Association for Counselling*, 6 (1): 38.

Littlewood, R. (1990) 'From categories to contexts: a decade of the 'new cross-cultural psychiatry', *British Journal of Psychiatry*, 156: 305–27.

McLeod, J. (1993) *An Introduction to Counselling*. Buckingham: Open University Press.

Moodley, S.R. (1991) 'A theoretical model for transcultural counselling and therapy'. Unpublished MPhil thesis, University of Nottingham.

Moodley, R. (1992) 'Interpreting the "I" in counselling and guidance: an anti-racist approach'. Unpublished keynote speech at Derbyshire FE Counselling and Guidance Conference.

Moodley, R. (1998) '"I say what I like": frank talk(ing) in counselling and psychotherapy', *British Journal of Guidance and Counselling*, 26 (4): 495–508.

Pankhania, J. (1996) 'Black feminist counselling', in M. Jacobs (ed.), *Jitendra: Lost Connections, In Search of a Therapist*. Buckingham: Open University Press.

Patterson, C.H. (1978) 'Cross-cultural or intercultural counseling or psychotherapy', *International Journal for the Advancement of Counselling*, 3: 231–47.

Pedersen, P. (1985) *Handbook of Cross-Cultural Counseling and Therapy*. New York: Praeger.

Pedersen, P. (ed.) (1991) 'Multiculturalism as a fourth force in counseling (Special Issue), *Journal of Counseling and Development*, 70: 4–250.

Phillips, M. (1991) 'Counselling the ethnic minority client . . . a response', *Counselling: The Journal of the British Association for Counselling*, 2 (1): 10–11.

Phung, T.C. (1995) 'An experience of inter-cultural counselling: views from a black client', *Counselling: The Journal of the British Association for Counselling*, 6 (1): 61–6.

Pomales, J., Claiborn, C.D. and LaFromboise, T.D. (1985) 'Effects of black students' racial identity on perceptions of white counselors varying in cultural sensitivity', *Journal of Counseling Psychology*, 33: 58–62.

Ponterotto, J.G. (1997) 'Multicultural counselling training', in D.B. Pope-Davis and H.L.K. Coleman (eds), *Multicultural Counselling Competency*. London: Sage.

Rogers, C.R. (1951) *Client-centred Therapy*. Boston: Houghton Mifflin.

Rowe, D. (1983) *Depression*. London: Routledge and Kegan Paul.

Rycroft, C. (1988) 'Comments on Farhad Dalal's "Jung a racist"', *British Journal of Psychotherapy*, 4 (3): 281.

Saadawi, N.El (1980) *The Hidden Face of Eve*. London: Zed Books.

Said, E.W. (1978) *Orientalism*. London: Routledge and Kegan.

Said, E.W. (1993) *Culture and Imperialism*. London: Chatto and Windus.

Samuels, A. (1988) 'Comments on Farhad Dalal's "Jung: a racist"', *British Journal of Psychotherapy*, 4 (3): 280.

Sashidharan, S.P. (1990) 'Race and psychiatry', *Medical World*, 3: 8–12.

Shapiro, E.T. and Pinsker, H. (1973) 'Shared ethnic scotoma', *American Journal of Psychiatry*, 130: 1338–41.

Smith, E.M.J. (1985) 'Counseling black women', in P. Pederson (ed.), *Handbook of Cross-Cultural Counseling and Therapy*. New York: Praeger.

Sue, D.W. (1981) 'Evaluating process variables in cross-cultural counseling psychotherapy', in A.J. Marsella and P.B. Pedersen (eds), *Cross Cultural Counselling and Psychotherapy*. Honolulu: East West Centre.

Sue, D.W. and Sue, D. (1990) *Counseling the Culturally Different: Theory and Practice*, 2nd edn. New York: Wiley.

Sue, D.W., Arrendondo, P. and McDavis, R.J. (1992) 'Multicultural counseling competencies and standards: a call to the profession', *Journal of Counseling and Development*, 70: 477–86.

Sue, S., Zane, N. and Young, K. (1995) 'Research on psychotherapy with culturally diverse populations', in A.E. Bergin and S.L. Garfield (eds), *Handbook of Psychotherapy and Behavior Change*, 4th edn. New York: Wiley.

Thomas, A. and Sillen, S. (1972) *Racism and Psychiatry*. New York: Bruner and Mazell.

Wade, P. and Bernstein, B.L. (1991) 'Culture sensitivity training and counselor's race: effects on black female clients' perceptions and attrition', *Journal of Counseling Psychology*, 38: 9–15.

Woolfe, R. (1995) 'New directions in counselling: a roundtable', *Counselling: The Journal of the British Association for Counselling*, 6 (1): 34.

Yee, A.H., Fairchild, H.H., Weizmann, F. and Wyatt, G.E. (1993) 'Addressing psychology's problem with race', *American Psychologist*, 48 (11): 1132–40.

14
INTEGRATION AND ECLECTICISM IN BRIEF/TIME-FOCUSED THERAPY

Jenifer Elton Wilson

> But at my back I always hear
> Time's wingèd chariot hurrying near.
> (Marvell, 1681)

Brief therapy has a distinguished history within the development of psychotherapy and counselling. It has been explored and developed within all the major orientations, although psychoanalytic and cognitive-behaviourist therapies have contributed more explicitly and for a longer time to this field than therapies with a humanistic orientation. In this chapter, the maturation of time-focused psychotherapy and counselling will be traced and current theoretical beliefs and practical applications described and explored. Subsequently, the author's own particular integration of classic and innovative psychotherapy approaches will be described and illustrated by a central case study. The chapter will close with a commentary on the broader consequences likely to ensue from the increasing use of a *focused, contractually committed* and *time-conscious* approach by practitioners of counselling and psychotherapy.

The presence of finite time as a major factor in all counselling and psychotherapy provides an inescapable integrative element in itself. In 'time-limited' or 'brief' therapies, time itself becomes the focus of the therapeutic encounter. Psychotherapy can be described as time focused whenever there is a designated closing date or a defined number of sessions. The circumstances demanding this precise specification may be client or practitioner driven, although the time limit is often set by a third party in the form of the agency or the organization funding the therapy. This apparent intrusion by an external agent into the working alliance between practitioner and client is one of the factors which has made the use of a time-focused contractual commitment an *issue* rather than an *approach*.

A more relaxed and flexible form of time-focused therapy is one in which there is an agreement between client and practitioner that there will be as few sessions as are necessary to resolve the client's present psychological distress and enable the individual to return, professionally unaccompanied, to their own journey through life, which can itself be engaged with as a therapeutic process. This agreement can be explicitly verbalized or may be a covert and pragmatic condition of the environment in which the therapeutic encounter takes place. Services providing crisis or trauma counselling, counselling services for students, employee advisory programmes (EAPs) or bereavement counselling agencies are all examples of the latter circumstance. For integrative and eclectic practitioners a *contractual commitment* defined by time offers an invaluable opportunity to practice with clarity and focus and to test out their own overarching combination of theory and practice for effectiveness and elegance. With this attitude, the apparent intrusion of the needs or demands of an external agency or organization into the therapeutic encounter can be made creatively useful.

History of time-limited therapies and their development towards current theory and practice

There is now a respectable body of literature describing the wide range of innovative developments in the field of brief psychotherapy. As mentioned above, these explorations have mainly been fostered under the umbrella of two of the three main theoretical orientations which inform the psychological therapies. Arising from a scientifically biased environment of academic and applied psychology, the *cognitive-behavioural* forms of psychological intervention have always been interested to arrive at clearly specified outcomes in the briefest amount of time and with the most economic expenditure of energy. From an early date, particular practitioners of *psychodynamic psychotherapy* have consistently questioned the received orthodoxy of psychoanalytic theory regarding the superiority of long-term psychotherapy (see Coren, 1996, for a brief overview of this process). A dazzling example of this challenge to post-Freudian orthodoxy is the work of Alexander and French (1946: 33–55) who boldly recommended the use of an 'Economic Psychotherapy', with its 'interruptions and termination of treatment' and its use of 'extra-therapeutic experiences'. Alexander and French (1946: 66–70) also introduce the more widely acceptable concept of a 'corrective emotional experience' as forming the main curative factor in any psychoanalytic therapy. In addition, their assumption that an emphasis upon a *core conflictual issue* is essential to effective psychoanalytic therapy now forms one of the main tenets of all time-conscious therapies, whatever the theoretical orientation.

It is at first surprising to note that the powerful and challenging influence of humanist and existential theorists upon the practice of counselling and psychotherapy has not extended to any widely accepted and significant model of brief psychotherapy. Although often unacknowledged, the influential concepts of Carl Rogers and his successors have modified the psychoanalytic therapies towards an acceptance of the centrality of the 'intersubjective' (Stolorow et al., 1994) realities operating in the therapeutic relationship. Above all, Rogers's emphasis upon the therapist's own congruence and genuine respect for the client as necessary, if not sufficient, conditions for psychological change have been adopted or discovered anew by most psychological therapists. However, these very conditions, of unconditional positive regard from the therapist and of the natural growth processes inherent in clients in receipt of therapeutic benevolence, have tended to work against the explicit use of clearly stated limitations of time by humanistic practitioners. This reluctance has recently been challenged by the demand for counsellors to maintain inflexible time boundaries in obedience to the resource restrictions of healthcare providers, insurance schemes and EAP agencies. Humanistic practitioners are searching for a practical approach which can be made congruent with their basic client-centred roots. Rogers himself only rarely acknowledges the need for an agreed time limit and then only when the therapeutic process had reached the final 'characteristic step', step 12:

> There is a feeling of decreasing need for help, and a recognition on the part of the client that the relationship must end ... there is neither compulsion on the client to leave, nor attempt on the part of the counsellor to hold the client. ... A time limit is set for the contacts, and they are brought to a reluctant but healthy close. Sometimes, in the last contact, the client brings up a number of old problems or new ones, as though in a gesture to retain the relationship, but the atmosphere is very different from that in the first contacts, when those problems were real. (Rogers, 1990: 66–77)

Humanist practitioners who are primarily influenced by Carl Rogers are doomed to struggle with engagement in any time-limited therapeutic encounter as long as they believe, with Rogers, that 'constructive personality change' will only take place if the six conditions which he describes as necessary and sufficient exist and continue *'over a period of time'* (Rogers, 1957: 96; emphasis added). The clear implication is that the period of time should always be open ended and not bound by a specific closing date.

Given this seemingly irreconcilable gap between the root source of humanistic theory and the development of a brief therapy approach, it is interesting to note that the cost-effective and time-limited methodology of behaviour therapy has, from its origins, incorporated as an essential component an almost humanistic emphasis upon warm and trusting relations between therapist and client. Clients were found to willingly engage in processes of desensitization or to fulfil homework projects only if they felt understood, accepted and respected by their therapist or counsellor (Bohart and Todd, 1988: 90). Indeed, an early comparative study found that behaviour therapists were scored slightly higher than psychotherapists trained in other orientations in measures of warmth, empathy and genuineness (Sloane et al., 1975). Similarly the most time-limited and structured of all the cognitive therapies as developed by Aaron Beck (Beck et al., 1979) used Rogerian conditions as a necessary aid and source of learning.

Cognitive-behavioural therapists pioneered a flourishing and influential version of brief therapy which was heavily influenced by *systems theory* as explored within the schools of strategic and structural family therapy (Minuchin, 1974; Watzlawick et al., 1974; Haley, 1976). These approaches encouraged the use of pragmatic problem-solving interventions into the immediate social environment or system within which clients were experiencing psychological distress and behaving dysfunctionally. Brief therapies were also developed within the highly structured approaches of Ellis's rational emotive behaviour therapy (1970) and the hypnosis-based work of Milton Erickson (Erickson and Rossi, 1979). Literature describing these original time-limited, cognitive-behavioural therapies tends to portray the therapist as a skilled change artist with the client as grateful recipient.

The continuing development of brief therapy has taxed therapeutic creativity and encouraged both eclecticism and integration throughout the profession of psychotherapy and counselling. Psychoanalytic theorists and practitioners have rediscovered and taken forward Alexander and French's (1946) radical discovery that an intensive and deliberate cultivation of the curative therapeutic relationship, combined with flexibility and openness to external life changes, can be effective over a comparatively short time. Influential developments have been the explorations of Malan (1975) and Davanloo (1980). For an excellent overview, see Peake et al. (1988) who have used their clinical experience and research (Malan, 1975) to generate an explicit theoretical justification for their particular forms of short-term psychodynamic brief therapy. These psychoanalytically based approaches emphasize the importance of *selection* for client suitability and swift *interpretation of defences* and a deliberate focus on *transference* issues. Meanwhile, cognitive-behavioural therapists have been elegantly developing the brief therapy approaches of Erickson (Erickson and Rossi, 1979) and Haley (1976) into models of *solution-focused* (de Shazer, 1985) and *brief-strategic* (Cade and O'Hanlon, 1993) therapies. These therapies, popular with hospital and health insurance providers, have featured an optimistic outlook towards the future and the evidence, drawn from the client's own narrative, of previously established strengths and coping strategies.

Current applications of brief time-focused therapy

At the present time, one of the most influential models of an integrative approach to short-term psychological therapy is the creative innovation of Anthony Ryle (1990). He has selected from psychoanalytic, cognitive and behavioural theory in order to present a highly structured and clearly delineated approach. Ryle's seminal text (1990) on cognitive analytic therapy (CAT) demonstrates a method whereby clients are included as co-workers throughout a clearly negotiated and time-limited process of therapeutic change. CAT therapists are encouraged to use and share their thinking with clients. Explicitly negotiated contractual commitments are made, with some flexible potential, although only within the parameters of 12 to 16 therapy sessions. Clients are all offered a theoretical understanding of their psychological patterns through the use of the 'psychotherapy file' (Ryle, 1990: 3–7), which combines the interpretations of psychoanalytic practice with the analysis of faulty beliefs typical of the cognitive therapies. CAT therapists share their thinking openly with clients, offering *'reformulations'* and *'goodbye letters'* to be mutually redesigned. Ryle maintains that this approach can be beneficial to most clients and argues (1990: 122–4) that even the personality disordered client may be reassured by a combination of optimism and trust in their capacity for self-reflexivity. The theoretical understanding and skill of the CAT practitioner is the crucial component of effective CAT brief therapy. This approach is highly manualized and uses somewhat rigid terms, abbreviations and procedures which can prove a drawback when adopted by a trainee therapist lacking theoretical conviction and personally unconvinced of the philosophical principles underlying CAT.

Contemporary innovative models of brief therapy include Peake et al.'s (1988: 223–9) own summary of *'brief psychotherapy by design'* which is the culmination of the overview mentioned above. Although primarily located in the problem-solving pragmatism of the cognitive-behavioural orientation, this is undoubtedly an attempt to integrate the 'effective therapeutic components shared by all psychotherapies' (Frank, 1985). The search for *effectiveness* is a fundamental spur towards the adoption of an integrative or eclectic approach to psychotherapy or counselling. Competent eclectic practitioners seek to have available a wide range of therapeutic methodologies with which to serve their clients as appropriate, following Paul's (1967) stricture that a conscientious therapy provider should attempt to answer the question: 'What treatment, by whom, is most effective for this individual with that specific problem, and under which set of circumstances?' Lazarus's multi-modal therapy (1981) is still probably the most clearly described model of effective eclecticism which implicitly aims to meet each client's individual needs in as short a time as possible. Integrative therapists are more concerned to ground their techniques in their own personal synthesis of the powerful theoretical explanations offered by the main schools of psychotherapy and counselling. This process of individualized integration can satisfy a practitioner's need for a personal approach which can be owned and explained theoretically as well as being useful and effective.

Another example of short-term therapy, which is currently highly influential and somewhat more palatable to the humanistically inclined eclectic or integrative practitioner, is the *existentially orientated* model developed by James Mann (1973, 1981). Mann is an experienced psychoanalyst who does not insist upon the usual principles of brief psychodynamic psychotherapy, careful selection followed by a deliberate focus upon transferentially acquired defences (Mann, 1973; Davanloo, 1980). His approach provides an interesting exception to these fundamental psychoanalytic precepts. Mann is in agreement with most short-term therapists that there is a need to find and stay with a *'central issue'* (Mann, 1973: 17–20), but it is the sequence of dynamic events which he follows most closely, always remaining in touch with the poignant and universal human longing for a timeless golden past which will need to be relinquished in order that reality can be effectively addressed. He emphasizes the practitioner's empathic engagement with the existential reality of a time-limited contract as the major curative factor. It may be that Mann's approach to time-conscious therapy provides humanistic practitioners with a brief therapy methodology based on a real I–Thou relationship, and an existential explanation which justifies the use of time limits.

Surprisingly, one of the most genuinely person-centred descriptions of a time-focused therapy can be found in Moshe Talmon's (1990) *Single Session Therapy*. Specializing in a systematic approach, this busy psychiatric practitioner noticed that a high proportion of his clients, as well as those of his psychoanalytic and humanistic professional colleagues, only attended for a single session of psychotherapy or counselling. His research into this phenomenon led him to discover that a majority of these apparently dissatisfied customers had benefited from their brief encounter with psychotherapy. This led him to revise his initial assessment process radically by offering the possibility of single session therapy at the outset of the first session. The opportunity is left open for more therapy sessions but the client is offered the optimistic prediction that a single session may be enough to resolve the present impasse. Talmon's aim (1990: 120) is to facilitate the 'smallest, simplest step towards change' so that the client 'leaves the session remembering one new point (or tries out one new behaviour)'. Nevertheless, Talmon describes his own theoretical formulations as typically those of an integrative practitioner: 'On the basis of my training, I might entertain multiple formulations of the present problem, ranging from dynamic to behavioural, cognitive to systemic' (Talmon, 1990: 120). Talmon omits humanistic explanations from his 'multiple formulations' and yet his concluding advice to single-session therapists seems redolent of a genuine person-centred belief system:

1 This is it.
2 View each and every session as a whole, complete in itself.
3 All you have is now.
4 It's all here.
5 Therapy starts before the first session and will continue long after it.
6 Take it one step at a time.

7   You do not have to rush or reinvent the wheel.
8   The power is in the patient.
9   Never underestimate your patient's strengths.
10 You don't have to know everything in order to be helpful.
11 Life is full of surprises.
12 Life, more than therapy, is a great teacher.
13 Time, nature and life are great healers.
14 Expect change. It's already well under way. (Talmon, 1990: 134–5)

Talmon probably represents the culmination of the humanistic here-and-now emphasis and basic optimism demonstrated in de Shazer's (1985) *solution-focused* and Cade and O'Hanlon's (1993) *brief-strategic* approaches to time-limited therapy. Ryle (1990: 1–2) is a self-confessed integrationist across orientations, while Mann (1973: 12–15) was willing to explore the broadest applications of psychoanalytic practice. These influential brief therapists seem much less concerned with maintaining an allegiance to one particular orientation and more with finding out how to intervene therapeutically in a client's life with sincerity and skill and in the shortest amount of time. Table 14.1 offers the reader a comparison of significant writers in the field of brief or time-conscious therapy. Readers are invited to add to this comparison wherever they can find more points in common between theorists.

A theoretically integrated and practical approach to time-focused therapy

Time-focused psychological therapy lends itself naturally to an eclectic or integrative approach. The demand for effective technique and the search for meta-theoretical principles are enhanced by the awareness, of practitioner and client, that the time available for this therapeutic engagement is itself a focal issue. As described in the previous section, there has already been a considerable amount of integrative synthesis and selection of key interventions by brief therapists. However, there is still a tendency for some practitioners to adopt a brisk problem-solving stance, firmly rooted in principles of behaviour change, in the belief that neither searching insight nor fundamental character change are likely to result from a contractual commitment with a time limit. Others adapt psychoanalytical preoccupations with firm boundaries around a psychotherapeutic 'frame' (Casement, 1985: 61) and transplant wholesale a somewhat punitive interpretation that any resistance to the agreed time boundaries is in itself a defence. Both these approaches fail to take advantage of the full range of theoretical and technical knowledge available to the practitioner of brief therapy who accepts that all psychotherapeutic engagements are only episodes in a client's life-time search for personal development. Each client's *life process* of psychological evolution is inevitable, central and

Table 14.1 *Comparison of approaches to brief therapy. Main aspects of shared theory and method showed at meeting points between theorists. Italics indicate features exclusive to an approach, shown where the theorist's name meets itself*

	Alexander & French	Malan	Davanloo	Cade and O'Hanlon	Mann	Ryle	de Shazer	Talmon
Alexander and French	*Flexible and economic Time-out promoted*	Selection – neurotic issues – oedipal and loss	Discusses real-life issues	Willing to problem solve	Corrective emotional experience	Face-to-face; one session a week	Problem solving	Problem solving
Malan	Transference interpretations	*Research approach (20+ sessions)*	Triangles of impulse and insight	Active	Fixed contract	Psychodynamics central		
Davanloo	Focus on relationship change	Triangles of impulse and insight	*Relentless healer catalyses and confronts defences*	Focal issue sought	Extended intake period	Psychodynamics central	Confrontative	Concentrated and swift
Cade and O'Hanlon	Discusses real-life issues	Critique of passivity	Confrontative	*Designed, goals central*		Aims and goals explicit	Aims and goals explicit	
Mann	Discusses real-life issues	Transference interpretations	Broad selection criteria	Broad selection criteria	*Existential approach; time as universal issue*	Focal issue made central		Focal issue made central
Ryle	Discusses real-life issues	Psychodynamic approach	Severe pathology accepted		Fixed contracts	*Therapist shares theory and insights*	Broad selection criteria	Intermittent therapy client as customer
de Shazer	Avoids regressive dependence	Pragmatics replace perfection	Confrontative	Solution focused; problem solving			*Future focus – the miracle question*	Optimistic approach
Talmon	Life as main teacher		Swift and skilled	Less is more *not more of the same*	Focal issue made central	Active and open	External life key issue	*Single session (2 hrs)*

Source: Jenifer Elton Wilson, 1997

independent of any particular practitioner's expertise. It is the practitioner's role to judge, with humility and sensitivity, where and how to enter this lifelong process (see Table 14.2).

Acceptance of a 'peripheral position' (Elton Wilson, 1996: 158) allows the counsellor or psychotherapist to reframe a time-focused contractual commitment as an imaginative, flexible and rewarding piece of work, replacing quantity and endurance with *quality and intensity*. From the expertise and theoretical rigour of the behaviourist, the practitioner can make an empathic and here-and-now assessment of the client's present concerns as well as exploring the social system and personal history from which they arise. In addition, the practitioner explores the immediate needs of their clients and their readiness for even a time-limited encounter with psychological therapy. Out of this assessment a time-focused contractual commitment can be designed, with opportunities for collaboration, discussion and mutual review. Essential to this process are the relationship skills of the humanistic practitioner as well as the psychoanalytical therapist's sensitive ability to discern transference issues and to develop an enduring working alliance. Exploration of early history can swiftly reveal, and make available to cognitive inquiry, the belief systems which underlie the client's present psychological distress. This combination of skills are needed so that client and practitioner can together work through these illusory blocks towards a more realistic and fulfilling person-to-person relationship. The main principles of the author's integrative approach to a brief time-focused therapeutic commitment are listed below.

- Make a clear contractual commitment to work together.
- Remain flexible regarding readiness, motivation and aims.
- Offer abundance rather than poverty while accepting and working with the concept that time is limited.
- Work within the client's life stage of personal development.
- Focus on a central issue, a survival strategy from the past which operates both in the client's external life and in the consulting room, and can be replaced by alternative strategies in future.
- Work together within a variety of therapeutic relationships.
- Be realistic and consider the context.
- Negotiate goals which are small but powerful.
- Facilitate fears as well as hopes.
- Use every moment of contact to build trust.
- Accept high expectations at first, and stay firm through disillusionment and retreat.
- Offer warmth and non-possessiveness.
- Believe in the efficacy of time-limited counselling.

The fictionalized case history of Paula is given below to illustrate some of these principles, which are offered as vital to a time-conscious approach.

Table 14.2 Working with a client's life process of psychological evolution

STAGE Possible point of entry/ area of focus (after intake)	FOCAL TASK Issues relevant to this stage tied into a focal theme based on earlier experiences	FOCAL RELATIONSHIP Working Alliance (WA), Real Relationship (RR), Transference Relationship (TR)
PREPARATION *Build trust*	Work on present problems. Defences/symptoms understood as strategies. Re-education about power issues and child development.	WA – main mode and essential focus. RR – explore factual/cultural components; and put aside. TR – note clues.
DISCLOSURE *Respect and listen as the 'story' is told objectively by the adult survivor*	Experiences named/labelled. Descriptions of situations and sensations with associated self-image. Original strategies for survival described and validated.	WA essential to cushion vulnerability of disclosure and insights. TR noted but not made focal: countertransference contained. RR only needed if modelling required or for cultural enquiry.
CATHARSIS *Facilitate contact with client's early emotional reality*	Re-experiences as child did. Queries and, with practitioner as witness, ally and advocate, reframes experience. Natural needs expressed versus adapted needs/reactive patterns.	TR likely to be central for both participants. WA in background and used to maintain coping strategies outside sessions. RR cautiously contained.
SELF-CARE *Share in the 'corrective' emotional experience (Alexander and French, 1946)*	Punitive and critical internal monitors replaced by insightful acceptance. Identity and related needs affirmed and re-structured within cultural and social parameters.	TR central – practitioner used to replace authority figures and previous models. RR can be introduced to balance idealistic transference. WA must be re-stated and used overtly.
RENUNCIATION *Encourage grieving, raging and letting go*	Sorrow and anger for lost ideals of childhood and parenthood. Acceptance of reality in past events. Allowing practitioners to step down from being the replacement ideal parent.	RR can become more focal to replace idealization. WA maintained and wound down. TR unpacked and worked with overtly, especially by client.
EMPOWERMENT *Observe the client getting on with existential issues of life*	Self-support and environmental support in place. Restructured relationships/partnerships. Confrontation/re-contracting with external social systems. Use of groups/other networks/future therapy.	WA available if required. Offer follow-ups/reviews. TR likely to remain operational. Avoid intimate or financial connections. RR contacts may be possible if abstinence maintained.

Source: Jenifer Elton Wilson, 1996: 36

This account of a time-focused engagement is drawn from a variety of experiences in this field and has been adjusted so that no identification should be possible.

Case study

Make a clear contractual commitment to work together

Charlotte Sills (1997: 11–36) has expanded upon Berne's (1966) categorization of three levels of contractual commitment between practitioner and client. In establishing the *'administrative contract'* the time-focused counsellor or psychotherapist needs to agree practical arrangements which are consistent with the demands of the setting and yet emotionally acceptable to both participants. The *'professional contract'* defines the issues which concern the client and the outcome sought within the concentrated and intensive experience of a time-focused therapeutic encounter. At the level of the *'psychological'* contract, the short-term practitioner needs to manage profound levels of existential dread in themselves as well as in their clients. All three types of contractual commitment were problematic in establishing a therapeutic engagement with Paula.

> Paula's initial contact with the practitioner was disguised as a social visit. She managed to find the door of the psychotherapy department's consulting room on the one day of the week on which it was used by this particular therapist, and to enter the room between sessions. She smiled her way confidently through a casual invitation to coffee based on a mutual friendship. However, the therapist was not free to accept the invitation and the following week Paula booked herself in for an assessment interview, still claiming that she was only making contact because their mutual friend had told her to do so. To establish clear contractual arrangements was difficult from the outset and remained problematic throughout. The smiling bid for friendship quickly became a fraught crisis counselling session as Paula offered a rapid and self-mocking description of her life with a dependent and alcoholic partner. During the last few weeks, she had tried to end the relationship only to find herself threatened with violence, and was now in fear of returning to her own home although she was the official owner of the apartment. She blamed only herself and had been tempted to take an overdose. Any discussion regarding length and availability of therapy was inappropriate until practical information about the availability of legal advice and temporary accommodation had been offered and her own coping abilities and supportive network of friends explored. It seemed,

initially, that Paula was more in need of holding through a period of crisis rather than any structured form of psychological therapy. She was offered an 'in crisis' (Elton Wilson, 1996: 12–14) appointment with another psychotherapist in the department for the very next day so as to offer support and check for suicidal impulse.

Remain flexible regarding readiness, motivation and aim

In this approach to time-conscious contracting (Elton Wilson, 1996: 13), practitioners are urged to remain open, from the very first moment of contact, to the possibility that all clients presenting for psychotherapy or counselling may only be 'visiting' the consulting room. A person, a couple or family may need help to recoup their own strengths and find practical ways through a time of trauma. Where there is no apparent immediate distress, the individual may be tentatively interested in what psychotherapy might offer and not fully 'willing to engage' in the self-exploration and expansion required. The humanistic skills of empathy, respect and accurate listening are essential in order to respond professionally to these 'visitors' and to people who are 'in crisis'. Any offer of continuing therapy, time-limited or otherwise, often needs to be shelved or postponed.

Paula reacted positively to the attention and assistance she was offered. She contacted two of her closest friends and, with their support, regained possession of her flat, succeeded in ejecting her partner and made a more determined attempt to end the relationship. A month later, she was back at the reception desk of the psychotherapy department. She wanted to book in for long-term therapy with the practitioner she had first contacted and would not accept an appointment with any other psychotherapist. The receptionist explained that the practitioner was available only for an assessment interview, likely to be followed by a referral to another therapist. Long-term therapy was unlikely to be on offer. Paula appeared to accept this arrangement with a good grace, but once in the consulting room insisted that she would only ever be able to trust this particular psychotherapist, and claimed that their mutual friend had advised her on this.

Offer abundance rather than poverty

Any offer of a brief period of counselling needs to be made in a relaxed and optimistic manner. If time-limited practitioners have some degree of freedom in the contractual arrangements they can make, then it is easier to match the offer to the needs of the client. Offering a period of extended exploration, culminating in a mutual opportunity to review progress, can convey a sense of unhurried and optimistic confidence to the client. Above all, time-focused practitioners should avoid giving an impression that therapy is being rationed. This requires the practitioner to hold to a strong humanistic belief that every client's life lies ahead with its potential for personal growth and development. In addition, the practitioner working with an eclectic or integrative approach knows that there is an abundance of professional methodologies and theoretical explanations to put at the service of their clients. Above all, time-conscious practitioners value and convey their commitment to the process and the potential of every session even if it is only a 'single session' (Talmon, 1990).

The assessment part of the session went well. Paula was calmer now, and showed both motivation and insight as she described a lifetime of abandonment and chaotic, confusing relationships. She acknowledged that she would need to explore some painful issues, and that some of her patterns of interaction might need to be explored. She was dubious about initially being offered only six weekly sessions which would culminate in an opportunity for her and the practitioner to evaluate progress and to agree a further specific amount of sessions. However, she accepted the offer with a knowing smile and the practitioner was left feeling somewhat manipulated.

Work within the client's life stage of personal development

The author has delineated elsewhere (see Table 14.2; Elton Wilson, 1996: 36) six stages of personal change and evolution which are traversed by most clients in their own personal journey, ranging from 'preparation' for change through the 'disclosure' and 'catharsis' stages and on into 'self-care', 'renunciation' and 'empowerment'. For each stage there are focal issues for the client to work through, and the practitioner's task is to offer the alliance and intervention to the stage in progress.

It became apparent within the first two sessions that Paula was deeply distrustful that any person was really willing to offer her respect and attention. Her belief that she needed long-term therapy sprang from her disbelief in the existence of a trustworthy helper. Impressively but superficially friendly and confident in herself, Paula was deeply suspicious of close relationships unless there was a clear imbalance of power. She was either the dominant carer in a close and often claustrophobic relationship or she was the cowering victim. The one exception was the mutual friend she shared with the practitioner. She had known this person as the one stable and helpful presence encountered during her chaotic early childhood. Recently she had made contact with this benevolent and steady friend again, and it was this influence that had indeed drawn her into this somewhat shaky and undecided therapeutic engagement. It seemed probable that, despite her apparent sophistication, Paula was at the very preliminary preparation stage in her therapeutic journey. She needed above all to learn to trust the practitioner and perhaps to gain some understanding of her present predicament as stemming from an early 'strategy for survival'. (Elton Wilson, 1996: 81–5)

Focus on a central issue, a survival strategy from the past which operates both in the client's external life and in the consulting room and can be replaced by alternative strategies in future

The psychoanalytic 'triangle of insight' (Jacobs, 1988) can be used to explain and clarify the client's adherence to a pattern of behaviours and cognitions which have become crippling to their progress. Figure 14.1 shows an extension of this concept which includes the future focused notions of de Shazer (1985). Discerning this crippling belief system, its roots in the past and how it is operating here and now between client and therapist, as well as in the client's present external world, is the primary insight needed within a time-focused therapeutic engagement. Close attention is needed to a repetitive communication offered by the client in the consulting room, to a similar pattern of interaction outside the room and to its probable origins in the client's past. Ideally, this realization occurs spontaneously from the careful commentary of the therapist on the client's progress and the story being told. However, it is the practitioner's task to find a way of exploring this understanding with empathy and, above all, acceptance that this belief and the consequent behaviour patterns were once in truth contributory to the client's survival strategy, and may even now be useful. A gentle but continuous commentary upon this central fact is a powerful tool for transformation. A client in the early stages of the therapeutic journey may at first use this knowledge only to make some sense of their present pain. Hope is fostered by the practitioner's parallel exploration of the *exceptions* pertaining in the past and how these might be linked to a range of alternative strategies, or *solutions* in the future. Very often this experientially gained intelligence is enough to take away and use as a lever for change in the future.

Paula described her painful life, past and present, with humour and wit. She showed a complete lack of empathy for the frightened child she had been and amused self-contempt for her present mode of existence. Any compassionate comment by the therapist was refused and Paula seemed almost to look forward

266 INTEGRATIVE AND ECLECTIC COUNSELLING AND PSYCHOTHERAPY

(Future)
IN VIEW

*solution
*solution
*solution
*solution
*solution

Expanded strategies →   ← Changes

IN HERE ←——— New learning ———→ **OUT THERE**
(Present) ←——— Focal theme ———   *(Present)*

Strategies for survival (focal themes)   Strategies for survival (defences/patterns)

*exception
*exception
*exception
*exception

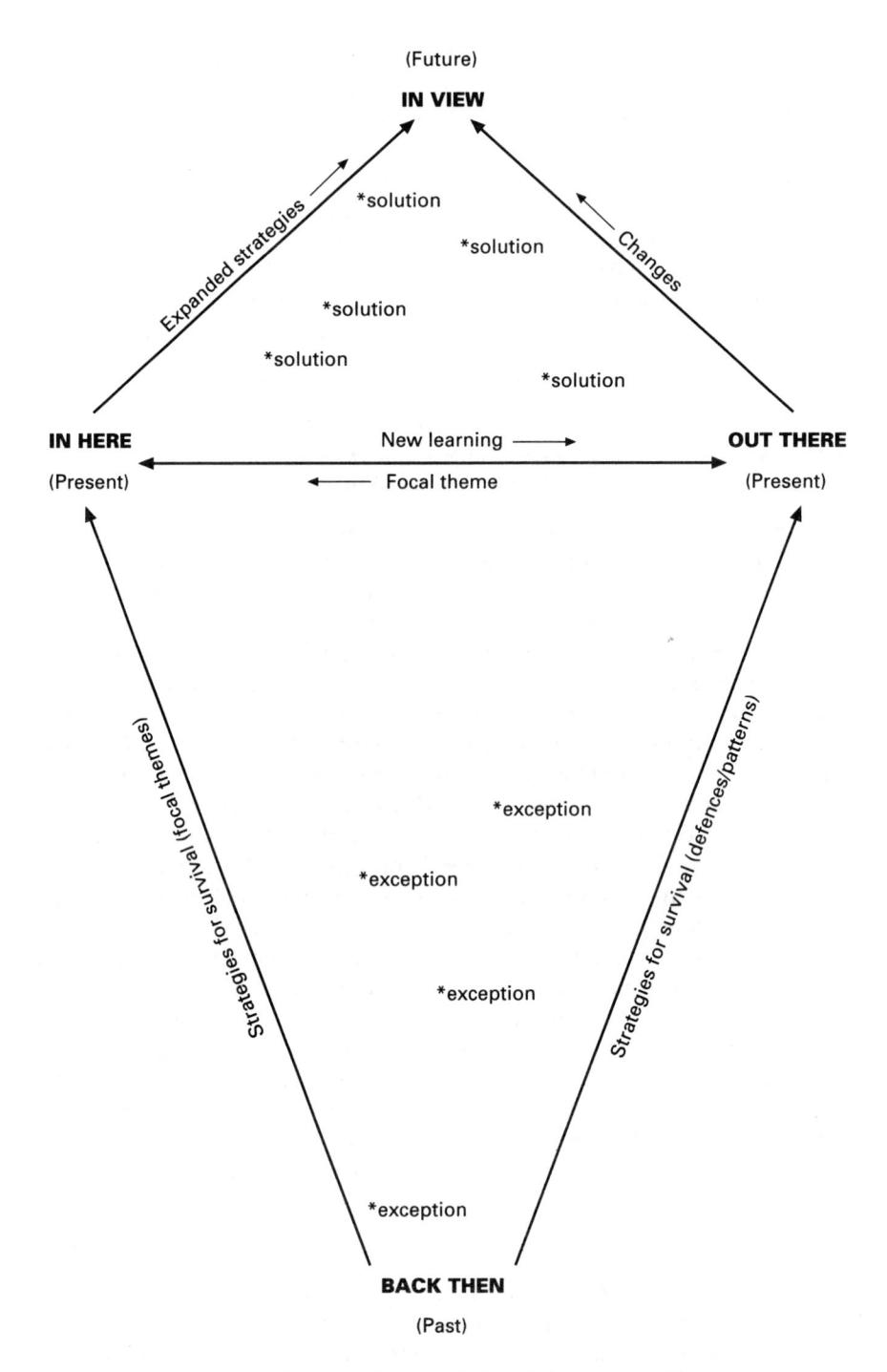

BACK THEN
(Past)

Figure 14.1 *From triangle to kite of insight (Elton Wilson, 1997 with acknowledgement to Jacobs, 1988 and de Shazer, 1985)*

to her next encounter with betrayal. She laughed as she admitted that she would feel comfortable with the therapist only when she could put her down verbally. She was anxious to differentiate her relationship with the practitioner from that of any other client, citing their social links through their mutual friend. She talked about her friendships in terms of who was in control and viewed most other encounters as battles which she had to win. She seemed to enjoy describing the risky situations she had been in and was even now inviting. In the fourth session the therapist asked Paula what she would want to embroider on her banner next time she 'went to war'. Paula suggested 'life's a laugh' followed by 'I'm invincible' and then, more tremulously, 'You can't hurt me' and 'I don't care'. Together they arrived at the formulation 'I will show you that no one can hurt me now!' For the first time, Paula was without a caustic comment and she became quiet and tearful.

Work together within a variety of therapeutic relationships

The 'working alliance' (Gelso and Carter, 1985: 161–9) is the primary mode of relationship necessary for time-focused therapy. It is an acknowledged pact between client and therapist to work together towards agreed goals. To maintain this emotional bond the practitioner must use every moment of contact to build trust or there is likely to be very little achieved within a limited period of time. It is important to negotiate goals which are small but powerful following Talmon's (1990: 119–20) discovery that most people need only take the 'smallest simplest step towards change' within the therapeutic frame. Malan was one of the first short-term therapists to note the surprising and beneficial influence when rapid transference of intense interpersonal patterns by the client on to the practitioner took place in the context of brief psychotherapy. The client's awareness of time limitation encourages the swift re-emergence of the unsatisfactory past experiences engendering present emotional distress. In time-focused work, practitioners initially allow and welcome this 'transference relationship' (Gelso and Carter, 1985: 170–82) to erupt, no matter how unreal and inappropriate, so that the underlying assumptions can be explored together and repetitions confronted. There are, however, always 'real relationship' (Gelso and Carter, 1985: 183–91) components to the client's experience of the counsellor which may obstruct the working alliance unless they are recognized. Usually this entails the practitioner's swift and open exploration of areas of difference or similarity between participants. Typically the process of a successfully negotiated time-focused commitment involves the ascendancy of the working alliance over unreal transferential issues.

Unsurprisingly, Paula tried to avoid the review session, first by postponing the sixth session through a series of cancellations and then by producing a new crisis situation. She had picked a quarrel with her closest friend who had cut off contact. Paula now felt abandoned and desperately angry with herself. She claimed to be contemplating suicide again. The practitioner focused first upon the way Paula had tried to 'show you that no one can hurt me now!' and then wondered aloud if she would like to pick a quarrel with the therapist rather than discuss the painful work they had done together. An alternative to conflict was to avoid all meaningful contact by leaving the scene. Paula ruefully agreed that she had tried to achieve this through cancellations and by suicidal ideation. The session was filled with a struggle between Paula's habitual defensive distrust and her ability to work insightfully and co-operatively with the therapist. She accepted the therapist's offer of a further six sessions to consolidate these insights. Paula realized that she would find the closing sessions difficult but wanted to try out a new way of saying goodbye.

A short-term therapeutic engagement invites idealistic optimism and the therapist often has to accept high expectations at first, stay firm through disillusionment and retreat especially as the agreed closing date approaches. By alluding calmly and confidently to this final session at regular intervals, time-focused practitioners demonstrate that they must sincerely believe in the efficacy of a time-focused approach and trust their clients to achieve what is possible, and necessary, in the time available. It is necessary for the practitioner to combine compassionate sensitivity and warmth with a high level of non-possessiveness so as to work within the intimacy of a therapeutic alliance which is dedicated to its own dissolution in service of the client's progressive resolution of their problematic life issues.

Paula's next few sessions were not, of course, easy. Her moods lurched between a manic euphoria in which she claimed to have changed beyond recognition, and a cynical despair during which she denigrated the therapy, the therapist and herself as a client. At times she claimed to be completely cured and suggested the closing session be brought forward immediately. However, the working alliance held and Paula's last session became a celebration of the changes which had taken place, both inside and outside the consulting room. She had re-established contact with her friend, this time on a more real and equal level. She was able to admit her sadness about the end of this therapeutic encounter as well as her fear of dependency. Paula was offered a follow-up session in three months time, to report progress and for which no crisis was necessary. She did not take this up, although she continues to send occasional cards and letters to the practitioner.

The future of integrative and eclectic approaches to time-conscious psychological therapy in Britain

If psychotherapy and counselling are to continue as professional services to the British public, then they will need to prove themselves to be as necessary, effective, economically viable and as valuable to society as other professions and service industries. At present, the future is uncertain. Counselling has become increasingly popular with the general public and psychotherapy, especially when labelled 'analysis', still commands a somewhat uneasy respect. However, the profession has hedged itself with untested assumptions and hypotheses and appears, to the outsider, to be divided against itself through its own preoccupation with distinctive 'schools of psychotherapy'. Employers and health service providers seek a service that can provide evidence for the competence of its interventions and can fit in with budget requirements. Psychotherapy and counselling which is open ended and somewhat vague in its promises of effectiveness is unlikely to be popular. Members of the public able to pay for their own therapy are increasingly likely to be intelligent users only willing to pay for therapists who can explain how their service works and who facilitate reasonably speedy relief from current pain and discomfort. The preference will be for a psychotherapist or counsellor who can explain their approach cogently, work effectively within the time frame available and draw on a range of professional experience.

References

Alexander, F. and French, T.M. (1946) *Psychoanalytic Therapy: Principles and Applications.* New York: Ronald Press.
Berne, E. (1966) *Principles of Group Treatment.* New York: Oxford University Press.
Beck, A., Rush, A.J., Shaw, B.F. and Emery, G. (1979) *Cognitive Therapy of Depression.* New York: Guilford Press.
Bohart, A.C. and Todd, J. (1988) *Foundations of Clinical and Counseling Psychology.* New York: Harper and Row.
Cade, B. and O'Hanlon, W.H. (1993) *A Brief Guide to Brief Therapy.* London: W.W. Norton.
Casement, P. (1985) *On Learning From The Patient.* London: Tavistock.
Coren, A. (1996) 'Brief therapy – base metal or pure gold?', *Psychodynamic Counselling.* 2: 1.

Davanloo, H. (1980) *Current Trends in Short-term Dynamic Therapy*. New York: Jason Aronson.
de Shazer, S. (1985) *Keys to Solution in Brief Therapy*. New York. W.W. Norton.
Ellis, A. (1970) *The Essence of Rational Psychotherapy: A Comprehensive Approach to Treatment*. New York: Institute for Rational Living.
Elton Wilson, J. (1996) *Time-conscious Psychological Therapy: A Life Stage to Go Through*. London: Routledge.
Erickson, M.H. and Rossi, E.L. (1979) *Hypnotherapy: An Exploratory Casebook*. New York: Irvington.
Frank, J. (1985) 'Therapeutic components shared by all psychotherapies', in M.J. Mahoney and A. Freeman (eds), *Cognition and Psychotherapy*. New York: Plenum.
Gelso, C.J. and Carter, J.A. (1985) 'The relationship in counseling and psychotherapy: components, consequences and theoretical antecedents', *Counseling Psychologist*, 13 (2): 155–243.
Haley, J. (1976) *Problem-solving Therapy*. San Francisco: Jossey-Bass.
Jacobs, M. (1988) *Psychodynamic Counselling in Action*. London: Sage.
Lazarus, A.A. (1981) *The Practice of Multimodal Therapy*. New York: McGraw-Hill.
Malan, D.H. (1975) *A Study of Brief Psychotherapy*. London: Plenum.
Mann, J. (1973) *Time Limited Psychotherapy*. Cambridge, MA: Harvard University Press.
Mann, J. (1981) 'The core of time-limited psychotherapy: Time and the central issue', in S. Budman (ed.), *Forms of Brief Therapy*. New York: Guilford Press.
Minuchin, S. (1974) *Families and Family Therapy*. Cambridge, MA: Harvard University Press.
Paul, G. (1967) 'Strategy of outcome research in psychotherapy', *Journal of Consulting Psychology*, 31: 109–18.
Peake, T.H., Borduin, C.M. and Archer, R.P. (1988) *Brief Psychotherapies: Changing Frames of Mind*. London: Sage.
Rogers, C.R. (1957) *On Becoming a Person: A Therapist's View of Psychotherapy*. London: Constable.
Rogers, C.R. (1990) 'Characteristic steps in the therapeutic process', in H. Kirschenbaum and V.L. Henderson (eds), *The Carl Rogers Reader*. London: Constable.
Ryle, A. (1990) *Cognitive-Analytic Therapy: Active Participation in Change*. Chichester: Wiley.
Sills, C. (1997) 'Contracts and contract making', in C. Sill (ed.), *Contracts in Counselling*. London: Sage.
Sloane, R., Staples, F., Cristol, A., Yornkston, N. and Whipple, K. (1975) *Psychotherapy versus Behavior Therapy*. Cambridge, MA: Harvard University Press.
Stolorow, R., Atwood, G. and Brandchaft, B. (eds) (1994) *The Intersubject Perspective*. New York: Jason Aronson.
Talmon, M. (1990) *Single Session Therapy*. San Francisco: Jossey-Bass.
Watzlawick, P., Weakland, J.H. and Fisch, R. (1974) *Change: Principles of Problem Formation and Problem Resolution*. New York. W.W. Norton.

15
INTEGRATION AND ECLECTICISM IN SUPERVISION

Val Wosket

Supervision is a structured interpersonal process with the primary purpose of enhancing the effectiveness of the therapeutic encounter through the growth in competence of the counsellor, whose work is monitored and facilitated by the supervisor. The British Association for Counselling (BAC) describes supervision as:

> A formal arrangement for counsellors to discuss their work regularly with someone who is experienced in counselling and supervision. The task is to work together to ensure and develop the efficacy of the counsellor/client relationship ... supervision is a process to maintain adequate standards of counselling and a method of consultancy to widen the horizons of an experienced practitioner. (British Association for Counselling, 1996)

Counselling supervision has recently come of age and within the last decade has 'earned the right to be considered as a distinct discipline' (Page and Wosket, 1994: 9). Supervision now exists as a separate and discrete branch of the counselling profession commanding its own body of theory, research and literature. While yet in its adolescence, supervision is fast growing into adulthood (Inskipp, 1996). Perhaps not surprisingly, since identity in adolescence is fluid, a clear definition of integrative or eclectic supervision has yet to emerge. The counselling world, as this book testifies, is still vigorously debating the differences and similarities between eclecticism and integration and arguing the relative merits of each. I will not endeavour to carry this debate into the supervision arena in any detail, although it is a debate which does call for attention from researchers and practitioners.

For the purpose of this chapter I will regard the two terms as loosely synonymous, while, on the whole, favouring the expression *integrative* over *eclectic*. The term integrative allows for a broadening of the horizons of supervision beyond the confines of models, processes and skills to encompass the wider contextual field. A flexible and supervisee-responsive approach to supervision may be more accurately defined by the use of the term integrative rather than the expression eclectic as the former more truly reflects the nature of the work undertaken by supervisors who see themselves as operating from more than a single school or orientation of counselling or supervision. I have rarely, if ever, met a supervisor who would use a variety of differentiated approaches (e.g. developmental, behavioural, systemic) or techniques with different supervisees, or even on different occasions with the same supervisees and who might therefore call themselves eclectic. More usually, competent supervisors who claim not to adhere to a single orientation strive to work in a wholistic and integrated manner in which they aspire to offer a consistent style and manner of supervision which can nonetheless be adjusted to the needs of individual supervisees, their clients and the contexts in which they work.

This chapter will attempt to delineate some thoughts towards an approach to counselling supervision which may be of relevance to both the counsellor (as supervisee) who practices from an integrated or eclectic stance and the supervisor who aspires to offer supervision from such a stance. Such a supervisor may also be an eclectic or integrative therapist, but not necessarily. I have discussed elsewhere (Page and Wosket, 1994) how supervisors trained and working in a single therapeutic orientation may educate themselves to offer an integrated approach to supervision if they are serious about rising to the challenge of offering supervision which truly matches the needs of the eclectic or integrative practitioner. While much of what is included in this chapter is applicable to group supervision, in order to maintain a focus I will direct my comments principally to the conduct of one-to-one supervision.

A profile of the integrative supervisor

Borders (1992) makes the simple but cogent point that in making the transition from counsellor to supervisor counsellors need to make a cognitive shift from thinking like a counsellor to thinking like supervisor. This involves, primarily, a shift in focus from the client to the counsellor. Supervisors who think like supervisors rather than counsellors 'ask themselves "How can I intervene so that this counsellor will be more effective with current and future clients?" 'rather than approaching sessions' well prepared to tell the counsellor what they would do with this client' with the result that 'supervisees become surrogate counselors who carry out supervisors' plans for counseling' (Borders, 1992: 137–8). Beginning to think like a supervisor is an important prerequisite to the ability to integrate and use a conceptual, integrative framework of supervision.

Even beginning supervisors, if they are experienced counsellors (which they should be), are hopefully less bound by skills and techniques than beginning therapists. This is not to say that skills and techniques do not have a place in supervision, but as Williams (1995: xiii) reminds us:

'Supervision and therapy are only partially matters of technique: for technique to be successful, just as for life to be successful, it must also submit to the creative, the experiential world of things imagined.' A view which encompasses the broader perspective of creative discovery envisages the acquisition of supervisor competence as a process whereby the supervisor develops an 'integrated personal theory' (Williams, 1995: 6) which extends far beyond the 'how to do it' school of learning.

> Supervision teaches people how to carry on therapeutic activity, rather than how to perform a series of specific interactions. There is nothing wrong with 'tips for supervisors' but tips on their own dry out, and the supervisor who is fed exclusively on tips becomes like the diner who dines exclusively on confectionery. (Williams, 1995: xiv)

The ability to operate as an integrative supervisor is less about the acquisition of an extensive tool kit than about acquiring clinical wisdom as a practitioner. Williams provides a useful breakdown of the components of clinical wisdom into four criteria which, for our purposes, could usefully be applied to evaluate the extent to which a supervisor is truly integrative:

- theoretical and technical knowledge;
- procedural knowledge;
- judgement;
- perspicacity.

Key aspects of the four categories are defined as follows:

1 *Theoretical and technical knowledge* are indicated by:
   - Profound insight into human development.
   - Excellent knowledge of theory.
   - Familiarity with previous work and techniques in the field.
   - Very high ability to construe a client's difficulties within an intellectual framework.
   - Evidence of development of an integrated theory of therapy.

2 *Procedural knowledge* is evidenced by:
   - Knowledge of the fundamental pragmatics of life and of the profession.
   - Unwillingness to become obsessed by a single theory.
   - High ability with routine and advanced professional operations and skills.
   - Flexibility in applying theory to practical work with clients.

3 *Judgement* is demonstrated in wise clinicians through:
   - High quality of judgement, understanding and commentary about difficult life problems.
   - Judgement based on deep and complex grasp of the issues involved.
   - Possession of a sense of where future progress is possible for clients.
   - Self-knowledge.

- Awareness of own limitations.
- 'Inner' sense of ethics and exemplary ethical practice based on good judgement.

4 *Perspicacity* is characterized by:
- Exceptional insight into persons.
- Systemic understanding of actions, beliefs and feelings.
- Ability of clinician to see his or her own part in system.
- Exceptional ability to understand and interpret one's environment.
- Resolution of major conflict in own life sufficiently to help others.
- Spontaneity. (Williams, 1995: 9–11)

The achievement of such a profile presents quite a tall order for any practitioner and it is heartening for nascent integrative supervisors to be reminded that 'clinical wisdom is not something that one *has*, but a state towards which one *aspires*' (Williams, 1995: 9, original emphasis). Nevertheless Williams presents a valuable profile against which aspiring supervisors can attempt to model themselves and supervisees can evaluate their supervisors. Happily the days are beginning to be over when supervisees had to put up with what they were given, partly from lack of knowing what they could expect from competent supervision. As the demystification of supervision proceeds apace, profiles like the one provided by Williams and evaluation processes such as those incorporated in the 'Cyclical Model' discussed below can provide valuable tools to help practitioners discover if they (and therefore their clients) are receiving supervision of a good enough standard.

Supervision competence, we might say, is therefore a combination of that which can be learned from external sources (reading, conferences, training courses, discussions with colleagues), clinical experience (both as a therapist and a supervisor) and the development of personal awareness and attributes. The essence of the effective supervisor is the ability to offer flexibility, rather than dogma, while demonstrating creativity, consistency, acceptance and containment.

A flurry of integrated models and approaches to supervision has recently emerged on both sides of the Atlantic (Inskipp and Proctor, 1994, 1995; Page and Wosket, 1994; Holloway, 1995; Carroll, 1996; Rapp, 1996) and this chapter will later consider Page and Wosket's Cyclical Model in some detail. Having a usable model to guide the process and conduct of supervision is, as I have already argued, only part of the picture of an integrative approach. A truly comprehensive integrative approach to supervision is *supervisee-responsive*, *client-responsive* and *context-responsive*. Such an approach has prerequisites and parameters which extend beyond the use of a model, although an effective integrative model provides the vehicle for their consideration and operationalization. I would like now to consider three further key aspects of an integrated approach to supervision which take account of the broader contextual issues:

- supervisor and supervisee matching;
- applicability across professions;
- adaptability to the systemic or organizational context.

Each of these will be considered in turn.

Supervisor and supervisee matching

In order to work together effectively in a co-operative and well-intentioned supervision relationship, the supervisor and supervisee need to be well matched. This means that they need to share sufficient common ground and understanding to speak the same 'language'. For the purist supervisor this may start with, or be predominantly determined by, the match of therapeutic orientation. The purely psychodynamic supervisor, for example, is likely to work most effectively with counsellors or psychotherapists who conceptualize the client and the therapeutic process in a similar way. There is also a strong argument for the trainee counsellor, if their training is approach specific, to be supervised by someone experienced in the same therapeutic orientation. For the integrative supervisor and/or supervisee, on the other hand, matching may be more concerned with acknowledging a broad range of multicultural issues. It is helpful to consider these under a number of headings.

Transcultural issues

In a recent chapter on 'Developments in psychotherapy integration', Newman and Goldfried reported on the 'increasing awareness that the psychological functioning of the individual is set in a sociological context that must be acknowledged, examined and respected' and they contend that 'heightened awareness of cross-cultural issues is both a cause and an effect of the growth of interest in rapprochement into an international movement.' (Newman and Goldfried, 1996: 253). While the literature on rapprochement (the search for common factors across diverse approaches) in psychotherapy which acknowledges and affirms cultural contexts currently far outstrips that on supervision, it is heartening to find a range of recent publications which are now starting seriously to address this topic in supervision (Bernard and Goodyear, 1992; Cook, 1994; Brown and Landrum-Brown, 1995; Lago and Thompson, 1996; Pope-Davis and Coleman, 1997). The stirring of interest in multicultural approaches to supervision was given a welcome further vigorous turn by the British Association for Supervision Practice and Research's second international conference in July 1997 which carried the theme of 'engaging with diversity in the practice of supervision' throughout the keynote addresses and workshops of the two-day event.

Bernard (1994) makes the point that when discussing transcultural supervision precise definition of terms is essential. Not only does the 'large umbrella of culture' (p. 167) cover race, but it also needs to encompass a broad range of cultural variables including ethnicity, class, education, socio-economic status, sexual orientation, mental and physical ability, religion, gender and age. She therefore favours the term multicultural over cross-cultural as the former allows for the consideration of a multiplicity of cultural variables while the latter may imply that race or ethnic background are the only important variables to be taken into account.

Taking this broader definition of multicultural, as adopted by Bernard, it becomes important for an integrated approach to supervision to take account of the wider world views of supervisor, supervisee and client as these form the backcloth to awareness of and attitudes towards cultural variables.

World view of supervisor and supervisee

The matching of supervisor and supervisee is to a large extent influenced by the proximity of the world view and person view of both participants. World view is determined by the cultural frame of reference of the individual and governs the way the individual perceives and construes their relationship with the world and its animate and inanimate phenomena (e.g. plants, animals, God). Person view is how the individual views the human condition, human development and behaviour. In counselling and supervision it is also about how they understand the determinants of psychological distress and disturbance; their understanding of how this is alleviated therapeutically and how they see the helping process operationalized.

Brown and Landrum-Brown argue that the matching of supervisor and supervisee needs to take greater account of possible discords and tensions generated by conflicting cultural frameworks. They see these as potentially ranged across three broad dimensions of difference: 'differences from the general population; differences from one's cultural group, and differences from either or both of the other parties in the [triadic] supervisory process' (Brown and Landrum-Brown, 1995: 266). They point out the need for acknowledgement that psychologically meaningful differences within cultural, racial or ethnic groups occur as frequently as cross-cultural differences and that these can seriously affect the supervisory process through 'misperceptions and wrongly applied culturally specific knowledge and experience' (p. 269).

Even supervisors/counsellors who work mainly or exclusively with same race supervisees/clients are not exempt from rigorously examining assumptions and prejudices which fail to acknowledge and take account of aspects of intra- as well as inter-cultural difference and disadvantage. These may be aspects of class, education, socio-economic status, age, sexuality, gender, religion, spirituality, mental and physical ability or appearance, urbanicity, norms relating to marriage and childbearing, and so on. Supervision is a triadic relationship and it is important to think about how complimentarity and conflict between any two of the participants will impact on the supervisory and therapeutic process.

> World view conflicts within the triadic relationship may result in distrust, hostility, and resistance. Although it is not always necessary for all parties in the relationship to have congruent worldviews, it is critical that the supervisor and counselor/supervisee be aware of potential worldview incongruities that might disrupt the therapeutic and supervisory process. Knowledge of one's own worldview perspectives is an initial step, with assessment of the worldview of the other parties in the triadic relationship as a secondary step. (Brown and Landrum-Brown, 1995: 272)

Hilde Rappe presents a similar argument and points to research which suggests that 'cultural differences between two people who speak the same language can make for greater misunderstandings than differences where the need to translate from one idiom into another is clearly marked' (Rapp, 1996: 59). There is a danger that the supervisor will become complacent in assuming that understanding and agreement exist when both supervisor and supervisee share a common language. She highlights the importance of vigilance on the part of the supervisor in adjusting to the differing meaning systems and learning styles of the supervisees: 'The *good enough . . .* supervisor, is sensitive to the need to shift relational styles in response to their dialogic partner's learning style, learning level and developmental need in a given task cycle' (Rapp, 1996: 9, original emphasis). What it comes down to is that the supervision will be most effective and the client therefore best helped if the supervisor and supervisee are sufficiently 'in synch' to be fully and constructively engaged for, as Rapp comments, 'solutions informed by the trainee's full participation are more enduring than solutions that the supervisor attempts to impose' (p. 60). The responsibility for ensuring that the necessary ongoing calibration occurs rests largely with the supervisor.

The organizational context of supervision

Supervision does not take place in a vacuum. Counsellors and supervisors – even those who work in independent practice – have organizational issues thrust upon them. While they may eschew such issues in their own arrangements to work privately, their clients and supervisees will invariably bring dilemmas which are influenced by their work or organizational contexts. The broadly integrative supervisor needs to add an ability and willingness to work with organizational issues to her or his repertoire of competencies. Holloway reminds us that 'both participants of the [supervisory] dyad must understand and be motivated to function in roles prescribed to them by their organizations. Organizational norms and politics often intrude on the supervisory relationship' (Holloway, 1995: 100).

Supervisors who supervise counsellors who work in organizations need to face up to a number of organizational realities. Their supervisees are not free agents within organizations which, today, are typically driven by financial efficiency. Whether we like it or not, and whether or not it fits with our traditional orthodox background and training, time-limited counselling contracts and problem management approaches appear to be here to stay – at least for the foreseeable future. Supervision models are already appearing specifically designed to take account of this change of climate in which brief and solution focused therapy may become the norm in counselling contexts where time and financial resources are strictly limited, such as employee assistance programmes and primary healthcare (Selekman and Todd, 1995; O'Connell and Jones, 1997).

Counsellors who work in organizations may, at times, bemoan their lot as undervalued, under-resourced and misconstrued employees working to line managers or departmental heads who do not appear to share their values, allegiances or priorities. It is sometimes difficult for supervisors, who may have similar crosses to bear as practitioners, to refrain from colluding and taking the traditional, if arguably outmoded, perspective that counsellors should invariably be their own case work managers and able, in almost regal seclusion, to decide about case management issues such as: length of counselling contracts; when and how to refer clients on; parameters of confidentiality; assessment procedures; how records should be kept and stored and how the flow of information should be managed. While it is important for supervisors to affirm supervisees as autonomous practitioners, they also have a responsibility to help them to understand that working for an organization involves at least some accountability to that organization and willingness to consider the employer's frame of reference.

Unwitting supervisors who operate from basic assumptions that their supervisees are, or should be, totally free agents may be doing them a gross disservice. Such an approach can create uncomfortable dissonance for supervisees who may already be struggling to achieve a reasonable fit between the demands of their organization and the ethical imperatives of their profession. Supervisors who take this line may end up, albeit inadvertently, fuelling supervisees' stress, frustration and confusion when what the supervisor appears to be advocating as in the best interests of clients seems impossible to put into practice because of organizational constraints and realities. Far healthier is an attitude where the supervisor acknowledges the existence of accountability to both organization and clients and is proactive in helping supervisees balance and manage the needs of both.

Michael Carroll has suggested a number of areas where counsellors working in organizations frequently need help and support from their supervisors:

1 Enabling supervisees to live and work in organizations.
2 Helping supervisees control the flow of information within the organization.
3 Helping supervisees manage the delivery of counselling provision.
4 Working with supervisees at the interface between the individual and the organization.
5 Ensuring supervisees look after themselves while working within an organizational setting. (Carroll, 1996: 122)

The reader is referred to Carroll's work for a helpful discussion of how supervisors may help supervisees manage these issues and dilemmas.

Supervision across professions

There are signs that counselling supervision is fast migrating from its place of inception and making inroads into other helping professions. This is particularly evident in nursing. The United Kingdom Central Council for Nurses, Midwives and Health Visitors has recently suggested that 'clinical supervision will play an increasingly important part in clinical care' and the Department of Mental Health Nursing Review Team now 'consider it an integral part of mental health nursing practice' (Hardy and Park, 1997: 133). Supervision is becoming more common, either as an ongoing requirement, as occasional consultative support, or in response to particular events such as trauma and disaster within the fields of police welfare, the prison service, clinical psychology, bereavement care, drug and alcohol agency work. It also features for managers in a variety of commercial, industrial, educational and voluntary organizations.

An invitation to provide supervision to professionals and volunteers working in such diverse settings provides the counselling supervisor with the challenge of developing an approach which is not only integrative in relation to therapeutic orientations but also conveys a range of generic and transferable competencies which are adaptable to the supervision requirements of individual work roles within different organizational contexts.

This may sound alarming if it suggests that integrative supervisors need to be experts in a great number of skills and processes pertaining to organizational cultures. It is important for supervisors who work across professions to do their homework and ensure that they are at least minimally knowledgeable about the work settings, responsibilities and activities of their supervisees in order not to operate from unexamined attitudes derived from narrow, even if in-depth, counselling training and experience. However, of equal if not more importance is the need to have a flexible and pragmatic approach or model which can be readily adapted to the needs of different supervisees who may or may not have a counselling role. The Cyclical Model described below is a generic framework which, while emerging from a counselling context, has been seen to transcend that context and to be transferable to a range of situations where a process of consultative support is to be delivered.

Having considered the wider context of supervision, the remaining part of this chapter will delineate a conceptual framework for understanding the process and activity of supervision. What follows is an overview of a model of supervision more fully detailed in *Supervising the Counsellor* (Page and Wosket, 1994). The reader is referred to this book for a full account of the model and how it is used to inform the practice and process of supervision.

An integrative model of supervision

The cyclical model of supervision (see Figure 15.1) was originally construed as a framework for the supervisor looking for guidance when attempting to navigate the multilayered and sometimes bewildering facets of the supervision process. It evolved from a Certificate in Supervision course as a template for training supervisors in the steps and stages of supervision practice. It soon became apparent that many counsellors were finding the language of the model equally useful in forging a dialogue with their supervisors about how they wished to explore their work in supervision. Others began using it as a tool to evaluate their supervision and give feedback to their supervisor or supervisees and it has been used as the basis for a structured questionnaire in research studies. It can be adapted for use in group supervision and has been used to induct counselling students into supervision and as a framework to help them reflect on their counselling practice or supervision sessions with external supervisors.

It is seen as a useful model to present as a template for integrative and eclectic supervision as, not only does it lend itself to the different counselling-supervision related activities and contextual elements as outlined above, but it has also been adapted to supervision across professions, including clinical psychology and nursing (e.g. Hardy and Park, 1997). It is a model which can be used to guide the process of individual supervision sessions or to make sense of the process over a number of sessions. While it is presented here as a sequential model, this is for ease of articulation. In reality the model can be accessed at any point within the five stages and twenty-five substeps. It can be fairly scrupulously adhered to or loosely held in mind to be called forth as and when it might be useful to give shape and movement to the supervision process. A summary of the five stages of the model with some examples of how it may be used follows.

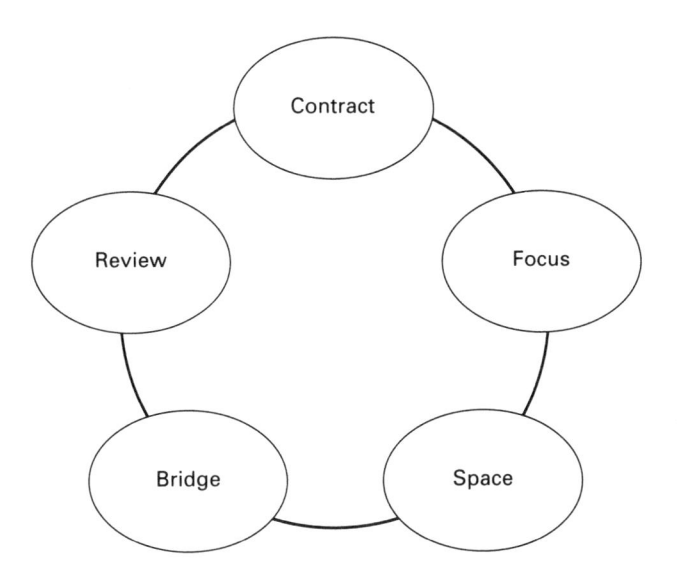

Figure 15.1 *A cyclical model of counsellor supervision (Page and Wosket, 1994)*

Stage 1: Contract

The supervision process needs to begin with a contract which establishes the groundrules for the process and relationship and ensures that the work gets off to a good start. Contracting is as much a qualitative as a quantitative term. The process by which it happens is as important as the content and the integrative supervisor will be flexible and supervisee-responsive in negotiating the contract. Depending on the needs and preferences of the supervisee and on whether there are any organizational imperatives, the initial meeting of the supervisor and supervisee may be largely about contractual issues or merely touch on these sufficiently to kick-start the process, with further elements of the contract then being forged in later sessions.

The supervision contract is important in establishing a structure that provides safety and containment for the exploratory work which follows. Both participants are more likely to be honest, open and vulnerable with one another and to take creative risks if a firm and holding contract is in place to support and sustain the supervisory work and relationship. The supervision contract encompasses the following elements, some of which may be redundant depending on the nature and context of the supervision, for example, whether it is with a trainee or an experienced, independent practitioner.

- *Boundaries*: clarifying differences and interfaces between supervision and training, counselling, and line management.

- *Confidentiality*: reaching a common understanding and agreement about the parameters of confidentiality governing the supervisory relationship.
- *Fees*: amount and when and how these are to be paid.
- *Time, place, duration and frequency*: of meetings and clarification of procedures for between session contact.
- *Codes of ethics and practice*: agreement on adherence to professional codes of practice. If supervisor and supervisee work to different codes they will need to have sight of one another's and negotiate some common ground.
- *Accountability*: clarity and understanding about any lines of accountability (e.g. where the supervisor may be accountable to an employer or training institution). Agreement about where the clinical responsibility for clients is held.
- *Expectations*: discussion and clarification of supervisor's and supervisee's hopes, expectations and responsibilities towards one another and for the supervisory process.
- *Relationship*: some early indications of the quality of relationship to be offered by the supervisor, taking account of the supervisee's preferences.

Stage 2: Focus

The focus in integrative supervision is normally what the supervisee chooses to bring for the attention of the supervisor. The supervisor may then help the supervisee to shape and clarify the focus or, unusually, alter it if she or he feels strongly that a different focus requires attention: for example, if there appears to be some danger to the supervisee, a client or another person which is not being addressed by the supervisee.

Supervisees' issues can be wide ranging. In counselling supervision they need to be related in some way to the work with clients in order to preserve the purpose and function of supervision and to prevent it straying into and becoming lost in associated activities such as training or counselling. Here are some examples of issues which supervisees might focus on:

- a sense of stuckness;
- a feeling of being out of depth;
- a boundary problem;
- a difficulty with endings;
- a relationship problem;
- strong feelings – e.g. of anger, fear, shame, despair or sexual arousal;
- an organizational issue;
- a transcultural concern;
- feelings of stress or impending burnout;
- lack of motivation;
- a sense of over-functioning for the client;
- awareness of transference or countertransference issues;

- a personal issue affecting the client work;
- a sense of achievement or success.

In my experience too much supervision time is often unnecessarily given over to protracted presentation of background material and case history, thereby cutting back on the more valuable space for exploration and the working through of current issues. I admit I also often get bored and struggle to retain the information when I am given a lot of detail about clients and past events without being engaged in a lively way with an immediate focus. I therefore frequently use questions like the following with my supervisees when we are in danger of talking too much *about*, and thereby objectifying the client, rather than engaging with him or her in an immediate, caring and responsive manner:

- 'What is your dilemma with your client?'
- 'Could you try putting your issue in one sentence?'
- 'What do you need help with to work more effectively with your client?'

Stage 3: Space

The exploratory space is the heart of the supervision process. It is the place where supervisees and their clients are held and supported and helped to move ahead and to grow. The key aspects of the supervision space are:

1 *Collaboration*: working together in a co-operative relationship.
2 *Investigation*: exploring possibilities and following hunches, stray thoughts, images, feelings and associations which may throw light on client issues.
3 *Challenge*: providing supportive challenges and, ideally, helping the supervisee to self-challenge in order to open up blindspots.
4 *Containment*: helping the supervisee and thereby their client(s) to feel supported and held.
5 *Affirmation*: helping the supervisee to feel valued and restored.

These elements are addressed and worked with using a variety of counselling and communication skills and the integrative supervisor may have a broad range with which to work. There is also a place here for intuitive approaches which draw on the symbolic power of objects, images and art work. The supervisee may, for example, be invited to handle and place stones or shells which in some way are chosen to represent the client and his or her systemic background. Role play or two-chair work may be introduced and while the supervisee is engaged in visual or active supervision the supervisor is wise to offer minimal facilitation, rather than direction or interpretation. A supervisee working intuitively within the supervision space is normally able, with the respectful holding and attention of their supervisor, to bring forth fresh awareness and find their own answers to dilemmas with clients.

It is important that this part of the supervision process is preserved as a place for opening up and exploring possibilities, issues and dilemmas, rather than attempting to resolve any of them. Getting caught up at this stage in action planning can shut down the creative process and prevent important new material from coming to awareness.

Stage 4: Bridge

The bridge stage of the supervision model is concerned with opening a channel from the exploratory space at the centre of the supervision process back into the work with the client or, if this is not counselling supervision, back to the original situation or dilemma that was presented at the focusing stage. A question I often ask at this point in the process is 'What would you like to do with what we have covered today?' This is an open question which may generate any number of responses. Often the supervisee will take the opportunity to sift through what has been discussed or worked with and sort out what seems useful to register or to have in mind when next seeing the client or grappling with the issue presented. Sometimes the supervisee will welcome further interventions from the supervisor to help him or her work out a possible way forward in managing the situation or dilemma, in which case the following key aspects may come into play:

1. *Goal setting*: identifying what possibilities may be workable and realistic.
2. *Information giving*: where the supervisor may offer to share her own ideas and experience, perhaps giving suggestions for a way forward or recommending some reading.
3. *Action planning*: where, having identified a goal, the supervisor and supervisee together wordstorm a range of strategies for achieving the goal and from these create a tentative action plan.
4. *Considering the client's perspective*: here the supervisor encourages the supervisee to imagine how any change might affect the client. Goals and action plans may then be reviewed following consideration of their likely impact on the client.

Stage 5: Review

The review stage of the supervision process is concerned with evaluation. If the supervisee is a trainee it may also have an assessment function. Ongoing review and evaluation is an important and sometimes neglected aspect of supervision. It is best operationalized through *mutual* feedback where the supervisee is encouraged to give their feedback to the supervisor as well as vice versa. Feedback should happen regularly to develop the relationship between supervisor and supervisee and enhance the efficacy of the supervision task. Feedback has a number of important functions, some of which are to:

- highlight what is going well and progress that has been made;
- indicate where there are weaknesses or omissions to be addressed;
- challenge blindspots or uncover missed opportunities;
- develop and deepen the supervision relationship;
- clear the air through releasing pent up feelings;
- clarify misunderstandings and check assumptions;
- provide an opportunity for the sharing of appreciations.

The ability to give feedback which is welcomed and well received requires the skills of empathy, assertiveness and good timing. Feedback will be most acceptable to either recipient when it is:

- *balanced* – positive with the negative;
- *constructive* – helps the recipient to see what they might do differently and the benefits of that;
- *specific* – given using concrete examples based on behavioural observations;
- *managed with good timing* – given when the other person is likely to be most receptive and open to hearing it;
- *given regularly* – not saved up and 'dumped' in a punitive or accusatory manner.

Mutual constructive feedback in supervision will often lead to recontracting or adjustments made to the initial contract. In this way it closes the circle and recycles back to the first stage of the supervision model.

This brief summary of the cyclical model has been included to provide a possible starting point for the supervisor who is beginning to provide an integrative or eclectic approach to supervision and requires some guidance as he or she develops their own way of working. There is no set formula for the integrative supervisor to follow. There are only pointers in a certain direction which may help to get him or her launched on their own unique voyage.

There follows an extract from a supervision session which demonstrates how the model may be used in a flexible way to frame and structure the work and to guide the supervisor's interventions. Stages of the model are indicated in bold and process notes are added in brackets. The supervisor is Val and the supervisee is Ella.

The **contract**, which has been established in previous sessions, has encompassed the possibility of the supervisee bringing personal material into sessions insofar as it seems to impact on her work with clients. Ella is discussing her work with a new client who, in the first session, has presented with issues of low self-esteem and role overload.

> *Ella*: She says to me things like 'I don't know who I am any more. I have so many different hats to wear. I feel as if there's nothing there that's me. How can I build up my self-esteem and learn to value myself?'

Val: [**Focus**] And what is the issue for you when she says things like that?

Ella: I seem to panic and go blank. I feel scared and useless and quite defensive. I start thinking that counselling can't really help her with all this. I feel as if I have nothing to offer her.

Val: [**Space**] It sounds like she really throws you. How would you normally help someone build up their self-esteem and learn to value themselves?

Ella: I don't really know. It seems to happen in a roundabout way – not because of anything specific.

Val: So when you have had clients who, at the end of counselling, feel greater self-esteem and a more solid sense of themselves, what happened in the counselling that contributed to this?

Ella: It seems to be the quality of the relationship more than anything – offering them warmth, genuineness, respect . . .

Val: Through the way that you value them, they learn to value themselves more.

Ella: Yes, that's it. But somehow it doesn't seem enough with this client.

Val: What else do you do that helps? Do you ever use specific techniques or interventions?

Ella: [*Sounding thoughtful and hesitant*] Well things like role play – if it's in response to a specific situation, say, a job interview.

Val: I was thinking, as you said that, that if this very general stuff that they bring, like 'I want to find out who I am', is broken down into concrete and specific instances, you *can* deal with it.

Ella: Yes, that's true. It's just how to get to the specific.

Val: What might you say that could enable that to happen?

Ella: [*Hesitantly*] Perhaps . . . 'Can you tell me what it's like to feel . . .?'

Val: Yes, that's a good question, it helps to get under the surface of what's presented. It's like when someone came to see me recently and said 'I want to learn to value myself more' and I said 'What's brought you to see me today?' The person said: 'Something that happened this week that I feel devastated about'. So then I could say 'Tell me some more about that.'

Ella: Yes, I feel so stupid. I know I could do that. It's really simple. Why couldn't I work that out for myself?

Val: It seems like we hit some kind of blindspot – or maybe there's something else going on, like it's really a different issue.

Ella: Maybe – I'm not sure. It's certainly a blindspot.

Val: [**Bridge**] Maybe if there is something else it will come up as we talk about your client. Do you have a sense that you'd be able to handle that sort of thing differently with her now that we've looked at it?

Ella: Yes, I'm sure I could.

Val: How about trying it? Say I am your client and I come to you and say 'The problem is, sometimes I wake up in the morning and just don't know who I am any more?'

Ella: I'd probably say something like 'Can you tell me about a time recently when you felt like that?'
Val: And what if she says 'I just feel like it all the time?'
Ella: [*Looking uncomfortable and speaking hesitantly*] I'm finding this really difficult. I feel anxious and embarrassed and I've gone blank.
Val: [**Space**] Is that how you feel when you're with your client?
Ella: Yes it is . . . but there's something else. I'm not sure what.
Val: I'm wondering if you feel that I've put you on the spot.
Ella: I *do* feel put on the spot, but there's another feeling that's coming up sitting here now with you [*beginning to look tearful*]. I feel just like I did when Chris [*her partner*] died. After Chris died I just thought 'I don't know who I am any more'. I'd wake up and think 'I'm nobody'.
Val: [*gently*] It's OK if you need to cry about this.
Ella: [*weeping*] It's so hard at the moment. I feel as if I'm dealing with the real mess deep inside and it's all so difficult. And I'm trying to be all these different people – a competent student, a good counsellor, a mother.
Val: It sounds like you have so much to cope with that it's almost overwhelming [*sits quietly with Ella, who cries for a few moments*]. . . . And I'm struck with how much you sound like the client you described at the beginning, wearing so many hats.
Ella: Yes, and because of that I find it so hard to deal with that kind of client. I just go blank.

[Some discussion of the supervisee's need for support follows and she lets the supervisor know that she is working through her personal issues in her own counselling. The supervisor asks her how she feels about continuing to see clients while she is doing this difficult personal work. Ella considers this carefully and decides that she is still able to counsel effectively as long as she looks after herself and remains alert to how her client's issues might impact on her own. Together they consider a range of strategies [**bridge**] that Ella might use if she again goes blank or feels panicky with her client. These include looking at ways to manage her own feelings and planning in advance a number of possible interventions she might use with the client if she suddenly feels she has temporarily lost her ability to respond spontaneously. Supervisor and supervisee then move to **reviewing** the session.]

Val: What I didn't get around to saying while we were dealing with all that stuff is how lucky I think your clients are to have a counsellor who is so sensitive to the way that her own issues come into the work and also willing to address them – as you've done with me today.
Ella: It felt OK to tell you that stuff because I knew you wouldn't be critical or try to counsel me. I needed to say what was going on for me, but I also wanted to keep on with the supervision. I was glad you let me cry because I needed to offload but I was also glad you didn't let

me wallow and that you brought us back to the client. I feel a lot clearer now because I understand what all that was about. For a while I just thought I'd lost it!

Val: I never, for an instant, thought you'd 'lost it' but I *was* puzzled that you couldn't see your way ahead with this client. Maybe because of that I pushed you a bit hard to come up with ideas when I might have picked up earlier that something else was troubling you.

Ella: I *did* feel put on the spot, but it wasn't until you did that that the other feelings came up and I knew what it was about. I'm glad you didn't back off, even though I felt uncomfortable and defensive, because if you had done I don't think I'd have had such a strong reaction.

Val: I guess it's about trusting the process. Although I like to think I might do it a bit more sensitively next time.

Ella: And I hope there *isn't* a next time like that. That was bloody hard work! [*Both laugh*].

The supervision relationship in integrative and eclectic supervision

I would like to give the last word in this chapter to the supervision relationship, as in my opinion good supervision, like good counselling, rests on the quality of the relationship established between supervisor and supervisee and that this is of paramount importance in determining the effectiveness of the work. In counselling, the relationship is the heart of the therapy; in supervision it is the cornerstone upon which all else is constructed. The ability of the supervisor to build and maintain an enabling relationship with the supervisee is determined by their willingness and capacity to involve themselves in the process and I have written elsewhere about the importance of the use of self in supervision (Wosket, 1999).

Trainee supervisors I meet on courses often lament the coldness and distance of a current or previous supervisor who might offer excellence in terms of clinical astuteness and judgement but in a way that is unpalatable to the counsellor who may wish for more humanity, warmth or support in the relationship. These observations are supported by recent research conducted into the preferences for supervisory style and emphasis of 274 qualified and experienced counsellors in the USA (Usher and Borders, 1993). The researchers in this study found that 'respondents indicated that they preferred a supervisor who is collegial and relationship oriented over one who is task oriented' (p. 74). I agree with Williams (1995) who argues that 'opacity may fit psychoanalysis and "draw the transference", but it is not appropriate for supervision'. He admonishes the supervisor not to treat supervisees 'as if you were not there; pretty soon they will wish you weren't, or worse, develop such a mystique about you that they become obsessed with you' (Williams, 1995: 65).

As supervision becomes more commonplace in other professions and as supervisors gain experience and reputation, they are increasingly called upon to supervise professionals in highly demanding positions. Often this work is with individuals who are called upon to give greatly of themselves in their work situation while receiving little in return to sustain them. Burnout hovers uncomfortably close for many practitioners, managers and professionals in today's pressured work environments.

Supervision can be a significant provider of sustenance to supervisees and we should not underestimate the importance of good listening and rapport in the provision of this. Warm and respectful attention can be hugely nourishing to someone who has no other space in which to offload and explore the pressures and stresses of their work without feeling they may be depleting others, for example, a spouse or partner. If as a supervisor I can be a sufficiently sound and strong container there is less likelihood that my supervisee will need to act out their own unexpressed stress or distress, or leak confidential client material in inappropriate contexts. There is an issue of quantity as well as quality here. Supervisees need to see enough of their supervisors on a regular basis for this restorative process to make a difference (BAC recommends one and a half hours per month as a minimum). While supervision is often afforded high priority by the practitioner who receives it, it is frequently accorded less importance by a line manager who may not have experienced the benefits of supervision at first hand or may begrudge the time and money spent on it. While we may, at times, have to fight for and justify the right to supervision, the tenacity with which this aspect of our professional development is preserved is one important measure of how we value ourselves, our clients and the work that we do.

References

Bernard, J.M. (1994) 'Multicultural supervision; a reaction to Leong and Wagner, Cook, Priest and Fukuyama', *Counselor Education and Supervision*, 34 (2): 159–71.

Bernard, J.M. and Goodyear, R.K. (1992) *Fundamentals of Clinical Supervision*. Boston: Allyn and Bacon.

Borders, L.D. (1992) 'Learning to think like a supervisor', *The Clinical Supervisor*, 10 (2): 135–48.

British Association for Counselling (1996) 'Supervision, Rugby: BAC. (Information Sheet 8.)

Brown, M.T. and Landrum-Brown, J. (1995) 'Counselor supervision: cross-cultural perspectives', in J.G. Ponterotto, J.M. Casas, L.A. Suzuki and C.M. Alexander (eds), *Handbook of Multicultural Counselling*. Thousand Oaks, CA: Sage.

Carroll, M. (1996) *Counselling Supervision: Theory, Skills and Practice*. London: Cassell.

Cook, D.A. (1994) 'Racial identity in supervision', *Counselor Education and Supervision*, 34 (2): 132–41.

Hardy, S. and Park, A. (1997) 'Supervision and professional practice', in B. Thomas, S. Hardy and P. Cutting (eds), *Stuart and Sundeen's Mental Health Nursing: Principles and Practice*. London: Mosby.

Holloway, E.L. (1995) *Clinical Supervision: A Systems Approach*. Thousand Oaks, CA: Sage.

Inskipp, F. (1996) 'New directions in supervision', in L. Bayne, I. Horton and J. Bimrose (eds), *New Directions in Counselling*. London: Routledge.

Inskipp, F. and Proctor, P. (1994) *Making the Most of Supervision*. Twickenham: Cascade.

Inskipp, F. and Proctor, P. (1995) *Becoming a Counsellor Supervisor*. Twickenham: Cascade.

Lago, C.O. in collaboration with Thompson, J. (1996) *Race, Culture and Counselling*. Buckingham: Open University Press.

Newman, C.F. and Goldfried, M.R. (1996) 'Developments in psychotherapy integration', in W. Dryden (ed.), *Developments in Psychotherapy: Historical Perspectives*. London: Sage.

O'Connell, B. and Jones, C. (1997) 'Solution focused supervision', *Counselling*, 8 (4): 289–92.

Page, S. and Wosket, V. (1994) *Supervising the Counsellor: A Cyclical Model*. London: Routledge.

Pope-Davis, D.B. and Coleman, H.L. (eds) (1997) *Multicultural Counseling Competencies: Assessment, Education and Training, and Supervision*. Thousand Oaks, CA: Sage.

Rapp, H. (1996) 'Integrative supervision: intersubjective assessment in a reflective learning space'. Unpublished paper.

Selekman, M. and Todd, T. (1995) 'Co-creating a context for change in the supervisory system: the solution focused supervision model', *Journal of Systemic Therapies*, 14 (3): 21–33.

Usher, C.H. and Borders, L.D. (1993) 'Practicing counselors' preferences for supervisory style and supervisory emphasis', *Counselor Education and Supervision*, 33 (2): 66–79.

Williams, A. (1995) *Visual and Active Supervision: Roles, Focus, Technique*. New York, W.W. Norton.

Wosket, V. (1999) *The Therapeutic Use of Self: Counselling Practice, Research and Supervision*. London: Routledge.

16
INTEGRATION AND ECLECTICISM IN COUNSELLING TRAINING

Mary Connor

Integration appears to be the favoured concept in the 1990s with eclecticism often frowned upon as if it implies a lack of centredness and sophistication in the counsellor. I often wonder whether those who call themselves integrative are, in fact, eclectic, but dare not admit this. Eclecticism involves using what seems appropriate and works best, from a variety of sources. One could argue that the eclectic counsellor stays most open to the needs of the client without using the filters of a purist perspective of, for example, the psychoanalyst, humanist and behaviourist or from the conscious frameworks of the integrative therapist. On the other hand, the dangers of eclecticism lie in the way in which choices are made. Eclecticism requires choice. It is possible that the eclectic counsellor does not make choices as consciously as the counsellor who knows that he or she is 'psychodynamic', 'person-centred', 'behavioural' or 'integrative'. It is possible that choices are made almost subconsciously, according to the fit with the personality or needs of the counsellor at a particular time. If this is the case then effective eclecticism will require a good supervisor, both internal and external.

Lazarus (1989) is an example of someone who proudly proclaims his eclecticism, arguing that research evidence has shown the merits of specific types of interventions with specific client problems. His eclecticism has been developed into what he calls *multimodal* therapy. Hollander (1997: 16) reviews the literature on definitions of integration and eclecticism and notes that there is a fundamental difference between them: '"Eclecticism" is a process of selecting out, with the implication of taking something apart; "Integration" is the process of bringing together, with the implication of making something whole and new.' He argues that integrationists seek synthesis and that this can be sought in two ways in counselling, either by bringing different approaches together so that eclecticism is incorporated in the notion of integration, or by a 'superordinate theory which goes beyond a blending of techniques from different therapies'. The integrative counsellor will be using judicious choices, based on the evidence of what is likely to be effective with this particular counsellor and this particular client, in these particular circumstances at this particular time and in this particular place.

The little that we know about counselling effectiveness points to the therapeutic significance of the counsellor as a person, rather than to a purist, integrationist or eclectic stance. If this is so then perhaps integration is what happens when any counsellor develops to the advanced stage of unconscious competence, whether they use a specialized approach, an integrative framework or an eclectic approach. In this sense, integration implies integrity or wholeness: the sort of synchronicity that one experiences in a superb performance where the heart, mind and soul are in tune to produce the thoughts, feelings and behaviours that reflect this. Such performances may be with clients, or with music, dance, poetry, art, engineering or even, dare we say it, politics. Such high level integration is characteristically idiosyncratic and therefore not readily amenable to analysis in a way that will produce transferable data which could be empirically verified. However, the challenge for integrative training is to assess competence in relation to this synchronicity.

What about the core theoretical model?

I wish to argue for an integrative approach to counsellor training which is open to and incorporates eclecticism. Such an approach gives trainee counsellors the opportunity to develop their own integrity as a counsellor, using the approaches and methods which are best for them, rather than those which are imposed by a training organization with a narrowly focused way of viewing, the world, clients, development, learning, change, systems and contexts.

What about the insistence of the British Association for Counselling (BAC) that all accredited training courses demonstrably operate from a core theoretical model? Feltham (1997: 121) argues that there are both philosophical and clinical reasons for him to have come to the conclusion that training in a core theoretical model is 'ultimately untenable and oppressive'. He cautions against the certitude with which certain schools of counselling and psychotherapy portray their efficacy, when there is so much research evidence pointing towards what he terms 'non-specific' factors and what Garfield and Bergin (1994) refer to as 'common therapeutic' factors:

> Many of these are about the client's belief in the therapist, confidence in the status of the therapist, therapist qualities ... working alliance, the protected setting, etc. Some are about simple human needs for attention, warmth and acceptant interest (Howe, 1993). Karasu (1992: 27) argues that the therapist's passionate belief in his or her theories and methods is crucial, since the aura of

conviction conveys itself to the clients. Conviction, not theoretical correctness, is what counts according to Karasu's argument. (Feltham, 1997: 123)

Other arguments put forward by Feltham include: the dangers of having a limited worldview which may be helpful with some clients, but harmful with others; the limiting nature of traditionally held views of what works, rather than a spirit of open enquiry into future possibilities; the newness of so much counselling and psychotherapy theory and the lack of cross-fertilization with other connected disciplines, e.g. philosophy, theology, anthropology. He criticizes the imposition of white, Western psychological concepts and states that core theoretical models are 'self-evidently productions of a patriarchal society':

Virtually all current psychotherapeutic theory reflects white, Western psychology and implicit assumptions about the universal correctness or desirability of autonomy, assertiveness, insightfulness, and emotional freedom, qualities which are not in fact valued by all individuals in all cultures at all times. Core theoretical models in psychotherapy and counselling encourage monolithic, ethnocentric and patriarchal thinking and tacitly discourage and marginalise (even forbid) any kind of anarchic (Feyerband, 1993), personalistic (Smail, 1978), radically feminist (McLellan, 1995), politicised (Newman, 1991) and dialogical (Sampson, 1993) accounts of human functioning, distress and healing. (Feltham, 1997: 123)

While acknowledging the dangers outlined above, I do recognize the advantages of training counsellors in a core theoretical model. A core model provides a base, an initial map from which the trainee can begin to explore the territory. Without a starting point and an integrating framework there is a greater possibility of becoming lost or fragmented. Mapping the territory assumes that there is some agreement about a core body of knowledge which has been developed, scrutinized and researched. Being integrative does not mean being unclear. It assumes that existing knowledge can be brought together in new, creative ways, thus establishing the possibility of innovative configurations. The 'loose hold' that counsellors offer to clients is what I also advocate that training courses offer to trainees with the use of a core model or integrating frame. It needs to be held in a spirit of openness, of enquiry, a source of comparison and contrast, which maps the territory and leads to uncharted places.

Counsellor training – towards integrity

I have developed an integrative model for counsellor training (Connor, 1994). It is designed to develop competent and reflective counsellors. Having been involved in early discussions about course recognition by BAC, I recognized the key elements in training which they identified. But I was also aware that it is often the *relationship between* particular elements of training that provides coherence and a developmental framework for training, for example: the link between theory and practice; the relationship between personal awareness and growth in supervision; the manifestation of the core conditions of genuineness; warmth and empathy in work with clients, but also in interactions with course tutors and the peer group.

Where there were difficulties with assessing the competence of trainees it was often because of a lack of consistency *between* key elements. I therefore tried to develop a framework which would integrate the key elements through the core activity, which is of course the relationship of counsellor and client. Models are criticized because they can appear to oversimplify (McLeod, 1992); they can induce conformity; they can too easily be applied mechanistically; they can give the impression of being linear rather than spiral or holistic. This cyclical model is a framework for the training process within which a variety of approaches and skills may be located. It allows for eclecticism within an integrative context.

All counsellor training starts with underlying assumptions about what counselling is and what the process and outcome of training may be. My aim is to develop competent and reflective counsellors. I therefore have an intentional view about counsellor training. It is a professional activity and as such it is accountable. The trainees will also become accountable for the quality of their work with clients. Work with the client is at the heart of all training. The focus is upon learning rather than teaching. Learning encompasses learning about self, client and self-with-client. The responsibility of the trainer is to provide the necessary conditions and resources for learning to take place. I believe that the trainee is able to take responsibility for her or his own learning. The ethos to be developed on the course is that of a collaborative learning community. I believe that trainers and trainees are both robust and vulnerable and that they respond positively to affirmation and high expectation. They are capable of achieving results beyond the ordinary. Finally, I believe in learning as a lifelong process.

The integrative model has been developed from the assumptions and beliefs outlined above. The core of the model is the client and counsellor in relationship. The model uses theories of learning as well as theories of counselling to provide integration. Kolb's (1984) learning cycle provides the frame for experiential learning, beginning with concrete experience, reflection upon experience, formulation of hypotheses and the opportunity to test these out in new situations. The rhythm of this cycle brings integrity to the learning process. Honey and Mumford's (1984) work on learning styles helps in the understanding of trainee preferences for certain activities during training and helps trainees to understand why, as activists, theorists, pragmatists or reflectors, they may have preferred ways of counselling.

I have identified four stages in the training process within a cyclical model, each contributing to the intrapersonal and interpersonal development of the

PROFESSIONAL DEVELOPMENT

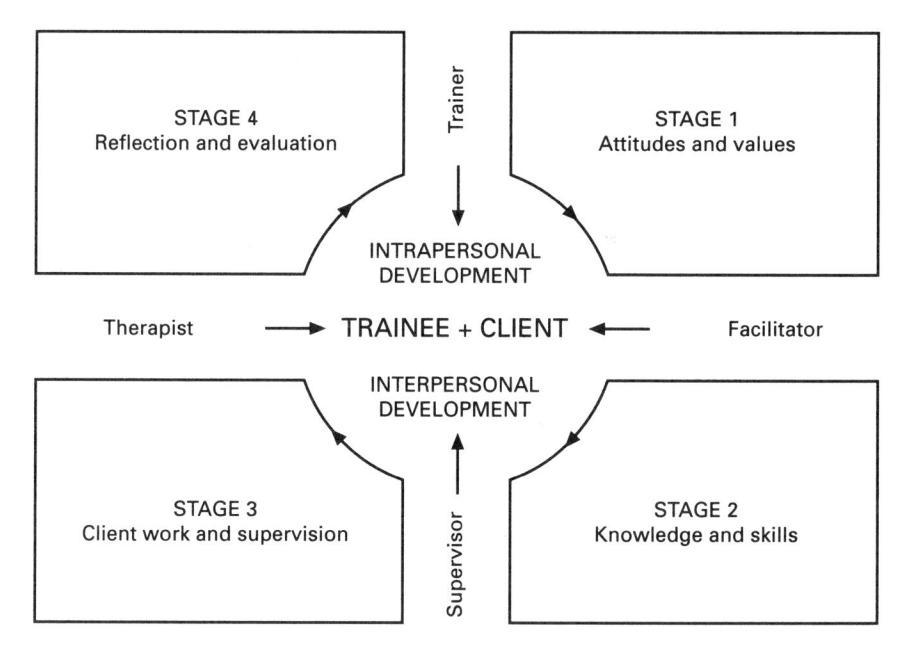

```
┌─────────────────────────┐   Trainer   ┌─────────────────────────┐
│      STAGE 4            │      │      │      STAGE 1            │
│ Reflection and evaluation│      ▼      │ Attitudes and values    │
│                         ╲             ╱                         │
└──────────────────────────╲───────────╱──────────────────────────┘
                      INTRAPERSONAL
                      DEVELOPMENT

Therapist      ──────▶   TRAINEE + CLIENT   ◀──────   Facilitator

                      INTERPERSONAL
                      DEVELOPMENT
┌──────────────────────────╱───────────╲──────────────────────────┐
│      STAGE 3            ╱      ▲      ╲     STAGE 2             │
│ Client work and         │      │      │  Knowledge and skills   │
│ supervision             │  Supervisor │                         │
└─────────────────────────┘             └─────────────────────────┘
```

COMPETENT REFLECTIVE COUNSELLORS

Figure 16.1 *The integrative model (Connor, 1994: 57)*

counsellor, which is at the heart of the ability to develop the therapeutic relationship. The four stages are:

- development of attitudes and values;
- development of theory and skills;
- client work and supervision;
- reflection and evaluation.

Contributing to all stages would be the course tutors, supervisors, groupwork facilitators and personal therapists/counsellors.

This is an integrating framework within which a whole variety of theories, approaches, ideas, techniques and skills may be explored, tried and tested. Providing a framework does not of itself ensure integration. The integration comes from the way in which it is modelled and used by trainees. The processes of learning and assessment have to be woven together into a seamless garment of exploration and discovery. Internalization will occur through active participation by learners, involvement, commitment, belief in and ownership of the process and systematic reflection upon learning. (See Figure 16.1.)

Intrapersonal and interpersonal development

At the heart of counsellor training are specific aspects of intrapersonal and interpersonal development which will enhance the ability to develop and sustain the therapeutic relationship (Rogers, 1961; Clarkson, 1995) and the working alliance (Bordin, 1979). Garfield and Bergin draw attention to the 'common factors' revealed by research across a variety of therapies. The research does not reveal significant differences in outcome across the approaches and writers have suggested looking at common therapeutic factors such as: 'the creation of hope, the opportunity for emotional release, explanations and interpretations of one's problems, support, advice, the trying out of new behaviours, and the modification of cognitions' (Garfield and Bergin, 1994: 8). I have specified some learning objectives in the areas of intrapersonal and interpersonal development, which give an integrating framework for various activities which occur throughout training:

Intrapersonal development

- To develop understanding and appreciation of self.
- To become aware of and utilize personal strengths and assets.
- To become aware of blindspots, blocks and vulnerabilities.
- To identify areas to work on in personal counselling.
- To appreciate experientially the significance of developmental stages in personal development.

Interpersonal development

- To understand areas of strength and areas for development in a range of interactions: with peers, staff, clients and in personal and professional relationships.
- To gain confidence in appropriate self-sharing.
- To develop skills in giving and receiving feedback.
- To facilitate growth in self and others through active participation in personal development groups.
- To develop helping relationships with clients.
- To reflect continuously upon successes and setbacks and to use such reflection as the basis for setting realistic objectives for development.

These lists are not meant to be exhaustive, nor are they intended to be value free. All counsellor training is based on assumptions and beliefs. The integrity of the training is in the conscious manifestation of those beliefs and in the openness to the possibility of other, different and perhaps better ways of thinking, feeling and doing. The learning objectives above demonstrate the integration of learning about self with learning about clients; the integration of 'being' with clients and 'being' as a member of a course group; the interaction of using skills both with other course members and with clients. Personal counselling, experiential groupwork and personal reflections in a learning journal are all vehicles for reflection and practice in relation to core counselling attributes, skills and approaches. The implications for course tutors are that if the course is to be truly integrative, the tutors will model to trainees a way of being which is consonant with that which is taught, so that learning can be from that which is 'caught' by observation as well as 'taught' by explicit methods of teaching and learning.

The four stages of the integrative model feed in to intrapersonal and interpersonal development: that is, the development of attitudes and values; the development of knowledge and skills; client work and supervision; reflection and evaluation. The first two stages prepare the trainee for client work and supervision. The final stage integrates and evaluates learning from all the other stages.

Developing attitudes and values

The model provides opportunities throughout training: to become aware of personal assumptions and beliefs; to explore and clarify values and attitudes; to develop core therapeutic qualities; to be aware of ethical and professional issues and expectations; and to develop a personal code of counselling ethics. One of the earliest exercises on the course is intended to challenge philosophical beliefs by addressing issues such as freedom, determinism, altruism, goodness and power.

When values are explored trainees may be unaware of the dissonance between espoused values and values 'in use'. They may have only had a hazy idea about what it is that they truly prize. Attitudes are, by definition, settled ways of thinking and therefore not easily amenable to change. However, counselling research indicates that it is the communication of certain attitudes towards clients that may be the most powerful impetus for change (Rogers, 1961; Garfield and Bergin, 1994). An integrative approach, which incorporates eclecticism, will explore a variety of therapeutic attitudes and qualities, and will not confine this exploration to topics examined within a lecture or seminar. Certain attitudes and values are particularly pertinent for the integrative counsellor and so there will be a focus upon decision making, choice, integrity and pluralism.

> Attitudes are not changed just by talking about them, or indeed by getting tutors feedback. Qualities are not developed by just practising skills or writing essays. They develop through the sum total of the learning experience and they are more likely to develop if there is intentionality in the learning process through ongoing structured experiences for reflection, reviewing and objective-setting. In this model this would be through regular entries in a learning journal and regular review with a learning partner. This would include reflections upon taught sessions, practice, work with clients, supervision, experiential groupwork and reflections upon reading. (Connor, 1994: 37)

Developing knowledge and skills

There was a lively debate in the 1989 *British Journal of Guidance and Counselling* between eclectics (Lazarus, 1989) and integrationists (Beitman, 1989). Lazarus cautioned against the 'fusionist' tendencies implied by integration and argues for the validity of technical eclecticism, noting that, contrary to false conclusions drawn from meta-analyses, there is evidence that specific treatments are effective for specific client problems. He describes fusionists as those who try to weld notions from two disparate orientations. Beitman identified three different forms of integration: systematic eclecticism; common factor integration; and theoretical integration. His own preference is for common factor integration and he explains several integrative principles: the principle of convergence among approaches; the principle of stages in counselling; and the interpersonal nature of counselling. He stresses the importance of flexibility to client need and as a means of counteracting rigid thinking.

A cautionary note, however, is sounded by Messer (1989) who sees obstacles to integration and eclecticism in: competing concepts of the therapeutic relationship; what constitutes knowledge; and visions of reality. He pinpoints these problems in the psychoanalytic, behavioural and humanistic approaches to psychotherapy. Norcross and Grencavage (1989: 236) pinpointed recurrent obstacles to psychotherapy integration and reported research from Norcross and Thomas (1988) in which 58 prominent integrationists rated twelve potential obstacles in terms of severity. The top five were, in order of severity: the investment of individuals in their own private perceptions and theories; inadequate commitment to training psychotherapists in more than one approach or system; divergent assumptions about psychopathology and health; inadequate empirical research on integration; and the absence of a common language among psychotherapies.

Such obstacles have not prevented Clarkson (1995) from developing integrative psychotherapy training at both initial and advanced levels. She describes her model as *integrating* rather than *integrative*, with emphasis upon a dynamic process rather than a finished product. This accords with my own view, that one of the characteristics of being integrative is constantly to look at ideas in new ways and through different lenses. This is not to deny the value of well-researched knowledge and skill, but to approach all knowledge in the spirit of active enquiry. 'The main sensitivity of a training structure is not to discount any of people's experience but to allow them a place where they can bring it, make sense of it and integrate or relinquish what they no longer need' (Clarkson, 1995: 280). She has developed an integrative model which focuses upon five aspects of the therapeutic relationship and from this framework she explores the similarities and differences between major psychotherapeutic approaches. The differentiated aspects of the therapeutic relationship are: the working alliance; the transference/countertransference relationship; the developmental/reparative relationship; the person-to-person (real) relationship; and the transpersonal relationship.

Like myself, she views the cyclical stages of learning as integrative and whereas I use Kolb's (1984) learning cycle to integrate learning activities, she uses the three phases of awareness, accommodation and assimilation as ways of viewing change and learning. She elaborates on the specific integrative skills of learning which are encouraged:

- *awareness* both of their own process and the fullest possible perception and intuitive awareness of the client(s)
- *accommodation* which can range from the introjection of earlier caveat(s) to later opposing or contradictory views
- *assimilation* which concerns making the acquired skills, knowledge and information an integral part of their individual psychophysiological system. This is of course again followed by phases of increased awareness and so on as long as the psychotherapist is learning and growing (Clarkson, 1995: 279)

My approach to integrating knowledge and skills is to start by introducing trainees to the spectrum of major counselling theories and approaches, noting areas of similarity and difference and focusing upon the historical development of counselling and psychotherapy. The next stage is to develop a thorough working knowledge of the counselling process and my preference here is for a transtheoretical model such as Egan's (1998) Skilled Helper model. The focus here is upon the therapeutic process in relation to valued change in the client. Once trainees have demonstrated proficiency in the basics of the counselling process, they can then explore contributing theories in more depth. At a later stage of development they are able to undertake specialist training in one or more specific counselling or psychotherapeutic approaches with a particular focus upon the therapeutic use of self in counselling.

Alongside the development of knowledge of the counselling process is the need to increase knowledge about clients, their development, the systems and contexts in which they live, major causes and manifestations of client problems and an understanding of mental health and mental illness. Appreciation of the work of helping agencies is important. Trainees are encouraged to learn and apply appropriately a variety of helping strategies and interventions. They are assisted in identifying and owning their personal strengths and limitations in relation to skills and strategies. They move from the state of unconscious incompetence to the more painful awareness of conscious incompetence, and then (hopefully) with training towards conscious competence. At this point they are developing an integrated counselling style. But my experience of training leads me to believe that many trainees need much more experience of counselling before they move to the synchrony of unconscious competence. Of course, there is a danger at this stage that without ongoing training and supervision unconscious competence could revert back to unconscious incompetence.

The role played by training institutions is key. If future counsellors and psychotherapists are to be able to function in a coherent but pluralistic way they need to be introduced to concepts of complementarity, convergence, systematic practice, prescriptive matching, empiricism and the ability to take the 'long view' (Norcross and Grencavage, 1989: 238). Complementarity involves looking at the strengths and liabilities in different approaches, including client as well as therapist variables.

Norcross and Grencavage discuss the view of integration as *systematic practice*. This implies that counsellors are competent in several approaches and they select their interventions based upon wise clinical decisions, informed by reading and research. *Prescriptive matching* is the attempt to fit the appropriate treatment to the appropriate client. As regards *taking the long view*, the writers note that there is inherent resistance to change from those who cling tenaciously to the dogmas of therapeutic effectiveness but what is needed in order to take these ideas forward is the 'promotion of open inquiry, informed pluralism, empirical research, and intellectual relativism' (Norcross and Grencavage, 1989: 243).

This view matches the later view of Samuels (1993) who writes about 'What is good training' in the *British Journal of Psychotherapy*. He identifies three components: authenticity, openness and pluralism. He offers six specific suggestions about how pluralism could be engendered in training: conflict-oriented training organized around major disputes that have characterized the field; using dispute as a teaching tool; use of polemical books and texts; use of some inexperienced teachers to free up discussion and creative uncertainty; distinguishing between the social and ideological functions of leadership to allow for more creative thinking away from those who also exercise power; and the use of plural interpretation, that is, competing alternative interpretations. Pluralism without authenticity could lead to haphazard eclecticism. The integrating factor is the authenticity of the developing counsellor's own integrity or wholeness.

Client work and supervision

It is in this area that most difficulties can occur when trying to integrate theory and practice, and learning on the course with learning in the actual counselling setting. If a course is truly integrative it will incorporate learning from all areas of the course, including the personal or experiential development group and learning from supervision sessions which are normally held separately from the course. How can we say that a trainee counsellor is competent unless we have direct evidence of personal development work in a group, of work with clients in situ and of work with a supervisor?

The learning from client work and supervision will include: the ability to distinguish between counselling and other helping activities; the ability to set up contracts with real clients; the opportunity to practise counselling competencies in real counselling situations; the ability to reflect regularly upon counselling practice through use of a counselling log, case notes, and a learning journal; the experience of regular supervision, both individual and group; the development of the internal supervisor; and finally the development of confidence as a counsellor. One trainee, Rod, talks about the way in which his learning is being integrated through reflections upon supervision:

> I feel that there has been a strong development in the intentionality of my counselling work. This I believe comes from a better theoretical foundation and perhaps more significantly a firmer grasp of the counselling process. I have found that the framework for writing up each counselling session allows for the examination of my own and the client's objectives, feelings and thoughts, also outlining the outcome of the session and any learning that has taken place. I feel that this has proved invaluable in enabling me to examine the dynamics within my counselling relationships. I have found a valuable aspect of supervision has been the constant challenge for me to examine my relationships with various clients, particularly those presenting from diverse backgrounds and with diverse problems. (Connor, 1994: 181).

Reflection and evaluation

One of the characteristics of any training which calls itself 'integrative' must be an emphasis upon constant reflection and evaluation. Otherwise there are all the dangers of 'wild eclecticism' which is not the result of considered, informed and judicious choice. I am reminded of the saying that there is no learning without action, but action does not promote learning unless there is reflection upon action. Reflective processes need to be built into the structure of the training course or programme to ensure that they occur with regularity.

Systematic reflection in a learning journal is a most effective integrating force. Trainees set learning objectives and constantly reflect upon these, noting what has and has not been achieved and what has helped or hindered learning. This includes factors in the self, in others and in the contexts and settings where learning takes place. Another process for integrating learning is the regular peer review that takes place with a trusted learning partner. Such structures reflect intentionality in counsellor training, which is necessary for a professional training with accountability to clients and to professional associations. I realize that others would not wish to have such a structured approach to reflections upon learning, and that some of the 'looser' approaches to systematic integration offer a different richness of experience.

Implications for assessing counsellor competence

The integrative approach espouses: openness and pluralism; the ability to hold ambiguity; the ability to distinguish without devaluing; the capacity to cross boundaries and to work collaboratively; the ability to make informed and wise choices; and the integrity demanded by remaining true to specific counselling approaches rather than adapting them in a way which dilutes or contaminates their efficacy. These are high-level competencies.

I have a developmental approach to the assessment of competence. It is incremental. In the initial stages of training (for example, the end of the first year of a counselling diploma) trainees are expected to demonstrate discrete behaviours which communicate the core therapeutic qualities and which demonstrate proficiency in the basic steps and stages of the counselling process. By the completion of the diploma, a higher order of competence is expected which reflects the ability to identify and work with the intrapersonal and interpersonal dynamics in the counselling relationship; to integrate relevant skills and strategies as appropriate; and to demonstrate the effective use of immediacy to support and challenge the here-and-now relationship.

These competencies give evidence of some integration. However, I would argue that being an effective integrative counsellor is something that only develops with considerable experience and is unlikely to be achieved in initial training. We need to be realistic about what can be expected. Both Hollander (1997) and Clarkson (1995) focus upon 'integrating' as a process rather than being 'integrative' as an outcome. This is a useful way of viewing competence, with a focus upon the qualities required in order to integrate. It is then possible to look for ways in which these qualities may be assessed through different elements of training – the qualities of openness, pluralism, collaborative enquiry, judicious choice – leading to therapeutic wisdom. These qualities will be evidenced in several aspects of the course: relationships with tutors and course members; input and participation in seminars and discussions; the way of being in the personal development group; reflections in the learning journal; case notes in a supervised practice file; joint learning statements with the supervisor and group facilitator; and finally the summative account of all learning in the personal and professional development profile.

Ethical and professional considerations

The British Association for Counselling (BAC, 1994) highlights three ethical values which inform standards: integrity, impartiality and respect. These are derived from ethical principles concerning autonomy (the exercise of maximum choice); fidelity (faithfulness to promises made); justice (fair distribution of benefits); beneficence (doing good to, or for, the other); nonmaleficence (doing no harm to the other). Integrity implies wholeness, honesty, transparency and congruence. An integrative training which operates from this value will be clear and upfront about what can be achieved. There will be a sense of coherence and consistency in the training. The values of the course will be lived by both tutors and students.

Impartiality implies fairness and equal access. An integrative training which operates from a value of impartiality will give trainees equal access to all relevant approaches and will highlight strengths and limitations across the spectrum of approaches. Respect implies valuing. An integrative training operating from respect will communicate valuing to trainees, clients and to all relevant counselling approaches. Learning will take place within the ethos of a collaborative learning community which values difference and creativity and which is characterized by its openness to new ideas.

The integrative approach to training should carry a trainee health warning. It is risky, it is demanding, it will always be at the cutting edge of thinking if it is to be really effective. It will require of the counsellor: receptiveness; skill; judgement; and tenacity. The capacity for synchronicity in counselling comes from a profound sense of personal integrity. This will not just be a product of integrative or eclectic training, it will be a lifelong process of learning and development.

References

Beitman, B.D. (1989) 'Why I am an integrationist (not an eclectic)', *British Journal of Guidance and Counselling*, 17 (3): 259–73.

Bordin, E.S. (1979) 'The generalisability of the psychoanalytical concept of the working alliance', *Psychotherapy: Theory, Research and Practice*, 16 (3): 252–60.

British Association for Counselling (1994) *Code of Ethics and Practice for Trainers*. Rugby: BAC.

Clarkson, P. (1995) *The Therapeutic Relationship*. London: Whurr.

Connor, M. (1994) *Training the Counsellor*. London: Routledge.

Egan, G. (1998) *The Skilled Helper*. Pacific Grove: Brooks/Cole.

Feltham, C. (1997) 'Challenging the core theoretical model', *Counselling*, 8 (2): 121–5.

Garfield, S.L. and Bergin, A.E. (1994) *Handbook of Psychotherapy and Behavior Change*. New York: Wiley.

Hollander, H. (1997) 'Eclecticism/integration among counsellors in Britain in relation to Kuhn's concept of paradigm formation'. Unpublished doctoral thesis, Keele University.

Honey, P. and Mumford, A. (1984) *A Manual of Learning Styles*. Maidenhead: McGraw-Hill.

Kolb, D.A. (1984) *Experiential Learning*. London: Prentice-Hall.

Lazarus, A. (1989) 'Why I am an eclectic (not an integrationist)', *British Journal of Guidance and Counselling*, 17 (3): 248–58.

McLeod, J. (1992) 'Issues in the evaluation of counselling skills courses', *Employee Counselling Today*, 4 (5): 14–19.

Messer, S.B. (1989) 'Integration and eclecticism in counselling and psychotherapy: cautionary notes', *British Journal of Guidance and Counselling*, 17 (3): 274–85.

Norcross, J.C. and Grencavage, L.M. (1989) 'Eclecticism and integration in counselling and psychotherapy: themes and obstacles', *British Journal of Guidance and Counselling*, 17 (3): 227–47.

Norcross, J.C. and Thomas, B.L. (1988) 'What's stopping us now? Obstacles to psychotherapy integration', *Journal of Integrative and Eclectic Psychotherapy*, 7: 74–80.

Rogers, C.R. (1961) *On Becoming a Person*. London: Constable.

Samuels, A. (1993) 'What is good training?', *British Journal of Psychotherapy*, 9 (3): 317–23.

17
ECLECTIC, INTEGRATIVE AND INTEGRATING PSYCHOTHERAPY OR BEYOND SCHOOLISM

Petruska Clarkson

> Tolstoy: 'I know that most men, including those at ease with problems of the greatest complexity, can seldom accept even the simplest and most obvious truth if it be such as would oblige them to admit the falsity of conclusions which they have delighted in explaining to colleagues, which they have proudly taught to others, and which they have woven, thread by thread, into the fabric of their lives.'
>
> (Gleick, 1988: 38)

Some hundred years after Freud, Moreno and Pavlov birthed the three great lineages of psychotherapy, more than 450 different approaches have been identified (Corsini, 1984). Polkinghorne's (1992) words summarize those of many thinkers since: 'The large number of theories claiming to have grasped the essentials of psychological functioning provide *prima facie* evidence that no one theory is correct' (p. 158).

Against this background, the perceived or actual orthodoxy of 'pure forms' of psychotherapy have engaged in more than 100 years of sometimes even fundamentalist rivalry with extremely ambiguous results. We can now say that Eysenck's challenge to the effectiveness of psychotherapy from the 1950s has been overcome, because there is substantial evidence of various kinds that psychotherapy seems to help many people (see *Consumer Reports*, 1995; Parry and Richardson, 1996; Roth and Fonagy, 1996 for reviews). While it is sometimes claimed that techniques such as exposure have advantages in certain kinds of cases (Duckworth and Charlesworth, 1988), it is also true that there appears to be no significant evidence that a *theoretical* approach is relevant to the successful outcome of psychotherapy – no matter how measured (Heine, 1953; Norcross and Goldfried, 1992; Barkham, 1995; Elkin, 1995; Seligman, 1995; Parry and Richardson, 1996; Roth and Fonagy, 1996; Shapiro, 1996; Arundale, 1997; Clarkson, 1997b). In fact there is evidence that there are experiences of psychotherapy by which people feel harmed. One of the most salient facts here is that the harmfulness seems to have to do with the extent to which a psychotherapist entrenches into a theoretical position when challenged or questioned by their client (see Winter, 1997 for review).

Three major meta-categories of solution to this problem have emerged: (a) eclecticism, (b) integration, and the more pluralistic (c) after schoolism movement.

Eclecticism

Various forms of so-called *eclecticism* have emerged, ranging from well-considered and arguably justified approaches such as that of Lazarus (1989) to the slipshod variety which characterizes the intellectually lazy magpie kind that takes indiscriminately and without rigour or discipline from whatever 'comes to hand'. This is legitimized with the claim that they are playing it by ear. This latter kind has obviously attracted opprobrium and while the term 'eclectic' can still be used with some pride in North America to describe a certain kind of open-mindedness, in Britain it tends to evoke an unremitting negative connotation which makes practitioners avoid using the term – even if it may be best descriptive of their practice.

Integrative psychotherapy

The denomination 'integrative psychotherapy' is now being hailed as the most popular descriptive term of psychotherapists (Norcross, 1997). However, this is also leading to another infinite proliferation. In 1984, Dryden estimated that there were about a dozen different forms of integrative psychotherapy, and the number has probably increased. Unfortunately many of these integrative theories have little to recommend them and equally consist of a hotchpotch of other people's ideas (often unacknowledged) brought together without coherence, systemization or integrity. This contrasts with serious and rigorous attempts to achieve integration of which Ryle, Barkham and Shapiro, and Beutler are only some examples.

In the same way as every solution contains the seeds of the next problem, these experiments and models of integration have been bedevilled with philosophical, ethical, scientific and practical problems. Not least is the competition and rivalry between different forms of integration, the thorny issue of whether it is the psychotherapist or the client who is actually doing the integration, and the intrinsic immeasurability of the project. There are also criticisms of a perceived unending commitment to exploration versus the desire for some kind of definitive statement which can withstand the demands for replicable evidence-based psychotherapy in an increasingly commercially oriented market.

One of the thorniest issues has concerned the training of so-called integrative psychotherapists with two usually opposite positions: (a) *integration after a training in one or more of the 'pure' forms of psychotherapy has been completed* and (b) *integration from the beginning of psychotherapy training*. Proponents of the first view contend that integration is exclusively the fruit of maturity and substantial experience which can only be accomplished if solid foundations have been built in singular approaches. Such early adoption of a 'pure form' it is argued, will emotionally and ideologically provide a sense of early security and later disillusionment as the practitioners experience the practical and theoretical limitations of any one particular system. Proponents of the second view maintain that students who are educated in an integrative orientation from the beginning are better able to develop both academically and professionally because they have to learn early on the required skills of intellectual questioning and tolerance for other perspectives.

Based upon the experience of designing psychotherapy programmes from both perspectives, I would offer the following opinion. I believe that immersion in the 'pure forms' before 'integration' has great benefits – clarity, purity, conviction. It also has ambiguous side-effects. One gets to learn from the 'classic' teachers who often require total ideological commitment. There is an enormous security in knowing that you are 'right' (on the authority of your doctrine) and that all critics are unquestionably wrong and of course that if your patient does not fit your theory it is the patient who is wrong, lacking in ego-strength or commitment or psychological mindedness, psychopathic, narcissistic, etc. Unless one learns more than one approach equally thoroughly, these side-effects can become iatrogenic diseases – seriously infecting and debilitating the profession of psychotherapy. If one learns two or more approaches thoroughly, integration at an advanced level can be both desirable and feasible.

On the other hand, since learning *one* approach thoroughly now takes many years of training, the potential – even for gifted individuals – to acquire equally thorough training in two or more approaches plus years of further training in psychotherapy integration means the dedication of practically half a professional life to this endeavour.

Farrell (1979) points out that participants, 'trainees' or clients are usually considered to be 'cured' or 'trained' or 'analysed' or 'qualified' by one single criterion: they have adopted the WOT or 'way of talking' of the leaders, governing bodies, examination boards and others of perceived status or power. An empirical study by Silverman (1997) also found repeatedly that 'rather than being a deviant case, such adoption by clients of the professionals' rhetoric is common. . . . Each centre [of counselling] offers an incitement to speak structured according to its own practical theories' (p. 209). The implications of these ideas for psychotherapy training have hardly begun to be imagined. However, they make somewhat of a nonsense of any 'pure form' approach which has exclusive claims to the 'truth'.

One of the most profound and recurring findings from *the research* is that it is the *psychotherapeutic relationship* rather than diagnosis or technique which potentiates the beneficial effects of psychotherapy. (See Fiedler, 1951, Clarkson, 1990, 1995a, 1996b, and Norcross, 1997 for more detail.) Recently, the evidence is also growing that there are different kinds of relationship required for different kinds of clients. This factor appears to be even more important than diagnosis in predicting effectiveness of psychotherapy (Norcross, 1997).

Clarkson (1975, 1990, 1996b, 1997b) has identified five different universes of discourse or kinds of psychotherapeutic relationship spanning all approaches: Working Alliance, Transference/Countertransference, Developmentally Needed or Reparative, Person-to-Person, and Transpersonal.

After schoolism (back to psychotherapy)

There is a third possibility which I believe can take these issues into account and move us beyond them – what I have termed 'after schoolism'. This way of viewing our world and our work is more the pluralistic (Samuels, 1993) or post-modern (Polkinghorne, 1992), an engagement with the co-existence of metaphorically many different languages – each with its own right to existence. It requires a willingness to be self-reflexive, an ability to consider meta-theoretical issues and an openness to explore the philosophical assumptions, value commitments and ideological bases of even our firmest 'scientific' findings.

Several psychotherapy organizations and many conferences are structured around the notion of different theoretical approaches – whether integrative or not. Psychotherapy school syllabuses and curricula specify theory. Few, if an, specify demands for research capabilities, understanding or performance. At conference after conference dozens of intelligent people passionately expound on the differences (usually 'theory') and commonalities (usually 'high standards') between their schools. Numerical and geographical popularity arguments abound. There is the semiotically rich use of 'flag' statements as distinguished emblems of theories. *Yet there is no evidence to date that theory is actually relevant to the delivery of effective psychotherapy.*

It often seems that psychotherapy's standards are judged by democratic votes, not accountability to internal and external critique. Indeed, standards ordinarily applicable to judging academically accountable theories are usually not mentioned. These include elegance, economy, explanatory power, academic rigour or effort (judging by the number of quality texts), freedom from (or awareness of) presumptive and logical errors, provability, the relationship to research (whether scholarly, quantitative, qualitative or philosophical), critical self-reflection and freedom of expression, the relationship to other theories – or even to the scientifically proven facts within the contemporary culture and sciences.

Much of psychoanalysis and academic psychology are of course handicapped by having harnessed themselves exclusively to Newtonian and Cartesian models, which the hard sciences such as physics actually relinquished some 70 years ago. The new paradigms of quantum physics, chaos and complexity (Clarkson, 1995a) as well as developments in computer and qualitative methodology (Denzin and Lincoln, 1994) have opened possibilities of research upon which psychotherapy can thrive. The use of these with conceptual shifts such as Shotter's (1992) meta-methodology would offer a contribution to the next millennium, rather than attempting to emulate a historically passé ideal of science or religion (exclusively logical positivism or exclusively ideological beliefs) (Hauke, 1996).

Tantam, at the 1996 UKCP professional conference, as reported by Smith (1997), suggested that:

> 1. Differences in technique are increasingly trivial and unimportant 2. theoretical knowledge has been over-emphasised and 3. we have overlooked the kind of practical knowledge that the media is interested in, the knowledge of outcomes. We each have our particular myths and rituals of healing; so long as they are valid for us and our patients, which we use does not really matter. This can also be said of theoretical knowledge. (Smith, 1997: 6)

This is consistent with the quantitative and qualitative psychological research evidence and with the psychotherapy values and practice which have been called 'after schoolism' (Clarkson, 1997a, 1997b). This is a working title to refer to a situation in psychotherapy where 'schools' or 'orientations' or 'approaches' will be acknowledged as less important than the therapeutic relationship itself, and when a common value commitment to the alleviation of human suffering and the development of human potential will have replaced factionism, rivalry and one-up-one-down politics. The attendant destructiveness to creativity and innovation of the latter tendencies hardly needs pointing out.

Schoolism in psychotherapy is the result of passionately held convictions of being right whatever the facts. Schoolism outlaws questioning and expels dissidents (Grosskurth, 1986). It is only by stepping outside the inherited or introjected frame of schoolism that psychotherapy can offer something equivalent or better. It is of course usually in the interstices and liminal spaces where the creative discoveries of any art or science are made (Koestler, 1989; Gleick, 1992).[1]

> The major problem with the notion of 'school' is its relative inflexibility in response to new ideas in psychotherapy. Schools have responded to varying degrees of psychotherapy innovation, but the value of schools has been to preserve good ideas. At this point in psychotherapy's history, these good ideas within schools have been preserved well enough. (Beitman, 1994: 210)

Rationalizations for schoolism

Information in psychotherapy and psychology is being produced at the rate of hundreds of books and thousands of papers and research reports per year. If one is unable or unwilling to read, there is a problem. Research of any kind is notoriously difficult. It is far more comfortable to avoid its multiple risks by adherence to ideological statements claiming the status of 'philosophy'. Philosophy is an ancient academic discipline; it is not a gratuitous statement of unquestioned preferences. It is indeed very difficult to make research relevant to practitioners (Morrow-Bradley and Elliott, 1986). *But, this bridge between the academy and the clinic is precisely what psychotherapy organizations who take research into account are uniquely equipped to sponsor* (Clarkson, 1995b; Lepper, 1996).

Schoolism is comfortable because it can relieve the existential burden of thinking and free choice (see the Grand Inquisitor's speech in Dostoevsky's *The Brothers Karamazov*). As the histories of our world and our professions prove, it is infinitely more comfortable to be *bystanders* to malpractice and injustice than to risk the responsible engagement with such demanding issues (Clarkson, 1996a).

The frequently heard statement that 'we must give the trainees a secure base' has enormous face validity. It is perhaps even true at a certain level. However, the epistemological nature of this vaunted security deserves profound investigation, not an unquestioning culture-blind acceptance (Ani, 1994). Every West European psychotherapeutic narrative minimizes the 'radical differences between egocentric Western culture and socio-centric non-Western cultures and [the disclosure] *that culture exerts a powerful effect on care*' [italics added] (Kleinman quoted in Helman, 1994: 279). Helman continues: 'Whether this narrative is short (as in spirit exorcisms) or lengthy (as in psychoanalysis) it summarizes *post hoc* what had happened to them, and why, and how the healer was able to restore them to happiness or health' (p. 280). (See also Gergen, 1994.)

All these perspectives are of course in line with the seminal work of Lyotard (1989) and Foucault (1980, 1988) who laid bare the power of social processes to constitute certain kinds of realities and distinctive kinds of human subjects in situations where professional knowledge is used, such as clinics and prisons. Unless psychotherapy training and supervision are done with these considerations in mind, they are likely to suffer from the very defects and destructive consequences entailed by short-sighted ignorance of these issues or adoption of unquestioning compliance with potentially fundamentalist ideologies. Indeed, what research there is about psychotherapy supervision suggests, for example, that developmental models of supervision are not empirically supportable, but it has been found again that it is the 'quality of the supervisory relationship [which] is paramount to successful supervision' (Watkins, 1997: 495).

The time may be ready for a transcultural, transtheoretical, transdisciplinary perspective which is genuinely based on **learning by enquiry** *(dierotao) –*

research in the widest, most philosophical, objective and most subjective sense of the term. There is little if any evidence that theory has an appreciable effect on the effectiveness of psychotherapy. There is an increasing valuing of exploratory research and felt need for professionals to collaborate across disciplines, across orientations and across cultural divides. Although not necessarily wanting to give up specializations and loyalties to specific 'psycholanguages', there is an increasing number of people who want instead, or also, to be *independent* of such languages, concentrating on transtheoretical and epistemological aspects as well as fundamental empirical questions and methods (see Clarkson, 1997b, 1997c). This moment might even mean recognizing and celebrating our essential and inescapable *interdependence* on each other (Hahn, 1997). As Stewart (1996) pleaded: 'We must get away from the simplex [or even complex] emphasis on the differences between areas of human culture, and begin to construct a multiplex vision founded on their similarities' (p. 80).

> We will have to come to terms, as we stagger into the postmodern era, with the hard-to-avoid evidence that there are many different realities, and different ways of experiencing them, and that people seem to want to keep exploring them, and that there is only a limited amount any society [or psychotherapy organization] can do to insure that its official reality is installed in the minds of most of its citizens [members] most of the time. (Anderson, 1990: 152)

Conclusion

The narratives of theory are located in a different universe of discourse from that of facts or even research. Theory cannot properly substitute for these or be conflated with them. Theories are the stories we tell about the facts, about how we constitute the phenomena, about how the observer perceives and co-creates the field of the research. It surely behoves psychotherapy to avoid the simplistic category errors which Gilbert Ryle (1960) pointed out decades ago in his philosophy classes at Oxford. To honour the value of theory appropriately, it should not be abused in the service of work it is ill-equipped and perhaps even dangerous to do.

This chapter is not intended as a call to the abandonment of theory or a non-theoretical kind of eclecticism. Theory is too important and too necessary to abandon. However this chapter *is an invocation to take philosophical and empirical research* **seriously** – not as a luxurious special interest, but as a depth charge challenge to our foundational assumptions and organizational structures. Each well-developed theory, as each well-developed question, has its own language, grammar, rhetoric and poetry. At the very least theories can be essential, beautiful and useful as tools are to the artist and the craftsman. They can live, die or be improved. This is also true for 'integrative psychotherapy' and the moment after 'integrative psychotherapy'.

The Greek work *theoreo* (the root of theory) indicates a show, a spectacle or a sacred procession around the temple – a story told or performed for the audience. The concept is closely linked to the ancient idea of theatre. A *theoros* was an ambassador sent by the state to consult the oracle. *Theoria* was the office of such an ambassador (Liddell and Scott, 1996). But we all know how oracles can instruct *or* deceive. Indeed, contemporary psychotherapy theories could be equated to what we would now understand as their socially constructed narratives or stories (Harré and Gillett, 1994; Winter, 1997). As the map is not the territory, so the story is never what actually happened.

Separating our philosophical universes of discourse for their proper differential uses of theoretical languages, forms of rational research and experientially based beliefs, the mystery remains intact (Marcel, 1950; Tillich, 1973).

When we bridge the academy/clinic divide through research, we find that it is about relationship again – the researched itself with the researcher (Einstein – see Schlipp, 1949). As Jung (1928) wrote: 'Learn your theories as well as you can, but put them aside when you touch the miracle of the living soul' (p. 361).

References

Anderson, W.T. (1990) *Reality Is Not What It Used To Be*. San Francisco: Harper and Row.

Ani, M. (1994) *Yurugu – An African-centred Critique of European Cultural Thought and Behavior*. Trenton, NJ: Africa World Press.

Arundale, J. (1997) Editorial, *British Journal of Psychotherapy*, 13 (3): 305–6.

Barkham, M. (1995) 'Editorial: Why psychotherapy outcomes are important now', *Changes*, 13 (3): 161–3.

Beitman, B.D. (1994) 'Stop exploring! Start defining the principles of a psychotherapy integration: Call for a consensus conference', *Journal of Psychotherapy Integration*, 4 (3) : 203–28.

Clarkson, P. (1975) 'Seven-level model'. Invitational paper delivered at the University of Pretoria, November.

Clarkson, P. (1990) 'A multiplicity of psychotherapeutic relationships', *British Journal of Psychotherapy*, 7 (2): 148–63.

Clarkson, P. (1995a) *The Therapeutic Relationship*. London: Whurr.

Clarkson, P. (1995b) 'Counselling psychology in Britain – the next decade', *Counselling Psychology Quarterly*, 8 (3): 197–204.

Clarkson, P. (1996a) *The Bystander (An End to Innocence in Human Relationships?)*. London: Whurr.

Clarkson, P. (1996b) 'Researching the "therapeutic relationship" in psychoanalysis, counselling psychology and psychotherapy', *Counselling Psychology Quarterly*, 9 (2): 143–62.

Clarkson, P. (1997a) 'Integrative psychotherapy, integrating psychotherapies, or psychotherapy after schoolism?', in C. Feltham (ed.), *Which Psychotherapy?* London: Sage.

Clarkson, P. (1997b) 'The therapeutic relationship beyond schoolism', post-conference seminar: *Psychotherapy in Perspective*, 29 June 1997, at the Seventh Annual Congress of the European Association for Psychotherapy, Rome.

Clarkson, P. (1997c) 'Dierotao – learning by inquiry – concerning the education of psychologists, psychotherapists, supervisors and organisational consultants', in P. Clarkson (ed.), *Counselling Psychology: Integrating Theory, Research and Supervised Practice*. London: Routledge.

Consumer Reports (1995, November) 'Mental health: Does therapy help?', pp. 734–9.

Corsini, R. (ed.) (1984) *Current Psychotherapies*. Itasca, IL: F.E. Peacock.

Denzin, N.K. and Lincoln, Y.S. (eds) (1994) *Handbook of Qualitative Research*. Thousand Oaks, CA: Sage.

Dryden, W. (ed.) (1984) *Individual Therapy in Britain*. Milton Keynes: Open University Press.

Duckworth, O.H. and Charlesworth, A. (1988) 'The human side of disaster?', *Policing* 4: 194–210.

Elkin, I. (1995) 'The NIMH treatment of depression collaborative research program: major results and clinical implications', *Changes*, 13 (3): 178–85.

Farrell, B.A. (1979) 'Work in small groups: some philosophical considerations', in B. Babington Smith and B.A. Farrell (eds), *Training In Small Groups: A Study of Five Groups*. Oxford: Pergamon.

Fiedler, F.E. (1951) 'A comparison of therapeutic relationships in psychoanalytic, nondirective and Adlerian therapy', *Journal of Consulting Psychology*, 14: 436–45.

Foucault, M. (1980) *Power/Knowledge: Selected Interviews and Other Writings 1972–1977*. New York: Pantheon.

Foucault, M. (1988) *Politics, Philosophy, Culture: Interviews and Other Writings 1977–1984*. (Lawrence D. Kritzman, ed.), London: Routledge.

Gergen, M. (1994) 'Free will and psychotherapy: complaints of the draughtsmen's daughters', *Journal of Theoretical and Philosophical Psychology*, 14 (1): 13–24.

Gleick, J. (1988) *Chaos: Making a New Science*. London: Heinemann.

Gleick, J. (1992) *Genius: Richard Feynman and Modern Physics*. London: Abacus.

Grosskurth, P. (1986) *Melanie Klein*. London: Maresfield Library.

Hahn, H. (1997) Meeting of *Choreo* Committee, 21 June 1997.

Harré, R. and Gillett, G. (1994) *The Discursive Mind*. Thousand Oaks, CA: Sage.

Hauke, C. (1996) Book review of *The Therapeutic Relationship* by Petruska Clarkson, *British Journal of Psychotherapy*, 12 (3): 405–7.

Heine, R.W. (1953) 'A comparison of patients' reports on psychotherapeutic experience with psychoanalytic, nondirective and Adlerian therapists', *American Journal of Psychotherapy*, 7: 16–23.

Helman, C.G. (1994) *Culture, Health and Illness: An Introduction for Health Professionals* 3rd edn., Oxford: Butterworth-Heinemann.

Jung, C.G. (1928) 'Analytical psychology and education', in *Contributions to Analytical Psychology* (H.G. Baynes & F.C. Baynes, trans.). London: Trench Trubner.

Koestler, A. (1989) *The Act of Creation*. London: Arkana. (First published 1964.)

Lazarus, A.A. (1989) *The Practice of Multimodal Therapy*. Baltimore, MD: Johns Hopkins University Press.

Lepper, G. (1996) 'Between science and hermeneutics: Towards a contemporary empirical approach to the study of interpretation in analytical psychotherapy', *British Journal of Psychotherapy*, 13 (2): 219–31.

Liddell, H.G. and Scott, R. (1996) *Greek–English Lexicon* (abridged). Oxford: Oxford University Press.

Lyotard, J-F. (1989) *The Postmodern Condition: A Report on Knowledge*. Manchester: Manchester University Press.

Marcel, G. (1950) *The Mystery of Being* (G.S. Fraser and R. Hague, trans.). Chicago, IL: Regnery.

Morrow-Bradley, C. and Elliott, R. (1986) 'The utilization of psychotherapy research by psychotherapists', *American Psychologist*, 41 (2): 188–97.

Norcross, J.C. (1997) 'Light and shadow of the integrative process in psychotherapy', post-conference seminar: *Psychotherapy in Perspective*, 29 June 1997, at the Seventh Annual Congress of the European Association for Psychotherapy, Rome.

Norcross, J.C. and Goldfried, M.R. (1992) *Handbook of Psychotherapy Integration*. New York: Basic Books.

Parry, G. and Richardson, A. (1996) *NHS Psychotherapeutic Services in England*. London: Department of Health.

Polkinghorne, D.E. (1992) 'Postmodern epistemology of practice', in S. Kvale (ed.), *Psychology and Postmodernism*. London: Sage.

Roth, A. and Fonagy, P. (1996) *What Works for Whom? A Critical Review of Psychotherapy Research*. New York: The Guilford Press.

Ryle, G. (1960) *Dilemmas: The Tarner Lectures*. Cambridge: Cambridge University Press.

Samuels, A. (1993) 'What is a good training?', *British Journal of Psychotherapy*, 9 (3): 317–23.

Schlipp, P.A. (ed.) (1949) *Albert Einstein, Philosopher-Scientist*. Evanston, IL: Northwestern University Press.

Seligman, M.E.P. (1995) 'The effectiveness of psychotherapy', *American Psychologist*, 50 (12): 965–74.

Silverman, D. (1997) *Discourses of Counselling – HIV Counselling and Social Interaction*. London: Sage.

Shapiro, D.A.. (1996) Foreword to *What Works for Whom? A Critical Review of Psychotherapy Research* (A. Roth and P. Fonagy). New York: The Guilford Press.

Shotter, J. (1992) '"Getting in touch": the meta-methodology of a postmodern science of mental life', in S. Kvale, *Psychology and Postmodernism*. London: Sage.

Smith, E. (1997) 'Knowing what we're doing', *The Psychotherapist*, 8: 6.

Stewart, I. (1996) 'Signing off', *Tate Magazine*, winter: 80.

Tillich, P. (1973) *The Boundaries of Our Being*. London: Collins.

Watkins, C.E. (ed.) (1997) *Handbook of Psychotherapy Supervision*. New York: Wiley.

Winter, D.A. (1997) 'Everybody has still won but what about the booby prizes?', inaugural address as Chair of the Psychotherapy Section, British Psychological Society, University of Westminster, London.

18
PRINCIPLES AND PRACTICE OF A PERSONAL INTEGRATION

Ian Horton

Counsellors and psychotherapists, even those who espouse pure form models, tend to develop their own individualized and personalized conceptual systems and styles of working (Skovholt and Ronnestad, 1995). While they may not necessarily describe themselves as integrative, many (or even most) appear to draw on aspects from more than one theoretical perspective (Garfield and Kurtz, 1977; Norcross and Prochaska, 1988; Arnkoff and Glass, 1992; Poznanski and McLennon, 1997). Some practitioners have responded to the bewildering proliferation of approaches and increasing diversity of opinions, theoretical languages, research findings, methods and philosophical positions by deliberately formulating an integrative theoretical model of their own. The purpose of this chapter is to discuss the issues, principles and practice of an approach to formulating a personal theoretical integration. I comment briefly on the influences on personal choice before discussing the complexity of theoretical orientation. Next, I examine the possible elements of a theoretical model which can be used as a meta-framework for the development of a personal integration. Finally, I outline some principles for developing a personal integration. In the Appendix to the book is a self-review checklist for the construction of a personal integrative model.

Choice of theoretical orientation

Why do counsellors and psychotherapists choose a particular theoretical orientation? There is some evidence to suggest that both personality and opportunity are significant determinants (Chwast, 1978). Quenk and Quenk's (1996) review of studies into preferred models of counselling using the Myers Briggs Type Indicator revealed no significant relationship between personality and theoretical orientation, although there were clear associations between type preferences and specific dimensions. For example, 'feeling types' tend to be drawn towards humanistic approaches and a preference for thinking is strongly associated with more cognitive/behavioural approaches that emphasize logical and analytic processes.

Poznanski and McLennon (1997: 7) argue that therapists' choices of orientation seem to be influenced by their underlying epistemological value structures. They identified two dimensions concerned with preferred ways of knowing or views of reality: objective–subjective and rational–intuitive. They found that these dimensions 'emerged consistently from research into therapists' attitudinal determinants of their approach to practice'. The first dimension is concerned with an emphasis on objective or observable data rather than on subjective experience. The second is concerned with a primary reliance on rational judgement rather than on intuitive therapeutic practice. Their findings suggested that cognitive-behavioural and psychodynamic adherents appear to be the most epistemologically pure in approach. Cognitive-behavioural practitioners reported clear preferences for concepts which emphasize objective reality rather than subjective experience and a focus on rational judgement rather than on intuition as their main process of understanding. Generally, psychodynamic practitioners had a much greater preference for concepts that give primacy to intuitive rather than rational processes than adherents of any other orientation.

Cummings and Lucchese (1978) acknowledge that personality and value systems play a part in the choice of orientation, but they argue that inadvertent or situational factors play an important if not primary role in the choice of an orientation which may be inconsistent or in conflict with personality. Inadvertent factors include basic training, the orientation of the practitioner's supervisor or personal therapist, as well as social, cultural and historical events in the practitioner's life. But espoused theoretical orientation is not a static entity. Mahoney and Craine (1991) reported widespread and significant changes in beliefs about psychological change and the ingredients of optimal therapeutic practice. This view is clearly demonstrated in Skovholt and Ronnestad's (1995) model of the evolving professional self. A personal integration is part of this evolving process.

Complexity of theoretical orientation

Conceptualizing and measuring theoretical orientation is problematic. Even reducing the myriad of approaches to psychodynamic, cognitive-behavioural, humanistic-existential, systemic-family and eclectic-integrative mainstream schools does little to ease the problem of measuring models of counselling or psychotherapy in a way that discriminates adequately between theoretical orientation. Few of the multi-item, self-report instruments intended to measure theoretical orientation show evidence of reliability and even fewer have been shown to have evidence of validity (Poznanski and McLennon, 1995: 411). This is not surprising as definitions of theoretical orientation are ambiguous and there is no consensus on what constitutes the elements of a model.

The idea of a personal integration compounds the complexity of the concept of theoretical orientation. 'Counsellors and therapists do not always believe and practice what they say they do' (Cummings and Lucchese, 1978: 324). While theory may provide the base for clinical practice, the link between theory and practice or what therapists actually do is tenuous at best (Fonagy and Higgett, 1984). Poznanski and McLennon (1995: 428) explain this, at least partially, when they suggest that theoretical orientation is not a simple or pure concept, but made up of four multifaceted and hierarchical elements.

1 *Personal therapeutic belief systems*: this they define as 'a schema-based organisation of declarative and procedural knowledge and epistemic beliefs and values that are not necessarily articulated clearly or accessible to rational inquiry'.
2 *Theoretical school affiliation*: this is the practitioner's self-reported adherence to one (or more) theoretical schools.
3 *Espoused theory*: this is what practitioners say they do. It is the self-reported use of theoretical concepts and therapeutic operations, and does not necessarily reflect accurately the practitioner's theory-in-action.
4 *Theory-in-action*: this is what is inferred by people observing the practitioner's behaviour when working with clients. It describes what others believe the practitioner actually does.

Poznanski and McLennon (1995) reviewed research evidence that demonstrates a relatively strong link between theoretical affiliation and espoused theory, but they reported contradictory evidence and a much weaker link between a practitioner's espoused theory and the externally perceived theory-in-action. This suggests that endorsing the therapeutic operations of a particular approach may not necessarily reflect accurately the nature of a therapist's theoretical orientation. The concept of personal integration used in this chapter is concerned primarily with espoused theory.

Elements of a model

What is a model of counselling? What is being integrated? An answer to these questions may be a prerequisite for developing a personal integration. Four constituent elements have been identified: personal belief system, formal theory, clinical theory and therapeutic operations (Gilmore, 1980; Neimeyer, 1993; Bond, 1995). A personal integration may be developed in one or more of these elements or levels.

Personal belief system (philosophy)

This is the ideological element which describes the meta-assumptions that underpin the other elements. It is typically concerned with two aspects: worldview and the therapeutic process. Worldview is about an individual's unique way of construing reality and making meaning in the world. Understanding your own worldview as a therapist and that of your clients is the key to enhancing effectiveness with a wide range of clients across cultures (Ivey et al., 1997). Bernard and Goodyear (1992) cite Sue's model of worldview that combines the concepts of internal or external responsibility and locus of control. So, for example, people with a high internal worldview will attribute responsibility (blame or achievement) to themselves and view themselves as having control over their own destiny and over their own behaviours, feelings and experiences. People with a high external worldview will attribute responsibility for failure or success to external sources or reasons and do not see themselves as having control over what happens to them. A personal belief system may account for the impact of sociocultural and sociopolitical factors as well as psychological and developmental influences. Larsen (cited in Bernard and Goodyear, 1992: 195) argues that people carry three identities within themselves: a (unique) individual identity, a (cultural) group identity and a universal sense of connectedness with humanity. Some therapists seek to integrate all three views when working with a client. Locke's (1992) model of multicultural understanding implies the need for a personal belief system to incorporate an individual's attitude and position on those factors regarded as personally significant such as economics (poverty), religion, politics, racism and prejudice, social context, child-rearing practices, family structure and dynamics and cultural values. The various broad schools of counselling and psychotherapy offer different and sometimes exclusive or contradictory positions on worldviews and the therapeutic process, but 'provide rich ways for practitioners and their clients to think, feel and act differently' (Ivey et al., 1997: 2).

The second aspect of a personal belief system includes the practitioner's definition of counselling or psychotherapy and her or his basic assumptions about the therapeutic process, characteristics of an effective relationship between therapist and client and what constitutes appropriate goals.

A therapist's personal belief system sets the stage for the selection and adoption of theoretical concepts and related therapeutic operations. However, it is an amorphous element and hard to define in a way that delineates theoretical orientation.

Bond's (1995) pictorial metaphor of a 'pond' demonstrates the relationship between the four elements of a theory (see Figure 18.1). He illustrates the personal belief system as the dark, murky and stagnant water at the bottom of the pond. Yet he describes it as 'containing rich and fertile soil, living creatures, flora and fauna and the unregenerate sludge and detritus

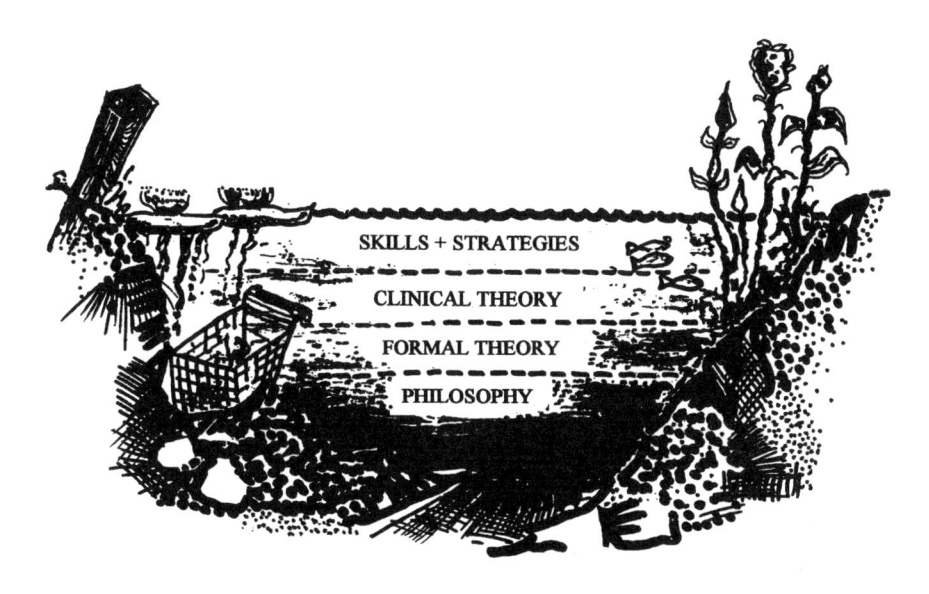

Figure 18.1 *Bond's Pond: elements of a model (Bond, 1995)*

of our own culture'. The formal and clinical theory elements occupy the middle depths with the therapeutic operations or skills and strategies as the clearly visible water on the surface of the pond. It is this element of a model of counselling or psychotherapy that is observable and which impacts directly on clients. It is what the therapist actually does. Theoretical orientation and a practitioner's personal belief system are not synonymous with therapeutic operations for the simple reason that what the therapist actually does seems to represent only a practical expression of espoused theory (Poznanski and McLennon, 1995).

Formal theory

This is the theory of human development which describes those characteristics of a person that account for consistent patterns of behaviour. It is the therapist's explanation of how both normal or functional and abnormal or dysfunctional thoughts, feelings and behaviours are acquired and how they are perpetuated or sustained. The explanation may include psychological, genetic and social or environmental determinants and motives. What seems important is that therapists are aware of the position they take on these issues. Some therapists who espouse pure or single-system models may have clearly articulated views on human development which attribute the origin and maintenance of psychological problems to specific determinants. However, other therapists may adopt the position that psychological problems are multidimensional and seldom attributable to one source, situation or factor and that people are too complex to be explained by any one theory. They may emphasize the importance of social and cultural determinants. It is this position that typically reflects an integrative view of human development. However, other approaches assume that attempts to understand the genesis of psychological problems are not necessary or even useful and that problems do not represent underlying pathology (George et al., 1990). So a critical issue in developing a personal integration is that therapists have a view on human development and its importance or otherwise to the therapeutic process.

Skovholt and Ronnestad (1995: 75) suggest that as counsellors and psychotherapists become more experienced they make less use of abstract concepts and greater use of guiding principles that have evolved from past experience of what works best with clients. This supports the view that a theory of counselling or psychotherapy is more than just a (formal) theory of personality (Mahrer, 1989; Beitman, 1994).

Clinical theory

This interprets the personal belief system and formal theory in a set of guiding concepts that define practice. Clinical theory may usefully contain some account of the following:

- general principles of change;
- processes of change;
- mechanisms of change;
- developmental stage-related process goals.

Beitman (1994: 221) presents seven general principles that underpin the process of change and which are adapted and summarized here (see also Horton, 1996: 287 and for multicultural principles Ridley, 1995: 82).

1 *Identify a focus or target of change and potential areas for intervention.* Prochaska and DiClemente (1992) describe possible levels of change: symptom or situational problems, maladaptive cognitions, interpersonal conflicts, systems or family conflict and at the deepest level, intrapersonal conflict. Particular models of therapy focus on specific levels; for example, cognitive therapists would tend to focus on maladaptive cognitions. Integrative practitioners may argue that the areas and levels are interrelated and that change in one may result in changes at other levels and that the therapist should respond to the needs of clients at a multiplicity of levels. A related issue in developing a personal integration is whether it is the therapist or client who should determine the goals of therapy.

2 *Assume the client is responsible for change.* Prochaska and DiClemente (1992) provide a useful model for the assessment of a client's level of readiness to change. Most approaches accept that therapists can only facilitate change and cannot make changes for their clients or make their clients change. Integrative practitioners may use different strategies according to the client's level of readiness.

3 *Utilize client resources.* This assumes that the practitioner needs to build on clients' strengths and resources and to enable them to utilize existing ways of coping.

4 *Explore and confront reluctance to be a client and resistance to change.* Many clients come reluctantly to therapy and frequently drop out. Most clients do not find change easy. The need to deal with these issues may be a key principle for some practitioners.

5 *Recognize social influences.* Increasingly, therapists recognize the influence of a client's cultural history and social variables such as gender and family. This principle acknowledges that clients do not live in isolation and that human development is a function of the interaction between the individual and his or her environment (Egan and Cowan, 1979).

6 *Facilitate learning and new perspectives.* Whatever the theoretical orientation, any positive outcome includes some change in how clients think about themselves or the world.

7 *Encourage application and generalization of learning.* Some therapists believe that it is not enough to enable clients to think, feel or behave differently in the therapy room and that they may need to enable some clients to apply their learning in everyday life.

The clinical theory element of a personal integrative model must include some explanation of the process of change which enables the practitioner to account for what he or she does. Stiles et al. (1993) describe an integrative process model that explains the way in which problematic experiences are assimilated into schemas or well-organized and familiar patterns of experiences, feelings and behaviours which are developed in the therapeutic process through a series of predictable stages. The model does not prescribe any particular theoretical approach or method to produce the sequence of increasing levels of awareness towards eventual assimilation. Assimilation is a common process in all theoretical approaches and draws concepts from developmental psychology and the main schools of psychotherapy and counselling.

An integral part of any account of the process of change is the mechanism or mechanisms that the therapist regards as the key to change. Garfield (1992: 185–92) describes the common mechanisms of change as:

- quality of the relationship between client and counsellor.
- expression of emotions or catharsis.
- provision of some explanation, interpretation or rationale for the problem.
- reinforcement of client strengths and resources.
- increasing levels of exposure to the problem, working towards greater understanding and 'desensitization' by facing and confronting what is being avoided.
- skills training and information giving.

Prochaska and DiClemente (1992) present a similar list of ten transtheoretical and separate mechanisms of change that are relevant for producing change at different stages of the process of change. Particular theoretical schools will tend to emphasize one mechanism of change over the others, whereas integrative practitioners may see particular mechanisms as relevant to particular goals.

Clinical theory provides a cognitive map of the therapeutic process that grounds practitioners with a sense of direction and purpose. Although individual preference and personality type will inevitably determine the level of detail and structure, a personal integration will need to include some indicative framework for intervention. The concept of process stages and stage-related process goals or tasks which may need to be achieved as a prerequisite of forward movement (Power, 1989; Beitman, 1990; Brammer et al., 1993; Orlinsky et al., 1994) may provide a useful starting point for the therapist attempting to articulate how he or she works with clients. Some personal integrations may delineate detailed maps of what the therapist and client needs to achieve at each stage of the process (for example, Egan, 1990; Horton, 1996; Ivey et al., 1997) while other descriptions of the process may only imply developmental goals through the beginning, middle and end of the process (Mearns and Thorne, 1988).

Therapeutic operations (skills and strategies)

This is the most concrete element of a model of counselling or psychotherapy. It is concerned with what the therapist actually does with clients – the skills and strategies for facilitating the change process and the methods used to implement the guiding principles of clinical theory.

Principles for developing a personal integration

This section outlines some basic assumptions and principles that may help practitioners to develop their own personal integration. While it may be possible to start from the beginning and invent a wholly new personal integration, this is a demanding and potentially risky approach which may result in an incoherent, inconsistent and confusing combination of theory and techniques (Lebow, 1987: 5). An alternative approach is to start by assimilating into the practitioner's primary orientation or within an atheoretical process model (Horton, 1996) a few concepts or techniques from another model.

1 *The development of a personal integration is an integral part of the development of a therapist's professional self.* Skovholt and Ronnestad (1995) describe an eight-stage career life span model of the evolving professional self. It starts with the untrained lay helper, the transition to professional training, imitation of experts and achieving conditional autonomy as a practitioner through to the exploration, integration, individuation and integrity stages of the post-training period. Each stage is characterized by a central task, predominant feelings, sources of influence, role and working

style, conceptual ideas used, process of learning and measures of effectiveness and satisfaction. They describe the process as long, slow and often erratic and involving the development of theory as the basis for professional functioning. As practitioners gain more experience they learn to rely on their own 'accumulated wisdom' (1995: 108).

2 *Ongoing professional development involves a progressive internalization of self and orientation*. Skovholt and Ronnestad's (1995: 131) model suggests that therapists are constantly in a process of moving towards a personalized way of functioning in which theoretical and conceptual structures are 'anchored' to an individual's value base. This is a process of gradual internal integration between the practitioner's personality, value system, philosophical base, theoretical orientation, methods and techniques. Theoretical orientations have been shown to be not very stable over time. The more time that has elapsed since basic professional training, the more likely it is that change in orientation will occur (Skovholt and Ronnestad, 1995: 109). A practitioner's own individuality and personality will be increasingly demonstrated in her or his work with clients and will emerge in a unique way which may be expressed differently depending on the client's needs.

3 *Any personal integration should enable therapists to account for what they do and why they do it*. This assumes that therapists are accountable to themselves, their clients, professional colleagues and employers. If therapists offer to intervene in the lives of their clients they cannot expect to be taken seriously unless they are able to explain what they are doing and why they are doing it. They must be able to provide a plausible account of the sometimes complex and subtle processes with which they are working (Horton, 1996: 282). Every intervention involves a working microtheory. A simple reflection of feeling is underpinned by some theoretical rationale that defines the purpose and intended impact on the client. In this sense no approach to counselling or psychotherapy can be described as atheoretical. Even the most intuitive practitioner would find it hard to argue that they should be permitted to tamper with processes which, at least in retrospect, they have not made a serious attempt to understand.

4 *The nature of a personal integration may vary from an individualized style or adaptation of a particular orientation to an integrative open systems model*. At one extreme personal integration may be little more than a less rigid individual role and style that remains essentially within a single approach. At the other extreme, a personal integration may be a genuinely open systems model with a meta-framework that can incorporate theoretical concepts and/or techniques from different orientations. Common forms of integration occur at the level of formal theory (theoretical integration) or therapeutic operations (technical integration).

5 *A personal integration needs to have some kind of core theoretical framework*. Any approach to developing a personal integration needs to have a clear and internally consistent theoretical framework which provides a

rationale for the way in which concepts and techniques are combined (Lebow, 1987: 3). The framework could be the practitioner's primary orientation acquired in basic training and into which selected aspects of another approach might be gradually and progressively assimilated. Alternatively, it could be a form of process model that does not contain any explanatory frameworks or imply any one formal theory of human development (for example, see Egan, 1990; Horton, 1996; Ivey, et al., 1997). Such a model provides a set of organizing principles in the form of a map of the process. The adoption of any concept or technique must be considered only in terms of how it contributes to achieving the stage-related goal or task. This is an essentially bottom-up empirical strategy that emphasizes what Neimeyer (1993) refers to as 'clinical observables as the foundation for integrative models' rather than at the more abstract levels of formal theory and belief systems. Beitman (1990) presents a useful integrative framework in the form of the stages and elements of the psychotherapeutic process.

6 *A personal integration can be created by combining the concepts, strategies and techniques from other approaches.* Integration can take place within any of the elements of a model, but not all of them. It does not seem possible to incorporate as an entity, one complete theoretical model with another. Neimeyer (1993: 144) argues that 'a high-level synthesis of any two theories is only feasible to the extent that they share deeper levels of theoretical assumptions and belief systems'. Most commonly, integration takes place at the level of therapeutic operations (skills and strategies) and clinical theory. Clearly some concepts and techniques are more amenable to integration than others. For example, 'action oriented process directive therapeutic operations mix readily', so behaviourists add cognitive and Gestalt interventions to their repertoire without presenting an inconsistent and disjointed plan (Lebow, 1987). What distinguishes theoretical orientation is not the use of particular interventions and strategies from different approaches, but rather the meaning which the intervention has for the therapist (Poznanski and McLennon, 1995). Many concepts and techniques identified as unique or belonging to particular schools or models actually overlap with those of other models. This relates to the 'common factors' approach to integration (Garfield, 1992).

7 *A review of current thinking and practice is a prerequisite for starting to develop a personal integration.* The four elements of a model of counselling or psychotherapy provide the building blocks for a personal integration. Before seeking to incorporate concepts and techniques from other approaches, practitioners may find it useful to review the position they take on each of the four elements of a model. The exercise in the Appendix to this book provides a framework for review. Therapists will vary in how they describe their approach. It is not assumed that the greater the detail and sophistication, the better. Clear and simple models delineating key ideas in each element may provide an effective basis for practice. Beitman (1994: 204) is critical of complicated theories which he suggests

have 'tended to obfuscate what actually transpires during the therapeutic hour and have served only to give the therapist an aura of wisdom and expertise'.

8 *A personal integration can begin with incorporating an additional perspective or strategy from another approach.* Especially with beginning practitioners, a personal integration can be developed with the gradual and progressive incorporation of one or two selected aspects from other approaches. Attempting to use as many concepts or techniques as possible will not necessarily lead to greater effectiveness and may well result in a confused therapeutic plan and potential harm to the client (Lebow, 1987). It is important to begin by adopting tentatively additional perspectives that are most in harmony with the practitioner's own values and clinical preferences. Incorporating additional techniques should be done with care. Therapists need to be aware of the purpose and intended impact of the intervention and how it relates to their integrative framework. More comprehensive forms of integration will probably come about only after many years of experience (Andrews et al., 1992).

9 *A personal integration is not a static entity but an evolving process.* (Lebow, 1987; Skovholt and Ronnestad, 1995). One of the advantages of a personal integration is that it can be constructed as an open systems process model which can accommodate change. In this way practitioners are less likely to impose their own ways of working on every client. As someone said, 'If you have only a hammer then everything has to be treated like a nail!' Ivey et al. (1997: 417) argue that from a multicultural perspective therapists need to try to involve clients in finding a therapeutic plan that best fits their needs. Integrative practitioners who are aware of current research findings may find ways in which they can accommodate alternative perspectives. However, it is essential to balance flexibility with coherence of approach.

10 *Developing a personal integrative model in training can be based on a core process model.* In integrative training the first step is to develop the ability to establish, maintain and use the therapeutic relationship (Andrews et al., 1992; Horton, 1996). This implies the acquisition of generic interpersonal and communication skills and qualities such as active listening, empathy, reflection of feeling, paraphrase of meaning, nonverbal communication, congruence and respect.

Alongside the acquisition of generic relationship skills is the need to understand fully the conceptual framework that underpins the therapeutic process. A process model provides a map of the clinical theory and therapeutic operations elements of a model of counselling or psychotherapy. Stage-related process goals or tasks are identified, together with the necessary strategies and skills needed to implement them. An integrative model of process needs to explicate the organizing principles and rationale for the gradual assimilation of explanatory concepts and techniques. Andrews et al. (1992) provides a summary outline of this approach to integrative training.

The next step involves exposure to the various contributions of the broad theoretical schools and to develop a working knowledge of some of the models of human development, behaviour and change. Different accounts of formal theory need to be examined critically, yet within a paradigm of comparison and potential for integration (Andrews et al., 1992). Practitioners may consider ways of incorporating those perspectives that reflect their own personal belief systems and views on the principles and mechanisms of change (Beitman, 1994).

These steps in developing a personal integration are only the beginning of a lifelong process of reflection.

11 *Reflection on the application of theory to practice is the key to the development of a personal integration.* Winter and Maisch (1996: 48) describe professional development as the accumulation of concrete experiences through a 'cyclical movement in which practice and reflection both develop by mutually informing one another.' Developing a personal integration either within training or more typically during post-training, requires an intensive period of active searching, exploration, testing out, self-monitoring and reflection (Skovholt and Ronnestad, 1995). Technical understanding of therapeutic operations should be acquired through training and supervision, rather than through experimentation with clients. Clinical supervision provides the opportunity for the therapist to articulate his or her approach to integration and the ramifications of assimilating alternative perspectives or techniques.

Conclusion

Models of counselling and psychotherapy are only views or constructions of reality. Despite the not infrequent claims to the contrary, there is no evidence that anyone has found the 'ultimate truth' about how best to conduct counselling or psychotherapy. A personal integration is an individual construction that can be developed to reflect the thinking and practice of the individual therapist in the service of her or his clients. Thinking through your own view of counselling or psychotherapy can be an exciting and worthwhile process. The Appendix at the end of this book provides a comprehensive checklist intended as a vehicle for reflection and self-review of current thinking and practice. It is based on the four elements of a model of counselling or psychotherapy discussed in this chapter. The aim is to provide an exercise designed to help the reader to work towards a personal integration. The questions are only indicative of the four elements, so attempting to answer all of them is likely to be daunting, if not confusing and ultimately counter-productive. The structure and categories and how the questions are formulated reflect how the author construes the range of potentially relevant aspects. The reader may need to adapt the checklist, perhaps using only the basic categories or subheadings to stimulate reflection and self-review, while ignoring or rewriting specific questions, yet remaining open to change and self-examination.

The central premise of this chapter is that the basis of constructing a personal integration is the need to clarify first just what constitutes a model of counselling or psychotherapy and then to use it as an organizing framework for an analysis and synthesis of thinking and practice. Continuous reflection is seen as a fundamental developmental process in an evolving personal integration.

References

Andrews, J.D.W., Norcross, J.C. and Halgin, R.P. (1992) 'Training in psychotherapy integration', in J.C. Norcross and M.R. Goldfried (eds), *Handbook of Psychotherapy Integration*. New York: Basic Books.

Arnkoff, D.B. and Glass, C.R.. (1992) 'Cognitive therapy and psychotherapy integration', in D.K. Freedheim (ed.), *History of Psychotherapy: A Century of Change*. Washington, DC: American Psychological Association. pp. 657–94.

Beitman, B. (1990) 'Why I am an integrationist (not an eclectic)', in W. Dryden and J.C. Norcross (eds), *Eclecticism and Integration in Counselling and Psychotherapy*. Loughton: Gale Centre Publications.

Beitman, B.D. (1994) 'Stop exploring! Start defining the principles of psychotherapy integration: call for a consensus conference', *Journal of Psychotherapy Integration*, 4 (3): 203–28.

Bernard, J.M. and Goodyear, R.K. (1992) *The Fundamentals of Clinical Supervision*. Boston: Allyn and Bacon.

Bond, T. (1995) 'Integration and eclecticism in counselling theory: Bond's Pond'. Unpublished handout for postgraduate counselling students. University of Durham.

Brammer, L.M., Abrego, P.J. and Shostrom, E.L. (1993) *Therapeutic Counseling and Psychotherapy*, 6th edn. Englewood Cliffs, NJ: Prentice-Hall.

Chwast, J. (1978) 'Personality and opportunity in psychotherapist's choice of theoretical orientation or practice', *Psychotherapy: Theory, Research and Practice*, 15 (4): 375–82.

Cummings, N.A. and Lucchese, G. (1978) 'Adoption of a psychological orientation: the role of the inadvertent', *Psychotherapy: Theory, Research and Practice*, 15 (4): 323–8.

Egan, G. (1990) *The Skilled Helper: A Systematic Approach to Effective Helping*, 4th edn. Pacific Grove, CA: Brooks/Cole.

Egan, G. and Cowan, M.A. (1979) *People in Systems: A Model for Development in the Human-Service Professions and Education*. Monterey, CA: Brooks/Cole.

Fonagy, P. and Higgett, A. (1984) *Personality Theory and Clinical Practice*. London: Methuen.

Garfield, S.L. (1992) 'Eclectic psychotherapy', in J.C. Norcross and M.R. Goldfried (eds), *Handbook of Psychotherapy Integration*. New York: Basic Books.

Garfield, S.L. and Kurtz, R. (1977) 'A study of eclectic views', *Journal of Consulting and Clinical Psychology*, 45: 78–83.

George, E., Iveson, C. and Ratner, H. (1990) *Problem to Solution*. London: BT Press.

Gilmore, S.K. (1980) 'A comprehensive theory for eclectic intervention'. Unpublished conference paper, Thessaloniki, Greece.

Horton, I.E. (1996) 'Towards the construction of a model of counselling', in R. Bayne, I. Horton and J. Bimrose (eds), *New Directions in Counselling*. London: Routledge.

Ivey, A.E., Ivey, M.B. and Simek-Morgan, L. (1997) *Counseling and Psychotherapy: A Multicultural Perspective*. Boston: Allyn and Bacon.

Lebow, J.L. (1987) 'Developing a personal integration in family therapy: principles for model construction and practice', *Journal of Marital and Family Therapy*, 13 (1): 1–14.

Locke, D.C. (1992) *Increasing Multicultural Understanding: A Comprehensive Model*. London: Sage.

Mahrer, A.R. (1989) *The Integration of Psychotherapies*. New York: Human Sciences Press.

Mahoney, M.J. and Craine, M.H. (1991) 'The changing beliefs of psychotherapy experts', *Journal of Psychotherapy Integration*, 1 (3): 207–21.

Mearns, D. and Thorne, B. (1988) *Person Centred Counselling in Action*. London: Sage.

Neimeyer, R.A. (1993) 'Constructivism and the problem of psychotherapy integration', *Journal of Psychotherapy Integration*, 3 (2): 133–58.

Norcross, J.C. and Prochaska, J.O. (1988) 'A study of eclectic (and integrative) views revisited', *Professional Psychology: Research and Practice*, 19: 170–4.

Orlinsky, D.E., Graw, K. and Parks, B.K. (1994) 'Process and outcome in psychotherapy: Noch Einmal', in A.E. Bergin and S.L. Garfield (eds), *Handbook of Psychotherapy and Behavioural Change*, 4th edn. New York: Wiley.

Poznanski, J.J. and McLennon, J. (1995) 'Conceptualizing and measuring counselors' theoretical orientations', *Journal of Counselling Psychology*, 42 (4): 411–22.

Poznanski, J.J. and McLennon, J. (1997) 'Theoretical orientation of Australian counselling psychologists'. Unpublished paper, School of Social and Behavioural Sciences, Swinburne University of Technology, Victoria, Australia.

Power, M.J. (1989) 'Cognitive therapy and dynamic psychotherapy', *British Journal of Psychotherapy*, 5 (4): 544–56.

Prochaska, J.O. and DiClemente, C.C. (1992) 'The transtheoretical approach', in J.C. Norcross and M.R. Goldfield (eds), *Handbook of Psychotherapy Integration*. New York: Basic Books.

Quenk, N.L. and Quenk, A.T. (1996) 'Counselling and psychotherapy', in A.L. Hammer (ed.), *MBTI Applications: A Decade of Research on the Myers-Briggs Type Indicator*. Palo Alto, CA: Consulting Psychologists Press.

Ridley, C. (1995) *Overcoming Unintentional Racism in Counseling and Therapy*. Thousand Oaks, CA: Sage.

Skovholt, T.M. and Ronnestad, M.H. (1995) *The Evolving Professional Self*. Chichester: Wiley.

Stiles, W.B., Elliott, R., Firth-Cozens, J.A., Llewelyn, S.P., Margison, F.R., Shapiro, D.A. and Hardy, G. (1993) 'Assimilation of problematic experiences by clients in psychotherapy', *Psychotherapy*, 27 (3): 411–20.

Winter, R. and Maisch, M. (1996) *Professional Competence and Higher Education: The ASSET Programme*. London: Falmer Press.

19
THE PERSONAL, THE PROFESSIONAL AND THE BASIS OF INTEGRATIVE PRACTICE

Rhona Fear and Ray Woolfe

This chapter seeks to explore two themes. Each addresses the subject of integration from a different perspective. The first concerns the relationship between the personal and professional selves of the counsellor. We explore the implications of a state of affairs where the two are not in a state of internal integration and harmony and suggest what might underlie such lack of congruence. The second relates to the concept of an integrative as opposed to a purist theoretical orientation. It promulgates the notion that there are certain conditions which facilitate this situation. This involves a discussion of the visions of reality or worldviews held by counsellors.

The counsellor's development

There is considerable literature on the professional development of the counsellor (Hogan, 1964; Loganbill et al., 1982; Friedman and Kaslow, 1986; Stoltenberg and Delworth, 1987; Goldberg, 1986; Skovholt and Ronnestad, 1992). A consistent theme in this literature has been the use of the metaphor of a journey to describe this development. Like all journeys, this is seen to have recognizable stages and landmarks. Skovholt and Ronnestad (1992) refer to this journey undertaken by counsellors as 'the evolving professional self'. They identify eight stages which move from an initial imitation of experts and exploration through to the final three stages of integration, individuation and a position which they describe as integrity. A key characteristic of these final stages is that individuals become increasingly inner-directed and less influenced by external forces. In terms of role and working style the counsellor tends to become increasingly self-focused, abides less by 'the rules' (Kinnetz, 1988) yet remains aware of professional boundaries.

A similar model to Skovholt and Ronnestad's is that of Kitchener and King (1981). In their seven-stage model, which they describe as 'reflective judgement theory', the earlier phases (stages one to three) are characterized by the way in which truth is assumed to be fixed, certain and attainable from 'experts'. At these stages, theories put forward by trainers who are deemed as 'seniors' tend to be swallowed whole and contradictory and rival views are judged as right or wrong dependent upon their consonance with the 'experts'. In the middle stages (stages four and five) thinking is relativistic, knowledge being viewed as impermanent, uncertain and contextual. During this phase, counsellors will be considering different theories, engaging on voyages of discovery as they chart new waters in terms of theoretical approach, but not yet certain whether to commit to a single theory or to search for an integrative approach.

When the individual reaches the final stages of Kitchener and King's model (stages six and seven), rational, reflective judgements are formed after critical examination and evaluation of the supporting evidence. At this stage of mature intellectual development the individual will tend to commit to a particular theory, or construct his or her own integrative practice. However, he or she will accept the undeniability of relativism and have the humility to accept that others may adopt other theories which work equally well for them.

This journey is as much a personal as a professional one. Rippere and Williams (1986) suggest that helpers tend to be wounded people, hence the concept of the wounded healer. Goldberg describes it as an attempt to work through unresolved personal issues without some of the hurt and disappointment experienced the first time.

Personal and professional selves

Another way of looking at this journey is to understand it as a process in which the counsellor's personal and professional selves move into some sort of harmony or congruence if the person is to prosper as a counsellor. We argue that for this to happen, each individual counsellor needs to operate within a theoretical orientation which encompasses the same underlying meta-theoretical assumptions as their personal philosophy. Imagine, for example, a state of affairs in which a counsellor was trying to practise in a person-centred fashion, yet deep down did not believe in some of the key principles inherent in the person-centred position, such as the inherent goodness and potential of human beings. If such a situation remained unresolved for any length of time, one would expect that the person in question would experience considerable inner conflict, cognitive dissonance and stress.

One response to this proposition is that it is unlikely that such a state of disharmony could come about. We would contend, however, that this is far from impossible or unusual. Indeed, we shall suggest that the theoretical orientation in which counsellors are trained owes as much to opportunity factors such as availability of courses as it does to personality variables and choices made in terms of consonance with one's philosophical underpinnings. This is particularly likely to be the case outside Greater London.

Cognitive dissonance occurs when an individual is faced with competing cognitions, as in the above example where the practice of one form of therapy is accompanied by a set of beliefs which is largely inimical. To sustain such a position is difficult without a great deal of internal conflict and some form of adaptation is likely to result. Vasco et al. (1993) suggest that in a situation like the one outlined, one of four scenarios is possible: revision or enlargement of one's paradigm; selective inattention or retrenchment; career crisis; or abandonment of one's career. While the first scenario can lead to positive movement for the therapist, the others are less felicitous in their effects, tending to lead to burnout or drop-out.

It follows from this that the process of selecting applicants for training courses might be more effective if it involved a search for individuals whose personal philosophy shares the same meta-theoretical assumptions as that of the theoretical orientation of the proposed training course. In this way, it is far more likely that the trainee counsellor will at least have the potential to create this harmony between his or her personal and professional selves (Barron, 1978).

Epistemology

To reach the higher stages of development described by Skovholt and Ronnestad (1992), it would thus appear desirable and probably crucial for the counsellor to operate in their practice in a manner which is consistent with their personal philosophy about life. In this context, the concept of epistemology is relevant.

Epistemology refers to the nature or grounds on which knowledge is based. Each person has what has been described as their own 'epistemological commitments' which in turn provide a conceptual framework for their 'personal myth'. This term is used by McAdams (1993) to describe the way in which each individual makes sense of their experience and creates an overarching theme for their own 'sacred story which embodies personal truth' (p. 34). The epistemological commitments which underlie this story refer to a composite collection of beliefs around a series of linked variables. These include such topics as the extent to which change in adult life is possible and what constitutes such change; the extent to which individuals are free agents and have freedom of choice or are social beings prescribed to act in certain ways by the dictates of society; whether individuals perceive themselves to hold an internal or external locus of control and whether human beings are basically bad or good. Responses to these variables tend to be in clusters and it is the existence of these clusters which gives rise to what we describe as visions of reality.

In the example described previously, where a person-centred counsellor did not believe in the inherent goodness and potential existing within human beings, it could be said that there was an inconsistency between philosophy and practice, or alternatively that the individual's epistemological commitments were confused. Festinger (1957) talks of 'cognitive dissonance' occurring when there is not a high degree of fit between one's beliefs and one's behaviour. He makes the point that 'the presence of dissonance gives rise to pressures to reduce or eliminate the dissonance' (p. 18). This is due to the fact that dissonance is uncomfortable and gives rise to internal conflict from which the individual seeks to escape. In consequence, the individual who experiences cognitive dissonance tends to take one of two possible courses. He or she may seek to alter his or her behaviour so that it ceases to be at odds with his or her belief system. To transfer Vasco et al.'s (1993) terminology, it leads to 'enlargement or revision of one's paradigm'. Alternatively, he or she may become engrossed in a process whereby there is an attempt to hide from aspects of the held value system. This approximates to the 'selective inattention' referred to by Vasco et al. (1993).

The counsellor who demonstrates consonance between the underlying epistemological commitments of his or her chosen theoretical orientation and his or her own personal philosophy is one whose practice is likely to be well grounded. We are suggesting that, to use Skovholt and Ronnestad's developmental model, such counsellors are likely to be able to achieve the advanced stages of integration, individuation and integrity.

It is arguable, however, that in order for this consistency of epistemological commitments to be achieved, the individual needs to undergo a process of consciously examining and addressing philosophical issues. Cooper and Lewis (1983) suggest that trainers should see a crucial part of their role as being to encourage such a process to take place, noting that 'epistemological innocence is lost if one is to grapple with pluralism' (p. 293).

Integration (1)

The relevance of this discussion to the concept of integration in an holistic sense is that the counsellor who is able to bring together the personal and professional aspects of themselves would appear to be engaging in an integrative, harmonious process. We would contrast this with the rather hodgepodge eclecticism which in our experience as trainers often characterizes the work of novitiate counsellors. This frequently involves 'a bit of this, a bit of that and give it a stir', with little or no attention as to whether the final produce holds together in a coherent fashion. To continue the culinary metaphor, the mix of ingredients may provide a tasty dish but may equally prove to be disastrous. We are suggesting that if there does not exist a congruent set of epistemological commitments which bind the different ingredients together, then the new recipe may prove ineffective or inedible to the client.

In this context we are making a value judgement in arguing that a practitioner who is integrated in this manner is operating at a higher level of sophistication than one whose practice is not characterized by the harmony to which we have referred.

Integration (2)

However, as we have already indicated, there is another sense in which we employ the term integration. This relates to its use in terms of the integration of different theoretical approaches into a form of practice, which can be contrasted with the so-called pure approaches such as psychodynamic, humanistic or cognitive-behavioural. We shall suggest that an integrationist practice perspective is associated with a particular philosophical outlook on the world (*weltanschauung*) or vision of reality.

It seems appropriate at this point to make it clear that we are not suggesting that such a practice perspective is superior to purer approaches or to more mature forms of eclecticism such as Lazarus's multimodal therapy (Norcross and Goldfried, 1992: 232–63) or Prochaska and DiClemente's transtheoretical approach (Norcross and Goldfried, 1992: 300–34). For the purposes of this discussion, we are linking together integrative and mature eclectic approaches under a single umbrella and making a comparison between this and pure approaches.

Choosing a theoretical orientation

The reason that counsellors elect to follow one theoretical orientation rather than another is complex. However, the question does bear on our discussion in its focus on personal philosophy. Feltham (1997) provides a list of reasons underlying theoretical allegiance which lists no less than fifteen items. These consist of the following variables: original training, personality fit, truth appeal, selecting the best, accepting research evidence, clinical experience, retraining, eclecticism, relationship factors, conservatism, novelty, theoretically consistent eclecticism, certitude, respect, atheoretical/agnostic stance. Apart from the first one, the tenor of these variables is to suggest that individuals make consciously informed choices.

More generally, the literature appears to adopt one of two positions. The first is that choice is largely dependent upon opportunity and accidental factors which are largely external to the individual. Schwartz (1978) identifies some of the important factors as geographical location, availability of a charismatic leader, professional setting, socio-political climate and the ascribed theoretical orientation of one's supervisor.

Many of these factors are adventitious, based upon taking what is available rather than making a conscious choice. Cummings and Lucchese (1978) in their paper on adoption of a psychological orientation refer to 'the role of the inadvertent' and suggest that while the choice of theoretical orientation is a complex process, it is one given to 'the whims of fate' (p. 323).

The second and contrasting position which is more congruent with Feltham's variables is that choice is heavily influenced by and even perhaps dependent upon personality and personal philosophy. Norcross and Prochaska (1983) while acknowledging the importance of opportunity nevertheless see the counsellor as responding to the available opportunities by making deliberate choices predicated on clinical experience, *personal values* (our emphasis) and graduate training. Lindler (1978) perceives the choice as resulting from psychic determinism: that a decision emerges from the individual's need to work through their own dysfunctional needs and drives in order to arrive at a resolution. Marks (1978) makes a similar point, arguing with regard to psychoanalysis in particular, that the therapist is in his own unconscious, remembering, repeating and working through his struggle with man's essential helplessness and aloneness. Many writers emphasize the link between personal philosophy and choice of theoretical orientation (Messer and Winokur, 1980, 1984, 1986; Messer, 1983, 1986, 1992; Vasco and Dryden, 1994; Fear and Woolfe, 1996).

If choice of theoretical orientation is influenced by personal philosophy, the question is raised as to which philosophies are associated with which theoretical orientation. This is of interest to any individual who wants to be able to integrate his or her professional and personal selves by finding a theoretical approach of which the meta-theoretical assumptions are consonant with his or her personal philosophy. However, as this chapter is focused on the subject of integration, the question of particular relevance is which philosophy, if any, fosters an integrative as opposed to a purist approach. Messer and Winokur suggest that integrative practice is difficult to achieve because the various orientations are built upon different and conflicting philosophical positions. Messer's position is encapsulated in the 'cautionary notes' he provided in the *British Journal of Guidance and Counselling* (1989, 17 (3)). Both Messer and Winokur used a four-part typology of worldviews or visions of reality to grapple with this issue. We have adopted this typology and developed it.

Visions of reality

The idea of visions of reality offers a framework through which we can construct a typology of personal philosophy based upon the clusters of issues described earlier. In the typology outlined, the four visions of reality identified each tell of a type of journey or quest taken by the individual as s/he moves through life. Each vision can be thought of as a life script or response to questions such as the purpose of life, the extent to which individuals are free or constrained by external circumstances, the essential goodness or otherwise of human nature, what constitutes change and the ease of effecting it.

The concept of visions of reality is an old one which is present in classical Greek literature. In more recent times it has been developed in the service of Shakespearean literary criticism, most noticeably by Northrop Frye (1957, 1965). Four visions of reality are identified: romantic, tragic, comic and ironic.

The romantic vision

In this script, life is seen as an exciting adventure in which the actor or actress is a free individual who is in control of their own destiny. External constraints are perceived as obstacles which can be overcome through personal endeavour and individuals are capable of reaching a state of what Shafer (1976) refers to as 'exhaltation'. The way in which evil is converted to good (Frye, 1957: 110) is indicative of the way this vision takes an essentially optimistic view of life. It is, as Frye (1957: 186) says, 'the nearest of all literary forms to the wish-fulfilment dream'.

There is a consistency between this vision and the epistemological assumptions of humanistic therapies. Read 'fully functioning person' (Rogers) and 'self-actualization' (Maslow) for 'exhaltation' and the correlation becomes clear and explicit.

The tragic vision

In this script, the overall mood of the journey through life is 'sinister and sombre' (Frye, 1965: 49). A fatalistic and pessimistic stance is adopted. There is a notion of inevitability (Frye, 1965: 124). Shafer (1976: 45) describes a process of repetitious compulsion in which the individual, driven by unconscious forces, is seen endlessly to enact the same rituals. Unlike the romantic vision, the ideal self or ego ideal is unreachable and given the power of the unconscious the ability to master the external world is limited.

In the same way as the romantic vision offers a set of meta-theoretical assumptions which underlie humanistic practice, the tragic vision can be seen to offer a philosophical framework underlying the psychodynamic project. To paraphrase Freud, the purpose of therapy is not to make people happy but rather to translate neurosis into ordinary unhappiness. As Messer (1989: 282) points out about the belief system of psychoanalysis, 'not all is possible or redeemable'. It is the task of the individual to come to terms with these limitations and to accommodate them.

The comic vision

In this script, life's drama involves three phases. In the first, the individual fails to achieve their objectives because he or she is operating dysfunctionally, perhaps because of being at odds with societal norms. This leads to a second phase characterized by confusion and loss of identity. The third phase involves the acquisition of self-knowledge. It focuses upon the manner in which the individual develops an increased capacity to understand what is needed in order to fulfil social roles more adequately and to adapt accordingly.

While constraints are acknowledged, Shafer (1976: 29) emphasizes the optimism inherent in this vision: 'No dilemma is too great to resolve, no obstacle too firm to stand up against effort and good intention, no evil so unmitigated and entrenched that it is irremediable, no suffering so intense that it cannot be relieved, and no loss so final that it cannot be undone or made up for.'

However, unlike the emphasis of the romantic vision upon self-actualization, the emphasis here in terms of self-knowledge is upon learning and adaptation. We are, therefore, in the domain of the cognitive-behavioural tradition of therapy. Social learning theory tells us that because behaviour is learned, it can be unlearned and replaced by new behaviour. Similarly, irrational cognitions can be replaced by more functional ways of thinking.

The ironic vision

The ironic vision is unlike the other three in that good and bad are seen as existing at the same time. In a sense, it could be said to contain elements of the other three visions. While acknowledging the bad, it seeks to look at the other side of the coin and ask the question how good can come from it. Shafer encapsulates this by noting the 'readiness to seek out internal contradictions, ambiguities and paradoxes . . . aiming at detachment, keeping things in perspective, taking nothing for granted, and readily spotting the antithesis to any thesis so as to reduce the claim of that thesis upon us' (1976: 50–1). An ironic view offers what Stein describes as 'clear view of contradictory principles and a tolerance for the tension created by our attempts to accommodate them'.

The essence, therefore, of the ironic stance lies in its ability to encapsulate and hold contradictions, to see beyond them and to marry them together into some sort of harmony and to arrive at a synthesis. Here in a nutshell is the basis of an integrationist model of practice with its emphasis on combining disparate parts into new and coherent wholes.

Dialectical thinking

The process of working within an ironic framework seems to us to involve the development of an ability to think dialectically. A dialectic is a philosophical system of working towards the resolution of differences. Its starting point is a thesis; for example, the post-1945 view that collectivist welfare policies were an essential basis for social cohesion. This led eventually to an opposing view, to an antithesis: the New Right position that only an emphasis on individuality could free people to be creative and thus generate sufficient resources to support social welfare policies. However, through a process of dialectical thinking, a theory and methodology is developed which works towards the resolution of opposing factors and seemingly irreconcilable differences. The contemporary philosophy of New Labour with its favoured slogan of 'tough yet caring' seeks to reconcile the two opposites and represents the process in action. With the passage of time, it is likely that this view will become the new orthodoxy, the new thesis awaiting its antithesis.

This process can also be seen to be operative within the world of counselling. When Norcross and Grencavage (Dryden and Norcross, 1990) refer to integration as 'more than the sum of its parts', they are asking us to engage in a process which requires resolution of the seemingly opposed methodologies, rationales and visions of reality which ground each theoretical orientation. It is the ability to perceive the world from an ironic perspective which facilitates this task.

It is important to acknowledge that while we are suggesting that the integrationist perspective involves the ability to engage in a sophisticated cognitive process, we are not suggesting that such persons are necessarily more sophisticated than those operating from a purist perspective. There may be all kinds of reasons why the purist practitioner prefers to operate in such a fashion. However, we are saying that not all purist practitioners have the potential to work in a manner that can be described as integrative.

Conclusion

The past two decades have seen a steady growth of counsellors who designate themselves as eclectic or integrationist. There has been a distinct growth of books on psychotherapy integration such as Norcross and Goldfried (1992) and Stricker and Gold (1993). The increase in debate, courses and societies to promote the interests of integrative approaches has been accompanied by a proliferation of integrative theories. It would seem that the majority of therapists ascribing to eclecticism and integration do so because they seek to find an individualized mix of therapies which suit their personality type, philosophical beliefs, client population and preferred style of working.

We have suggested in this chapter that in order for counsellors to reach advanced developmental stages they need to develop the capacity for reflective judgement. They will then be at a stage of mature intellectual development which will enable them to find a theoretical orientation which marries up their personal epistemological commitments with the underlying metatheoretical assumptions of a chosen orientation. In this way, counsellors will be able to achieve an integration of their professional and personal selves. Given this mature stage of relativistic thinking and reflective judgement, the counsellor will be capable of choosing whether to develop an eclectic or integrative practice, or to commit to a pure theoretical approach. We have suggested that this will depend to some extent upon the counsellor's ability to engage in dialectical thinking. This is encapsulated in the ironic vision of reality. However, perhaps it is wise to bring attention to Wachtel's (1991: 44) note of caution that even for the committed integrationist 'the habits and boundaries associated with the various schools are hard to eclipse, and for most of us integration remains more of a goal than a constant daily reality'.

This chapter has followed a dual theme: that of integration in the holistic sense involving the process of achieving harmony of one's professional and personal selves, and that of the counsellor's propensity to develop an integrative theoretical approach. Whichever theme is addressed, it is fascinating to note that the counsellor's journey towards integration mirrors the client's central if unconscious task in therapy; to join up the discontinuities of one's life, so that inconsistencies are remedied and 'cut off' parts reintegrated and accepted. Thus, we might hypothesize that clients seek in therapy to achieve their own personal integration. In like vein, we suggest that it is the task of the counsellor to tease out the philosophical inconsistencies in their lives, and to find a theoretical approach which matches their own epistemological commitments: in short, to achieve a personal integration.

References

Barron, J. (1978) 'A prolegomenon to the personality of the psychotherapist: choices and changes, *Psychotherapy: Theory, Research and Practice*, 15 (4): 309–13.

Cooper, T.D. and Lewis, J.A. (1983) 'The crisis of relativism: helping counselors cope with diversity', *Counselor Education and Supervision*, 22: 290–5.

Cummings, N.A. and Lucchese, G. (1978) 'Adoption of a psychological orientation: the role of the inadvert', *Psychotherapy: Theory, Research and Practice*, 15 (4): 323–8.

Dryden, W. and Norcross, J. (eds) (1990) *Eclecticism and Integration in Counselling and Psychotherapy*. Loughton: Gale Centre Publications.

Fear, R. and Woolfe, R. (1996) 'Searching for integration in counselling practice', *British Journal of Guidance and Counselling*, 24 (3): 399–410.

Feltham, C. (1997) 'Introduction: irreconcilable psychotherapies', in C. Feltham (ed.), *Which Psychotherapy*. London: Sage.

Festinger, L. (1957) *A Theory of Cognitive Dissonance*. Evanston, Ill: Row, Peterson.

Friedman, D. and Kaslow, N.J. (1986) 'The development of professional identity in psychotherapists: six stages in the supervision process', in F.W. Kaslow (ed.), *Supervision and Training: Models, Dilemmas, and Challenges*. New York: Haworth.

Frye, N. (1957) *Anatomy of Criticism*. Princeton, NJ: Princeton University Press.

Frye, N. (1965) *A Natural Perspective: The Development of Shakespearean Comedy and Romance*. New York: Columbia University Press.

Goldberg, C. (1986) *On Becoming a Psychotherapist: The Journey of the Healer*. New York: Gardner Press.

Hogan, R.A. (1964) 'Issues and approaches in supervision', *Psychotherapy: Theory, Research and Practice*, 1: 139–41.

Kinnetz, P.L. (1988) 'Saving myself versus serving the client in T.M. Skovholt and P.R. McCarthy, Critical incidents: catalysts for counselor development', *Journal of Counseling and Development*, 67: 69–110.

Kitchener, K.S. and King, P. (1981) 'Reflective judgement: concepts of justification and their relationship to age and education', *Journal of Applied Developmental Psychology*, 2: 89–116.

Lindler, H. (1978) 'Therapists and theories: I choose me', *Psychotherapy: Theory, Research and Practice*, 15 (4): 405–8.

Loganbill, C., Hardy, E. and Delworth, U. (1982) 'Supervision: a conceptual model', *Counseling Psychologist*, 10: 3–42.

McAdams, D.P. (1993) *The Stories We Live By*. New York: Morrow.

Marks, M.J. (1978) 'Conscious/unconscious selection of the psychotherapist's theoretical orientation', *Psychotherapy: Theory, Research and Practice*, 15 (4): 354–8.

Messer, S.B. (1983) 'Integrating psychoanalytic and behaviour therapy: limitations, possibilities and trade-offs', *British Journal of Clinical Psychology*, 22: 131–2.

Messer, S.B. (1986) 'Eclecticism in psychotherapy: underlying assumptions, problems and trade-offs', in J.C. Norcross (ed.), *Handbook of Eclectic Psychotherapy*. New York: Brunner-Mazel.

Messer, S.B. (1989) 'Integration and eclecticism in counselling and psychotherapy: cautionary notes', *British Journal of Guidance and Counselling*, 17 (3): 275–85.

Messer, S.B. (1992) 'A critical examination of belief structures in integrative and eclectic psychotherapy', in J.C. Norcross and M.R. Goldfried (eds), *Handbook of Psychotherapy Integration*. New York: Basic Books.

Messer, S.B. and Winokur, M. (1980) 'Some limits to the integration of psychoanalytic and behaviour therapy', *American Psychologist*, 35 (9): 818–27.

Messer, S.B. and Winokur, M. (1984) 'Ways of knowing and visions of reality in psychoanalytic and behaviour therapy', in H. Arkowitz and S.B. Messer (eds), *Psychoanalytic Therapy and Behaviour Therapy: Is Integration Possible?* New York: Plenum.

Messer, S.B. and Winokur, M. (1986) 'Eclecticism and the shifting visions of reality in three systems of psychotherapy', *International Journal of Eclectic Psychotherapy*, 5:115–24.

Norcross, J.C. and Goldfried, M.R. (eds) (1992) *Handbook of Psychotherapy Integration*. New York: Basic Books.

Norcross, J.C. and Prochaska, J.O. (1983) 'Clinician's theoretical orientations: selection, utilization, and efficacy', *Professional Psychology*, 14: 197–208.

Rippere, V. and Williams, R. (eds) (1986) *Wounded Healers*. Chichester: Wiley.

Schwartz, B.D. (1978) 'The initial versus subsequent theoretical positions: does the psychotherapist's personality make a difference?', *Psychotherapy: Theory, Research and Practice*, 15 (4): 344–9.

Shafer, R. (1976) *A New Language for Psychoanalysis*. New Haven: Yale University Press.

Skovholt, T.M. and Ronnestad, M.H. (1992) *The Evolving Professional Self: Stages and Themes in Therapist and Counselor Development*. Chichester: Wiley.

Stoltenberg, C.D. and Delworth, U. (1987) *Supervising Counsellors and Therapists: A Developmental Approach.* Oxford: Jossey-Bass.

Stricker, G. and Gold, J.R. (eds) (1993) *Comprehensive Handbook of Psychotherapy Integration.* New York: Plenum.

Vasco, A.B. and Dryden, W. (1994) 'The development of psychotherapists' theoretical orientation and clinical practice', *British Journal of Guidance and Counselling,* 22 (3): 327–41.

Vasco, A.B., Garcia-Marques, L. and Dryden, W. (1993) '"Psychotherapist know thyself!": dissonance between metatheoretical values in psychotherapists of different theoretical orientations', *Psychotherapy Research,* 3(3): 181–96.

Wachtel, P.L. (1991) 'Towards a more seamless integration', *Journal of Psychotherapy Integration,* 1: 43–54.

APPENDIX
Exercise: developing a personal integration

Ian Horton (see Chapter 18)

The following exercise provides a checklist for building a personal integration. It is intended only as a vehicle for reflection and self-review. The questions provide indicators of the substance of each of the four elements of an integrative model. One way to use this checklist is to answer only those questions that relate to aspects you regard as personally significant. Many questions or issues may not be relevant or useful to you and can be deleted. Other questions may feel important to you in some way, yet you cannot immediately articulate your ideas or how you want to respond. These questions or subcategories can be reviewed later. However, what may be important is to review your position on each of the *four elements* of a model of counselling or psychotherapy.

1 Personal belief system

It may be helpful to start by reading quickly through the questions in this section and identifying those to which you react almost immediately as being interesting or significant to you in some way. You may need to modify the question before considering your response.

(a) About your worldview

- What gives you a sense of meaning and purpose in life? How important are goals in life? Is the meaning of life about doing, being or becoming? How would you describe the 'good life'?
- What is your view of human nature? At birth do you consider people to be basically good, bad, neutral or mixed? What kind of people do you value and respect?
- How do you define the 'self'? How is a person's identity determined?
- To what extent do you see people as having control over their own destiny, behaviour and experiences?
- To what extent do you attribute responsibility for achievement or blame to yourself or to external factors or reasons? (Think about specific situations.)

(b) About your values

- What are the main values you live by? How did those values become yours?
- Why did you become or why do you want to train as a counsellor or psychotherapist? What needs of yours are met or do you see being met by being a counsellor or psychotherapist?

(c) About cultural identity and differences (Bernard and Goodyear, 1992: 195)

- How do you describe yourself culturally?
- Who in your family influenced your sense of cultural identity?
- Which groups other than your own do you think you understand best?
- Which characteristics of your culture/ethnic group do you like most and which do you like least?
- How do you think members of your family would react to having therapy?
- In what way are any of the following themes relevant to you personally and in your work as a therapist: cultural values and attitudes, family structures and dynamics, religious practices, child-rearing practices, sociopolitical factors, racism and prejudice, language and arts, history of oppression, poverty and economic concerns (Locke, 1992: 6)?

(d) About developmental mapping (Egan and Cowan, 1979)

Significant life events may form an important part of your worldview. The developmental map you generate is an important part of the environment you provide for your clients.

- What is your chronological stage of life development?
- As you reflect on your life, what central concerns emerge? What concerns do you know or suspect to be most important to the lives of those with whom you are involved?
- Do certain systems (e.g. family, friends, work, community, education, politics) seem crucial to your development and that of others?
- What crises or developmental transitions have you experienced or anticipate in your life? How did you or do you think you will cope? What systems or personal resources, qualities or skills helped you to cope?

Please note: as you explore your personal belief system and reflect on your answers to these questions, you may notice that a pattern of words or key concepts emerges. How do you think these patterns or concepts influence your choice of theory and impact on your work with clients?

(e) About the counselling process

- How do you define counselling or psychotherapy?
- What do you regard as the purpose or goals of counselling or psychotherapy?
- What are the most important functions of a therapist? How do you define your own role?
- What do you think are the most essential characteristics of an effective relationship between client and therapist?

2 Formal theory

What position do you take on the following questions? Which do you regard as important for you to be able to answer? Which do you regard as irrelevant?

- How do you define normal or healthy human development?
- How do you explain the origin and development of dysfunctional thoughts, feelings and behaviours?
- How do you explain how psychological problems are perpetuated or sustained?

An alternative way of exploring these aspects has been proposed by Mahrer (1989).

- What kind of material do you want to elicit from clients? What do you observe and listen for? (For example: dreams, free association, recollection of parental injunctions, bodily sensations, irrational beliefs, internal conflicts, childhood traumas, positive self-statements.)
- What explanatory frameworks do you use to account for the origin and/or perpetuation of client problems?
- What are your broad targets for change?

3 Clinical theory

- What general principles of psychological change inform your practice?
- What mechanisms account for psychological change?
- How do you explain the function of the therapeutic relationship?
- How do you describe the therapeutic process? What types of process goals or tasks do you have at each stage of the therapeutic process? Are particular process goals more important at one stage than at others?
- Do you develop clinical formulations or assessments? How do you see the purpose of assessment? What constitutes an assessment?
- Do you formulate therapeutic plans? How does your therapeutic plan relate to assessment?

- How do you listen to a client? (For example, do you pay full attention to the facts of the client's story or do you listen to the underlying feelings or what the story means to the client; do you listen as if you are the person the client is talking about; do you listen to your own emotional response to the client's story and to your own internal flow of private thoughts and ideas? Mahrer, 1989.)
- What are your targets for change?
- If therapy is successful, what type of outcome goals would the client have achieved? Would the type of outcome goal vary with particular clients? Are outcome goals made explicit? Who decides?
- Do you have explicit business and/or therapeutic contracts with clients? What form do they take?
- Do you evaluate progress and your therapeutic plan? How? When?
- What do you see as the purpose of clinical supervision? How do you use supervision?

4 Therapeutic operations (skills and strategies)

- Are there any skills you regard as core to the therapeutic process?
- What general therapeutic strategies do you use at various stages of the therapeutic process. (For example, at the beginning, middle and end of the process.)
- What strategies or techniques do you use to help achieve particular process goals and outcomes?
- What procedures or techniques do you employ in certain situations? (For example: if the client is crying, silent, anxious, persistently talking about another person, adopting a particular position or physical movement or if you sense something is going on between you and the client.)
- What skills do you use to implement particular therapeutic strategies? (For example: to build rapport or enable the client to gain a new perspective.)

The final task is to identify any potential conflicts or tensions between aspects of the four elements and the extent to which each interprets or is at least consistent with the previous element.

References

Bernard, J.M. and Goodyear, R.K. (1992) *The Fundamentals of Clinical Supervision*. Boston: Allyn and Bacon.

Egan, G. and Cowan, M.A. (1979) *People in Systems: A Model for Development in the Human-Service Professions and Education*. Monterey, CA: Brooks/Cole.

Locke, D.C. (1992) *Increasing Multicultural Understanding: A Comprehensive Model*. London: Sage.

Mahrer, A.R. (1989) *The Integration of Psychotherapies*. New York: Human Sciences Press.

INDEX

ABCDE model, 184–6, 188
abundance motivation, 220
acceptance, 117, 186
accommodation, 129, 299
accountability, 282, 323
actions, disclaimed, 64
affect modality, 142, 145, 152
affective/emotional experiencing, 14, 167, 171
Alexander, F., 5, 253, 255, 259
alexithymia, 66
'aloneness togetherness', 59
American Association for Humanistic Psychology, 219
American National Institute of Mental Health (NIMH), 17
analytical psychotherapy, 50
Anderson, W.T., 311
Andrews, J.D.W., 15, 325, 326
Anna (case study), 241–7
Annie (case study), 132–3
anxiety, 49–50, 156
Arkowitz, H., 7, 8, 9, 11, 13, 36, 41
Arnkoff, D.B., 8, 13, 36, 315
Asen, K., 75, 83
Assagioli, R., 219, 222
assimilation, 15, 22, 129, 131, 132, 299
association, 143–4
Association of Cognitive Analytic Therapists (ACAT), 22, 214–15
Association for Humanistic Psychology (AHP), 219, 229
Association for Humanistic Psychology Practitioners (AHPP), 229
associations and networks, 17–18, 42–3
attachment theory, 23, 59, 94–5, 123
attitudes, development of, 295, 297
Austen, C., 127–39
authenticity, 300
awareness, 223, 299
awfulizing and anti-awfulizing, 185, 186
Ayer, A.J., 35

Barkham, M., 20, 44, 58, 71, 173, 305
BASIC I.D. modalities, 142, 143, 145–6, 147, 149, 153–5
Bateson, G., 75, 76, 79, 85
Beck, A.T., 8, 255
behaviour modality, 142, 145, 152
behavioural approaches, 3, 4–6, 7–10, 12–13, 49, 93, 142, 152, 164, 218, 254–5
behavioural change, 14, 167–8, 170–1, 172
behavioural regulation, 171
Beitman, B.D., 16, 33, 37, 38, 93, 94, 95, 96, 98, 298, 309, 320, 322, 324, 326
Bergin, A.E., 5, 8, 292, 296, 297
Bernard, J.M., 275–6, 318, 342
Berne, E., 98, 262
Bernstein, B.L., 240, 241
Beutler, L.E., 15, 16
bibliotherapy, 150
Bill (case study), 137–8
bioenergetics, 219
bipolar affective disorder, 66
Birk, L., 9
'blank wall' visualization, 170
bodywork, 219, 224, 225
Bond, T., 317, 318–19
Borders, L.D., 272, 288
Bott, D., 74–90
boundaries in supervision, 281
Bowen, M., 78, 83, 84, 86
Bowlby, J., 94, 113, 114, 115, 116
brainstorming, 170, 183
bridge stage of supervision, 284
bridging, 155–6
brief therapy, 15, 49, 103, 107, 108, 203, 252–69, 278
brief-strategic therapy, 255, 258
Brinkley-Birk, A., 9
British Association for Counselling (BAC), 45, 271, 292, 302
Brockman, B., 48, 214
Brown, M.T., 275, 276, 277
Buber, M., 14, 19, 58, 112, 119
Byng-Hall, J., 78, 83

Cade, B., 255, 258, 259
Carroll, M., 274, 278–9
Carter, E., 76, 77, 87
Carter, J.A., 100, 267
Carter, R.T., 234, 237, 238
Casement, P., 115, 116, 118, 119, 258
Centre for Multimodal Therapy, 147, 160
change, 117, 163; behavioural, 14, 167–8, 170–1, 172; levels of, 130–2, 138–9, 320; mechanisms of, 321–2; process of, 98, 100, 102, 147, 167–8, 170–1, 193–4, 320–1; readiness for, 320; resistance to, 321
child–carer relationship, 94–5, 96–7, 113, 113–14
circular questioning, 79, 83
Clarkson, P., 14, 23, 39, 41, 111, 112, 122, 127, 223, 296, 298, 302, 305–12
client work, learning from, 300–1
client-centred therapy *see* person-centred therapy
clinical theory, 320–2, 324, 343–4
clinical wisdom, 273–4
'coaching', 87
cognition modality, 142, 146, 152
cognitive analytic therapy (CAT), 20, 21–2, 37, 48–9, 202–15, 256
cognitive behavioural therapy (CBT), 23, 47, 49, 50, 130, 132, 142, 163, 173, 181, 225, 253, 255, 336
cognitive dissonance, 331, 332
cognitive mastery, 14, 171
cognitive psychology, 13, 203
cognitive reframing, 167
cognitive therapy, 8, 10–11, 13–14, 142, 152
Collingwood, R.G., 65
comic vision of reality, 23, 335–6
commitment, 41–2
common factors approach, 3–4, 7, 14, 37, 292, 296, 324
communications theory, 142, 143, *see also* metacommunication
competence, counsellor, 302
complementarity, 300
confidentiality in supervision, 282
congruence, 111, 117, 146, 222, 223, 245, 254
Connor, M., 177, 291–303
contracts: supervision, 281–2; therapeutic, 65, 116–17, 169, 262
conversational model, 19–20, 47, 57–73
coping, forms of, 182
core conditions, 111, 117, 146, 163, 171, 172, 222, 244–5
core interpersonal schema, 93, 95, 96, 98–9
core theoretical framework, 292–3, 323–4
cost-benefit analysis of beliefs, 190

countertransference, 62, 118, 124, 223, 241, 244, 298, 308
couple counselling, 107, 120
Cowan, M., 164, 166, 321, 342
crisis intervention, 107
Crossley, D., 202–15
cultural fit, 238–9, 248
cultural identity, 342
cultural issues, 233–48
cultural sensitivity, 240, 241
cultural values, 247–8
culture shock, 242–3
Cummings, N.A., 316, 317, 333–4
cybernetics, 75, 79–80
cyclical dynamics, 9–10
cyclical model of supervision, 279–88
cyclical psychodynamics, 23

Dalal, F., 236, 237
d'Ardenne, P., 234, 237, 239, 241
Davanloo, H., 255, 257, 259
Davison, G.C., 3, 11
De Shazer, S., 170, 255, 258, 259, 265
Dederich, C., 225
defence mechanisms, 114, 144
depressive disorders, 49, 66, 71, 156, 173
developmental mapping, 342
developmental/reparative relationship, 298–9, 308
dialectical thinking, 336–7
diaries, 207, 208
DiClemente, C.C., 16, 101, 172, 209, 320, 321–2, 333
'dilemmas', 205, 207
Dimond, R., 127, 130
disclaimed actions, 64
Dollard, J., 4–5
dreams, 245
Driscoll, R., 43
drugs/biology modality, 143, 146, 153
Dryden, W., 16, 17, 33, 36, 38, 45, 127, 141, 147, 148, 155, 156, 192, 230, 306, 334, 337
Durham, R.C., 50
dynamic exploratory therapy, 49
Dyne, D., 20–1, 33, 41
dysthymia, 66
D'Zurilla, T.J., 181, 182, 183, 184, 192

eating disorders, 156, 173
eclectic therapy, 15, 16
eclecticism, 306; defined, 31–2, 291; integrated, 127–39; versus integration, 32–3
Edmondson, E., 221, 226
Egan, G., 6, 11, 163–8, 170, 171, 172, 177, 299,

321, 322, 324, 342
ego psychology, 13, 57
Ellis, A., 2, 6, 8, 181, 182, 185–6, 190, 194, 199, 255
Elton Wilson, J., 101, 252–69
emotional responsibility, 187
emotional/affective experiencing, 14, 167, 171
empathic discussion, 84, 85
empathy, 81, 117, 146, 222, 223, 244, 245
employee assistance programmes, 107, 177, 198
empty chair technique, 13
encounter groups, 219, 225
Epictetus, 182
epistemology, 331–2, *see also* knowledge
Erickson, M., 78, 255
ethics, 225, 302–3; in supervision, 282
ethnicity, 233–48
evaluation and training, 295, 301
existential therapy, 219, 253, 257
existentialism, 219
experiential therapy, 130, 132
explanatory hypotheses, 63
exposure techniques, 190
externalizing, 191–2
Eysenck, H.J., 2, 305

failure attacking, 190–1
Fairbairn, D., 94, 113, 114, 115
family life cycle, 76–7, 81
family systems theory, 75, 76–80
family therapy, 74–90, 128, 130, 255
Farrell, B.A., 307
Fassinger, R.E., 234, 235
Fear, R., 23, 329–38
Feather, B.W., 11
feedback in supervision, 284–5
Feldman, L., 9
Feltham, C., 112, 292–3, 333
feminist movement, 236
Festinger, L., 332
Fiedler, F.E., 4, 308
Firth, J., 15, 47, 66, 173
focus in supervision, 282–3
focused treatment, 8
Fonagy, P., 49, 305, 317
Foucault, M., 79, 310
frameworks, eclectic integrative, 37
Framo, J., 78, 86
Frank, J., 7, 99, 256
Freedheim, D.K., 1, 2
French, T.M., 3, 4, 253, 255, 259
Freud, S., 3, 14, 112, 236, 237
Friedman, M., 14, 23

Frosh, S., 245
frustration tolerance, 185, 186
Frye, N., 23, 335

Garfield, S.L., 8, 15, 16, 37, 45, 127, 292, 296, 297, 315, 321, 324
Gelso, C.J., 100, 267
gender issues, 173, 236, 243–4
geneograms, 83
general systems theory, 142
generalized anxiety disorder (GAD), 50
Gergen, K., 23, 35, 79
Gestalt therapy, 6, 11, 13, 14, 152, 219, 223
Gilbert, M., 93–108
Glass, C.R., 8, 36, 44, 315
Gleick, J., 305, 309
Glickauf-Hughes, C., 14
Gold, J.R., 16, 23
Goldberg, C., 329, 330
Goldfried, M.R., 3, 14, 16, 17–18, 32, 33, 38, 43, 93, 96, 98, 275, 333
'goodbye letters', 208, 256
Goodyear, R.K., 275, 318, 342
Greening, T., 221
Grencavage, L.M., 32, 46, 298, 300, 337
group work, 120, 124, 224–5, 305
Guthrie, E., 66, 72
Guttman, H., 75, 77

Haley, J., 75, 77, 78, 81–2, 83, 255
handbooks, 16
Hardy, S., 279, 280
Heidegger, M., 113
Heron, J., 19, 120, 128
Hinshelwood, R.D., 23, 34, 39
Hobson, R., 19–20, 47, 57–60, 62– 3, 64, 65, 67, 71
holistic work, 220, 224
Hollanders, H., 1–24, 31–51, 219, 291, 302
Holloway, E.L., 274, 277–8
Holmes, J., 23, 94, 127, 130
Horton, I., 316–28, 341–4
humanistic therapy, 6, 10–11, 13– 14, 85, 93, 112, 218–31, 253–4, 335
Hunt, H.F., 12
hypotheses, generation of, 62–3

'I Thou' relationship, 14, 58, 129, 257
identity, 42; cultural, 342
imagery modality, 142, 146, 152
imagery techniques, 191
immanent mind, 76
impartiality, 302, 303
inference chaining, 188–9, 196
information, missing, 145

Inskipp, F., 167, 173, 271, 274
integrated eclecticism, 127–39
integration: defined, 32, 291; locus of, 37–40; as a position, 40–1; as a process, 41; versus eclecticism, 32–3
integrative psychotherapy, 306–8
integrity, 302–3, 303
interdependence, 311
International Academy of Eclectic Psychotherapists, 17
interpersonal and intrapersonal development, 294–5, 296–7
interpersonal modality, 142, 146, 153
interpersonal therapy, 49, 112, 130
intuition, 316
ironic vision of reality, 23, 336, 338
Ivey, A.E., 318, 322, 324, 325

Jenkins, H., 75, 83
Jenkins, P., 163–78
John (case study-integrated eclecticism), 134–5
John (case study-multimodal therapy), 154, 157–9
John (case study-systemic thinking)), 86–9
Jones, D., 218, 219, 230
Jones, E.E., 245
journals, 16–17
judgement, 273–4
Jung, C., 57, 58, 236–7, 245, 312

Kahn, M., 13–14, 112
Karasu, T., 14, 171, 292–3
Kareem, J., 234, 244
Keeney, B., 76
King, P., 329–30
Kitchener, K.S., 329–30
Klein, J., 245
Kleinian theory, 129
knowledge: development of, 295; procedural, 273; theoretical and technical, 273, *see also* epistemology
Koestler, A., 247, 309
Kohut, H., 13, 14, 98, 112
Kolb, D.A., 294, 299
Kuhn, T.S., 2, 34, 74

Lago, C., 114, 233–48, 275
Lambert, M.J., 37, 38, 44, 47, 48–9
Landrum-Brown, J., 275, 276, 277
Lane, D., 248
language, 63–4; of integration, 43, *see also* metaphor
Lazarus, A.A., 7, 11, 15, 16, 33, 36, 37, 48, 141–8 *passim* , 153, 160, 182, 256, 291, 298, 306
learning, 6, 8–9, 10, 163, 294, 296–301, 321; by enquiry, 310–11, *see also* social learning theory
learning cycle, 294
learning styles, 294
Lebow, J.L., 322, 324, 325
life process of psychological evolution, 258, 260, 261
Lindler, H., 334
linking hypotheses, 63
'living-learning' concept, 58
Locke, D.C., 318
locus of control, 318
Louise (case study), 67–71
Luborsky, L., 14, 37, 127
Lucchese, G., 316, 317, 333–4
Lyotard, J.-F., 310

McAdams, D.P., 331
McGoldrick, M., 76, 77, 87
McKinney, M.K., 16, 36
McLennon, J., 315, 316, 317, 319, 324
McLeod, J., 41, 173, 219, 225, 231, 234–5, 238, 239, 294
Mahrer, A., 15, 320
Mahtani, A., 234, 237, 239, 241
Maisch, M., 326
Malan, D.H., 8, 255, 259
management, business, 177, 229
Mann, J., 257, 258, 259
Margison, F., 57–73
Marks, M.J., 5, 335
Marmor, J., 5, 8, 13
Maroda, J., 118, 119, 124
Martin, J., 57–73
Maslow, A.H., 112, 113, 219, 220
matching: cultural, 241; prescriptive, 300; supervisor and supervisee, 275–7
meaning, construction of, 128
Meares, R., 59, 60, 67
Mearns, D., 117, 322
mental schemas, 129
Messer, S.B., 2, 8, 13, 16, 23, 43, 127, 298, 334, 335
meta-methodology, 309
metacommunication, 84–5, 144
metaphor, 63–4, 70, 71, 72, 79
Milan models, 78, 79, 80
Miller, N.E., 4–5
Minuchin, S., 78, 82, 83, 255
'miracle question', 170
misinformation, 144–5
Mitchell, S.A., 111, 112, 114, 115–16

modalities, BASIC I.D., 142, 143, 145–6, 147, 149, 153–5
modality profiles, 142, 149, 153–4
Moodley, R., 233–48
multicultural issues, 233–48; in supervision, 275–6
Multimodal Life History Inventory (MLHI), 150
multimodal therapy, 7, 15, 16, 37, 38, 47–8, 141–60, 256, 291
Murphy, K., 93–108
mutuality, 124
'myself', sense of, 60

narrative approaches, 79, 80
Neenan, M., 181–99
Neimeyer, R.A., 199, 317, 324
Nelson-Jones, R., 173, 177
networks and associations, 17–18, 42–3
Newman, C.F., 17, 33, 275
Nichols, M., 79, 90
Nicola (case study), 120–2
non-conscious processes, 144
Norcross, J.C., 15–16, 32, 33, 36, 38, 45–6, 96, 199, 298, 300, 305, 306, 308, 315, 333, 334, 337

object relations theory, 13, 14, 111, 204, 205
objective view of reality, 316
O'Hanlon, W.H., 255, 258, 259
organizational context of supervision, 277–9
organizational problem solving, 177
Osborn, A., 183

Page, S., 271, 272, 274, 280
Palmer, S., 141–60, 181–99
Palo Alto group, 75, 78, 79
panic disorder, 50
paradigms, incommensurability of, 34–5
paradoxical techniques, 79, 84
parity, principle of, 143
Park, A., 279, 280
Patterson, C.H., 6, 33, 238, 246
Paul, G., 5, 150, 256
Paul, S., 110–24
Paula (case study), 262–9
Pavlov, I., 3
Peake, T.H., 255, 256
Pedersen, P., 233–4, 236, 238
Pelham, G., 110–24
'people in systems' framework, 166–7
Perls, F., 2, 6, 219
Perry, W., 42
Person-Centred Approach Institute, 229

person-centred therapy, 6, 10, 50, 111, 117, 129, 163, 171, 172, 219
person-to-person (real) relationship, 100, 299, 308
personal beliefs/philosophy, 317, 318–19; and choice of theoretical orientation, 318–19, 334–6; integration with professional philosophy, 330–3, *see also* world views
personal construct theory, 203
personal theoretical integration, 23, 315–27, 338, 341–4
personality of therapist, 3, 10; and theoretical orientation, 315–16, 334
perspicacity, 274
Peterson, L.E., 36
phenomenology, 218
Phillip (case study), 209–13
phobias, 49, 225
Phung, T.C., 241
Piaget, J., 59, 129
Pilgrim, D., 2, 18, 123
Pinsof, W., 127, 128, 130, 132
planograms, 192
pluralism, 35–7, 300
Pocock, D., 75, 80, 81
Polkinghorne, D.E., 305, 308
post-modernism, 79–80
Poznanski, J.J., 315, 316, 317, 319, 324
pre-countertransference, 244
preference, 45–6
problem-focused counselling, 181–99
procedural knowledge, 273
Procedural Sequence Object Relations Model (PSORM), 202, 203, 205
process model, 325
processing, depth of, 130–1
Prochaska, J.O., 16, 32, 38, 42, 45–6, 101, 172, 209, 315, 320, 321–2, 333, 334
professional development, 322–3, 329–30; and the personal self, 330–3
projective identification, 205
psychoanalysis/psychodynamic therapy, 3, 4–6, 7–10, 11, 12–13, 47, 78, 93, 112, 129, 130, 132, 152, 218, 236, 253, 255, 335
psychodynamic interpersonal (PI) tradition, 57
psychotherapy file, 207, 256

Quenk, N.L. and Quenk, A.T., 325
questioning, 189

racial issues, 233–48
racism, 236–8, 245
Rappe, H., 277

rational emotive behaviour therapy, 6, 8, 142, 152, 181, 182–6, 194, 255
rational judgement, 316
reactive distance, 84, 86
real relationship, 100, 299, 308
reality, 128; client's view of, 221; construction of, 203; rational-intuitive view of, 316; subjective-objective view of, 316; visions of, 23, 331, 333, 334–6, *see also* world views
reciprocal role procedures, 205–6, 207, 208
reciprocity, 124
referral, 81
reflection, 295, 301, 326
reflective judgement theory, 329–30, 337
reflexivity, 222
reformulation letters, 206, 207–8, 210–12, 256
Reich, W., 219, 224
Reimers, S., 81, 86
relational models, 110–24; systematic integrative relational model, 93–108
relaxation techniques, 190
religion, 59, 220, 231
repertory grid technique, 21
'repetition phenomenon', 173
repetitive interactive patterns, 93, 97–8
representation of interactions (RIGs), 95–6
research, 310–11, 312; eclectic/integrative, 44–50
resistance, 13, 321
respect, 302
responsibility: emotional and therapeutic, 187; internal or external, 318
Rhoads, J.M., 12, 13
Richard (case study), 226–9
Richie, B.S., 234, 235
Rogers, C., 6, 11, 14, 19, 98, 100, 112, 114, 117, 172, 219, 229, 296, 297; core conditions, 81, 85, 146, 171, 222, 223, 229, 244, 254; groupwork, 224–5; concept of self-actualization, 220; on a sense of self, 113, 115
role behaviour, 204, 205
role play, 193, 208, 283
romantic vision of reality, 23, 335
Ronnestad, M.H., 315, 316, 320, 322–3, 325, 326, 329, 331
Roth, A., 49, 305
Rowan, J., 218, 219, 220, 225, 229, 230, 231
Ryle, A., 20, 21–2, 37, 43, 127, 202–3, 204, 205, 208, 209, 214, 255–6, 258, 259
Ryle, G., 311

Saadawi, N. El, 246–7

Sadie (case study), 133–4, 137
safety, 225
Said, E.W., 238
Samuels, A., 35, 36, 123, 237, 300, 308
Sandy (case study), 174–7
Sara (case study), 194–8
Schacht, T.E., 36
schemas, mental, 129
schizophrenia, 66, 156, 198
schoolism, 308–11
Schutz, W., 225
self, sense of, 59–60, 113, 114, 115
self-acceptance, 145
self-actualization, 110–11, 123, 219, 220
self-awareness, 144
self-confirmation model, 15
self-disclosure, therapist, 243
self-esteem, 7, 59
self-monitoring, 207
self-psychology, 13
self-regulation, 75
self-states, 204
sensation modality, 142, 146, 152
Sequential Diagrammatic Reformulation, 208, 212, 213
Shafer, R., 23, 335, 336
shame attacking, 191
Shapiro, D.A., 15, 47, 66, 173, 305
Shear, M.K., 50
Sheffield Psychotherapy Project, 15, 20, 22, 47, 49
Sheila (case study), 104–7
Shostrom, E., 6, 32
Shotter, J., 309
Sills, C., 262
Silverman, D., 307
single session therapy, 257–8
six-category intervention analysis, 19
skilled helper model, 11, 163–78, 299
skills, development of, 295
Skovholt, T.M., 315, 316, 320, 322, 323, 325, 326, 329, 331
Sloane, R., 6, 9, 255
Smith, E., 309
Smith, E.M.J., 244
Smith, M.L., 14, 37, 47
'snags', 205–6, 207
Soames family (case study), 135–7
social constructionism, 75, 79, 80, 90, 128
social influence theory, 163, 164
social influences, 321
social learning theory, 142, 143, 336
Society for the Exploration of Psychotherapy Integration (SEPI), 17, 18, 42–3, 46

solution plans, 192–3
solution-focused therapy, 255, 258, 278
somatization, 66, 71
space, supervision, 283–4
spirituality, 219, 220, 231
stereotyping, racial, 237, 241
Stern, D., 95, 113
Steward, I., 311
Stiles, W., 14, 15, 22, 23, 127, 129, 130, 131, 204, 321
Stolorow, R.D., 97, 254
Stowell-Smith, M., 202–15
strategic interventions, 78–9, 83–4, 85, 255
stress mapping, 192
Stricker, G., 16
structural profiles, 142, 150, 151
structural therapy, 78, 82, 255
student counselling, 107, 177, 198
subjective view of reality, 316
subliminal stimuli, 144
Sue, D., 234, 236, 237, 238, 240–1
Sue, D.W., 234, 236, 237, 238, 240–1, 243
Sullivan, H.S., 10, 57, 112, 113, 114, 118, 124
supervision, 271–89, 300–1, 310, 326
systematic eclecticism, 37
systematic integrative relational model, 93–108
systemic integrative psychotherapy, 23
systemic thinking, 74–90, 93, 129
systems theory, 255
Szasz, T.S., 41–2, 43

Talmon, M., 257–8, 259, 264, 267
target problem procedures (TPP), 212
technical eclecticism, 7, 33, 37, 141
theoretical integration, 37
theoretical orientation, 45, 323; choice of, 315–16, 333–4; complexity of, 316–17; and personal philosophy, 334–6; and personality, 315–16, 334
theoretical school affiliation, 317
theoretical and technical knowledge, 273
theory, 308, 311–12; in action, 317; clinical, 320–2, 324, 343–4; core theoretical framework, 292–3, 323–4; espoused, 317; formal, 319–20, 343
therapeutic frame, 116–18
therapeutic operations, 322, 324
therapeutic relationship, 14, 23, 39, 110–24, 173, 296, 298–9, 308, 325; cognitive analytic therapy, 206; cognitive-behavioural approaches, 173; conversational model, 59, 71; family therapy, 80–1; humanistic therapy, 223; integrated eclecticism, 138; problem-focused counselling, 187; skilled helper model, 171– 2; systematic integrative relational model, 94, 108
therapeutic responsibility, 187
therapist as instrument, 223–4
Thomas, B.L., 46, 298
Thompson, J., 114, 233, 234, 239, 240, 245, 248, 275
Thoresen, C.E., 10
Thorne, B., 117, 322
three-stage model, 164–6, 173
thresholds, 14
time projection imagery, 192
time-focused therapy see brief therapy
Totton, N., 221, 226
touch, 224, 225
tracking, 155
tragic vision of reality, 23, 335
training, 291–303, 307; cognitive analytic therapy, 214–15
transference, 63, 100, 118, 221, 223, 255, 267, 298, 308
transpersonal psychology, 220
transpersonal relationship, 299, 308
transpersonal therapy, 219
transtheoretical approach, 16
'traps', 205, 207
Treacher, A., 81, 86
Treasure, J., 48
'triangle of insight', 265
triangulation, 84
Truax, C.B., 10, 163
two-chair work, 283

unconditional positive regard, 146, 222, 223, 244, 254
unconscious processes, 173
understanding hypotheses, 63
United Kingdom Council for Psychotherapy (UKCP), 219, 229
universal model, 238–9

values, 342; cultural, 247–8; development of, 295, 297
Vasco, A.B., 45, 331, 332, 334
visualizing, 191–2

Wachtel, P.L., 3, 4, 9–10, 13, 16, 23, 33, 36, 338
Wade, P., 240, 241
Walsh, B.W., 36
Watson, G., 4
Watzlawick, P., 79, 84, 142, 255
West, W., 218–31
Wheeler, S., 41, 112

'why?' questions, 192
Wiener, N., 75
Williams, A., 272–4, 288
Winnicott, D.W., 13, 14, 59, 94–5, 113, 114
Winter, R., 326
Wittgenstein, L., 58
Wolfe, B.E., 17–18, 32, 33
Woods, S.M., 13

Woolfe, R., 23, 170, 177, 248, 329–30
Wordsworth, W., 58, 59
working alliance, 100, 101–2, 267, 296, 298, 308
world views, 238–9, 318–19, 333, 334–6, 341; of supervisor and supervisee, 276–7, *see also* reality, visions of
Wosket, V., 271–89